# WHAT IT ALL MEANS

# WHAT IT ALL MEANS

**Semantics for (Almost) Everything**

PHILIPPE SCHLENKER

The MIT Press
Cambridge, Massachusetts
London, England

The MIT Press would like to thank the anonymous peer reviewers who provided comments on drafts of this book. The generous work of academic experts is essential for establishing the authority and quality of our publications. We acknowledge with gratitude the contributions of these otherwise uncredited readers.

This book was set in Adobe Garamond Pro by New Best-set Typesetters Ltd. Printed and bound in the United States of America.

Library of Congress Cataloging-in-Publication Data

Names: Schlenker, Philippe, author.
Title: What it all means : semantics for (almost) everything / Philippe Schlenker.
Description: Cambridge, Massachusetts : The MIT Press, [2022] | Includes bibliographical
    references and index.
Identifiers: LCCN 2021057611 | ISBN 9780262047432 (hardcover)
Subjects: LCSH: Semantics.
Classification: LCC P325 .S363 2020 | DDC 401/.43—dc23/eng/20211208
LC record available at https://lccn.loc.gov/2021057611

10  9  8  7  6  5  4  3  2  1

publication supported by a grant from
The Community Foundation for Greater New Haven
as part of the Urban Haven Project

To my parents, Claire and Michel Schlenker,
who might *still* wonder what semantics is for—but do know what it takes to have
a meaningful life.

# Contents

Acknowledgments  *ix*

Introduction  *xi*

Prologue: Primate Meanings  *xxiii*

1  **MEANING IN THE WILD**  *1*

**PART I: THE BUILDING BLOCKS OF MEANING**  *37*

2  **VISIBLE LOGIC: SIGN LANGUAGE AND PRONOUNS**  *39*

3  **ME, ME, ME! PERSPECTIVES IN LANGUAGE**  *69*

4  **NOUNS AND VERBS: OBJECTS AND EVENTS**  *91*

5  **BEYOND THE HERE AND NOW I: FROM OBJECTS TO SITUATIONS**  *111*

6  **BEYOND THE HERE AND NOW II: DESCRIBING AND CLASSIFYING OBJECTS AND SITUATIONS**  *127*

**PART II: USING MEANING**  *145*

7  **LOGIC MACHINE I: PREDICATE LOGIC**  *147*

8  **LOGIC MACHINE II: ENGLISH AS A FORMAL LANGUAGE**  *157*

9  **LOGIC MACHINE III: THE EXPRESSIVE POWER OF HUMAN LANGUAGE**  *173*

10  **NOT QUITE SAYING IT: FOCUS AND IMPLICATURES**  *197*

11  **NOT AT ISSUE: PRESUPPOSITIONS, SUPPLEMENTS, AND EXPRESSIVES**  *225*

**PART III: EXTENDING MEANING**   *245*

**12  ICONICITY REVISITED: SIGN WITH ICONICITY VERSUS SPEECH WITH
    GESTURES**   *247*

**13  GRAMMAR IN GESTURES**   *265*

**14  MEANING IN GESTURES**   *287*

**15  MEANING IN MUSIC**   *303*

**EPILOGUE: THE LIMITS OF TRUTH**   *339*

**16  THE LIMITS OF TRUTH I: THE RIDDLE OF PARADOXES**   *341*

**17  THE LIMITS OF TRUTH II: SOLVING THE RIDDLE OF PARADOXES**   *355*

Conclusion   *383*

Appendix: Phonology, Morphology, and Syntax in Speech and in Sign   *389*

Glossary   *405*

Going Further   *415*

Notes   *429*

Illustration Sources   *451*

Index   *455*

# Acknowledgments

I am extremely grateful to all the friends and colleagues who kindly provided encouragement, information, references, authorizations, and/or feedback in the course of this project: Sam Adue, Mark Baker, Chris Barker, Itai Bassi, Mélissa Berthet, Sam Blanc-Cuenca, Arthur Bonetto, Denis Bonnay, Marion Bonnet, Yann Cantin, Cristiane Cäsar, Lucas Champollion, Emmanuel Chemla, Gennaro Chierchia, Camille Coye, Shai Davidi, Guillaume Dezecache, Paul Egré, Andreas Ferus, Suzana Fong, Danny Fox, Xavier Gabaix, Carlo Geraci, Ted Gibson, Kirsty Graham, Patrick Grosz, Catherine Hobaiter, Henkjan Honing, Jonah Katz, Nathan Klinedinst, Jeremy Kuhn, Jonathan Lamberton, Alban Lemasson, Fred Lerdahl, Haoze Li, Diane Lillo-Martin, Hao Lin, Matthew Mandelkern, Salvador Mascarenhas, Jason Merchant, Léo Migotti, John Mikhail, Ulrich Miksch, Andrea Moro, Julien Musolino, Barbara Partee, Pritty Patel-Grosz, Lucie Ravaux, Daniel Rothschild, Laurent Roussarie, Wendy Sandler, Larry Solan, Benjamin Spector, Dominique Sportiche, Mark Steedman, Zoltán Gendler Szabó, Anna Szabolcsi, Lyn Tieu, Ronnie Wilbur, Zhuoye Zhang, Klaus Zuberbühler.

My research on sign language—LSF (French Sign Language) and ASL (American Sign Language)—would not have been possible without my Deaf consultants and coauthors: Yann Cantin (LSF), Ludovic Ducasse (LSF), Laurène Loctin (LSF), and Jonathan Lamberton (ASL).

Gennaro Chierchia provided important initial encouragement for this project. Sylvain Bromberger played a key role as well; I regret that he did not live to see the end result. Arthur Bonetto was crucial as a music consultant, and he helped improve and correct chapter 15. Nathan Klinedinst made very useful suggestions about chapter 1 and chapter 9, and Carlo Geraci did as well for the final appendix.

Hao Lin, Léo Migotti, Pritty Patel-Grosz, Laurent Roussarie, Mark Steedman, Zoltán Gendler Szabó, and Ronnie Wilbur all read the entire manuscript and provided extraordinarily helpful corrections, criticisms, and suggestions (several were inspired by Zoltán Gendler Szabó's philosophy of language students at Yale). Pritty Patel-Grosz and Ronnie Wilbur displayed endless (and heroic) patience in commenting on several versions of the manuscript, and they offered innumerable helpful suggestions.

Marion Bonnet, Léo Migotti, and Lucie Ravaux did considerable work on the references, figures, and audiovisual examples, with admirable patience and competence. In addition, Léo Migotti prepared the index. I am very grateful to Sandrine Allier-Guepin for giving us permission to use her drawing "Les Balcons" for the book cover. Finally, MIT Press (especially Marc Lowenthal and Anthony Zannino) helped at every stage of this project, including by finding two excellent referees, whose comments and objections are gratefully acknowledged. Skillful copyediting was provided by Karen Brogno, and production was expertly coordinated by Barbara Chernow.

A large part of the work reported here (and in part the book itself) was supported by two grants from the European Research Council, whose decisive contribution is gratefully acknowledged: ERC grant agreement No. 324115–FRONTSEM (PI: Schlenker); ERC grant agreement No. 788077–Orisem (PI: Schlenker). My research was primarily based at Institut Jean-Nicod and DEC (Ecole Normale Supérieure), which is supported by grant FrontCog ANR-17-EURE-0017. My work on ASL was made possible by regular visits at New York University, where I benefited from the helpful comments of students and colleagues.

# Introduction

In 2020, the world came to a halt: Widespread confinement was imposed to limit deaths caused by the coronavirus pandemic. For medical personnel and essential workers, acting meant saving lives and preventing societal collapse, often at considerable personal risk. For the rest of us, who had to stay at home, action primarily meant words: spoken, written, and for Deaf[1] people, signed. Never was *Homo sapiens* to such an extent *Homo semanticus*, a being that lives through complex meanings (i.e., through semantics). In fact, finding meaning in one's life often meant sharing meanings with others. This took diverse forms. From their balconies, Italians sang, gestured, and talked to each other. In several countries, people took to applauding medical personnel at a set time each night while taking this opportunity to wave at each other to regain a sense of belonging. Work often meant email, phone, and video meetings, while classes were moved to Zoom and other online video platforms.

The post–World War II generation had been called the baby boomers. The opaque term *Generation Z* was often applied to people born between the late 1990s and early 2010s, sometimes called *zoomers* by analogy with *boomers*. But suddenly this took on a whole new meaning: "We finally figured out what Z stands for in Gen Z," a college student once joked—young people's lives had entirely moved to the Zoom video platform, complete with Zoom classes, Zoom parties, Zoom dates, and even Zoom bar- and bat-mitzvahs.[2] Many other people's lives were moved online as well, and orchestras even gave Zoom concerts.

Despite the lockdown, much could be achieved online, where communication wasn't limited to spoken or written words. For Deaf people, words were signed, not spoken; for the rest of us, words were complemented with gestures, facial expressions, and sometimes even music. These diverse signals were experienced with heightened intensity because they were often one's primary connection to the rest of the world.

Our primary means of communication is of course through language, which has rightly been called "one of the wonders of the natural world."[3] While it has sophisticated properties pertaining to sound, word formation, and syntax (i.e., word combination), language's main practical interest is to convey meaning. But there is meaning beyond words: in gestures, in facial expressions, and even in music. From their balconies, Italians used all these means, be they linguistic or not, to regain a sense of community. Meaning isn't even restricted to humans. Animals too can convey meaning: with alarm calls, monkeys can communicate specific information about a threat, using different calls for eagles and for leopards.

This book explains how meaning works, from monkey calls to human language, from spoken language to sign language, from gestures to music. These are extraordinarily diverse forms of meaning, and yet they can be studied and compared within a unified approach, one in which the notion of truth plays a central role. Although you might not learn about the Meaning of Life, you will understand how meaning comes to life, and comes to permeate numerous aspects of human and even animal behavior.

### OUR INNER MEANING MACHINE

Philosophers and logicians have often bemoaned the vagaries of language. And not without cause: *Someone lies to everyone* can have two entirely different meanings. One is that everyone is lied to by someone or other—plausible enough. Another is that there is someone, maybe a compulsive liar (or a politician), who lies to everyone—a possible but less common occurrence. Ambiguities of this sort abound. This led to a long tradition of attempts to create formal languages, artificial systems devised to eschew the ambiguities of natural language, and to be optimal for the representation of precise thoughts in logic and science. This enterprise proved extraordinarily fruitful: it led to the development of modern mathematical logic and, later, to the formal languages of computer science.

But here is a well-kept secret: Despite initial appearances, human language is a formal language too, one with exquisitely precise and sophisticated rules that connect form to meaning. When analyzed in greater detail, even cases of ambiguity turn out to be governed by systematic principles that reveal how our inner meaning machine works. But because human language is so much more complex than standard logical languages, it was only after sophisticated tools were developed in mathematical logic that logicians and linguists came to understand human language itself as a fully systematic formal language.

Building on 50 years of research in formal semantics, the study of linguistic meaning as a logical system, this book explains how meaning is represented and computed. It introduces the main challenges and methods through the study of much simpler languages than ours, the communicative systems of monkeys and apes. It then turns to meaning in human language and lays bare its elementary building blocks, from pronouns to nouns and verbs, from person to tense and mood, from *the* to *if* and *when*. It explains how meaning divides information among different types of content, some asserted (i.e., presented as being under discussion or 'at issue') and some not, each with its own status and behavior. Finally, it compares standard linguistic meaning to less traditional types of meaning, such as pictorial information presented in gestures and even meaning effects found in music. Throughout, the approach follows contemporary semantics in treating human language as a logical system whose properties can be described and explained with great precision. It is thus fitting that the final chapter should discuss what turns out to be one of the hardest challenges for this enterprise—the meaning of logical paradoxes.

## WHAT IS SEMANTICS?

Semantics, the science of meaning, isn't quite a household name. *It's just semantics* is often used as a put-down to suggest that a point is merely a matter of words. But semantics as a field has an extraordinary history. It is an unsung success of modern linguistics, which transformed problems that were once thought too hard to tackle (*What is truth? What is meaning?*) into a science that combines the conceptual depth of philosophy, the formal rigor of mathematics, and the empirical breadth of philology and experimental psychology. It is a striking example of what one might call the 'scientific humanities,' the attempt to investigate some of the deepest questions about human nature with the most powerful tools from the empirical and formal sciences.

Modern semantics arose from three main insights. One is that *to know the meaning of a sentence is to know under what conditions it is true.* If you are in a soundproof basement, you might not know whether the sentence 'It's raining' is true. But you know what it would take to make this sentence true (e.g., there should be water drops falling down). In other words, while you don't know its truth *value* (i.e., whether it is in fact true or false), you know its truth *conditions* (i.e., what it would take to make it true). As a result, questions about meaning can be transformed into questions about truth conditions, and thus *What is meaning?* can be reduced to *What is truth?*

But doesn't this reduction make our question harder, not easier? After all, *What is truth?* sounds like . . . well, a very philosophical question. The reason the reduction of meaning to truth makes things simpler is because of a second insight, from the Polish logician Alfred Tarski. Tarski showed in 1933 that one can give a beautifully simple definition and theory of truth for some formal languages used in science: Starting from the smallest units, he devised a systematic procedure to extend truth conditions, step by step, to an entire language. In so doing, he radically transformed the question, *What is truth?*, from a possibly opaque problem in philosophy to a tractable one in logic.

The third insight, epitomized by the American philosopher Richard Montague, was that English and other natural languages can be treated as formal languages, and thus a theory of truth can be developed for them as well. Montague's proposal dates back to 1970, but it became plausible because of an earlier development in linguistics, the Chomskyan revolution of the 1960s. Back in 1933, Tarski couldn't think of applying his definition of truth to English because English wasn't a formal language to begin with. But one of Noam Chomsky's pioneering contributions was precisely to treat the form of English sentences (their syntax) as a formal language: He defined explicit rules that predicted which English sentences are syntactically possible (e.g., *What did Robin eat?*) and which are not (e.g., *Did what Robin eat?*). This paved the way for Montague's proposal about the meaning of English sentences (their semantics), which in turn gave rise to a systematic science strongly grounded within mathematical logic.

This program became gradually integrated with sister fields. After initial quibbles (as followers of Chomsky and Montague had somewhat different worldviews), syntax, the study of form, and semantics, the study of meaning, became part of a unified research program in the early 1980s, spearheaded by Barbara Partee, James Higginbotham, Arnim von Stechow, Angelika Kratzer, Irene Heim, and Gennaro Chierchia, among many others. Both fields, syntax and semantics, increasingly adopted a systematic approach to language comparison, seeking a theory of meaning not just in English but in every human language. Not an easy project, for sure, but an exciting one, as it led to detailed comparative studies of diverse languages. Semantics later became integrated with experimental psychology as well: The goal wasn't just to characterize the formal properties of language but also to explore how meaning is processed in real time, how semantic rules are learned by children, and how they are implemented in the brain. In short, semantics became one of the cognitive sciences.

Semantics in the strict sense is concerned with the literal meaning of sentences. By now, we are getting close to a systematic understanding of the rules by which literal meaning is built in English and other languages. This involves a beautiful architecture in which the same abstract categories make it possible to talk about entities (individuals or objects) and situations (be they present, past, future, or merely imagined). To give but one example, you might think that the category of pronouns (e.g., *I, he, she,* and *it*) is specifically designed to refer to individuals and objects. But this is not so: There are pronoun-like elements that refer to situations. In English, tenses and moods (e.g., *-ed, will, would*) can display a pronominal behavior and serve to refer to past, future, or merely imagined situations (as in *it rained, it will rain, it would rain*). As we will see, each use of pronouns has a direct counterpart with tense and mood. More generally, language makes available abstract but highly articulated categories that organize in a uniform way diverse aspects of human experience.

Semantics in a broader sense includes pragmatics, which goes beyond literal meaning to study additional information (or additional 'inferences') one typically draws by reasoning on the speaker's state of mind. Tarski's formal languages conveyed information in a simple and uniform way through logical entailments. Not all linguistic information is conveyed in this way, however. The philosopher Paul Grice famously noted that a letter of recommendation for John Smith won't help him a bit if it just mentions that *Smith's command of English is excellent, and his attendance at tutorials has been regular.* These are qualities all right, just not the best ones in this context, from which we infer that Smith has these qualities *but no better ones.* That he is no good isn't part of the literal meaning of the sentence: it isn't asserted, but it is still 'implicated'—that is, conveyed through a reasoning on the speaker's motives.

Whenever we say something, we must decide how the information will be conveyed: as an assertion (i.e., as being at issue) and, hence, as the main point of the utterance; or as an implicature, as in Grice's letter. But there are further possibilities as well. It is one thing to say, *Our president is lying, and he will be impeached*: You may agree or disagree with the statement, but the information that the president is lying and will be impeached is presented in a relatively neutral way, and someone who replies *No* won't be committed to any of it. If I say instead, *Our lying president will be impeached*, part of the information is presented as being at issue (the claim that the president will be impeached), but part of it isn't. It is now presupposed (i.e., taken for granted) rather than asserted that the president is lying. As a result, if you reply *No*, you will be understood to deny that there will be an impeachment but to tacitly accept that the president is lying. And if I say that *our damn president will be impeached*, I convey not just my belief that there will be an impeachment, but also my dislike for the president. Here, too, a negation will target the part that is at issue—namely, the occurrence of an impeachment, but not the part pertaining to my dislike. This is only the tip of iceberg: human language divides information among a rich typology of inferences that have no counterpart in standard formal languages such as those of logic and computer science.

Things can get rather sophisticated and even dizzying. If I tell you that *not all my friends spoil their dog*, I *presuppose* that all my friends have a dog, I *assert* that not all spoil their dog, and I *implicate* that some do. The full typology is richer and more subtle. It is fascinating in its own right, as each type of inference displays a characteristic linguistic behavior. But it also has consequences for human communication. Thus, if you wish to mislead without being caught red-handed, implicating may be a better strategy than asserting, as it will preserve plausible deniability; this has occasionally been used with some success in real-life trials.

Originally, semantics was primarily concerned with speech; only recently did it get extended to sign languages. Sign and speech will make up a large part of our discussion. But there is meaning beyond language, and a broader investigation has two benefits: It makes it possible to better appreciate the specificities of human language (be it signed or spoken), and it also yields an understanding of other meaning-bearing forms that matter to human experience. We will thus go on an adventurous expedition and explore the realm of Super Semantics, which applies the methods of semantics beyond its standard objects of study (just like a jet is *supersonic* if it goes beyond the speed of sound, Super Semantics goes beyond the traditional confines of semantics).

## THE ROAD AHEAD

Our journey starts in the heart of Africa, with the alarm calls of monkeys and the communicative gestures of apes (our closest relatives). Monkey calls are simple enough that they can illustrate key ideas in semantics and pragmatics, though possibly not ones that the founders of the field had quite anticipated. But how much more expressive human language will appear after this initial detour!

We will explore in detail how human meanings are constructed, but we will do so with an unusual guide: the sign languages used by Deaf people throughout the world. Before sign languages were properly studied and recognized, there was a widespread belief that they didn't have a real grammar and were expressively limited. The opposite is true. Not only do sign languages have the same kind of grammatical and logical structure as spoken languages; in some cases, they make this structure visible and thus give us more direct access to the building blocks of human meaning, which include pronouns, nouns, and verb; person, tense, and mood; and also words like *the*, *if*, and *when*, which make it possible to describe things and situations.

Having seen how meanings are constructed, we will explore how they simultaneously convey information and comment on the status of that information as being at issue, presupposed, implicated, and more. The simplest component, at issue meaning, makes it possible to compare human language to standard formal languages and to see in which respect human language is more expressive than some of them. At issue meaning forms the core of our inner "logic machine," and we will uncover its workings thanks to the discoveries of Tarski, Chomsky, and Montague. But there are many further component of meaning. We will thus investigate in some detail how human language divides information among this rich typology (including Grice's implicatures), with important consequences for human communication, from political and social slogans to jokes and to trials.

We will then go back to some fundamental issues raised by sign languages, which will motivate going beyond meaning as it is standardly conceived. On closer inspection, sign languages don't just have the same kind of logical and grammatical structure as spoken language. Along certain dimensions, they are more expressive as well, because often a conventional signed word can simultaneously be modulated so as to pictorially resemble what it refers to (this resemblance is called 'iconicity'). There are traces of this in English when you say that a talk was *looong* to mean that it was *very* long: The length of the vowel represents the length of the talk, which makes this use iconic. But this process is far richer in sign languages, and these are in a sense 'super languages,' because they have the same kind of logical resources as spoken languages but far richer iconic means.

This observation will force us to ask new questions about spoken language as well. The importance of iconicity in sign languages might just show that it was a mistake not to include gestures, an iconic device par excellence, as first-class citizens of spoken languages. We will thus embark on a study of the different gestures that can enrich the meaning of speech.

We will discover a surprisingly rich landscape, a sophisticated typology of gestural inferences, and even hints of a gestural grammar. At the end of this exploration, gestures and even visual animations embedded in sentences will provide new insights into human meaning. Still, there will remain respects in which sign languages are arguably more expressive than their spoken counterparts. Taking sign languages as a guide to semantic phenomena won't just help reveal the logical structure of language in general; it will also bring out aspects of meaning that are easily overlooked when we exclusively focus on spoken language.

If semantic analyses can illuminate such diverse objects as spoken and signed languages, primate calls and gestures, how far can we go in the exploration of nontraditional meaning forms? Very far indeed, as we will see when we revisit the vexed issue of meaning in music. It is often said that music is a language, and that it conveys meaning through emotions. This contains a bit of truth and a lot of confusion. While there are systematic ways of producing meaning in music, these are much closer to devices used in visual depictions than to standard linguistic rules. Once these differences are understood, however, we will be able to define a notion of truth in music, thus extending the analysis of meaning as truth conditions to the musical realm.

Having seen how far meaning can extend (from animal communication to music, through speech and signs and gestures!), we will ask about some of its limits. Because the theory of meaning is a theory of truth conditions, a special challenge is presented by paradoxes—statements like *This very sentence is false*. We typically assume that there are just two truth values, *true* and *false*. But the problem is that this sentence cannot be coherently treated as true (for, if so, it should be false) or as false (for, if so, what it asserts would be true). Semantics will rise to the occasion. Paradoxes can be dealt with, but they show that we need more than two truth values (standard sentences can be true or false, but paradoxes have a third truth value). Paradoxes also alert us to devious patterns of reasoning, including in a case that some people greatly cared about throughout history: a purported proof of God's existence, proposed by the eleventh-century monk Anselm of Canterbury.

We will conclude with some broader lessons that can be gained from semantics for science and the humanities. As I will argue, semantics offers a good model of how to help bridge the gap between the 'two cultures' of science and the humanities. This journey will hopefully give you an example of what the scientific humanities can look like.

## A NOTE ON REFERENCES, TERMINOLOGY, AND AUDIOVISUAL EXAMPLES

Virtually all the claims reported in this book have been published in scientific journals, and endnotes reference most of them. In the *Going Further* section at the end of the book, you can find some pointers to relevant textbooks and articles, which in turn contain further references. To say that a claim has been published in a scientific journal doesn't mean that it is uncontroversial: Science is a process, and debate lies at its core. In general, the more recent the articles cited, the more open the debates. To date, there has been a lot of work on the semantics of spoken languages, and many of the associated claims have withstood the test of time. In some cases, I present results in a way that may not be standard, but that I find easier to explain or more enlightening. Work on sign language semantics is more recent and thus based on a narrower set of works and data. Finally, the nonstandard topics I cover, from primate meanings to gestural and (even more so) musical meanings, are very recent and thus much more open and debatable—but hopefully exciting enough to be worth the effort (and risk).

The results reported in this book were discovered by an entire field, semantics—in fact, by several fields, as sign language research, psycholinguistics, primatology, musicology and logic have all played a role as well. It would have been impossible to cite all the researchers whose works are directly or indirectly reported here. With few exceptions, I only cited some of the pioneers, researchers who played a key role in establishing a new research program (I also cited specific researchers when my discussion mirrored theirs extremely closely). I apologize to the numerous colleagues whose research contributed to the results reported in this book but who are not directly mentioned. Systematic bibliographies can be found in works mentioned in the *Going Further* section.

Technical terminology has been kept to a minimum, and definitions are informally introduced to explain terms that may be unfamiliar. A *Glossary* at the end of the book recapitulates the main definitions.

Finally, the text makes reference to audiovisual examples that illustrate some aspects of the discussion on music, sign language, and gestures. These examples are stated in the text within brackets—for instance, [**AV1.10.1**]. This tells the reader to refer to the example labeled *AV1.10.1* on the website. The link to the companion website can be found at https://mitpress.mit .edu/what-it-all-means (this website also contains additional references or remarks about the text).


## HOW TO READ THIS BOOK

While the story develops from one chapter to the next, most chapters can be read independently without too much loss. Still, a few chapters presuppose earlier ones. This is transparent when the title includes *I*, *II*, or *III* (as in *Logic Machine I*, *Logic Machine II*, *Logic Machine III*). In addition, chapters 12, 13, and 14 all build on some earlier chapters. Each line below corresponds to a chapter or a set of chapters that can be read independently, with prerequisites listed if relevant.

Chapter 1
Chapter 2
Chapter 3
Chapter 4
Chapters 5 and 6 (Beyond the Here and Now I, II)
Chapters 7, 8, and 9 (Logic Machine I, II, III)
Chapter 10 (preferably after chapter 9)
Chapter 11
Chapter 12 (after chapter 11)
Chapter 13 (after chapters 2, 3, 4)
Chapter 14 (after chapters 10, 11)
Chapter 15
Chapters 16, 17 (The Limits of Truth I, II)
Appendix

# Prologue: Primate Meanings

*The program and methods of semantics will be introduced through an unusual case study: the meanings found in primate communication, especially in the alarm calls of some African and South American monkeys. These calls illustrate in miniature form the main theoretical questions of semantics. First, what are the elementary components (such as words and suffixes) from which the language is built? Second, how can these components be put together to form larger units; in other words, what is their syntax? Third, what are the meanings of simple and complex elements; in other words, what is (in a narrow sense) their semantics? Fourth, how does one choose a message when several are compatible with a given situation; in other words, what is the pragmatics of the language? In the case of human language, these questions are often quite complex and require detailed discussions of rich data. They can sometimes receive much simpler answers in primate languages.*

*This exploration will lead to surprising results. While primate languages are far less sophisticated than human language, some display an interesting structure (e.g., calls display suffixes), and primate pragmatics arguably relies on a principle that mandates that the most informative calls should be used whenever possible. Furthermore, in some cases the evolutionary history of primate calls and gestures can be reconstructed over millions of years, yielding a time depth that has to this day remained elusive for human language.*

# 1 MEANING IN THE WILD

## 1.1 A SNAKE ENCOUNTER IN UGANDA

In the heart of the Sonso forest in Uganda, a group of primatologists is following a group of chimpanzees. For both sides, this is a routine occurrence. This group of chimpanzees has long been 'habituated,' which means that they tolerate the presence of these human onlookers. The human scientists know the chimpanzees. They even know them by name: it is customary in studies of apes to give them proper names so as to keep track of who is who. But the chimpanzees know the humans, too: while they may do their best to keep their distance and avoid any disruption, their presence never goes unnoticed, and any newcomer is discretely but intensely scrutinized by the elders.

Suddenly, while most of the chimpanzees are away, the humans hear a soft call: *hoo . . . hoo . . . hoo . . . .* It is produced by a chimpanzee, but there is no other chimpanzee in the immediate vicinity. Rather, his eye gaze goes back and forth between the field assistant, Sam, and the ground. It may have been hard to discern, but when one looks more closely, the reason becomes apparent: A snake is crawling. And it looks like the chimpanzee is trying to warn Sam. *Hoo* is a snake alarm call, and the chimpanzee's eye gaze movement between Sam and the snake suggests that Sam was the intended audience.[1]

This real-life anecdote raises fascinating questions about the relationship between the chimpanzees and the humans who study them. The primatologists do their best to avoid interacting with their primate cousins: The goal is to observe, not disrupt, and primatologists do their best to be as transparent as possible to the apes. But could it still be that some chimpanzees treat some humans as their friends? We do not quite know. In fact, the precise nature of the relationship is still a mystery.

But this anecdote also highlights a remarkable fact about ape communication: Chimpanzees have signals that convey information about threats and can be used intentionally, as illustrated here by the chimpanzee's eye gaze going back and forth between the field assistant and the ground, possibly to check that the snake has indeed been spotted. Still, an anecdote is just an anecdote, and short of systematic studies, we will never know for sure what happened in the chimpanzee's mind on that particular day. To really understand how primate communication works, we need to harness the tools of science: systematic observations, field experiments, and precise theories. As it turns out, we humans are currently limited in our understanding of chimpanzee calls, possibly because they have social implications that escape us. Important headway was recently made in the understanding of ape gestures. But the most decisive progress was made when primatologists studied in detail the meaning of monkey calls (around the early 1980s).

### 1.2   OUR PRIMATE COUSINS

Before we plunge into monkey calls, we should pause to consider the primate family tree. Humans and chimpanzees have a common ancestor that lived between 6 million and 7 million years ago. That's a long time. As a point of comparison, all current humans have a common ancestor that lived a few hundred thousand years ago. Bonobos are relatively close cousins of chimpanzees, and both species are equally closely related to us. Further cousins (more remote ones) are gorillas, orangutans, and gibbons. All are apes, and like us they lack a tail. Monkeys have one, but they are more distant in our 'family' tree. To find a common ancestor between us and African and Asian monkeys (called 'Old World monkeys'), we need to go rather far back in time, 20 million to 30 million years ago. And to find a common ancestor with American monkeys (called 'New World monkeys'), we need to go back 30 million to 40 million years ago.

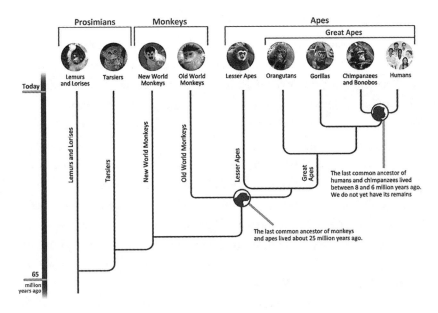

**Figure 1.2.1**

*The primate family tree*

You might ask, How do we know all this? The answer is through DNA analysis. Parents pass their DNA to their offspring, but the DNA isn't transmitted without modifications (called 'mutations'): Occasional random 'errors' are made in the copying process, as when monks in the Middle Ages copied manuscripts by hand but made small errors in the process.[2] The more mutations have accumulated, the more distant the original copy. Furthermore, once a mutation has occurred, it will typically be inherited by later copies. So, by studying which of these mutations are shared among individuals or species, we can reconstruct their family tree.

### 1.3 SEMANTICS: VERVET AND DIANA CALLS

Among primatologists interested in communication, the Vervet monkeys of Africa are real stars. It was by studying their calls that three pioneers, Robert Seyfarth, Dorothy Cheney, and Peter Marler, showed in the early 1980s how sophisticated monkey calls can be.[3] But Vervets are not always as popular with the locals. Unlike most monkeys we will discuss, they spend much time on the ground, so they are very good at eating cultivators' crops. On a field visit to Uganda, we were anxiously awaiting our first encounter with the Vervets. Our field assistant asked a peasant where they could be found. Helpful indications were provided, with a suggestion that we eat the Vervets for dinner (it was made in jest, since monkeys and apes are strictly protected from poaching in Uganda).

So why did the Vervets, who are not especially popular with the locals, become linguistic stars? Because they established the existence of a primate semantics: They have several calls, three of which are respectively associated with raptors, leopards, and snakes. This association can be ascertained by carefully observing the situations in which the calls are produced. But how do we know that the calls are not just physiological reactions, devoid of any informational content? To establish this point, we must show that Vervets understand the content of these calls and thus display the appropriate reaction when they hear them. So, the first thing to do is to observe how Vervets react when they hear, say, a raptor alarm call. But things aren't so easy: Many things happen simultaneously in the forest, and when a Vervet produces an alarm call, it may be hard to determine whether other Vervets are reacting to the call, or to what triggered it (the raptor), or possibly to something unrelated. To really understand what is going on, primatologists perform field experiments: They hide loudspeakers in trees, and they play back alarm calls in the absence of any real threat. In this way, they can determine whether the calls can convey information on their own, independent of any disturbance in the forest.

The results of Seyfarth, Cheney, and Marler's experiments were remarkable. The Vervets typically reacted appropriately. Not only this, their reactions suggested that they took into account both the informational content of the calls and their own situation to display the most appropriate reaction. In all cases, a Vervet that heard a snake alarm call tended to look down (what else would *you* do if you were told that there's a snake around?). By contrast, a Vervet that heard a leopard alarm call while on the ground didn't look down but, rather, ran for cover or looked up (as leopards can climb on trees). But looking down was a useful reaction if the Vervet heard the call while in a tree, since the leopard could be coming from the ground, and this reaction was indeed found. Similarly, a Vervet that heard an eagle alarm call looked down more often when the Vervet was in a tree (as the eagle could be down below) than on the ground.

These results show two things. First, alarm calls convey specific information to the Vervets. Not only do they produce calls in some situations but not in others, but they also understand the calls of others (including if these others turn out to be facetious primatologists who, in the interest of science, have hidden loudspeakers in the trees). In other words, Vervet calls have a semantics. Second, Vervet calls genuinely seem to convey information about the world rather than about the best reaction to display. One could imagine that calls are tantamount to orders, such as *run for cover* or *climb up*. But this is unlikely, since Vervets react to the same call in different ways depending on where they are in the tree: They don't look down when hearing a leopard call while on the ground, but they do look down if they are in a tree.

In order to drive home the point that there is a kind of equivalence in monkey minds between a raptor alarm call and the presence of a genuine raptor, a beautiful experiment was performed by Klaus Zuberbühler, Dorothy Cheney, and Robert Seyfarth in a different species, the Diana monkeys—distant cousins of the Vervets (they share a common ancestor from approximately 7.5 million years ago).[4] There are three sub-experiments, each involving two sounds played through a loudspeaker at times $t$ and $t$ + 5 minutes. The second sound was always an eagle shriek, but the first sound differed across experiment. The goal was to determine whether the second sound produced new information that licensed an alarm or not.

| | | |
|---|---|---|
| **1st experiment:** | **Eagle shriek at t = 0** | Eagle shriek at t = 5 min |
| | Dianas produce eagle alarm calls! | Dianas **don't** produce eagle alarm calls. |
| | | (Eagle presence is old information.) |
| **2nd experiment:** | **Diana eagle call at t = 0** | Eagle shriek at t = 5 min |
| | Dianas produce eagle alarm calls! | Dianas **don't** produce eagle alarm calls. |
| | | (Eagle presence is old information.) |
| **3rd experiment:** | **Diana leopard call at t = 0** | Eagle shriek at t = 5 min |
| | Dianas produce leopard alarm calls! | Dianas **do** produce eagle alarm calls! |
| | | (Eagle presence is new information.) |

In an initial experiment, the primatologists started by playing back to the Dianas some eagle shrieks. Understandably alarmed, the male Dianas produced eagle calls at a high rate. Five minutes later, eagle shrieks were played again. The Diana monkeys' reaction was muted—possibly because they already knew of an eagle's presence and had already warned the surrounding monkeys. This much is rather unsurprising.

In a second experiment, the shrieks played in the first one were replaced with Diana eagle alarm calls. Here, too, the target individuals were alarmed and responded with their own eagle alarm calls. But five minutes later, the primatologists played back eagle shrieks (rather than Diana calls) as they had in the first experiment. In that initial experiment, the monkeys were hearing the same type of sound for a second time, and thus it was unsurprising that they failed to react much. In the new version of the experiment, this wasn't the case: Diana eagle calls sound very different from eagle shrieks. But the Dianas' reaction to the shrieks was still muted, as if they had already known, thanks to the Diana eagle alarm calls, that there was an eagle around. As a result, hearing eagle shrieks didn't convey any new information. In other words, it seemed to be the conceptual equivalence between an eagle's presence and a Diana eagle alarm call that was responsible for this behavior.

Going one step further, the primatologists reasoned that if the initial Diana eagle call was replaced with a Diana leopard call, the reaction when hearing eagle shrieks should be anything but muted. This made sense because in that case, the eagle shrieks conveyed entirely new information. The prediction was borne out in a third experiment: having heard a leopard alarm call rather than an eagle alarm call, the Dianas reacted with high call rates when they heard eagle shrieks five minutes later.

At this point, you might wonder how the monkeys learn what these calls mean. This question too can arise in any semantic investigation: Once we know how the adults behave, we may want to understand how kids learn that behavior. With human language, nobody would think that we are born with a knowledge of what *car* or *dog* mean, but the situation is different with nonhuman primates. For starters, the form of their calls seems to be largely innate (i.e., genetically inherited). Monkeys of the same species that were raised in entirely different groups usually have the same calls. Not only this, but these calls also seem to have the same meanings. In addition, hybrids born to parents from different subspecies have calls that are determined by their genetic heritage rather than by the environment in which they are raised. Which calls they have does not seem to be much affected by which species they grow up with, and this highlights the plausibility of a genetic explanation. Things get even more surprising. In several of the monkey species we'll be discussing, males have different calls from females—they are louder, involve different sounds, and have different meanings as well. But juvenile males have female calls, and it's only around puberty that they start calling like males. How this happens in monkeys is still a bit of a mystery.

Still, we know something about call acquisition in Vervets. Seyfarth, Cheney, and Marler analyzed the situations in which infants and juveniles used raptor calls, and they found something interesting. Even infants didn't use raptor calls in situations involving mammals. On the other hand, they called 'raptor' in all sorts of situations that involved nonthreatening birds. Juveniles were more discriminating than infants, and adults only used raptor calls for predators that genuinely pose a threat. Is it that Vervet children have a different meaning for the raptor call than adults do? Or is it that for children and adults alike, the raptor call has a general meaning—akin to Bird!—but that children haven't yet learned that it's not worth calling attention to something that's not a threat? We don't know yet.

Much linguistic knowledge seems to be innate in primates. This is what explains the similarities among calls of socially unrelated groups (and also the calling behavior of hybrids). But one shouldn't conclude that *everything* about monkey calls is innate. There are definitely some examples of variation. Dianas and Vervets have another cousin species, the Campbell's monkeys, which are a bit closer to the Dianas than to the Vervets (the Dianas and Campbell's shared a common ancestor approximately 6 million years ago). Diana and Campbell's males have very different calls, but the Campbell's female calls are rather close to the Diana female calls, suggesting that calls can be preserved over millions of years (we will revisit this issue at the end of this chapter). But for all this biological determinism, Campbell's female calls were shown to be subtly different from one individual to the next. A genetic explanation would lead one to expect that call proximity reflects genetic relatedness. Family members should thus talk in similar ways. But this is not what was found when a group of captive (i.e., non-wild) monkeys were investigated in France. Just like human children tend to talk like their friends, so too were female Campbell's monkeys acoustically closer to their friends than to their family members.[5]

A more radical case of variation was found as well. In the same group of captive Campbell's monkeys, the females apparently created a new call never heard in the wild: It was specifically used to warn of unfamiliar or unpopular humans, such as . . . the local veterinarian.[6] This finding should be taken with caution because it is difficult to ascertain that a call is never used in the wild. Still, this case of linguistic innovation isn't isolated. In chimpanzees (who are much more closely related to us than to Campbell's monkeys), some captive groups 'invented' a call that primatologists called the 'Bronx cheer' (or 'raspberry' or 'splutter'). It was specifically produced when the chimpanzees needed to capture the attention of an inattentive human; the call seemed to be produced intentionally rather than as an automatic reaction to the presence of a threat or, for that matter, food.[7]

## 1.4  ELUSIVE SYNTAX: TITI CALLS

Stepping back, it seems clear that primate calls have meanings, just like words do (although words have very different meanings, obviously). But there is more to language than individual words. From *Robin, loves,* and *Casey,* we can form *Robin loves Casey* as well as *Casey loves Robin.* Not any order goes: *Loves Robin Casey* is not an English sentence. English has a syntax—that is, a set of rules that define what is and what isn't a possible sentence. Furthermore, new meanings can be obtained from these combinations. The meaning of the whole *Robin loves Casey* is derived from the meaning of its parts, but the combination isn't trivial—in particular, it cannot be analyzed as a succession of utterances meaning *There is someone named Robin. There is some loving relation. There is someone named Casey.* And of course different word orders would yield different meanings: It may be that *Robin loves Casey* even though the sentence *Casey loves Robin* is, alas, false. Do monkey calls have a comparable syntax?

The tiny Titi monkeys of Brazil initially suggested a positive answer. They are endearing little fellows. They mate for life and entwine their tails to strengthen their couple's bond. They 'sing' duets together (possibly to mark their territory) and produce soft alarm calls that sound like bird chirps. But their life isn't easy: they are eaten by catlike predators, and by eagles, and by some more famous monkeys, the Capuchins—notoriously smart primates that can eat meat.

Now the extraordinary thing is that with just two of their calls rearranged in different ways, the A- and the B-calls, the Titis encode information about the type of predator that's threatening them and about the predator's location. A beautiful field experiment was devised by Cristiane Cäsar and colleagues to demonstrate this.[8] This time the primatologists didn't hide loudspeakers in the forest; taking things a step further, they hid model predators—a model raptor and a model cat—that were as lifelike as possible. And they hid them in two positions: on the ground or in the canopy (high in the trees).

When primatologists and then linguists inspected the results, they were flabbergasted: By rearranging the calls in various ways, the Titi sequences encoded information about which kind of predator they saw and where it was located. The results are illustrated in figure 1.4.1, where each line represents the first 30 calls emitted by the Titis in the field experiment (any longer sequence just repeats the last calls).

Setting aside some extraneous calls (labeled C and O), the four blocks corresponding to the four experiments can be visually distinguished from each other rather easily. For a raptor in the canopy, it is a long series of A-calls. For a raptor on the ground, A-calls are followed by B-calls. For a cat on the ground, there is a long series of B-calls. And for a cat in the canopy, a single A-call is followed by B-calls.

Have we discovered syntax in monkeys? It sure doesn't look like human syntax because of the numerous repetitions: Humans don't go around saying things like *Robin Robin Robin Robin loves loves loves Casey Casey Casey Casey Casey Casey*. But maybe we shouldn't hold the repetitions against the Titis. When your interlocutors are far away and it's important that you be heard, it might make sense to repeat yourself quite a bit (if your airplane must make

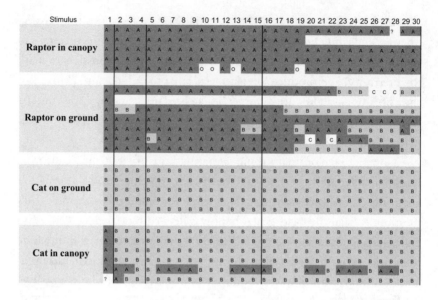

**Figure 1.4.1**

*Titi call sequences encode information about predator type and predator location*

Each line represents the series of (the first 30) Titi calls produced in reaction to the presence of a model predator: A-calls (dark gray), B-calls (light gray), and additional types without color: O, C, and ? in unclear cases.

an emergency landing, it's likely the pilot won't just say *Brace!* once, but rather *Brace! Brace! Brace!* . . . ). So maybe we should abstract away from the repetitions, writing $A^+$ for any number of repetitions of $A$ and using $B^+$ for any number of repetitions of $B$. With this notational trick, the Titi sentences start looking more orderly: $A+$ means 'there is a raptor up'; $A^+B^+$ means 'there is a raptor down'; $B^+$ means 'there is a cat down'; and $AB^+$ means 'there is a cat up.' The challenge for the primate linguist is to understand how these meanings come about.

On closer inspection, however, the prospects for a bona fide syntax appear bleak. The main problem is that these sequences are fairly slow, and because of the repetitions, it would take a really long time to know whether you are hearing a 'raptor up' ($A^+$) or a 'raptor down' ($A^+B^+$) sequence. The unfortunate Titis would often have to wait for about 15 seconds to know whether the threat is coming from above or from below. If you are a Titi, the stakes couldn't be higher: understanding the calls quickly enough will determine whether you'll end up as somebody else's lunch.

So it's likely that the Titis don't interpret sequences as wholes. Instead, researchers have explored an alternative hypothesis: Each call is a complete linguistic unit—a sentence if you will—and it provides information about the nature of the threat at the precise time at which the call is produced. But then what are the meanings of the A- and B-calls?[9]

At this point, we need to go beyond the beautiful field experiment we started out with and observe some natural situations. The first thing to notice is that the B-call is used in extraordinarily diverse contexts: when there is a predator, when there is a ground mammal that isn't a predator, when the Titis are feeding, and so on. Since these situations have so little in common, it makes sense to take the B-call to convey something very broad, such as *something is happening*—a kind of completely general alert call.

The remaining challenge, then, is to discover the meaning of the A-call. An observation gave scientists a clue: It was regularly observed that when hearing an A-call, the Titis looked up. So it was hypothesized that the A-call means something like: *There is a serious threat up*. Both parts—*serious* and *up*—are important, as we will now see.

Let's go back to the $A^+$ sequence produced in 'raptor in the canopy' situation. It is certainly used to signal that there is a serious threat up in these situations, so the repeated $A$ call makes sense. Furthermore, the model raptor is sure to stay put for as long as the primatologist desires. As long as the threat is present, the A-call can be produced—hence the long A-sequences we observe in the field experiment. In natural situations involving real predators, different patterns are found. For a flying raptor, we still find a sequence of A-calls, but it is much shorter: As soon as the raptor has flown away, there is no reason to keep calling anymore. When the raptor is perched and potentially in a hunting position, the sequences are much longer.

What about the $A^+B^+$ sequences we find in 'raptor on the ground' situations? Well, the main idea is that raptors don't usually attack by crawling but by flying. This might explain why the Titis signal a serious threat up, hence the repeated A-calls at the beginning of the sequence: A raptor that's on the ground would probably attack by flying, and thus the threat would usually come from above. In addition, if a raptor stays on the ground for a while, chances are that it isn't in a hunting position; it might also be that this just isn't a normal position for a raptor to stay in (unlike a perched position in a tree). Either way, after a while the Titi might decide that the threat isn't so serious, and thus the 'serious threat up' isn't licensed any longer. This explains why the sequence transitions to a B-call, which just says that there is something to pay attention to.

In 'cat on the ground' situations, the Titis don't have a choice, since it would be misleading to announce a 'serious threat up' by way of an A-call. So, only the B-call can be used. The last case to be explained in the data is the 'cat in the canopy' sequence, which involves a single A-call followed by B-calls: AB$^+$. The initial A-call is unsurprising because there is indeed a serious threat up. But why don't we find the same pattern as in the 'raptor in the canopy' situations, with a series of A-calls? One (somewhat speculative) possibility is that the threats involved are different. A raptor in a tree likely presents a danger as long as it stays there. But for monkeys, cats are thought to be far less dangerous once they have been detected since it is easy for the monkeys to climb in places that are hard to reach. In fact, in a different environment (Africa rather than South America), it was shown that leopards tend to abandon the hunt once they have been detected by monkeys. So while the cat in the canopy might initially be a *serious* threat, after its presence has been announced, it might become a more innocuous event. Announcing a serious threat would no longer be correct, and the A-call stops being appropriate— hence the appearance of the B-call.[10]

Titis teach us an important lesson: Not everything that looks like syntax is syntax. To understand Titi call sequences, we did without any Titi grammar of the kind needed to analyze *Robin loves Casey* or *Casey loves Robin*. All we needed were very simple call meanings, combined with plausible assumptions about the evolution of the threats in different situations.

This lesson has broader significance: Primates have sophisticated communication systems, but so far there are no clear cases of a complex syntax. Interestingly, birdsongs are different. Notes can be combined according to constrained and sophisticated rules. But as things stand, there is no evidence that these different combinations do anything but advertise the caller's quality, for instance to potential mates. In other words, there is no counterpart of our *Robin loves Casey* versus *Casey loves Robin* example: human language remains one of a kind in this respect as in many others.

## 1.5 PRAGMATICS: THE INFORMATIVITY PRINCIPLE

If you were hoping for extraordinary linguistic feats by monkeys, Titi calls might have come as a disappointment. They seemed to promise some beautiful primate syntax, and all I did was convince you that far simpler hypotheses can explain the findings. But if we dig deeper, the Titis can tell us something quite extraordinary about monkey abilities and the difference between semantics and pragmatics.

To introduce the phenomenon, it is best to start from human language. If I tell you, *It is possible that Russia influenced the 2016 election*, you will normally infer that I don't take this to be a certainty, because if so, I should have said: *It is certain that Russian influenced the 2016 election*. Now you could think that this is because *possible* means something like *conceivable but not certain*. But this wouldn't be quite correct. The reason is that I can say, without contradicting myself, *It is possible, and in fact even certain, that Russia influenced the 2016 election*. Linguists have come up with a better analysis in which *possible* competes with *certain*. On the assumption that *possible* means something like *there's at least a possibility*, *certain* is more informative. So if the speaker is cooperative and thus chooses the most informative sentence available, we can infer from the use of *possible* that *certain* wasn't open, presumably because it was overly strong—hence the *possible but not certain* inference we get in the Russia-related sentence.

This is a typical example of pragmatic reasoning (and an example of what the philosopher Paul Grice called an 'implicature'): The literal meaning of the words is enriched by reasoning on the speaker's motivations. In this way, we get the inference we wanted: *Possible* implies *not certain*, but this isn't due to a hardwired ('semantic') component of the meaning of *possible*. Rather, it is just due to a plausible reasoning about the speaker's behavior (and for this reason, it is no contradiction to say *possible and even certain*). The specific reasoning I outlined is based on what is called the Informativity Principle, which mandates that speakers should be as informative as possible. This principle makes its effects felt in numerous other examples. If I ask you how you found a movie we just saw, and you tell me that *it was nice*, I'll have reason to think that you didn't quite love it, because if you did, you should have said something stronger, such as: *It was great!* (We will revisit the Informativity Principle in detail in chapter 10.)

Remarkably, Titis seem to have a version of the Informativity Principle. Let's think again about the data we just discussed. The B-call appears in all sorts of contexts, and thus we took it to have a really broad meaning (*something is happening*). We gave the A-call a more specific meaning (*there is a serious threat up*), which did a pretty good job of explaining its distribution. But we didn't ask a simpler question: Why isn't the B-call used all over the place? Given its extraordinarily general meaning, it should be true whenever something is happening—including when there is a raptor that's about to attack! Now you might wonder, Why on earth would the Titis use a B-call in a raptor situation when they have a perfectly appropriate A-call that provides much more useful information? And I agree, that would be strange. But this is just another way of saying that *the Titis seem to obey a version of the Informativity Principle*: if they can use something more specific than the completely general B-call, they do so.

Now we can't conclude from this that the *reason* the Titi monkeys do such a thing is that they are trying to be cooperative with their audience, along the lines of the following reasoning: 'I could use A, and also B, but my interlocutor will acquire more useful beliefs if I say A, so that's what I am going to say.' This would require an ability to represent other animals' beliefs— or, in other words, a theory of other minds—which is something that researchers are not necessarily ready to ascribe to monkeys (although there is some evidence for it in apes, as we will soon see). But the Titis could still have a kind of instinct that tells them to use the most specific call they have, thus obeying the Informativity Principle without a detour through a reasoning on their interlocutors' minds.

While it is still the object of debates, the Informativity Principle seems useful to analyze the calls of further primates, including ones (from Africa) that bear little relation to the South American Titis. Often one finds a fairly general call and a specific raptor call. But one almost never finds the general call used in raptor situations; this might well be because all these monkeys obey the Informativity Principle. This principle might also offer the key to the remarkable call system of a very different species: the African Campbell's monkeys.

## 1.6  PUTTING IT ALL TOGETHER: CAMPBELL'S CALLS

While Vervets were stars of primate communication in the 1980s, in recent years they were eclipsed by Campbell's monkeys, studied in particular by Karim Ouattara and colleagues.[11] Their calls offer a case study in primate linguistics, with a tiny bit of syntax, some semantics, and some pragmatics combined in one system.

I briefly mentioned that female Campbell's monkeys talk with the mannerisms of their friends rather than of their family. But males are no less interesting. In the forest, a resident male warns his group—a harem of females and juveniles—of impending threats. His calls are loud, and invariably given by the same individual, as there is only one resident male per group. This makes male calls much easier to study than female calls, as the latter are much softer and often given by an entire group.

Male Campbell's calls are remarkable for several reasons. First, they include a non-predation call, *boom*, which is low in frequency, loud, and heard far away in the forest. Primatologists aren't sure of the precise meaning of *boom*, but it is never used in the presence of predators and seems to function to establish group coherence and possibly to defend territory ('I am here!'). Remarkably, *boom* usually appears at the beginning of call sequences, as a single pair (*boom boom*). So it seems that the Campbell's have a syntactic rule governing the use of *boom*—and this might be more robust than our initial impression that Titis have syntax! (Full disclosure: I try to remain cautious on this one, because besides *boom*, little order could be found in the call sequences of Campbell's monkeys, either because there is none or because we weren't smart enough to detect it.)

The second remarkable thing is that some Campbell's calls have an internal structure. This is a common occurrence in human languages: From *inform* you can derive *informative* and from that *informativity*, a word you read a few paragraphs back when I introduced the Informativity Principle. Here we obtained two new words by successfully adding the suffix *-ative* and then the suffix *-ity*. Linguists call this morphology, the rules by which words are made. But morphology *in monkeys*? That's more surprising. And yet Campbell's monkeys seem to have a suffix—namely, *-oo*. Just like male Dianas, Campbell's have a call warning of eagle presence: *hok*. But they also have a call *hok-oo*, warning of less serious non-ground (e.g., aerial or arboreal) threats. For instance, they use *hok-oo* when they encounter other monkey groups (Campbells, just like Dianas, live in trees, so the encounters will usually take place in the trees as well). Here, *-oo* genuinely seems to function like a suffix: It is added to a word to form a new word with a related meaning. From *green* you can form *green-ish* ('kind of green'), from *blue* you can form *blue-ish* ('kind of blue'), and *-ish* makes the same contribution in both cases. Similarly, the Campbell's use of *-oo* is reminiscent of *-ish*. Whereas *hok* is used for serious non-ground threats, *hok-oo* is used for attenuated versions and for less serious non-ground threats.

But couldn't it just be an accident that *hok* and *hok-oo* have a part in common? In English, the adjective *irate* (meaning 'very angry') is made of two syllables, and each syllable has an independent meaning (*I* = the first-person pronoun, *rate* = the verb), but that's a pure accident—nobody would dream of analyzing *irate* as being made of *I* + *rate*, since to be irate has nothing to do with any kind of rating! While we can't completely exclude that *hok-oo* presents a similar accident, two facts militate against this conclusion. For starters, there is a very brief pause between *hok* and *-oo* in *hok-oo*, as if the call acoustics were telling us that it's genuinely made of two parts. (Not that this is a requirement to be a suffix, mind you—you don't have such pauses in the English examples I discussed; but if we want to argue that *hok-oo* has two parts, finding a tiny pause between them is still helpful.)

But there is more. In the case of *green-greenish*, the main argument for an analysis with a suffix is that *ish* can be added to other adjectives, such as *blue*. As it turns out, *hok* is not alone in taking *-oo* as a suffix. There is another call, *krak,* which was initially analyzed as a leopard alarm call. And from *krak + oo,* Campbell's monkeys form *krak-oo*; and it too seems to be an attenuated call of sorts, used for all kinds of alerts, not just predator-related ones (we'll refine this point below).

So this is the language of Campbell's monkeys: *Boom* is used for situations of non-predation and appears as a pair, at the beginning of sentences. *Hok* is used for serious non-ground threats (eagle-related threats) and *hok-oo* for all sorts of non-ground alerts. *Krak-oo* is used even more generally, for all kinds of alerts, whether ground or non-ground, while *krak* is used for serious ground threats (leopards).

I have simplified things a bit, however. I described the call system of Campbell's monkeys as found in the Tai forest of Ivory Coast. But Campbell's monkeys were also studied in a different site, on Tiwai Island in Sierra Leone. And they had another surprise in store for the primatologists (Kate Arnold, Sumir Keenan, and colleagues): While most of the calls had the same form and meaning as in the Tai forest, there was one striking exception. *Krak,* which was used as a leopard alert in the Tai forest, appeared to be used as a completely general alarm call on Tiwai Island. Most surprisingly, although Campbell's monkeys of the Tai forest almost never used *krak* for eagles (reserving this call for leopards), their cousins of Tiwai Island produced lots of *kraks* when an eagle's presence was simulated. The rough meanings of Campbell's calls are thus the following (with a difference between Tai and Tiwai regarding *krak*):

**Campbell's calls**
boom boom (only at the beginning of sequences): situations of non-predation
hok: eagle presence
hok-oo: non-ground alert
krak: (i) leopard presence (Tai); (ii) general alert (Tiwai)
krak-oo: general alert

There is an interesting environmental difference between the Tai forest and Tiwai Island. While Tai and Tiwai both have eagles, leopards haven't been seen on Tiwai Island for dozens and dozens of years. Primate calls are thought to be largely innate. We saw an example of this when we discussed the use of the eagle call by infant Vervet monkeys: They know from the start that it should only be applied to birds. So what should we expect of the calling behavior of the Campbell's monkeys on Tiwai Island? If the meaning of the *krak* call is innate, and if it genuinely warns of leopard presence, we would just expect it not be used on Tiwai Island. But this isn't at all what primatologists found. The call was used all over the place, with a completely general meaning—so much so that on Tiwai, *krak* and *krak-oo* seemed to have roughly the same meaning (whereas in the Tai forest, *krak* was primarily used to warn of leopard presence).

When linguists and primatologists analyzed these data, they couldn't rule out that there was a bit of dialectal variation across Campbell's monkey populations. The Irish writer George Bernard Shaw famously quipped that England and America are two countries divided by a common language, and that is in part because it's not *quite* the same language. For instance, *pants* refers to trousers in the United States but to underpants in Great Britain. Since we already saw that there is a bit of linguistic innovation in primates (as in the case of the chimpanzee 'Bronx cheer' made to humans), we couldn't exclude that at some point one group 'invented' a new meaning for *krak*.

But on closer inspection, something else was puzzling about these calls, even just looking at their use in the Tai forest. *Hok* refers to serious non-ground threats and *hok-oo* to an attenuated version of these threats. In the Tai forest, *krak* refers to serious ground threats, so by parity of reasoning, we could expect that *krak-oo* refers to attenuated ground threats. But the facts were different: in the Tai forest, *krak-oo* was used as a genuinely general call, for ground and non-ground threats alike.

In the end, then, we have two puzzles on our hands: Why is there a difference in the meaning of *krak* between the Tai forest and Tiwai Island? And focusing on Tai, how is the meaning of *krak-oo* derived from the meaning of *krak* and *-oo*? This is illustrated in figure 1.6.1 (from which I have removed *hok-oo* for simplicity).

Linguists devised a solution to solve both problems. It makes crucial use of the Informativity Principle. To start with, consider *hok* and *hok-oo*. The idea is that *hok* is used for non-ground (e.g., aerial) alarms while *hok-oo* is used for aerial alarms that are not serious. If we stopped here, the analysis

# A Campbell's Puzzle

krak is used for leopards in Tai and for eagles on Tiwai

hok
krakoo

krak
hok
krakoo

krak
krakoo

Tiwai Island
Sierra Leone

Tai forest
Ivory Coast

**Figure 1.6.1**

*The puzzle of krak*

would be wrong: *hok* is used for raptor alarms, not for other non-ground alarms. But the Informativity Principle comes to the rescue: *Hok-oo* is more informative than *hok*, since if there is a *nonserious aerial alarm*, there is certainly an *aerial alarm*. By the principle, if *hok* is produced, this is because the more informative call *hok-oo* couldn't be, so the alarm wasn't nonserious: it was a serious alarm!

In figure 1.6.2, I've put *hok-oo* above *hok* because the former is more informative than the latter. The Informativity Principle tells us that *hok* can only be used when *hok-oo* can't, so if *hok* is used, there must be a serious aerial alarm.

When we come to *krak*, things get more interesting. We take its literal meaning to be the one it has on Tiwai Island—that is, *krak* is just a general alarm call. Since we want *-oo* to have the same effect when applied to *hok* and to *krak*, we have no choice but to say that *krak-oo* is used for nonserious alarms. Now let's go back to *krak*, taking into account the Informativity Principle. *Krak-oo* is of course more informative than *krak*. If there is a

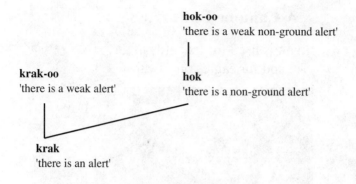

**hok-oo**
'there is a weak non-ground alert'

**krak-oo**
'there is a weak alert'

**hok**
'there is a non-ground alert'

**krak**
'there is an alert'

When taking into the Informativity Principle, the contribution of *krak* is:
krak and not krak-oo and not hok
i.e. there is a serious, ground-related alert.

**Figure 1.6.2**
*Informativity relations among Campbell's calls*
For two calls that are linked, 'higher' means 'more informative.'

nonserious alarm, there is an alarm (this is the same reasoning we used for *hok-oo* and *hok*). But *hok* is also more informative than *krak*: If there is an aerial alarm, there is an alarm. So *krak* can only be used when these two competitors cannot be. In other words, it can only be used when there is an alarm but it's *not* nonserious (so it's serious!) and it's *not* an aerial alarm (so it's ground-related!).[12]

Putting everything together, *krak* can only be used when there is an alarm, and it is serious, and it is ground-related. Now put yourself in the shoes (or fur) of a Campbell's monkey of the Tai forest, where the main predators are eagles and leopards. What could a serious alarm that's ground-related refer to? Leopards, of course! We have derived the correct use of *krak*.

The only thing that remains to be explained is why *krak* doesn't have the same overall meaning on Tiwai Island ('serious ground-related alarm'). Let's think about this a bit more. If there was such a meaning on Tiwai, it would be pretty useless, since there are no leopards and thus no serious ground threats on Tiwai. At this point, we must remember that the ground predator inference isn't hardwired in the meaning of *krak*: It's the Informativity Principle that leads to this inference. So, all we need to posit is that the enrichment of meaning that comes from the Informativity Principle doesn't take place if it gives rise to a useless result: monkeys aren't stupid.

In sum, Campbell's male calls have a semantics and also a tiny bit of morphology, with a suffix *-oo* that can modify the meaning of *hok* and of *krak*. They might have a syntactic rule: *Boom boom* comes as a pair at the beginning of sequences (although the rest of the syntax is . . . a mess). And a case can be made that they obey a pragmatic rule, the Informativity Principle, which mandates that the most informative calls should be used whenever possible. Campbell's monkeys thus offer a miniature system of what semantics (broadly construed) is all about.

## 1.7 BILINGUALISM IN THE WILD

Some of us know several languages, but these are languages used by our own species. Our primate cousins routinely understand the language of *other species*. Take the Diana monkeys. As we saw before, the males produce very different calls from the Campbell's males, with whom they share a common ancestor from approximately 6.5 million years ago. But Campbell's and Dianas often live in the same trees, and thus they have experience with each other's calls. And they have ample reason to understand the neighbors' calls, as these may warn of impending threats. Bilingualism might be a matter of life and death.

And bilingualism there is. Diana monkeys understand Campbell's calls, down to the details.[13] Let us go back to the Tai forest but turn our attention from the Campbell's monkeys to the Dianas. Hiding once again a loudspeaker in the trees, we play back a series of Campbell's *krak* calls, which in this environment are indicative of leopards. The Dianas respond with their own calls appropriate for ground predators. If instead we play back a series of Campbell's *hok* calls, the Dianas respond with their own eagle calls. Although the Dianas don't speak the Campbell's language, they clearly understand some of it.

But how detailed is their knowledge? It took us humans quite some time to understand the workings of *boom, krak, hok, krak-oo, and hok-oo*. Are the Dianas more gifted polyglots? Take *booms*. When they appear in Campbell's call sequences, they are a sure sign that the situation is not one of predation. The Dianas themselves don't have *booms*. But remarkably, they understand their meaning. How do we know? As before, we play back to the Dianas some Campbell's leopard- and eagle-related sequences. But now we artificially add to them *boom boom* at the beginning. This time the Dianas stop responding in anything like the same way as before: They know that *boom* is a non-predation call. In fact, they know something more precise—namely, that *boom* is indicative of non-predation *when it is produced by Campbell's monkeys*. How could we tell? We wish to exclude the more mundane possibility that they know that whenever *boom* is produced, there is no predator around. To test this, we now play back a hybrid sequence made of a Campbell's *boom boom* followed by a Diana sequence warning of the presence of a leopard or eagle. But now the Dianas react with alarm: They know that the *boom boom* pair doesn't belong in a Diana sequence, and they just ignore it. In other words, they interpret the Diana sequence without the extraneous Campbell's calls that were deviously added by the primatologists.

And it's not just that the Dianas understand the Campbell's. The Campbell's monkeys understand their Diana neighbors, too. So much so, in fact, that primatologists sometimes use Diana calls to trigger Campbell's calls—and the Campbell's immediately decode Diana call content and relay it with their own calls.

This kind of bilingualism might seem remarkable, but it is by no means exceptional. While our primate pride might suffer from this observation, some birds understand Diana monkey calls. Such is the case of the hornbill, a large, majestic bird with an impressive beak and a slow flight.[14] When you play back some Diana calls, the hornbill reacts with its own calls, but in a selective fashion: Diana eagle calls elicit a reaction, but Diana leopard calls don't. No wonder: Eagles are a threat to hornbills, but leopards are not (they may climb on trees, but they can't fly). Hornbills thus respond as they should; but this is possible only because they understand the difference between Diana leopard and Diana eagle calls.

## 1.8  CALL EVOLUTION

In 1876, the Linguistic Society of Paris famously prohibited any further debates on language evolution because this topic had only produced the wildest of speculations. The situation has improved, but not as much as one would have hoped. Take this long-standing question: Did human language originally start developing in sounds or in gestures? There have been endless debates and a bit of progress, but the question is still considered fairly open among scientists (which doesn't prevent some of them from having strong opinions on this matter; it's just that different scientists have strong opinions that go in opposite directions). Given how distant monkeys are from us, any hope of connecting their calls to human language is, of course, even more remote.

But there is a little scientific secret that even scientists have made insufficient use of: It is that the evolutionary history of some monkey calls can be reconstructed over millions of years. Think about it. In humans, the state of language 300,000 years ago is a very controversial topic, and one would be hard-pressed to find a strong argument that a particular word already existed at the time with a particular meaning. But, as we will now see, the situation is entirely different with Campbell's monkeys and their relatives.

**The Story of *Boom*:** Let's go back to the *boom* call, which may appear at the beginning of Campbell's male sequences and is a signal of non-predation. It's not hard to reconstruct its history over millions of years and to conclude with great certainty that it was already present 2 million to 3 million years ago.

*But you weren't there*, you might object, *so how could you know?* By combining two sources of information: DNA data to help reconstruct the history of species, and the distribution of *booms* in today's monkey species. The key observation is that the Campbell's are not alone in having *booms*. True, their cousins, the Dianas, don't have them—which makes it all the more remarkable that they still understand them. But many other members of the Diana and Campbell's family have *booms*. To get a glimpse of the situation, we start from a 'family tree' obtained with DNA methods, and we plot which species do and which species do not have *booms*. We immediately find something remarkable: there are two subfamilies all of whose members have *booms*.[15]

In the family tree in figure 1.8.1, I have boldfaced current members of the Campbell's and Diana family that have *booms* (this entire family is called Cercopithecines). Species that have *booms* cluster around two coherent subfamilies: one had a common ancestor 2.5 million years ago, the other

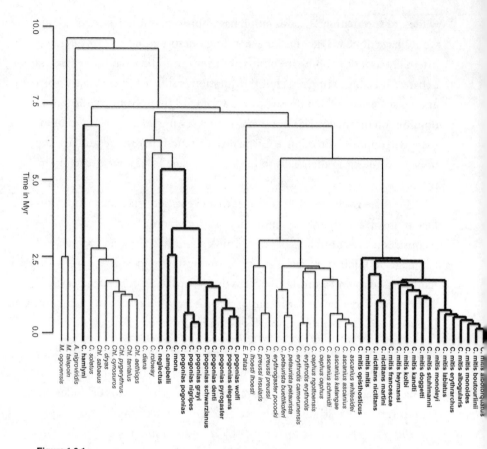

**Figure 1.8.1**

*The evolutionary history of boom*

'Family' tree of Cercopithecines, the group that includes Campbell's monkeys and Diana monkeys, with boldfaced names for species that have *booms*. C. is short for *Cercopithecus*, the general family name, complemented with the full official Latin name of the relevant species. It seems very likely that the most common recent ancestor of the rightmost boldfaced (= *mitis*) group (which lived about 2.5 million years ago) had *booms*, since all of its descendants do; similarly, for the most recent common ancestor of the boldfaced group in the middle (*C. pogonias, C. mona, C. campbelli, C. neglectus*).

had a common ancestor 5 million years ago. While it could be that these ancestors didn't have *booms* and these happened to appear independently several times, a more parsimonious and thus convincing theory is that both ancestors already had *booms*.

This method makes much sense if we think of calls as being part of monkey biology. Within our own primate lineage, the apes have in common the absence of a tail. Humans, chimpanzees, gorillas, and orangutans all share this property, unlike monkeys. We could, of course, imagine that the most recent common ancestor of the four groups had a tail, and that it was lost independently in several lineages. But a more parsimonious explanation is that the most recent common ancestor had no tail either (which is indeed what evolutionary biologists think). The same reasoning carries over to *booms*.

Can we go further and conclude that the most recent common ancestor of *all* the monkeys in the Cercopithecine family had *booms* as well? Here I'll have to say that we don't know. Maybe it did, and *booms* were lost in several subfamilies. The data are not overwhelming, because some subfamilies have *booms* while others don't. But if we limit our ambitions to 2.5 million to 5 million years ago, some solid inferences can be drawn because we find subfamilies whose members *all* have *booms*.

This is not an isolated case. Monkey calls are often preserved over millions of years and thus shared among close or distant cousin species. In fact, calls are so well preserved that in the 1970s and 1980s, when DNA methods were not as easily accessible as they are today, call similarity was sometimes used in lieu of DNA to reconstruct the family relationship among monkey species. Strikingly, the results converged with those of DNA methods.[16] Now that we have the luxury of easy access to reliable DNA methods, we can turn the problem on its head: Instead of using call similarity to reconstruct monkey evolutionary history, we start from well-established family relationships and use them to reconstruct the evolution of monkey languages.

## 1.9  APE COMMUNICATION: CALLS

If monkeys have sophisticated communication systems, we might expect to find something even more remarkable in our closest cousins, the apes, especially the chimpanzees, bonobos, and gorillas. Unfortunately, their call systems aren't well understood yet, although there might soon be progress on that front. Still, two important discoveries were made about ape communication. First, unlike the species we have discussed up to this point, apes have sophisticated means of gestural communication. This difference makes sense. Campbell's monkeys and their close cousins usually live in trees, and thus a speaker and its audience have little chance of seeing each other, so using predominantly vocal rather than visual signals is the thing to do. By contrast, chimpanzees, bonobos, and gorillas spend much time on the ground, in visual contact with each other, so both vocal and gestural signals can be useful. There is a second difference as well. As I noted when I mentioned the Informativity Principle ('pick the most informative call possible!'), there is no clear evidence that monkeys can represent what other monkeys think, and for this reason it was hard to argue that monkeys try to be as informative as possible *in order* to be cooperative with their audience (a standard assumption for humans). But it is increasingly likely that apes do have a representation of what their audience knows.

The evidence comes from experiments with chimpanzees and model snakes, conducted by Catherine Crockford and colleagues.[17] I started this chapter with the chimpanzee *hoo* alarm call, produced to warn of a snake's presence. The tantalizing possibility in this initial anecdote was that the intended audience was made of . . . a human. But in less extraordinary circumstances, it is made of other chimpanzees. In such cases, does the caller produce the call automatically, or does it adapt its calling behavior to what its audience knows? Automatic call production can't be ruled out for monkeys, but for chimpanzees it's unlikely to be the full story.

Think for a second about what you would do when your interlocutor is aware of a threat. Suppose you and I are walking together in the forest. Suddenly you see a snake, and it's obvious to you that I've seen it too—maybe because of my startled reaction. Will you then say, *Watch out, a snake!* Probably not, unless you think that I am really dense. That's another principle of pragmatics (call it the Economy Principle): Not only does one try to be as informative as possible, but one also doesn't go around stating the obvious. On the other hand, if I didn't see the threat, warning me explicitly will be appropriate and (hopefully) called for. Finally, if somebody else warned of the snake's presence, you might or might not reiterate the warning depending on whether you think I am aware of the danger.

In other words, you won't just produce the warning automatically: You will adapt the signal to what you can infer of my state of knowledge. You can do this because you have a theory of other minds. In this case, chimpanzees seem to behave like us. The primatologists hide a model snake and observe a target chimpanzee's reaction depending on what it could know about its intended audience—other chimpanzees. These other chimpanzees might not have seen the snake or heard a *hoo* call. If so, the target chimpanzee has no reason to believe they know anything about the danger, and it should produce lots of *hoos*. On the other hand, if the target chimpanzee can determine that the other chimpanzees have seen the snake, it would produce far fewer *hoos* because it doesn't want to state the obvious. Finally, if those other chimpanzees have heard some *hoo* calls but it's unknown if they have *seen* the snake, the target chimpanzee should produce an intermediate number of calls. This three-way distinction is exactly what was found: Chimpanzees, just like humans, take into account what their audience knows before saying something, and they don't go around stating the obvious. They go by the Economy Principle. That's one aspect of pragmatics that they seem to share with us.

Still, it is fair to say that the details of the chimpanzee call repertoire are not entirely understood yet. Chimpanzees have further calls besides *hoos*— they produce *grunts* and *barks* and *pants* in different situations, but the basic units as well as their meanings are still elusive.

### 1.10  APE COMMUNICATION: GESTURES

If ape calls are still a bit of a mystery, recent discoveries about gestures are revolutionizing our understanding of ape communication, thanks in particular to the work of Catherine Hobaiter, Richard Byrne, and colleagues.[18] So much so that primatologists now have a kind of 'chimpanzee gesture dictionary' comprising at least 60 or 70 communicative gestures, which are found in socially unrelated groups and are likely to be innate.

**Gesture use:** The first thing to note is that ape gestures, just like *hoos*, are produced while taking into account the state of knowledge of the addressee. If you want to express your enthusiasm at a suggestion I made, you might say *Great!* or use the thumbs-up gesture 👍. But if we are talking over the phone, you'll preferably use sound because you know I can't see you. Chimpanzees and bonobos do the same thing: They may use silent visual gestures when their audience is looking at them, but otherwise they preferably use calls (or contact gestures that can grab their audience's attention).

In fact, there is evidence that these gestures are used intentionally to achieve a specific goal. Thus apes typically repeat a gesture until the outcome is satisfactory. Researchers showed that orangutans take it one step further. Faced with a human keeper who partly understands their gestural request, giving them only half of the desired food, they just repeat the same gesture, hoping that their dense interlocutor will finally get the message. But faced with a completely incompetent keeper who continually hands the wrong food, they give up and switch to a different gesture, one that might be more effective with their linguistically challenged interlocutor.[19]

**Pointing and iconicity:** Two things often come to mind when one thinks of gestures: pointing and iconicity, which is the ability of a gesture to resemble what it denotes (as when you trace an imaginary path with your finger to tell your interlocutor which way to go). A striking anecdote, captured on video, suggests that some apes can master both. It involves a female chimpanzee at a zoo in the United Kingdom. This chimpanzee had early exposure to humans. At the beginning, one sees the chimpanzee pointing (humanlike, using the index) through a window at a visitor's bag—and to make sure that there is no ambiguity, the chimpanzee comes closer to the bag while continuing to point. The visitor takes a bottle of soda out of the bag, and the chimpanzee makes a beckoning gesture to tell the human to follow her, then points toward the bottle, then toward a small hole under the window: She wants the human to pour the liquid so she can get her share. Utterly charmed, the visitor complies. Having quenched her thirst, the chimpanzee would now like to fill her stomach, hence a new pointing gesture toward the bag. It contains a banana, but clearly it won't go through the hole. So now the chimpanzee points her finger upward, iconically tracing the imaginary path that the banana should follow: The humans are being instructed to send it over the glass wall. Charm doesn't quite do it this time, so the chimpanzee is content to ask for more soda ([**AV1.10.1**]).

There is a grain of general truth in this video. As in any anecdote, however, interpretation is difficult: How much early contact did this chimpanzee have with humans? Would other chimpanzees display similar abilities? Here the results are a bit conflicting. While this may come as a disappointment, a dog will likely understand your pointing gestures far better than a chimpanzee would. And this result was obtained experimentally: A group of dogs was compared to two groups of chimpanzees, one from a zoo in Germany, the other from a sanctuary in Uganda.[20] The animals were rewarded if they brought back an object that the experimenter had pointed at. Dogs succeeded above chance; chimpanzees just didn't. This is less surprising than it seems. Dogs have been domesticated for at least 10,000 years, and thus they have had ample time to evolve with humans and to adapt to their communicative cues, unlike chimpanzees.

Other experiments specifically focused on captive chimpanzees' understanding of iconic gestures. A chimpanzee had to maneuver a complex apparatus to get some food, and the human experimenter produced an iconic gesture resembling the correct action, such as pushing something in or pulling something down. To assess the role of iconicity, arbitrary gestures (whose form didn't provide information on what to do) were tested as well. Four-year-old children often succeeded at the task when seeing iconic but not arbitrary gestures. Chimpanzees were bad at the task in both cases (over time, they did make greater progress with iconic than with arbitrary gestures).[21]

But some results go in a different direction. The short of it is that apes reared by humans seem to routinely use pointing. Anecdotes are legion. The primatologist Robert Yerkes recounts a case in which a captive chimpanzee, Moos, had been ill and was refusing hard foods. Moos readily responded to a dental inspection by a caregiver, who was unable to detect anything wrong. "Satisfied with his examination he turned to leave the room, but Moos took hold of his coat, drew him back, and raising his upper lip with one hand pointed with a finger of the other hand to a spot on his upper jaw," where the caregiver found an erupting tooth—and was apparently "chagrined at having to be assisted in the diagnosis by the animal himself."[22] In one study, about half the chimpanzees living in zoos and research centers used pointing.[23]

Still, these observations only assess how apes understand or use human gestures. A more relevant question is whether there are instances of pointing and iconicity in the natural gestures that apes use in the wild. As a first approximation, these instances are extremely rare, although not entirely absent. Some of the most striking examples involve bonobos, a more quiet and considerably more promiscuous species than chimpanzees. Bonobos are known to go by the adage 'make love, not war' and use sex with partners of both sexes to foster social bonds and relieve tension. One signal is a beckoning gesture toward a location where they wish to invite their interlocutor to have sex—a pointing gesture of sorts.[24] Another X-rated example pertains to bonobo females that wish to initiate mutual genital rubbing with another female. The signal involves foot pointing (with the heel or toe) toward the initiator's sexual swelling. The same goal can also be achieved through a less subtle cue: By way of hip movement, the initiator will pantomime the action that takes place during genital rubbing—an iconic gesture of sorts.[25]

Despite these advances, the status of pointing and iconicity in ape gestures remains a matter of debate. And more generally, we don't know much about the relation between ape gestures and human language. Still, ape gesture research has led to another fascinating finding: Many ape gestures are shared among ape species. Using the same kind of argument we developed in our little evolutionary history of *boom*, we can draw the conclusion that most ape gestures are millions of years old.

**Evolution of ape gestures:** Unsurprisingly in view of their close family relationship (they shared a common ancestor approximately 2 million years ago), chimpanzees and bonobos have particularly similar gestures, despite the fact that they live in different areas. Not only do they have lots of gestures in common, but their meanings are often related as well.[26] How do we know what the meanings are? At this point, we don't have sophisticated linguistic analyses to offer. But primatologists took advantage of the fact that these gestures are produced with a goal in mind: They listed outcomes that count as satisfactory because they put an end to the gesturing. These 'apparently satisfactory outcomes' can serve as a first approximation of gestural meanings. I don't think they are likely to correspond directly to the apes' mental representations of these meanings, but they are still a very useful way to approach them.

To start with a simple example, in bonobos and chimpanzees alike, a hand gesture directed at an infant (figure 1.10.1, picture (a)) is a signal to climb on the gesturer. Similarly, a mouth stroke (figure 1.10.1, picture (b)) is in both species used as a signal that the gesturer wishes to acquire an object. A reaching gesture (figure 1.10.1, picture (c)) by a chimpanzee is primarily an indication that they want to acquire an object, whereas the same gesture used by a bonobo is an invitation to climb on them. In chimpanzees, shaking an object (figure 1.10.1, picture (d)) is primarily a way to suggest to the

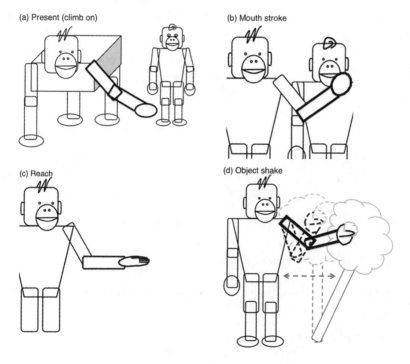

**Figure 1.10.1**

*Examples of bonobo and chimpanzee communicative gestures*

addressee that they follow the gesturer. True to form, the bonobos primarily give this gesture a more sexual meaning, although sometimes the satisfactory outcome just involves grooming. So there are similarities and differences between the meanings that the two species assign to a given gesture type, but researchers have still been able to show that shared meanings are much more common than would be expected by chance.

When it comes to form, shared gestures do not just occur in the bonobo and chimpanzee branch of the ape family tree: They are the norm among apes.[27] After a painstaking study of chimpanzee, bonobo, gorilla, and orangutan gestures, primatologists concluded that 36 gestures are typical of the entire ape family, from chimpanzees and bonobos to orangutans, while an additional 30 gestures are typical of the chimpanzee/bonobo/gorilla group. You can see this in the 'family tree' of apes that appears in figure 1.10.2: chimpanzees and bonobos are our closest cousins, then come gorillas, then come orangutans. The number of shared gestures in each subfamily appears in the tree as well.

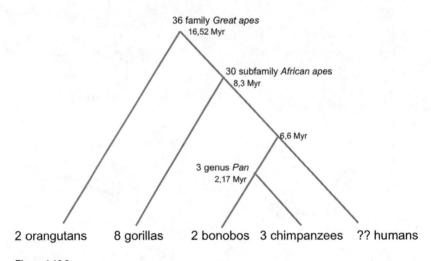

**Figure 1.10.2**
*Shared gestures of the great apes*
The distribution of gestures across living great ape species and genera, based on current knowledge: The number of gestures specific to each species are shown, revealing extensive overlap. Notably, 36 gestures are shared among all apes, 30 additional ones are shared by African apes, and three additional ones are shared by bonobos and chimpanzees.

The reasoning we developed to reconstruct the history of *booms* can be applied again. Very roughly, it is likely that approximately 36 gestures were already present in the most recent common ancestor of the great apes, which lived approximately 16 million years ago (Myr). And an additional 30 gestures are likely to have been present in the most recent common ancestor of African apes (chimpanzees, bonobos, and gorillas), which lived about 8 million years ago. While the state of human language a few hundred thousand years ago is still a mystery, we have now gained extraordinary time depth concerning the evolution of ape gestures.

**Back to humans:** But there is an important character missing from our discussion: us! We are more closely related to chimpanzees and bonobos than they are to gorillas, as seen in the tree in figure 1.10.2. The most recent common ancestor of chimpanzees, bonobos and gorillas also had *us* as descendants. If this common ancestor transmitted something like the 66 gestures to its ape descendants (the 36 great ape gestures and the 30 additional African ape gestures), shouldn't we have inherited some of these gestures as well?

This is the current frontier. Initial results are tantalizing. Researchers from Hobaiter's team observed 13 one- and two-year-old human babies interacting with each other—one group was in Germany, the other in Uganda.[28] They described their communicative gestures with the same methods and criteria as they had used when observing chimpanzees in the wild: 50 of the infant gestures they described (96 percent of the total) seem to be part of the great ape lexicon, and among those, 46 (89 percent of the total) are shared with chimpanzees. The next step will be to determine what relation, if any, these infant gestures bear to our linguistic communication. As things stand, we just don't know. They might be an entirely different system, or they might have the seeds of human language. These are exciting times in ape and gesture research.

### 1.11 CONCLUSION

Primate calls and gestures have meaning, in the sense that they convey information about the world. But does that make them language-like? After all, yawning, coughing, and laughing convey information as well, but we wouldn't treat them as being linguistic in nature. In the end, it all depends on what one means by 'language.' But more substantively, in the following chapters we will come to precise conclusions about how meaning works in human language, and how different it is from what we found in primate calls and gestures. In particular, one thing is clear: Human language is characterized by a sophisticated syntax that feeds into meaning—and thus *Robin loves Casey* doesn't mean the same thing as *Casey loves Robin*. There is currently no evidence for this sort of syntax in nonhuman primates. This doesn't mean that their communication system is uninteresting. First, there is at least one case in which Campbell's monkeys attach *-oo* as a suffix to a root (*krak* or *hok*) to form a new call with a different meaning. Second, there are arguments for an Informativity Principle in primates, one that is reminiscent of some principles of human communication (to be revisited in greater detail in chapter 10).

Do we know what relation these systems bear to human communication? No, with one possible exception. Like some primate calls, ape gestures are remarkably well preserved over millions of years. This makes it possible to reconstruct the evolutionary history of ape communicative gestures in chimpanzees, bonobos, and gorillas, among others. But this also suggests a tantalizing possibility: Gestures that are shared among these three species would be expected to exist in humans as well. Initial work on infant gestures suggests that this might indeed be the case.

Finally, primate communication raised some of the main questions of meaning studies in general, those we will be concerned with in the rest of this book (they are summarized in the table below). What are the elementary pieces of meaning? We saw quite a few calls and gestures, and even a call suffix, *-oo*. How are these elementary pieces put together—what is their syntax? Things were a bit disappointing in this respect, although Campbell's *boom* arguably comes with a syntactic rule. What do the calls and gestures mean— what is their semantics? And are there further principles that constrain their use—what is their pragmatics? We saw at several junctures that there was much interesting action in the interplay between semantics and pragmatics. In particular, postulating an Informativity Principle proved illuminating to explain calls by the Titi and the Campbell's monkeys. We even saw that chimpanzees appear to know another pragmatic principle (the Economy Principle), according to which one shouldn't state the obvious. Last, but not least, chimpanzees taught us to expand our view of communication so as to include the gestural modality. We will see all these questions arise in human communication—but in an incomparably richer form.

(The rest of this book is primarily concerned with meaning and thus with semantics and pragmatics, but an understanding of morphology and especially syntax will sometimes be important. In addition, rules pertaining to the elementary perceptual units of language—audible ones in spoken language, visible ones in sign language—are the realm phonology. If you wish to have a bird-eye's view of phonology, morphology and syntax, you can refer to the brief appendix at the end of this book.)

| | Definition | Nonhuman primate examples | English examples |
|---|---|---|---|
| **Morphology** | = rules to construct (some) calls/words from smaller meaningful units | Campbell's monkeys krak → krak-oo hok → hok-oo | inform → informative green → greenish blue → bluish |
| **Syntax** | = rules to construct sequences/sentences from calls/words | Campbell's monkeys *Boom boom* (usually) appears as a pair at the beginning of sequences. | *Robin loves Casey* and *Casey loves Robin* are well-formed. *Loves Robin Casey* is ill-formed. |
| **Semantics** | = rules that determine the literal meaning of expressions | Titi monkeys The A-call is true (appropriate) just in case there is a serious threat up. | *Robin loves* Casey is true just in case Robin loves Casey. |
| **Pragmatics** | = rules by which one reasons on the speaker's intentions to obtain further information | Informativity Principle Use the most informative call available (e.g., Campbell's monkeys, Titi monkeys). | Informativity Principle Use the most informative word available. *It is possible that Russia influenced the 2016 election* implicates that *it's not certain that Russia influenced the 2016 election.* |
| | | Economy Principle Do not state the obvious (e.g., chimpanzees use of the snake alarm call *hoo*). | Economy Principle Do not state the obvious. *Look, there's a snake!* shouldn't be uttered if it's already obvious that there's a snake. |

# I  THE BUILDING BLOCKS OF MEANING

*Animal languages are more complex than you might have thought, but they are incomparably less sophisticated than human language. The alarm calls and gestures of chapter 1 are interpreted one at a time, without structure to connect them; they come closest to our telegraphic use of* Danger! *or* Fire! *Language reduced to these formulas wouldn't be human language, which can convey complex and structured meanings. This part of the book introduces the main building blocks of human meaning, and it does so from a perspective that includes both sign languages and spoken languages. In several cases, sign languages make visible some key structures that must be inferred indirectly in spoken languages. For this reason, sign language will serve as a friendly and pedagogical guide to the structure of meaning in all languages, be they signed or spoken.*

*We start this exploration with the simplest words that make it possible to refer to people and things: pronouns. But their simplicity is deceptive: They lie at the heart of the meaning engine of language. First, they play the role of logical variables, akin to the little x's and y's you might have seen in mathematical formulas. The idea that pronouns play the role of logical variables has a long pedigree in linguistics, but its consequences are particularly striking in sign language, where these x's and y's are visibly realized. In this way, sign language helps make plausible the view of human language as a sophisticated formal language; this will be the topic of chapter 2. Second, pronouns offer a window into the interplay between meaning and context. The first-person pronoun* I *is an indicator of perspective, a notion that plays a crucial role in human meaning but not in standard formal languages. We will see in chapter 3 how perspectives work in language, and here too sign language will provide special insights.*

With pronouns alone, we can refer to people and to things, but we can't say anything general about them. To do so, we need nouns and verbs. While they are two very different types of words, their meanings are related. As we will see in chapter 4, nouns are to objects as verbs are to events. Just like the noun cloud is true of certain objects, the verb to rain is true of certain events. And some of the same grammatical distinctions are made in both domains, pertaining to singulars and plurals, for instance, depending on whether one is talking about one or several objects or one or several events. Sign language will help in this case as well because the very same grammatical marker can refer to a plurality of objects (when applied to a noun) or to a plurality of events (when applied to a verb).

With pronouns, nouns, and verbs, we can say lots of things, but only about the present moment and situation. Going beyond the here and now, we will discuss tense and mood in chapter 5. They make it possible to talk about past and future situations—I was wrong, I will be wrong. They allow us to describe possible or counterfactual situations—If I am wrong, I will own up to it; if I were wrong, I would own up to it. Here too, meaning has a beautifully simple architecture: Tense and moods behave in many ways like pronouns, just ones that refer to situations rather than to objects (and yes, here too sign language will help clinch the case). We will take this idea one step further in chapter 6, when we investigate in greater detail how we can describe arbitrary situations thanks to the words when and if. As we will discover, the little word if gives rise to surprising patterns of reasoning, ones that make human language a more complex system than standard logic. An explanation of these unexpected patterns will be gained by analyzing the words when and if as abstract versions of the word the, but used to describe situations rather than objects.

At the end of part I, we will have gained an understanding of the main building blocks of human meaning, and we will have seen that human meaning works by way of simple but abstract logical categories that are found in spoken and signed languages alike, and apply in nearly identical fashion to objects and events or situations.

# 2 VISIBLE LOGIC: SIGN LANGUAGE AND PRONOUNS

If you visit Gallaudet University in Washington, DC, you may encounter students who have developed an unlikely skill: They may walk around campus while holding their smartphone with one hand and silently chatting with the other hand. They are Deaf students, and Gallaudet is the only university in the world in which all classes are taught in sign language—in this case, American Sign Language (ASL). And just as in any other college, students spend much time on their smartphones; but to talk, they use silent videos rather than sound. While sign language involves both hands, fluent signers can recover information from just the dominant hand (left or right, depending on whether the signer is left- or right-handed). Hearing visitors at the university might miss out on some of the academic information, but if so, that's because their knowledge of sign language isn't quite up to the task, not because of the language itself. ASL can convey any subtleties or technical notions one wishes. In fact, along certain dimensions, sign languages are *more* expressive than spoken languages—they are 'super languages' of sorts, as we will see.

While sign languages raise very interesting questions in their own right, they will be our initial guide in our tour of human meaning because they make visible some key logical structures of language in general. So, after discussing how sign languages arose in history and how they relate to spoken languages, we will see that they have unique insights to offer into pronouns, one of the most basic building blocks of meaning. In spoken language and sign language alike, pronouns are arguably the realization of logical variables (such as the $x$ one uses in mathematical formulas). But as we will see, in spoken language, logical variables must be inferred indirectly, whereas they can be directly seen in sign language, which thus makes visible a key logical component of language. (Our primary focus in this chapter will be on meaning. If you wish to have a bird-eye's view of phonology, morphology, and syntax in sign language, as well as a comparison with spoken language, you can refer to the appendix at the end of the book.)

## 2.1 SIGN LANGUAGES IN HISTORY

What are sign languages, and how do they arise? Instead of articulating words with their mouth, signers articulate words with their hands and parts of their face (for instance, their eyebrows, which carry much grammatical information). While people sometimes think that there is a single, universal sign language, this is not so. Different groups of Deaf people have different sign languages. Just like English, French, and Italian have different grammars, so do American Sign Language, French Sign Language, and Italian Sign Language. And they are not derived from the surrounding spoken languages. In fact, British Sign Language and American Sign Language had completely different histories and are thus historically unrelated and not mutually intelligible. Thus sign languages are entirely independent linguistic and social objects from the spoken languages used by the surrounding groups. French and Italian are somewhat similar to each other because they are both descended from Latin. Similarly, French Sign Language, Italian Sign Language, and American Sign Language share some properties because they are all descended from (or were heavily influenced by) Old French Sign Language, which spread in the early nineteenth century. British Sign Language has an entirely different history and thus belongs to a different group.

There are other cases in which two societies that speak the same spoken language don't have the same sign language. Taiwan and mainland China both have Mandarin as an official language. But they have different sign languages: Taiwan Sign Language originated around 1895, when Taiwan was under Japanese rule (1895–1945). As a result, the Taiwanese and Japanese sign languages are still mutually intelligible, whereas Chinese Sign Language had a rather different history (as well as some influence on Taiwan Sign Language because of immigration from the mainland after the Chinese Civil War in 1949).[1]

It is likely that any group of Deaf people tends to develop its own sign language if it didn't have one to begin with. But the institutional history of French Sign Language started shortly before the French Revolution in Paris. An abbot, Abbé de l'Épée (1712–1789), was trying to find ways to teach religion to deaf children. He saw two young siblings communicating in signs, and in 1760, he started using signs to teach other deaf children, which led to the creation of several schools using signs in education.[2]

While some Parisians used a preexisting (and natural) sign language,[3] which Abbé de l'Épée borrowed from, he also tried to invent 'methodical signs' designed to follow the grammar of French.[4] But later his own schools switched to the natural sign language that the children had been using anyway. The initial institution became a network of schools using sign language in nineteenth-century France, combined with a vibrant Deaf culture. In the words of a specialist of sign language history, Yves Delaporte, in the eighteenth and early nineteenth century, "Paris was the center of the Deaf world."[5] As a result, different versions of French Sign Language (or LSF, for "Langue des Signes Française," as it is now called) spread throughout Europe. In fact, Italian Sign Language (or LIS, in Italian "Lingua dei Segni Italiana") has remained so close to LSF that signers of the two languages can understand each other with little effort.

Another consequence of this initial success was that Old French Sign Language was exported to the United States. This was in part serendipitous. The wealthy parents of a deaf daughter, Alice Cogswell, had asked their friend, neighbor, and minister, Thomas Hopkins Gallaudet (1787–1851), to explore teaching methods that were used in Europe to teach deaf children. British schools didn't use sign language but took their methods to be trade secrets, so Gallaudet ended up in Paris, where he saw the very public successes of sign language.[6] He convinced one of Abbé de l'Épée's teachers, Laurent Clerc (1785–1869), to go back to America with him to found a school for the deaf. Clerc was deaf himself, multilingual, and a brilliant scholar. He spent the rest of his life in the United States, and deaf children at his school used a version of Old French Sign Language.

This early form of American Sign Language was certainly influenced by a preexisting sign language that had been used in Martha's Vineyard. In the nineteenth century, with a high prevalence of hereditary deafness among the descendants of some immigrants from southern England, sign language was in common use. In fact, many hearing people knew sign language. For some years, town hall meetings were routinely conducted bilingually, in English and in sign language.[7] Besides the (probably small) influence from Martha's Vineyard Sign Language,[8] time led to an increasing separation between American and French sign languages. While still related, the two languages are not mutually intelligible in the same way French and Italian sign languages are.

The extraordinary cultural and pedagogical successes of sign language in the nineteenth century came to an abrupt end after a congress in Milan in 1880. In the years before, progress had been made in the oral method, which teaches deaf individuals to articulate and to lip-read, with the aim of allowing them to communicate with hearing people without sign language. The Milan Congress, which was devoted to deaf education but only included one deaf delegate,[9] decided that the oral method was the sole way to improve deaf education, and in effect it managed to virtually outlaw sign language in most of the world (signing became a clandestine activity in many schools for the deaf).

The Milan Congress had failed to take into account that lipreading is extraordinarily taxing and only yields a degraded signal; in effect, it condemned untold numbers of deaf children to be educated without easy or complete access to language—with devastating effects for a century. Nowadays, the research is clear—deaf children benefit from bilingual education that includes sign language (and this even applies to children who have cochlear implants).[10] But for a century after the Milan Congress, sign language was repressed, including in France, where deaf education and deaf culture receded until the revival of sign language in the 1970s and 1980s (which is known as the Deaf Awakening).

The United States was in part spared because its delegation rejected the conclusions of the Milan Congress—and Gallaudet University was thus able to thrive. Yves Delaporte and his coauthor Emily Shaw (a specialist of ASL) cite a poignant description of the situation by George Veditz, the former president of the National Association of the Deaf. In an address given in ASL in 1913, he said:

> For 33 years, the French Deaf have watched, with eyes full of tears, with hearts breaking, as the beautiful language of signs was wiped out of their schools. ( . . . ) The French Deaf look at us American Deaf with jealous eyes. They look at us as a prisoner, locked down with an iron chain about his leg, looks out at those wandering free.[11]

The remarkable role of Abbé de l'Épée in the history of LSF shouldn't give you the wrong idea. Sign languages tend to arise spontaneously in situations in which deaf people come together. One often thinks that a sign language is a code for the spoken language used in the same community, but as noted, nothing could be further from the truth. French Sign Language has a relatively free word order (just like Russian); French doesn't. Italian Sign Language has the basic order Subject-Object-Verb (Maria coffee drinks),[12] whereas Italian has, like English, the basic order Subject-Verb-Object (Maria drinks coffee). And as mentioned, despite the presence of English around both languages, British Sign Language is not mutually intelligible with American Sign Language. This doesn't mean that sign languages cannot borrow from surrounding languages—all languages do. When sign languages borrow from spoken language, one common device they employ is fingerspelling: A manual alphabet makes it possible to sign the letters of an English or French word borrowed by American or French Sign Language, for instance. But for the rest, signs have nothing to do with the words used by the surrounding spoken language.

People are often shocked to learn that sign language isn't universal, but that's because they have the wrong idea of what sign languages are. Once it is understood that they share general properties of spoken languages, it's not that surprising that they should differ from each other just like spoken languages do. Still, it *is* true that signers of different sign languages, even unrelated ones, understand each other more easily than speakers of unrelated spoken languages. Part of the reason is that the meaning of a foreign word is often easier to guess in sign than in speech. This is due to the iconic nature of some (not all) signs, which resemble what they refer to: The sign for *eat* in ASL and LSF evokes someone putting something in their mouth. Signers can purposefully choose more iconic words when talking to signers of different languages, which further facilitates communication. Another reason interlinguistic communication is often easier in sign than in speech is that historically unrelated sign languages still share some grammatical properties. Even without a common origin, they belong in a sense to the same language family (we will discuss in chapter 13 a possible reason for this similarity among the grammars of historically unrelated sign languages).

International contacts among Deaf people, especially at conferences, have led to the development of International Sign. Like Esperanto for spoken language, it is an international language with few, if any, native speakers (or rather native signers). It borrows words from established Western sign languages, with different influences depending on who the signer is. While America's role is such that ASL is often used at sign language conferences, International Sign is routinely used as well. Still, it had a very different emergence from other sign languages, which tend to arise naturally as soon as groups of Deaf people come together.

So how do sign languages naturally arise? Several sign languages arose recently and were studied almost from the start by linguists. One case in point is Nicaraguan Sign Language. In 1977, a center for special education opened, offering classes for deaf children but using the oral method. The children came from diverse families that each used home gestures to allow for some communication between the children and their hearing family members. As researchers who have studied these 'homesigners' found, communication is rather limited. But when the children came together in the school, they pooled the gestures they used at home, modified them, and started creating a sign language. And since their teachers used spoken Spanish, this sign language arose on its own. It was studied by linguists over the course of several generations.

Strikingly, the children invented a grammar. As an example, linguists studied the way in which signers of Nicaraguan Sign Language, as well as Spanish-speaking (hearing) non-signers, describe a cartoon in which a cat, having swallowed a bowling ball, goes down a street "in a wobbling, rolling manner." Asked to describe the scene, a typical Spanish speaker may use words but also gestures that mimic the situation, with a single hand movement conveying both the direction of movement (down) and the manner of movement (rolling); see figure 2.1.1A below. Quite a few students from the first generation of the school used a similar strategy in signs. But in later generations, another strategy became more prevalent: Two signs instead of one were used, one providing the direction of movement, the other the manner of movement (see figure 2.1.1B below). This decomposition is a grammatical strategy adopted by other languages. In fact, in English, one would naturally say that the cat *rolled down* the street, thus using the very same strategy as these deaf children: The first part of the verb, *roll*, indicates the manner of movement, and the second, *down*, the direction of movement. A similar decomposition can be seen in the signs of later generations of children at the Deaf school.[13]

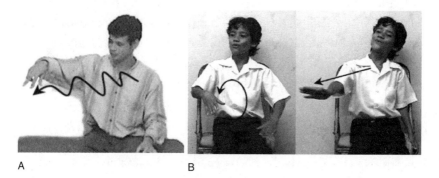

A           B

**Figure 2.1.1**
*Rolling down as expressed in gestures by a Spanish speaker (A) and in signs by a signer of Nicaraguan Sign Language (B)*

## 2.2 SIGN VERSUS SPOKEN LANGUAGES

While sign languages were for years treated as being impoverished and purely gestural, the experience of signers as well as scientific research show that this was a colossal mistake. Classes at Gallaudet University and scientific talks given in sign language can convey the same subtle information (including when it is extremely abstract) as talks given in spoken language. Two general scientific results further highlight these facts: one pertains to neuroimaging, the other to linguistic typology.

Starting from the least linguistic perspective, there have been for years detailed studies of the brain areas that underlie language using two primary techniques: neuroimaging studies, which make it possible to see which parts of the brain are activated in different behavioral tasks, and lesion studies, which investigate how brain lesions correlate with behavioral changes. In a review of the literature, Mairéad MacSweeney and colleagues stated that "overwhelmingly, lesion and neuroimaging studies indicate that the neural systems supporting signed and spoken language are very similar."[14] To see this point more concretely, let us look at the pictures below (figure 2.2.1), which represent the left hemisphere (on top) and right hemisphere (bottom) of a Deaf signer (i) seeing a video in British Sign Language and of a hearing non-signer (ii) listening to a recording in English.

The pictures display in very light gray those areas that are specifically activated by the linguistic input (by comparison with a nonlinguistic video or a nonlinguistic audio recording). It is a classic result that language is usually processed by the left hemisphere. If you look at the left hemisphere of the hearing non-signer (on the top), you see two classic areas of language in the brain called Broca's area (toward the left) and Wernicke's area (toward the right). But if you look at the left hemisphere of the Deaf signer, also on top, you see very comparable regions being activated. This makes concrete the striking similarity observed between brain areas activated in language for signers and non-signers, suggesting that sign language and spoken language are treated by the human brain as the same kind of object.

But you can also approach the comparison between sign and spoken language in a more linguistic fashion by exploring the formal properties of

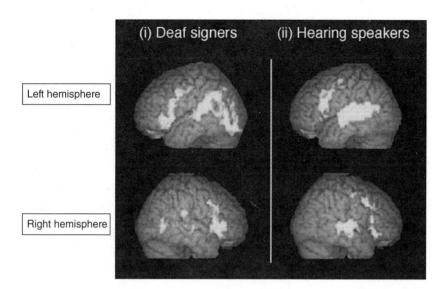

(i) Deaf signers　　(ii) Hearing speakers

Left hemisphere

Right hemisphere

**Figure 2.2.1**
*Brain areas that are specifically activated by sign language (i) and by spoken language (ii)*

the two language types. This linguistic investigation yields similar conclusions: While sign languages differ from each other just as spoken languages do, they also have properties that all languages share (some examples are discussed in the appendix at the end of this book). It is by now an old (if still controversial) idea, proposed by the linguist Noam Chomsky, that part of being human is to have an innate 'Universal Grammar' that constrains the grammar of all possible human languages (and might make them relatively easy to learn); "all languages have nouns and verbs" could be an example.[15] Now the precise list of properties that are universal in this way is a matter of heated debate, but it is generally accepted that not anything goes. A further (and possibly more controversial) idea is that even the part of language that is not universal is ruled by some abstract parameters. For instance, one of them specifies that a subject can be omitted (as in Italian or Spanish, where you can say *speaks* for *she/he speaks*) or that this is not a possibility (as in English or French). No wonder, then, that sometimes American Sign Language resembles, say, modern Hebrew or other languages it has absolutely no historical connection to: both are constrained by Universal Grammar and by its grammatical parameters.

Still, sign languages also share a lot with each other. It's well known that languages descended from Latin, called Romance languages (such as Italian, French, Spanish, and Portuguese), have some properties in common and can thus be treated as a language family. In some respects, sign languages form a language family of their own, even when they have no historical connection. One rather extraordinary property of sign languages explains part of their similarity to each other: They sometimes make visible some abstract logical structures of language in general, and they do so in remarkably similar ways from one sign language to the next (further reasons are explored in chapter 13). Since these abstract structures are key to the production of meaning, we will explore them using sign language as a friendly and pedagogical guide.

### 2.3 PRONOUNS AS LOGICAL VARIABLES

Let us embark, then, on an exploration of the logic of language from the joint perspective of spoken language and of sign language.

The animal systems we investigated in chapter 1 were more sophisticated than you might have thought, but they were still very limited: Each call seemed to be an autonomous utterance, and there was virtually no structure to be found in call sequences. In human language, by contrast, there is structure from the get-go. To start with the simplest possible structure, we attribute properties to people and objects, as when we say *Mary thinks* or *I smoke*. In order to do this, we first need to name things (including people). Proper names are one way to do it, but some things don't have names. Still, we can refer to *any* object that is in our environment thanks to pronouns. Seeing an animal I've never encountered before, I might not know what it's called, but I might still say, *It looks dangerous.*

Pronouns don't just serve as temporary names for things in our immediate environment. They also play a key logical role in language because they can serve as temporary names for any object whatsoever, as when we say, *Every human being knows that he/she will die.* In logician's talk, this has a meaning akin to saying, *For every x which is a human, x knows that x will die.*

For the logician, $x$ is a temporary name (called a variable), which can refer to any object, and the claim is tantamount to saying, "Give me anything which is a human, and let me use $x$ to name that object; then $x$ *knows that x will die* will be true."

Sometimes, it matters to logicians that they can use as many different variables (temporary names) as they like. If I point toward a man I dislike and say, *Everybody knows that he [pointing] will die,* the correct analysis is now different: *For every x which is a human, x knows that y will die,* where $y$ is a temporary name for the disliked individual. So, from a logician's perspective, pronouns may be ambiguous between different variables—$x$ and $y$ in this case. There are cases of genuine ambiguity in real life. If I say that *Sarkozy told Obama that he would win the election,* it's hard to tell whether *he* should be interpreted as $x$ = *Sarkozy* or as $y$ = *Obama.* In the first case, the sentence should be logically represented as *Sarkozy$_x$ told Obama$_y$ that **he$_x$** would win the election.* In this case, *he* plays the role of a variable $x$ introduced by *Sarkozy.* In the second case, the representation should be different, with *he* realizing the variable $y$ introduced by *Obama;* that is, *Sarkozy$_x$ told Obama$_y$ that **he$_y$** would win the election.*

The use of $x$'s and $y$'s to analyze English pronouns has the advantage of precision, but it might strike you as entirely artificial. Isn't this just a logician's way of talking about things that the human mind represents in a different and possibly simpler way? This is where sign language comes into play.

At first sight, sign language seems to use a completely different system. If I want to talk about myself in ASL or LSF, for instance, I will point toward my chest; to talk about you, I will point toward you. To talk about a person or object nearby, I will point in their direction as well. In fact, although you may have been taught that it was impolite to point at people, in sign language this need not be so, as one can point toward nearby people to express pronouns referring to them.[16] But how can a signer refer to Obama when he is not present? Easy. The signer arbitrarily introduces a position in signing space to refer to Obama and then points toward that fictional position to refer back to Obama (one only does this if the person isn't physically present; otherwise, one normally uses the person's real position to point). This position is called a 'locus,' which just means *place* in Latin (plural: loci, pronounced *low-sigh*).

While one can repeat the name Obama in such cases, just as in English, the natural thing to do is to just point toward the Obama locus.

While initially these pointing signs might seem to be entirely different from English pronouns, on closer inspection they provide a key insight into what pronouns do. Let's go back to our ambiguous example: *Sarkozy told Obama that he would be elected.* In LSF, Sarkozy is assigned a locus on the signer's left (by way of the index finger of the left hand held upright, ◊-left below), and Obama is assigned a locus on the right (using the index finger of the right hand held upright, ◊-right below). The verb *tell* in *he (Sarkozy) tells him (Obama)* is realized as a single sign linking the Sarkozy locus on the left to the Obama locus on the right (it is called an 'agreement verb' because its form involves a movement that goes through the subject and object positions). But now comes the interesting part: Depending on whether the expected winner is Sarkozy or Obama, the last pronoun is realized by pointing with one's index toward the Sarkozy locus (on the left) or toward the Obama locus (on the right).

Let's see how the result looks. I'll adopt the convention (standard in linguistics) of using capitalized English words to transcribe sign language words, and for the moment I'll be using finger icons to represent pointing (☞$_{left}$ or ☞$_{right}$); as you now expect, the word order is often very different from that of English (or French, for that matter). So here is how the LSF sentence looks in two versions: if *he* refers to Sarkozy, the signer points toward the Sarkozy locus on the left; if *he* refers to Obama, the signer points toward the Obama locus on the right ($_{left}TELL_{right}$ reminds you that this sign starts from the Sarkozy position on the left and links it to the Obama position on the right).

SARKOZY  ◊-left OBAMA ◊-right   $_{left}$TELL$_{right}$
    'Sarkozy told Obama . . .

    ☞$_{left}$ WILL WIN ELECTION.
    that he, Sarkozy, would win the election.'

    ☞$_{right}$ WILL WIN ELECTION.
    that he, Obama, would win the election.'
  [AV2.3.1]

(While the details wouldn't be the same in ASL, the use of loci on different parts of a horizontal plane—on the left or right—would be very similar.)

The sign language way of doing things should give us pause. On closer inspection, it bears an uncanny similarity to the logician's way of doing things.

Sarkozy$_x$ told Obama$_y$

that **he**$_x$ would win the election.

that **he**$_y$ would win the election.

If you think of the locus on the left as the logician's variable $x$ and the locus on the right as the variable $y$, the sign language sentence realizes visibly the two options I mentioned above: *Sarkozy* comes with a variable $x$ realized as a position on the left, *Obama* comes with a variable $y$ realized as a position on the right, and depending on whether one points toward the left or toward the right, we get the meaning *he = Sarkozy* or *he = Obama* (. . . *will win the election*).

Remarkably, then, sign language offers a window into the logical structure of language in general. It makes visible the abstract variables that had been posited by linguists on the basis of indirect arguments.

But isn't that too good to be true? How do we know that sign language pointing signs are genuinely expressions of the same mental system as spoken language pronouns? Grammar can help. In English, one can't say *Mary likes her* while intending that *her* refers to *Mary*. One has to say *Mary likes herself*, using the reflexive pronoun *herself*. This only happens when the pronoun is too close to the proper name: *Mary likes people who support her* can be understood with the pronoun referring to Mary. Now you might think that *Mary likes herself* is preferred to *Mary likes her* to avoid ambiguities, since the latter sentence could make reference to another female individual. But this isn't the right explanation: *You* is mostly unambiguous, and yet *You like you* is an odd thing to say, unlike *You like yourself*. Furthermore, the rule prohibiting *her* from referring to *Mary* seems to be very common across languages—you will find versions of it in historically unrelated languages such as Mandarin, for instance. This does not mean that everything about the pronouns of

Mandarin works as in English. For instance, while English speakers can't say that *Obama feels that himself will win* (*he* must be used in this case), the Mandarin equivalent of *himself*—*zìjǐ*—can be used in this configuration.[17] This is a common pattern in grammar: Some rules are found in many or all languages, such as the prohibition against *Obama likes him* to mean that Obama likes Obama; others give rise to more modulations, as in the precise use of the reflexive pronoun. These are precisely the kinds of facts that led to the view of Chomsky's Universal Grammar as a parametrized system with some universal properties and others that are subject to variation (how extensive this variation can be is a matter of current debate).

In ASL, a pointing sign is often as unambiguous as English *you*. And it must obey the same grammatical constraint. To say something like *Obama likes people who support him*, an ASL signer may associate a locus with Obama and then point toward that locus to realize the pronoun *him*. But if the signer wishes instead to say that *Obama likes himself*, the same strategy won't work well: The simple pointing sign is usually odd, as is the pronoun *him* in *Obama likes him* (with *him* referring to Obama) or the second-person *you* in *You like you*.[18] And just as in English, one has to use a reflexive pronoun. In ASL, it's realized not by a pointing index ☞ but rather by a thumbs-up sign 👍 (transcribed as *SELF*) oriented toward the appropriate position. And lest you think that this is just an imitation of English *himself*, let me add that linguists who have studied ASL *SELF* have concluded that its behavior is closer to that of the Mandarin reflexive pronoun *zìjǐ* than to English *himself*.[19] For instance, ASL *SELF* can be used to say something like *Obama thinks that SELF will win*. Although this would be impossible in English, it is a fine sentence in Mandarin!

So we finally have our argument that ASL pointing signs are genuinely part of the same system as English or Mandarin pronouns: They too avoid sentences such as *Obama likes him* when *him* refers to Obama, and they express this instead with a reflexive pronoun (closer to the Mandarin than to the English version). But now let's go back to our initial observation: pointing signs seem to give the key to the behavior of English pronouns, in the sense that they express visibly, by way of positions in signing space, the little variables *x* and *y* that linguists and logicians posited to explain the logical behavior of pronouns.

Given how different pointing signs are from English pronouns, you might have thought that this was really an accident—that it was a stretch to take ASL pronouns as the key to the logical behavior of English pronouns. But now we see that this wasn't so far-fetched after all: ASL and English pronouns are characterized by the same grammatical behavior, as in the case of *Obama likes him/himself.* And this is not an isolated finding. There are several complex grammatical behaviors that are shared by the pointing signs of ASL or LSF and by the vocal pronouns of English, Mandarin, and many other languages.

Let me add that ASL pronouns can, *if they want*, be as ambiguous as English pronouns. The reason is that one isn't always forced to use different loci to refer to different individuals. One can also use a neutral locus, roughly in front of the signer, which can be used and reused to refer to different individuals, a bit like the English pronoun *he* may be used in the same sentence to refer to different males. Being unambiguous is often an option in sign language, but it need not be an obligation.

## 2.4  ICONICITY

While sign language doesn't *always* make visible the logical structure of language (this would put semanticists out of business), we will encounter several cases throughout this book in which sign language will be a very helpful guide. But at this point, I would like to turn to a more radical finding: in the background of the shared logical structure we just discussed, sign languages are along some dimensions more expressive than spoken languages because they make greater use of iconicity.

What is iconicity? It is the resemblance between an expression and the things it denotes. If I tell you that *the talk was looong*, you will infer something rather different than if I tell you, without lengthening the vowel, that *the talk was long.* The *looong* version suggests that it was *very* long indeed, or at least felt that way. This is not accidental: You know a rule according to which the longer the vowel, the greater the size of the denoted thing. I could have produced an impression of still greater duration by making the vowel even longer, as in: *The talk was looooooong.* By contrast, if you try to say that *the talk was shooort,* or for that matter *the talk was shoooooort,* you might get a slightly puzzled look from your interlocutor. The reason is not hard to find: The iconic modulation evokes length, but the meaning of *short* goes in the opposite direction, so your interlocutor won't know what to make of your utterance. On the other hand, if you say that *the talk was looong, but the crowd was huuuge,* the intent will be clear: While the talk was overly long, it drew an enormous crowd. Similarly, if I tell you after having dinner at a restaurant that *service was slooooow,* you'll understand that it was extremely slow; saying that *service was faaaaast* wouldn't quite work.[20]

There are other cases of iconicity in English, as in the word *boom,* which bears some acoustic resemblance to the explosive sound that it evokes (primatologists working on monkey calls make use of iconic devices when naming the calls *krak, hok* or . . . *boom*). There are more subtle examples as well, as in the word *teeny,* whose initially *ee* is evocative of small things (as in *a teeny amount of butter*), possibly because you need to constrict your mouth to produce it. Still, these examples are a bit limited in spoken language. Most words, like *cat* and *dog,* do not in any way resemble the things they denote. And outside the evocation of sizes, durations, and acoustic effects, it is not easy to convey precise information with vocal iconicity. The situation is rather different in sign language, where the hands can be used to convey specific information about the world.

Consider the verb *GROW* in ASL. It is a conventional sign of the language, realized with the two hands forming a sphere and then moving away from each other. While this shape is already evocative of something growing, it is recognized by an ASL signer as a word, not an improvised gesture. Still, it can be modulated in ways that affect its meaning, just as is the case with *looong.* But the effects are much more subtle. For instance, the sentence *My group grew* could be realized in at least six different ways, with clearly distinguishable meanings (there are intermediate realizations, but we focus on six for simplicity; [AV2.4.1]).[21]

| | Narrow endpoints | Medium endpoints | Broad endpoints |
|---|---|---|---|
| | 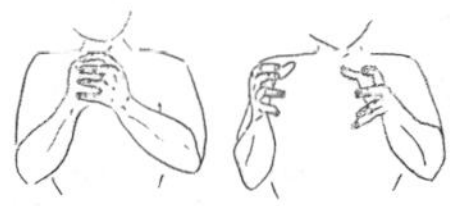 | 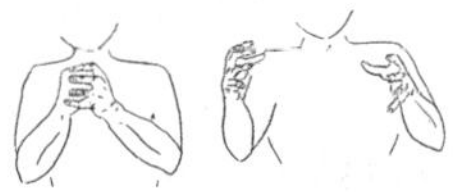 |  |
| **Slow movement** | small amount, slowly | medium amount, slowly | large amount, slowly |
| **Fast movement** | small amount, quickly | medium amount, quickly | large amount, quickly |

**Figure 2.4.1**
*Different iconic modifications of the sign* GROW *in ASL*

First, the final position of the hands after they have moved could be relatively close together or further or still further apart: The space between them can, in effect, be used to represent the final size of the group, just like the length of the vowel in *looong* could give an indication of the length of the talk. But in addition, the verb *GROW* can be realized more or less quickly in order to give an idea of the speed of the growth process. So, just considering a slow and a fast movement, combined with narrow, medium, and broad endpoints, we get six different meanings for a single verb. These examples were picked arbitrarily: There could be many other intermediate realizations. Still, these iconic modulations are optional: a neutral form of the verb (with moderate breadth and speed) could be used in very diverse situations, just like the English verb *grow*.

### 2.5 ICONIC VARIABLES: A FIRST LOOK

A peculiar form of iconicity is present at the logical core of sign language—on pronouns (we will return to the topic of iconicity in general in chapter 12). As we saw, loci play the role of logical variable, and they may be created at will by establishing arbitrary positions on a horizontal plane in front of the signer. But in some cases, ASL and LSF signers can do more: They can point upward for a tall, powerful, or important individual and downward for a short individual. Thus loci are not just logical variables; in some cases, they are simultaneously variables and simplified pictures of what they denote.

Importantly, this iconic component isn't an external add-on: It arguably has a grammar and in fact resembles grammatical gender in English, notably the distinction between *she*, *he*, and *it*. The first thing to note, however, is that LSF and ASL do not have gender distinction on pronouns, although we saw before that they distinguish between first, second, and third person (we will soon see that they also have plural pronouns). Nothing exceptional: In this respect, LSF and ASL resemble Mandarin, which also doesn't have gender distinctions in the third person, pronounced *tā*. Or rather, Mandarin doesn't have these distinctions in the pronunciation: Since its writing system is not based on an alphabet but on ideograms, there are different characters for *he*, *she*, and *it* written respectively as 他, 她, and它. It's just that they don't correspond to any distinction in the spoken language. This occasionally leads to amusing situations when, as is standard in China, Mandarin dialogues are subtitled with Chinese characters. There is a popular TV thriller about a Chinese Sherlock Holmes of sorts, Detective L, with powers of deduction no less impressive than those of his British model. In an especially breathtaking episode, he astounds his assistant by informing her that the fugitive in male attire is in fact a woman. Alas, more than a minute before the dramatic announcement, in the heat of the pursuit, Detective L had referred to the fugitive with the gender-neutral pronoun *tā*. But the unfortunate captioner, who was forced to make a choice, had transcribed this with the feminine character, thus fully ruining the suspense.[22]

With pointing signs, ASL and LSF encode gender as little as Mandarin does in the pronunciation. Still, ASL and LSF have a grammatical distinction that works very much like gender but pertains to people's heights rather than sex.

In English, if I point in the distance and say *She is smoking*, you might not know who I am talking about, but you will usually assume that this person is female. The feminine component of the word *she* makes a particular informational contribution, called a presupposition: It is typically taken for granted rather than asserted that the person I am pointing to is female. You can see this by contrasting the sentence *Is she smoking?* with *Is this a woman smoking?* The first question only asks about the smoking, taking the gender for granted, whereas the second question also asks about the gender.

Similarly, if I tell you that *I doubt that she is smoking*, I am just denying the smoking, not the gender. By contrast, if I were to say that *I doubt that this is a woman smoking*, the gender could be in doubt.

The 'tall' contribution of a high position in signing space behaves in the same way. If someone says in ASL or LSF the equivalent of *I didn't understand ⑴*, with a pronoun pointing upward, it will be taken for granted that the person referred to is tall (or important or powerful), and what will be denied is that the signer understood the person: The height contribution is a presupposition, just like the contribution of grammatical gender in English. The very same behavior is found in English if I say *I didn't understand her*. What is denied in this case is that there was understanding on my part, not that the person I am talking about is female. One small difference relative to English gender is that in ASL or LSF, using high pointing to talk about tall individuals is usually optional. With gender, using a neutral option is difficult in several spoken languages, but English does have the option of using neuter singular *they*, as in *Someone mentioned that they would come late*. The use of singular *they* is also common to refer to nonbinary people who so desire (in some circles, people routinely specify the pronoun—such as *he*, *she*, *they*—that they want others to use to refer to them).

In English, the distinction between *he*, *she*, and *they* is not just a matter of meaning but also of subtle grammar. The reason is that sometimes the choice of one pronoun over another is not determined by the meaning but by formal properties of the linguistic antecedent (i.e., the expression the pronoun depends on). Take the sentence *My colleagues all think that they are the smartest person in the world*—or to avoid complexities, its counterpart in French, which doesn't have neutral singular they: *Tous mes collègues pensent qu'ils sont la personne la plus intelligente au monde*. It is clear that the plural pronoun is used because *my colleagues* is plural, not because the content of any person's thought pertains to a plurality. The sentence thus asserts that of each of my colleagues' thought is something like, *I am the smartest person in the world*. The thought pertains to a single person, and the use of the plural pronoun is due to a grammatical process, the agreement of a pronoun with its antecedent. This agreement-based behavior is characteristic of grammatical elements such as pronouns and doesn't extend to other words.

For instance, a completely different meaning would be obtained from the (slightly awkward) sentence *My colleagues all think that these individuals are the smartest people in the world.* This one clearly attributes to each of my colleagues a plural thought—for instance, *These individuals are the smartest people in the world* (the individuals in question could be my colleagues themselves or other individuals; similar facts hold in French).

The ability of pronouns to inherit their properties (*he* versus *she* versus *they*) from their antecedent has consequences for further constructions. If I tell you that *John admires himself, but Peter doesn't,* the second clause is obviously missing a verb, but this doesn't cause a problem because you can retrieve it by copying it from the first clause, thus yielding: *John admires himself, and Peter doesn't ~~admire himself~~* (the barred words remain unpronounced). You can already see in this case that the copying is a bit more abstract than the literal repetition of words, since we need to copy *admires* without its third-person ending *-s*. But more generally, the copying process is allowed to disregard grammatical elements whose presence is motivated by agreement. For this reason, it is possible to say that *Your cats love themselves, but my dog doesn't,* even though one wouldn't usually say, *My dog doesn't love themselves.* In *My dog doesn't,* the plural component of *themselves* has been disregarded in the copying process.

Now consider a slightly different case: *John admires himself, but Mary doesn't.* This just means that Mary is not a self-admirer, with no implication that she is male; a good paraphrase is just that Mary doesn't admire herself. Things would be very different if we replaced *himself* with a nongrammatical expression: *John admires the man he has become, and Mary does too* definitely does not mean that Mary admires the woman she has become. The upshot is that the *him* component of *himself* can be disregarded as *admires himself* is copied from the first clause to resolve the missing part of the second, as shown below; and this seems to be possible because masculine gender is a grammatical element that can be inherited through agreement with an antecedent.

What is pronounced:   John admires himself, but Mary doesn't.
What is understood:   John$_1$ admires himself$_1$, but Mary$_2$ doesn't **admire ~~himself~~**$_2$.

Other grammatical elements can be disregarded in the same way. Take the sentence *John admires himself, but I don't.* This can be understood to imply that I don't admire *myself.* In this case, the copying process disregards the third-person component of *himself,* since *I don't admire himself* is an odd-sounding sentence.

The very same argument can be developed to suggest that high pointing in sign language behaves like a grammatical expression (I will discuss LSF, but similar data exist in ASL). Since we are interested in height rather than gender, we will be talking about a very tall and a very short person (I will assume in this case that they are males, but gender isn't marked in LSF). Making use of loci, we will associate the tall person with a position on the signer's right and the short person with a position on the signer's left. The first sentence just talks about the tall man and says that he likes himself, while making use of the option of pointing high in view of his height.

$\emptyset$-right$^{high}$ LIKE SELF$^{high}$-right.

Here, *he* is realized by pointing upward on the right, and the reflexive *SELF* (realized by the thumbs-up sign 👍) also targets a high position, so we write it as *SELF$^{high}$-right.* The superscript *high* is used to remind ourselves that the reflexive involves high pointing, and the suffix *-right* because it's signed on the right.

Next, we talk about the short person, so we point toward the left using a neutral height (which is possible since height marking is optional), and we add the negation to mean *he doesn't.* So the two sentences together now look like this:

$\emptyset$-right$^{high}$ LIKE SELF$^{high}$-right.    ☞$_{left}$ NOT.

This discourse is entirely acceptable and means that the short person doesn't like himself. But wait—if we just copied the missing words from the first clause, we would obtain *LIKE SELF$^{high}$,* which is definitely not appropriate when *SELF* refers to a short person (this is easy to establish independently). So the reason the sentence is acceptable is that, in the copying process, we were able to disregard the 'high' component of *SELF$^{high}$.* Strikingly, this is exactly what we saw in our earlier examples involving gender:

*John admires himself, but Mary doesn't* required that the *him* component of *himself* be disregarded as the missing words were copied to fill the gap in the second clause. The upshot is rather remarkable: the height specification of the pointing sign behaves very much like the gender specifications of pronouns in English.

What is signed: ∅-right$^{high}$ LIKE SELF$^{high}$-right. ☞$_{left}$ NOT

What is understood: ∅-right$^{high}$ LIKE SELF$^{high}$-right. ☞$_{left}$ NOT LIKE SELF$^{high}$ right.

(LSF)

But that's not quite the end of the story. We don't just need to disregard the 'high' component of *LIKE SELF$^{high}$-right* before we can apply it to the short person represented on the left. We also need to disregard the 'right' component, since the right-hand locus refers to the tall person, not to the short one. But this too shouldn't come as a big surprise: It is reminiscent of the operation we saw in *John admires himself, but I don't* (meaning I don't like *myself*). The third-person component of *himself* had to be disregarded in order for the verb phrase to apply to the speaker. Different third-person loci thus display the behavior of a grammatical person in general.

## 2.6  ICONIC VARIABLES: ICONICITY IN ACTION

There is still one last thing to check, however. What tells us that there is genuinely something pictorial in the use of high pointing? We saw that iconicity plays a role in the lexicon of English, as in *boom,* which sounds a bit like an explosion (when it is not used to refer to monkey calls, as in chapter 1). But nowadays the word is still a conventional part of English. Maybe the same thing happened with high pointing: it could have an iconic origin in history while being used with a conventional meaning in the contemporary language.

To test this possibility, we must consider once again one tall and one short individual, but now we add that the poor fellows are training to be astronauts and thus must get rotated in all sorts of weird positions. And we discuss their attitudes about themselves while they appear in these positions (as before, we'll say that the tall astronaut likes himself while the short one doesn't). The signer uses the combined index and middle fingers of the right hand to vividly represent the tall person, and the index and middle fingers of the left hand to represent the short person, with the knuckles corresponding to the head. The two individuals are represented in the same way at this point, and only pointing will later create height differences: one points above the knuckles to target the head of the tall person. By rotating the fingers, it is easy to indicate that the would-be astronauts get rotated as well, as you can see in the following pictures (from the addressee's perspective):[23]

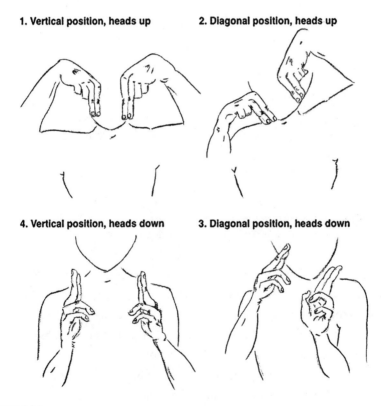

**1. Vertical position, heads up**   **2. Diagonal position, heads up**

**4. Vertical position, heads down**   **3. Diagonal position, heads down**

**Figure 2.6.1**
*Sign language representation of two persons training to be astronauts in four different positions*

When referring to the tall person (to say that *he likes himself*), the signer points high on his right, to target the tall person's head, as seen in part 1 of figure 2.6.2 (where the two positions are represented from the signer's perspective). But here is the remarkable thing: When the fingers get rotated, the high positions get rotated as well, as shown in the figure. As a result, when the fellows are in upside-down position, the 'high' position (corresponding to the person's head) ends up being . . . very low.

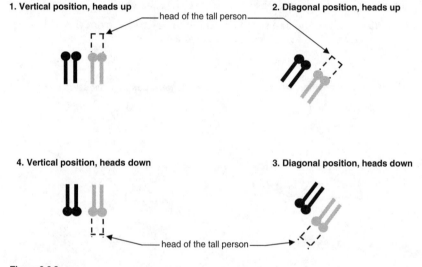

**Figure 2.6.2**
*Sign language representation of two persons training to be astronauts in four different positions (schematic representation, from the signer's perspective)*

This is exactly what we expect if the fingers serve to create a simplified picture of the astronauts and if high pointing is really pointing toward the head of the relevant person in the picture. As that person is rotated, so is that person's head, with the result that when the person is in upside-down position, 'high' pointing targets a low position!

There is an additional use of high loci that is rather extraordinary. In ASL, signers who are familiar with religion can use a locus for *God* which is . . . above their head. This is different from normal uses of high pointing. If you are talking about President Obama and wish to show respect, you can use a point to the side (corresponding to the Obama position) and upward *◌*. But for God, you will use an even higher pointing, orthogonally toward the sky *◌*. So, although there is a conventional word for *God*, if one wishes to refer to *Him* (with a pronoun), one just points upward. And it is easy to check that this isn't due to the form of the sign: *GOD* is realized with a downward rather than an upward motion—roughly, a flat hand orthogonal to the face goes down in front of the nose.

**Figure 2.6.3**
*GOD in ASL* ([**AV2.6.1**])

In fact, there is a sign that's minimally different from *GOD*: The ASL name of the linguist Noam Chomsky is a modification of *GOD*, with the C of the manual alphabet (for _Chomsky_) replacing the flat hand (no doubt because of the considerable respect he enjoyed in circles in which the proper name was created—and also because the signers involved had a good sense of humor!). But when ASL signers wish to use a pronoun to talk about Chomsky, even if they wish to show great respect, they wouldn't normally point toward the sky: there remains a considerable difference between the Chomsky locus and the God locus.

The God locus is occasionally very useful. In the Jewish tradition, God's name is so sacred that it should not be articulated. And in ASL, this prohibition naturally applies to the sign for *God*. But thanks to the God locus, one can talk unambiguously without violating the law: One just points toward the sky, using in effect a very exclusive pronoun rather than a proper name.

God's name hasn't been used, yet no ambiguity ensues. English would be hard-pressed to do quite the same thing.

In sum, whether they refer to God or to tall individuals rotated in all sorts of weird positions, sign language pronouns are remarkable in that they can simultaneously be visible logical variables and simplified pictures. This is a sense in which sign languages are 'super languages': They have the same type of logical resources as spoken languages, but seamlessly integrated with them are iconic resources that are far less common in spoken language. (We will revisit the role of iconicity in chapter 12.)

### 2.7 PLURAL PRONOUNS

So, singular ASL and LSF pronouns can simultaneously be logical variables and pictures of what they denote. Not to be outdone, plural sign language pronouns are no less remarkable: in some cases, they lead a dual life as logical symbols and as diagrammatic representations of the groups they denote.

ASL and LSF plural pronouns are realized by sketching with one's index finger a circular area (the use of plurals is generally optional, in the sense that a normal pointing sign can be used to refer to a group). Such a 'plural locus' is realized by having the finger trace a semicircular area, but I'll simplify things a bit and talk of circular ones.

**Figure 2.7.1**
*A plural locus in ASL*

Here, too, the interaction of grammar with iconic conditions gives rise to possibilities that do not exist in spoken language.

If I tell you in English that *Most of my students came to class*, I could continue by mentioning, proudly: *They are a serious group*. *They* is meant to refer to the entire group of students who collectively count as serious. Alternatively, I could continue the first sentence by adding, happily: *They asked good questions*. Here, *they* refers to the students who came to class, rather than to the entire group of students. So *they* can refer to the set of all students and also to the set of students who came to class. But can *they* also refer to the set of students that *didn't* come to class?

Let's try. *Most of my students came to class. They stayed home instead.* This discourse should make sense if *they* could mean *the students who didn't come to class*. But your gut reaction is probably that the second sentence doesn't make much sense. For whatever reason, it seems that the first sentence makes salient the entire set of students, and the set of students who came to class, but that referring with *they* to the set of students that *didn't* come to class just doesn't work.

In ASL and LSF, the very same facts hold if we use the ambiguous strategy that consists, as I mentioned above, in assigning a single default position to different pronouns (in this case, plural pronouns). This similarity between ASL, LSF, and English isn't surprising if we remember that unrelated languages of the world share numerous grammatical properties: this is just another case in which sign languages pattern with spoken languages.

But signers can also do something more interesting. They can explicitly set up a large locus—call it *ab*—to represent the entire set of students, and within it a smaller locus *a* to represent the set of students that came to class (the notations *a* and *ab* are just here to remind us that the smaller locus is within the large locus *ab*). But when you do this, something in the representation pops out: having represented the set of students as a big circular area and the set of students that came to class as a smaller circular area within it, a third area immediately becomes visible, corresponding to the set of the students that *didn't* come to class (a 'complement locus' relative to *a*), which is displayed below:

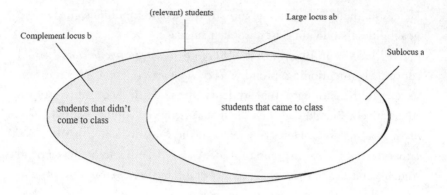

**Figure 2.7.2**

And remarkably, signers can point toward that third area with a completely normal plural pronoun to express the very meaning that we could *not* get in English, or for that matter in ASL or LSF with default loci.

The result looks like this: *My students* is expressed as *MY STUDENT* introducing a large circular position, the one we've called *ab*. Then *MOST* introduces a smaller circular area within *ab*, which we've called *a*. Finally, the pronoun corresponding to *they* points toward the third area made visible by the diagram (below): the *b* area corresponding to the students that didn't come to class.[24]

MY STUDENT ☞ ‾‾‾‾‾ **-ab** MOST ☞ ⋯⋯ **-a** a-CAME. ☞ ⋯⋯ **-b** b-STAYHOME.

'Most of my students came to class. They [the students that didn't come to class] stayed home.' (ASL)

The result is an extraordinary mix of grammar and iconicity. To understand the full sign language data, we need grammar: It is because sign languages have a lot in common with English and other spoken languages that it is odd, when one just uses a default locus, to utter a sign language equivalent of *Most students came to class. They stayed home.* But it is because of iconicity that a locus referring to the students that didn't come to class becomes salient when the positions are arranged in a diagrammatic fashion.

Now you might think that the last pointing sign in the ASL sentence for *they stayed home* just means 'the others stayed home,' which yields the desired reading in English. But ASL (or LSF, for that matter) has a word for *OTHER*, and it's not at all the normal pointing sign that is used here. For the same reason, it won't do to say that ASL just uses a diagram to realize the meaning that was missing in English. Rather, the plural loci are in this case *simultaneously* grammatical and diagrammatic.

Maybe you will now grant that sign language can do something that's not so easy to achieve with comparable resources in English. Still, it's worth pausing to ask what it would take for a spoken language to have pronouns that behave like ASL and LSF plural loci. The crucial fact was that a locus could be put within another locus. Without even getting into the issue of the third locus that pops up when this happens, what would it take to do the same thing with words? We would need to put one word within another word! Things could look like this. You ask me, *What did your students do today?* I reply, boringly, *Most of them came to class.* Here, *them* refers to the entire set of students. But then I continue, less boringly, saying, *Th-they-em asked good questions.* That's right: To mean that the students who came asked good questions, I embed the pronoun *they* within the pronoun denoting the entire group of students, hence *Th-they-em.* The sound rules of English definitely don't allow for this, but one can surmise that there are deeper reasons why such patterns have never been described in spoken language. And even if they were possible, there wouldn't be an obvious equivalent of pointing toward one part only of *th-they-em*, which was precisely what we were able to do in ASL with embedded loci. In this respect, then, sign language genuinely seems to have expressive resources that spoken language lacks.

### 2.8  CONCLUSION

Sign languages taught us two lessons. First, they made plausible the linguist's view that pronouns like *he* and *she* express logical variables, and thus come with unpronounced indices that determine their reference, hence the two representations *Sarkozy$_x$ told Obama$_y$ that **he**$_x$ would win the election* versus *Sarkozy$_x$ told Obama$_y$ that **he**$_y$ would win the election.* Depending on which variable we mentally pick, we will obtain the Obama-winning or the Sarkozy-winning meaning. Strikingly, these logical representations can be made distinctly visible by the use of space in sign language: *Sarkozy* and *Obama* are each assigned a position, and depending on where one points, one gets a meaning on which he = Sarkozy or he = Obama.

The second lesson is that sign languages have iconic resources that would have been hard to imagine had we thought of language as just speech. In several cases, our logical variables are not realized by points in space but by entire areas that simultaneously serve as simplified images (or diagrams) of what they denote. One can point upward to refer to a tall person because one indicates in this way where the head is represented (as for God, well, He is represented as being in the sky). But if the tall person is an astronaut in training and gets rotated in all sorts of positions, his head will correspondingly move, and this will be reflected in the pointing patterns as well. Plural pronouns provide another example: These are logical variables that may serve as diagrammatic representations of the denoted groups. A plural area embedded within another one serves to indicate that one group is included within another, as in the case of the students who came to class relative to the entire set of students. And by a kind of visual logic, a third area immediately pops up to denote the set of students that *didn't* come to class.

In sum, sign languages provide visible evidence for the hidden structure of language in general, but they also show that the vocal modality might be iconicity-challenged. In this domain, the full expressive resources of language might be better studied in sign languages: they are in some respects super languages.

# 3 ME, ME, ME! PERSPECTIVES IN LANGUAGE

"Dear, dear! How queer everything is to-day! ( . . . ) I wonder if I've been changed in the night? Let me think: was I the same when I got up this morning? I almost think I can remember feeling a little different. But if I'm not the same, the next question is, 'Who in the world am I?' Ah, that's the great puzzle!" And she began thinking over all the children she knew that were of the same age as herself, to see if she could have been changed for any of them.

Lewis Carroll, *Alice's Adventures in Wonderland*

## 3.1 THE FIRST-PERSON PERSPECTIVE

*I don't know who I am.* At the beginning of the 2002 action movie *The Bourne Identity*, a body is recovered by fishermen off the coast of Marseille, France. With two bullets in his back, the man is still alive but suffers from amnesia, and in the rest of the film he simultaneously learns about the world and about who he is. His only initial clue is a micro-projector implanted in his hip, which displays the number of a Swiss bank account. In the safe deposit box, he finds a passport with his picture and the name Jason Bourne. Unfortunately, the box contains multiple other passports that fit him just as well, and a gun. The survival skills that he soon displays (in several action-filled scenes) strongly suggest that his prior existence was anything but transparent and peaceful. He comes to understand that a powerful organization is out to get him. Three weeks later, in hiding in Paris, he reads in the French newspaper *Le Monde* an article on the assassination of an ex-dictator named

Wombosi. A young woman who has come to follow him asks him what the article says, and he tells her:

> *It says that three weeks before he was killed, Mr. Wombosi told police that a man came onto his yacht, five miles off the coast of Marseille, and tried to kill him. It says that he chased the man off the boat and shot him twice in the back.* **It says I am an assassin.**

As Bourne reads the article, he initially learns about the world. An assassin came onto Mr. Wombosi's yacht, with a clear goal: *He tried to kill Wombosi.* As Bourne starts putting two and two together, he comes to a horrifying conclusion: The assassin is none other than himself. Hence: *I tried to kill Wombosi. I am an assassin.*

In a sense, these two thoughts (*He tried to kill Wombosi* and *I tried to kill Wombosi*) say the very same thing about the world, since in this case *he* and *I* refer to the same individual. But the cognitive difference between them couldn't be greater. This is an old theme. In an ancient Greek myth, Oedipus is left to die after his parents Laius and Jocasta are told by a prophet that their son will end up killing his father and marrying his mother. But the servant tasked with the deed takes pity on the baby and passes him to a shepherd, who gives him away for adoption. As an adult, aware of the prophecy but not of his true parentage, Oedipus leaves his adoptive family and hometown to escape his tragic destiny and heads toward the city of Thebes. But not without incidents: Following an argument on the road, he kills a stranger; and before reaching the city, Oedipus finds out that Thebes is at the mercy of a monster, the Sphinx, that he can only defeat by solving its riddles. Having done so in ways that we need not get into, he wins the throne of the recently deceased king and marries the king's widow.[1]

Oedipus later learns that the king had been killed on a road and eventually infers that the king was the stranger he had killed, that the king was his birth father, and that the king's widow, now Oedipus's wife, is none other than his birth mother. As this change of perspective happens, he comes to think *I killed my father, I married my mother*—and in despair, he blinds himself. Throughout the myth, Oedipus learns about the world but also about which person in the world he is, and thus he learns which person *I* refers to.

Thousands of years apart, Jason Bourne and Oedipus epitomize the role of the first-person perspective. It is one thing for Bourne to think that an assassin tried to kill Wombosi: This is mere information about the world. It is quite another to think *I tried to kill Wombosi*. This is information about which individual he is.

There is no doubt that the first-person perspective immensely matters to human experience. We all like to think that we have a privileged access to ourselves, and possibly to our self, the source of conscious thought that has exercised philosophers for centuries. German refers to this mysterious entity as the *I* (*das Ich*), French as the *Me* (*le Moi*), while English occasionally uses the Latin pronoun, the Ego (or the Self, a more common term). One might be tempted to think that the first-person pronoun is a kind of private proper name for our self. The grammatical parallelisms that can be found between *I* and *you* suggest that this is not quite what is going on, as it doesn't seem very promising to take *you* to be a proper name of anything, as it changes its reference depending on one's interlocutor. But *I* and *you* highlight the role of perspectives in language: Any sentence usually comes with words that only make sense relative to the context in which they are uttered. *I* refers to different people, depending on who is speaking, and *you* refers to different people, depending on who is being addressed. Similarly, *now* depends on the time of utterance, and *here* on the place of utterance.

These perspectival elements are called 'indexicals,' expressions whose meaning depends on the context, and are easily understood from an utterance alone. Expressions that also depend on the context but usually require a pointing gesture to be understood are called 'demonstratives,' as in, *I'll invite her* [pointing to Ann] *but not her* [pointing to Mary], or *I'll invite this guy* [pointing to John] *but not that guy* [pointing to Bill]. Perspectives are essential to the analysis of thoughts, to their representation in language, and to our ability to report other people's thoughts and words. Interestingly, logical languages designed for science eschew context-dependency (i.e., perspectives) in an attempt to state observations and laws that are as universal as possible. But, in so doing, they also miss something essential about human thought and language, as we will now see. The upshot will be that while human language is a formal language, it is one with special properties and devices that are not found in standard logical languages.

## 3.2 PERSPECTIVAL THOUGHTS AND INDEXICALS

What is the informational content of a thought, or of somebody's beliefs? Philosophers often think about it in terms of the ways things could be, called possible worlds. In 1998, France won the soccer World Cup, but one could easily imagine that Brazil had won instead, or Italy, or Germany. There are possible worlds in which France won (among them, the actual world), other possible worlds in which the winner was Brazil, and still others in which it was Italy, or Germany. If someone—say, Sam—has no idea who won, then all four world types are compatible with Sam's beliefs. If Sam knows that the winner is European, then the 'France,' 'Italy,' and 'Germany' worlds are compatible with Sam's beliefs but the 'Brazil' worlds are not. And if Sam is completely informed in this respect, only the 'France' worlds remain. I write 'worlds' in the plural rather than 'world' in the singular because a possible world, a way things are, is entirely specific: It determines the truth value of every imaginable sentence (think of it as the complete specification of everything there is to know). There are certainly lots of things that Sam doesn't know about the world, so there must be multiple worlds compatible with Sam's beliefs.

But knowledge of the world isn't enough to characterize human thought. We also have irreducibly perspectival beliefs, which are beliefs about where in the world we are rather than just which world we are in. This is because one might know everything there is to know about the world but still lack some crucial bit of information about the *context*—namely, about where in the world or which individual in the world one is. You can think about it with a comparison: If you are lost in a forest, it won't suffice to give you a perfect map of it. What you really need is a map together with a dot that you can interpret as *This is where I am right now!* The map corresponds to the world you are in; the dot corresponds to the context within that world.

But how could we fail to know which individual in the world we are? In *Alice's Adventures in Wonderland*, Alice undergoes a series of magical transmogrifications and comes to wonder whether she could have been turned into somebody else: *'Who in the world am I?' Ah, that's the great puzzle.* Magic aside, the cases of Jason Bourne and of Oedipus begin to highlight the problem, but they involve additional complexities that we'll want to sidestep. So let's consider a more radical (if less exciting) fictional case whose original form was investigated by philosophers.[2] It involves Rudolf Lingens, an amnesiac who has the dubious privilege of being locked after hours in a dark computer room of Harvard's Science Center. Having access to excellent online resources, he can learn everything there is to know about the world—so for once we'll assume, fancifully, that there is a single world compatible with his beliefs. He might even learn that a certain Rudolf Lingens is locked in Harvard's Science Center. But this still won't put him in a position to say, *I am Rudolf Lingens, I am in Harvard's Science Center.* Besides knowing how the world is, Lingens needs to know which individual he is— or in other words, in which context he is located. For him, *Who in the world am I?* is the great question, just as it was for Alice.

Lingens, Bourne, and Oedipus (not to mention Alice) are all fictional characters. But examples closer to real life are not too hard to find. Oliver Sacks once told the poignant story of a former hospital director with Alzheimer's disease. Sacks writes:

> He is always "on the go," and for much of the time seems to imagine he is still a doctor here; [he] will speak to other patients not as a fellow patient but as a doctor would, and will look through their charts unless stopped.
>
> On one occasion, he saw his own chart, said "Charles M.—that's me," opened it, saw "Alzheimer's disease," and said, "God help me!" and wept. Sometimes he calls out, "I want to die. . . . Let me die."
>
> Oliver Sacks, *Everything in its Place: First Loves and Last Tales* (Sydney: Pan Macmillan, Kindle Edition, 2019, 1643).

In Sacks's telling, Charles M. (unlike Lingens) immediately gets the right perspectival thought, *I have Alzheimer's disease*, because he also has the thought *I am Charles M.* Without it, he would be in Lingens's situation: he would hold the belief that *Charles M. has Alzheimer's*, without thereby believing the first-person thought, *I have Alzheimer's*.

These examples show that the thought contribution of *I* is very different from that of a proper name. For Lingens, it is one thing to think *Lingens is locked in Harvard's Science Center* and quite another to think *I am locked in Harvard's Science Center*. And if Charles M.'s disease were more advanced, it might not be the same thing for him to think *Charles M. has Alzheimer's* and to think *I have Alzheimer's*.

Of course, we usually know who we are, which is why it takes uncommon examples (from Greek mythology to action movies) to find thoughts that are irreducibly perspectival (i.e., context-dependent). With texts, by contrast, there are more mundane situations in which the identity of the writer is initially unknown, and the first person may occasionally provide critical information. Take little Tommy Smith. Tommy (unbeknownst to his mother Ann) has an irrepressible desire to skip school, but he fears the consequences. He has the foresight to send his teacher a note: *Tommy will be absent today because he is sick*. But he signs it, *My mommy*. Unless the teacher is charmed, that won't quite do the trick. Here *my mommy* and *Ann Smith* refer to one and the same person. But *my mommy* can only be produced in a context whose speaker (or rather writer) is the mother's child, hence the giveaway. (Things won't work any better if the note ends with *My mother, Ann Smith*; by contrast, *His mother, Ann Smith* might be more successful, especially if the signature is forged well).

Further indexical expressions can provide crucial perspectival information as well. If I am furiously writing against a deadline, it's a very different matter to think *At 00:01am the deadline has passed* and *Now the deadline has passed*. The first thought needn't cause alarm: It just happens to be a midnight deadline, nothing out of the ordinary. The second sentence means that I have missed the deadline. Although one usually knows who one is, one doesn't always know at what time one is located. So, at 00:01am, chances are that I am not in a position to think, *Now it's 00:01am*. For this reason, although the two sentences say the same thing about the world (because unbeknownst to me, *now* refers to *00:01am*), they have very different perspectival implications; they say different things about the context one is in. This is a temporal version of Lingens's predicament: We may know about lots of things happening at lots of times, but this won't help much if we don't know where we are situated on the timeline. Similar examples could be constructed with spatial location. It is one thing for an explorer to think *the South Pole is 90-degrees south latitude* (this is just general geographical knowledge) and quite another to think *the South Pole is here* (the explorer's goal has been reached!).

The upshot is that thoughts are not just about the world—they are also about *our position in the world*, be it with respect to who we are, where we are located on the temporal line, or where we are located in space. Expressions such as *I, now*, and *here* are exquisitely suited to indicate the speaker's or thinker's perspective. And they are not just convenient abbreviations. If we try to eliminate indexicals by replacing them with proper names or descriptions, as in the Lingens case or the example involving the midnight deadline, we obtain different meanings, with different implications about the context of thought.

### 3.3 THOUGHT REPORTS AND LOGOPHORIC PRONOUNS

Thanks to indexicals, language seems remarkably well suited to the expression of perspectives; in this respect, it is a remarkable piece of cognitive engineering. Still, when we dig deeper, there are occasional cases that may give us grounds to doubt the engineer's competence. This is because when we *report* thoughts, there may be a conflict between the speaker's perspective and that of the individual whose thoughts are reported.

Let's think again about the unfortunate amnesiac Rudolf Lingens. We saw how different it was for him to think *I am locked in Harvard's Science Center* and to think *Rudolf Lingens is locked in Harvard's Science Center*. And yet both cases are naturally reported in the same way, as *Rudolf Lingens thinks that he is locked in Harvard's Science Center.*[3] To make things worse, if we use the first-person pronoun in the report, we get a completely irrelevant meaning. Take the sentence *Ruldolf Lingens thinks that I am locked in Harvard's Science Center.* It attributes to Lingens a thought about me, the speaker or writer, rather than about himself. This is an instance of indirect discourse, and as a result *I* refers to the speaker (or writer). In English, the word *that* (as in *that I am locked . . .*) suffices to indicate that we are not dealing with a mere quotation of Lingens's words. To preserve his perspective, we would need to use direct discourse—that is, a quotation—by saying, for instance, *Lingens thinks: "I am locked"* (if Lingens doesn't have a first-person thought, we could say instead, *Lingens thinks: "Lingens is locked"*). As we will see, there are limitations to what can be done with quotations because they are not grammatically integrated with the rest of the sentence. In addition, not all constructions that report thoughts can take quotations as complements: *Lingens has the impression that he is locked* is a natural thing to say, but *Lingens has the impression: "I am locked"* is rather odd.

Having noticed that indirect discourse as we know it was badly designed to report perspectival thoughts, the Guatemalan-American philosopher Héctor-Neri Castañeda proposed to add an artificial pronoun to English for the (admittedly narrow) purposes of philosophical analysis. He suggested that one should use *he\** (which I pronounce as *he star*) to report thoughts that involved a first-person perspective and to otherwise use *he*.[4] In our scenario, then, the philosopher could write that *Lingens thought that he was locked in Harvard's Science Center*, as Lingens knew, thanks to the rich information he got online, that Lingens was locked over there. But since he didn't know that he himself was Lingens, it wouldn't be true to say that *Lingens thought that he\* was locked in Harvard's Science Center*: This would require precisely the first-person thought that Lingens lacked. So *he\** has two properties. First, it can only be used in speech or thought reports to talk about the relevant speaker or thinker, and thus in *Lingens thought that he\* was locked in Harvard's Science Center*, the pronoun couldn't refer to any individual but Lingens. Second, it can only refer to this individual from the first-person perspective.

Now here is a remarkable fact: *he\** exists, just in other languages than English. If English may seem a bit philosophically challenged, lacking the distinction that was close to Castañeda's heart (and to that of many other philosophers), several languages passed the philosophy test with flying colors. One case in point is Ewe, a West African language spoken in Togo and North Ghana (*Ewe* is often pronounced *ayway*). Ewe draws an explicit distinction between *he* and *he\**. The normal third-person pronoun is a word written as *e* (corresponding to standard *he* or *she*). It can be used in *Lingens thought he* *was locked at Harvard* if *he* refers to somebody else, or to Lingens when his thought has the form *Lingens is locked at Harvard.* In the more usual case in which Lingens had a first-person thought, on the other hand, the report involves a different pronoun, *yè*, which is Ewe's version of *he\**.[5]

This is by no means an isolated case. Real-life versions of *he\** are called *logophoric* expressions, a term from Ancient Greek that means 'which carries discourse.' Such expressions are markers of indirect discourse (rather than of quotation). Logophoric expressions have been described in several languages. In Gokana, a language of Nigeria, the logophoric element appears as a suffix on the verb rather than as a pronoun.[6] So a sentence such as *Lingens said that he fell* will be realized differently depending on whether *he* refers to Lingens (under the first-person perspective, as *I fell*) or to someone else. With the first-person perspective, corresponding to Castañeda's *he\**, the suffix *è* must be added to the verb that follows the third-person pronoun: *Lingens said that he fell-è*, rather than just *that he fell* (in Gokana, the verb *fell* with the logophoric suffix is *do-è* rather than just *do*; I use English words to facilitate the discussion). Without the suffix, the verb is free to take as subject someone other than Lingens.

Even outside of cases that involve amnesiacs or people who don't recognize themselves, a logophoric expression can make all the difference. In Ewe stories, one may find long stretches of discourse with just one verb of thought, followed by several independent sentences that might otherwise seem to describe objective facts. But the presence of the logophoric pronoun is a telltale sign that these sentences continue to report the character's thoughts.[7]

Going back to our initial problem, logophoric expressions are an elegant grammatical solution to the problem we started out with: How can we preserve a thinker's first-person perspective when we report their thought, given that *I* is already taken to convey the *speaker's* (rather than the reported thinker's) perspective? The Ewe solution, which was also Castañeda's, is to use a 'new' pronoun just for this situation. Gokana achieves the same result by adding a suffix to the verb. But is there anything similar we can do in English?

## 3.4 THE PERSPECTIVAL NATURE OF THE ENGLISH INFINITIVE

On closer inspection, English has a simple way of unambiguously conveying first-person perspectives in indirect discourse, but it involves a different construction: the infinitive.[8]

To see how this works, let's imagine that we are attending an amateur piano competition on TV. Contestants sent in their recordings of a Chopin piece beforehand, and now the jury is listening to the top-ten audios, trying to decide which is best. Anyone watching can send in their votes as well. Ann took part in the competition, but as she watches it on TV, she doesn't know she was selected among the top-ten contestants. At some point, she hears a slightly flawed rendition and tells her friends, *Well, that contestant certainly doesn't deserve the prize, and ought to lose!* Alas, unbeknownst to her, the flawed contestant is none other than herself, and thus without realizing it, *Ann hopes that she loses.* This, of course, is but a new version of the problem we encountered with Jason Bourne, Oedipus, and Rudolf Lingens: Whether Ann thought *I ought to lose* or *That contestant ought to lose*, both thoughts can be reported in the same way, with the pronoun *she*. But this doesn't do justice to the complexity of the situation, where her thought about herself is in the third person (= *that contestant ought to lose)* rather than in the first person (= *I ought to lose*).

Strikingly, however, things are different if we use an infinitive and say, *Ann hopes to lose.* In the situation described, where Ann doesn't recognize herself, this sentence doesn't ring true. The reason is that the infinitive must report a first-person thought, and Ann's hope is definitely not of the form *I ought to lose.* With verbs of speech and thought, the perspectival implication of the infinitive can easily be found in further examples. As Jason Bourne reads about the attempted murder of ex-dictator Wombosi, he might think: *The assassin ought to be apprehended.* Since the assassin is none other than himself, in effect *Bourne hopes that he gets apprehended.* But it doesn't ring true to say *Bourne hopes to get apprehended.* This is because he definitely does not have the first-person thought: *I ought to get apprehended.*

This subtle contribution of infinitives that follow *hope* and related verbs is a general finding, in English as well as in several other languages. If we change the scenario a bit and now focus on Ann's reaction after the flawed (and still anonymous) contestant lost, we could say that, without realizing it, *Ann is happy that she lost*. But it won't do to say that *Ann is happy to have lost*. Here, too, the infinitive can only report a first-person perspective. In English, *hope* and *be happy* can take the infinitive, but *think* cannot (you can't say *Ann thinks to lose* to express something close to *Ann thinks that she will lose*). In French, things are different, and the literal translation of *Ann thinks to lose* ('Ann pense perdre') is acceptable, but as you can guess, it is only appropriate if Ann has a first-person thought (such as *I will lose*). In this case, too, the infinitive *to lose* behaves like Castañeda's *he\*/she\* loses*, as well as verbs with logophoric markers in Ewe and Gokana.

Similar effects can be found with still other verbs that take the infinitive. The great American actor Cary Grant once quipped, *Everyone wants to be Cary Grant. Even I want to be Cary Grant.* In effect, Cary Grant wanted to be the mythical character, something that didn't quite go without saying. As expected, *Cary Grant wanted to be Cary Grant* can only be used to report a first-person desire on the actor's part, unlike *Cary Grant wanted Cary Grant to be Cary Grant*.

### 3.5  THE ENGLISH FIRST PERSON

I started this chapter by arguing that some thoughts are irreducibly perspectival: They contain information not only about the world but also about the context we are in. Indexical expressions such as *I, now,* and *here* are exquisitely suited to the task, as they refer to elements of the context—its speaker, time, and location, respectively. But this also created a linguistic dilemma: In indirect discourse, how can we preserve their first-person perspective without conflating it with that of the speaker? Castañeda's *he\** was an artificial solution to the problem, with equally clever counterparts in natural language: Ewe and Gokana's logophoric markers, as well as the English infinitive.

But if perspective preservation is the name of the game, why don't we just use *I* in thought reports, but with a meaning that corresponds to the thinking agent rather than to the speaker? Initially, it might look like this option is open in English as well. For instance, if I utter the words *Ann said I should hire Sam*, the result will be ambiguous: *I* can refer to me, the speaker, or to Ann. Furthermore, in the latter case, there is no doubt that it reports Ann's first-person perspective. Granted, this doesn't unambiguously convey Ann's perspective (because *I* can also refer to the speaker), but certainly the broader context can help choose between the two interpretations.

In fact, something else is going on: When spoken (rather than written), the sentence is ambiguous between indirect discourse and direct discourse (i.e., quotation). The direct discourse interpretation could be written far more clearly with quotation marks: *Ann said, "I should hire Sam."* In bona fide indirect discourse, *I* may *only* refer to the speaker, and the simplest way to see that is to add a *that*, which grammatically connects an embedded clause with its environment. Just doing this makes it much harder to say *Ann said that "I should hire Sam."* Journalists sometimes write things like this, no doubt because of the pressure to show that they are faithful to the precise words used. Thus Reuters once wrote: *Trump said that "I love WikiLeaks"* (before dropping the *that* in a later update).[9] But if you pronounce aloud *Ann said that I should hire Sam*, your interlocutors will certainly understand *I* to refer to you, rather than to Ann.

Unlike indirect discourse, quotations don't need to be grammatically integrated with the rest of the sentence, and so they can quote words from a different language, as in *Kennedy famously said, "Ich bin ein Berliner"* (using in the quotation the German for *I am a Berliner*). Now try: *Kennedy famously said that ich bin ein Berliner*—it doesn't quite work. You can tweak the German as much as you want and it won't really help to make the entire sentence more natural. Similarly, the *Washington Post* once ran this title:[10]

Trump tweets 'covfefe,' inspiring a semi-comedic act of Congress

But it would have been very odd to write: *Trump tweets that covfefe*, because *covfefe* isn't a word, let alone a full clause.

There is another way to show that quotation rather than indirect discourse is involved in *Ann said, "I should hire Sam."* A quotation attributes not just the meaning but also the specific choice of words to the agent. This seems right in the case at hand. We are getting precise information about the words Ann used, not just *I*, but also *should hire Sam*. If Ann said something like *I ought to give Sam a job*, the quotation isn't entirely accurate. By contrast, the indirect discourse report *Ann said that she should hire Sam* isn't so picky: it allows for a different choice of words as long as the meaning is preserved.

The difference between indirect discourse and quotation becomes more striking if we modify the sentence a bit. I could tell you in the same situation: *Sam is the person who(m) Ann said she should hire*. However, it is far less natural to claim: *Sam is the person who(m) Ann said, "I should hire."* The reason is grammatical. In the first sentence, *who* (called a relative pronoun) is the object of *hire*. This is shown by the fact that you can replace it with *whom*, a form that is characteristic of objects. Thus, one can say *Whom will Ann hire _*, where *whom* asks about the hiree and corresponds to the object of *hire*, marked with the underscore _. But one cannot say *Whom will hire Sam*, where *whom* tries—and fails—to ask about the hirer and corresponds to the subject. So, in our initial sentence, there is a grammatical dependency between the verb *hire* and *who/whom*:

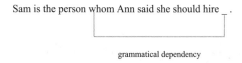

The reason we can't do the same thing with *Sam is the person who(m) Ann said: "I should hire"* is that a quotation is an opaque unit: Grammatical dependencies cannot cross quotation marks, so to speak. In order to encode the fact that this sentence sounds weird to native speakers of English, I'll adopt a convention from contemporary linguistics and mark it with a star at the beginning.

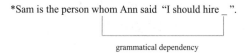

The conclusion at this point is that, in English at least, the word *I* rigidly conveys the perspective of the actual speaker. In indirect discourse, *I* just cannot convey the perspective of the agent whose thoughts or words are reported. The only way to use *I* with this function is to resort to a quotation, but this comes with some limitations, as a quotation is not grammatically integrated with the rest of the sentence.

In sum, to unambiguously report a first-person perspective in indirect discourse we need Castañeda's *he\**, or logophoric markers, or the English (or French) infinitive. The English word *I* is definitely not the way to go (unless we use quotation, of course).

### 3.6 CONTEXT SHIFT: THE FIRST-PERSON IN ZAZAKI AND AMHARIC

Surprisingly, not all languages use the first person in the same way as English. Quite a few languages allow the speaker to use *I* in indirect discourse to convey the perspective of another person whose thoughts or words are reported.

A case in point is Zazaki, an Indo-European language spoken in eastern Turkey. To start with, in Zazaki, it is possible to say something like *John said that I am-sick* to mean that John said that he, John, is sick (I write *am-sick* rather than *am sick* because in this case Zazaki has a single word where English uses two). While this could in principle be a case of quotation, the presence of a word analogous to English *that* already makes this a bit unlikely. But we can clinch the case against quotation by noting that the grammatical dependency that was impossible with English quotation is possible in this Zazaki sentence.

The crucial sentence is literally the following: *Girl that Hesen said I kissed is-pretty* (*Hesen* is the name of a male). Its English translation would be: *The girl who(m) Hesen said he kissed is pretty*. It involves a grammatical dependency between the embedded clause and *who(m)*, as can be seen by the fact that *whom* can be used. The existence of this grammatical dependency tells us that this is not a case of quotation. If we used similar words in English, including the first-person pronoun, we would get: *The girl who(m) Hesen said I kissed is pretty.* And in English, there is no doubt that *I* has to refer to the actual speaker, as it does in the examples we discussed before. But the facts are different in Zazaki: The word for *I* can, in this case, refer to Hesen, despite the fact that the grammatical dependency guarantees that quotation could not be the culprit.

The girl whom John said I kissed _ is pretty.

grammatical dependency

If you wish to see the real Zazaki sentence, it looks like this:[11]

čɛnɛkɛ [kɛ Hɛseni va **mɪ** paci kɛrda] rindɛka
girl that Hesen said I kiss did pretty.be-PRES
'The girl that Hesen said {Hesen, I} kissed is pretty.'

The first line is the Zazaki original, the second line is a word-for-word translation (with the English words aligned with the Zazaki original terms), and the third line gives two possible translations. One is the interpretation we've just discussed, where *I* refers to Hesen. But there is also an English-style possibility, which is to interpret *I* to refer to the actual speaker.

As you see, then, the sentence is ambiguous: *I* can either refer to Hesen or to the actual speaker (only the latter option is available in English, of course). One way to understand this ambiguity is to posit that one can optionally add an invisible word that shifts the context with respect to which indexicals are assessed. I'll write this invisible word as *C* to remind us that it shifts the context. Take a Zazaki sentence whose translation is schematically this:

Hesen said that I am-sick.

Without *C*, this sentence behaves like its English counterpart, *Hesen said that I am sick.* As is shown by the presence of *that*, this is an instance of indirect discourse, and *I* refers to the actual speaker. But Zazaki has the additional option of interpreting the sentence with *C* while *still* being in indirect discourse. Adding the invisible word, we will get this:

Hesen said that C I am-sick.

Now *C* tells you to shift the context of the embedded clause in order to adopt Hesen's perspective (as a first approximation, you can think of it as *Hesen said that he is in a context C in which 'I am sick' is true*—but remember that the Zazaki construction doesn't involve quotation, unlike my paraphrase). As a result, *I* refers to Hesen. Importantly, because this is indirect discourse, not quotation, it is possible to have a grammatical dependency between the complement clause and the rest of the sentence, as we saw above.

As you might expect, this 'shifted' *I* (which is evaluated relative to a shifted context, namely Hesen's) can only serve to report Hesen's first-person perspective. So it isn't fully accurate to translate this sentence as *Hesen said that he was sick*. The reasons is that the English *he* can be used in indirect discourse if Hesen thought, without recognizing himself, *This guy is sick*. This option is precluded in the Zazaki sentence, as was shown by the linguist Pranav Anand, who investigated these cases in great detail.[12] Anand gave Zazaki consultants a scenario reminiscent of the Oliver Sacks story mentioned above, along the following lines:

> Hesen, a doctor, happens to have had a checkup. He glances at the chart of a patient's blood work, and sees that the patient is clearly sick, but the name is hard to read. He tells the nurse: *This guy is really sick.*

In this case, the Zazaki sentence with *I* won't work, although if Hesen had a first-person thought, the sentence would be fine. In other words, Zazaki *I* can fulfill the same role as Castañeda *he\**, Ewe and Gokana logophoric expressions, as well as the English infinitive: It can unambiguously convey a first-person perspective in indirect discourse. But it has the advantage of showing more transparently (through the use of the first person) that context-dependency is at the root of the phenomenon.

Still, you might be uneasy about one aspect of this analysis—namely, the presence of the unpronounced word *C*. To reassure you, we will soon see that something rather similar can be made visible in sign language. But even in Zazaki, the effect of *C* can be felt indirectly. When two indexical expressions, *I* and *you*, both appear in the same clause in indirect discourse, they are both affected in the same way by *C* in case it is present.

It is independently interesting to note that not just *I* but also *you* can be evaluated with respect to *C*. This just highlights the parallelism between the first- and the second-person pronoun (I mentioned this parallelism at the outset to suggest that it's not too promising to take *I* to be a kind of private proper name for the self, as this wouldn't extend to *you*, whose reference changes from conversation to conversation). For example, a Zazaki sentence akin to *Rojda said to Bill that I am angry at you* can be understood with *I* referring to Rojda and *you* referring to Bill. This makes sense if the sentence is understood with the invisible word *C* (again, you can think of it, with some approximations, as *Rojda said to Bill that she is in a context in which 'I am angry at you' is true*). Another possibility is to understand the sentence without *C*, and in this case *I* and *you* refer to the actual speaker and actual addressee, not to Rojda and Bill. The two representations appear below, but they correspond to the same sequence of words in Zazaki:[13]

Representation with C:   yesterday Rojda to-Bill said that C   I at-you am-angry.

Representation without C:   yesterday Rojda to-Bill said that   I at-you am-angry.

Importantly, either *C* is present and both *I* and *you* are evaluated with respect to it, or *C* is absent and these two words behave like their English counterparts. In other words, in Zazaki at least, it's not possible to mix perspectives and thus to have *I* referring to Rojda while *you* refers to the actual addressee: both indexicals are affected by *C* in case it is present.

It's not clear that all languages that allow for shifting of perspectives follow the same pattern, however. In Amharic, the official language of Ethiopia, two first-person pronouns can be evaluated with respect to different contexts: *John said that my son will not obey me* has several possible meanings, including two on which *my* and *me* refer to different people. These two meanings can be conveyed in English by *John said that his (= John's) son will not obey me*, and *John said that my son will not obey him (= John)*. The correct analysis of these data is still a matter of debate, but it is clear that it is not compatible with the restrictive use of *C* we saw in Zazaki, since C would force *my son* and *me* to be evaluated from the same perspective, hence blocking the mixed readings we find.[14]

### 3.7  VISIBLE CONTEXT SHIFT IN SIGN LANGUAGE

While it was a bit surprising that we posited an invisible word in Zazaki— namely, *C*, the context-shifter—it was reassuring that you could see its effect indirectly: When it was present, it had to affect not just *I* but also *you*. But can we find more direct evidence for *C*? We had encountered a similar question in our initial analysis of English pronouns. We had postulated unpronounced symbols to capture the ambiguity of *Sarkozy$_x$ told Obama$_y$ that he$_{x/y}$ would win the election*: Depending on whether *he* was read as *he$_x$* or *he$_y$*, we obtained the meaning on which Sarkozy was to win or Obama was to win. But we quickly turned to sign language to argue that these little *x*'s and *y*'s could be visibly realized—namely, as loci in signing space.

Remarkably, a similar argument can be developed for the context-shifter *C*, thanks once again to sign language. In ASL, LSF, and other sign languages, context shift is visibly realized by an operation called 'Role Shift,' in which the signer shifts his or her body to adopt the position of a character whose thoughts or words are reported. A simple example is found below, with just four words:[15]

WIFE  SAY  **YOU**  **FINE**.

*WIFE* introduces a locus slightly on the signer's right. But something happens between the second and third word: The signer shifts her body to adopt the wife's position, with a corresponding change of eye gaze direction; so the boldfaced words (*YOU FINE*) are signed from this shifted position, which is an instance of Role Shift.

| WIFE | SAY | **YOU** | **FINE** |

**Figure 3.7.1**
***YOU FINE*** *is signed after rotating to adopt the perspective of the wife, who was established on the signer's right*

As a result, the rest of the sentence is interpreted from the wife's perspective, with the consequence that *YOU* refers to whomever the wife is talking to (and as you may expect, *YOU* is just a pointing sign referring to the addressee of the reported words).

Role Shift is an option but not an obligation. So the sentence *John told Mary I give you a-car* has different meanings depending on whether the signer performs a body shift to adopt John's perspective. Without the shift, the sentence has the same meaning as its English counterpart, namely: *John told Mary that I would give you a car*. But with the body shift, the meaning becomes: *John told Mary that he, John, would give her a car*. This is well captured if the body shift marks the effect of the unpronounced word *C* that we posited in Zazaki. With *C*, the sentence becomes *John told Mary C I give you a-car*, and because of the presence of *C*, both *I* and *you* are evaluated with respect to John's perspective—and, in fact, the signer literally produces them from John's perspective by rotating to adopt it. As a result, *I* refers to John and *you* refers to Mary. This case is thus remarkably similar to that of Zazaki, since when *C*, realized as Role Shift, is present, both pronouns have no choice but to be evaluated with respect to the shifted perspective. Similar facts hold in LSF as well. (You may have noted that Role Shift doesn't just correspond to *C* but also affects the words that depend on *C*: In our example *WIFE SAY C YOU FINE*, the last two words are signed from the wife's perspective. This is a common pattern in sign language, where for instance negation can be accompanied by a headshake that co-occurs with the negated words.)

You might recall that I also described a slightly different pattern: In Amharic, two indexical pronouns in an embedded clause can correspond to different perspectives. Interestingly, the Amharic pattern can also be found under Role Shift, but in sign languages other than ASL and LSF. In German and Catalan Sign Language, perspectives can be 'mixed' in the same way as in Amharic. So it looks like German and Catalan Sign Language are to ASL and LSF as Amharic is to Zazaki: The variation within sign language seems to mirror variation found in spoken language, with some languages (German and Catalan Sign Language, Amharic) allowing perspectives to be mixed in the presence of context shift while other languages (ASL and LSF, Zazaki) require all indexicals in a clause to correspond to the same perspective.

One last question is whether we could analyze away these examples as instances of quotation. Couldn't we just treat the ASL example above as *My wife said: "You are fine"*? For German and Catalan Sign Language, this analysis is unlikely. With quotation, the sentence *John told Mary: "I will give you a car"* doesn't really allow one to mix perspectives in the quoted sentence, so the quotation-based analysis couldn't explain the German and Catalan Sign Language facts. But since perspectives cannot be mixed in ASL, the argument is more complicated. One way to develop it is to apply the same tests with grammatical dependencies involving *whom*, as in our discussion of English and Zazaki. In ASL, the results sometimes seem to be the same as in Zazaki, but they hinge on complex data (in LSF, the facts are more favorable to an analysis based on quotation).[16]

Finally, there is a further twist to our sign language data, and it's particularly enlightening. Both ASL and LSF can also use Role Shift outside of indirect discourse. For instance, if I am talking about an angry person associated with locus *a*, I could use an English strategy and say *IX-a WALK-AWAY*, which literally translates to *he/she walked away*. Here, *IX-a* is just an index pointing toward a locus *a*, something I wrote before with an index icon ☞ (the notation *IX* abbreviates *index*). But I can also apply Role Shift after the initial pointing sign: By rotating my body, I can adopt the position corresponding to the angry person (in locus *a*) and sign from this position something like *I walk away*. The result has the unpronounced word *C* and boldfacing to remind you that the last expression is realized with Role Shift. The result looks like this:

IX-a **C 1-WALK-AWAY**

The expression *1-WALK-AWAY* is just a first-person version of 'walk away,' realized from the signer's shifted position, but the overall meaning is that the person associated with locus *a* (not the signer) walked away. By performing a body shift and adopting that person's position, the signer makes the description more vivid, as if she were embodying that person's action. Of course, in this case, there is just no possibility of a quotational analysis, since no words or thoughts are reported. In this respect, it seems that some sign languages go beyond the possibilities that have been described for spoken language, where no similar cases of context shift outside of indirect discourse have been described. Since this is an area of active research, the situation might well change in the coming years, but this is yet another case in which sign language offers unique insights into language in general.

## 3.8 CONCLUSION

I started this chapter by noting that some thoughts are irreducibly perspectival. In the simplest scenario, the amnesiac Lingens knows everything there is to know about the world, and he might even know that *Lingens is in Harvard's Science Center*, without thereby coming to the crucial realization: *I am Lingens, I am in Harvard's Science Center*. Jason Bourne and Oedipus were faced with different versions of the same situation. Thanks to the word *I* and other indexical expressions (e.g., *you, here, now*), language is exquisitely suited to the communication of such perspectives. But in English indirect discourse, *I* can only convey the speaker's perspective, not that of the agent whose thoughts are reported. As a result, we just use the third-person pronoun instead. But *Lingens thought he was locked in Harvard's Science Center* doesn't tell us whether Lingens's thought involved a first-person perspective or not. While philosophers invented an artificial pronoun, *he\**, to convey the first-person perspective in indirect discourse, some languages have expressions (namely, logophoric expressions) that do exactly this, so they are in this respect more 'philosophical' languages than English. Still, as we dig deeper in the grammar of English, it too reveals itself to be capable of such nuances, although just with the infinitive: *Ann hopes to lose* can only assign to Ann a first-person thought, unlike *Ann hopes that she loses*, which is underspecified in this respect.

In some further languages, such as Zazaki, an operation of context shift makes it possible to retain words like *I, you, here,* and *now* in indirect discourse so as to convey the perspective of the person whose words or thoughts are reported. Remarkably, sign language arguably has a visible version of this operation: a signer may literally shift their body to adopt the position of the person whose perspective is being conveyed. This is one more case in which sign language makes visible subtle logical tools of language in general.

Chapter 2 highlighted some similarities between human language and some logical languages. Both have logical variables such as $x, y$, and $z$, which can be visibly realized in sign language. In this chapter, we saw that when it comes to perspectives, human language goes far beyond standard logical languages: unlike them, it has diverse and very nuanced ways of conveying the irreducibly perspectival nature of thought. Does that make it less 'logical' than them? Not at all. Human language handles perspectives as precisely as it does variables. It just has formal mechanisms that are not used in standard logical languages. In that sense, human language is a *more sophisticated* formal language.

# 4 NOUNS AND VERBS: OBJECTS AND EVENTS

*A virus is spreading.* With pronouns, we can refer to persons and objects, but we cannot yet *say* anything about them. To make important statements such as the italicized one, we need nouns and verbs, adjectives and adverbs. With pronouns alone, we could talk about a virus as *it*, but we couldn't qualify it more precisely as a *virus*, or as a *dangerous virus*, let alone say what it does—namely, that it is *spreading* or *spreading rapidly*. We convey information about things by classifying them in terms of what they are and what they do. To take this further step, we first need nouns and verbs. These characterize entire sets of objects and entire sets of events. Thus, *I am a man* states that I belong to the set of men, while *I am reading* asserts that I take part in an event belonging to the set of reading events; similarly for *SARS-CoV-2 is a virus* or *SARS-CoV-2 is spreading*. In effect, verbs are just like nouns, but they characterize different kinds of things: events, not objects.

In simple cases, *verbs are to events as nouns are to objects.*[1] This parallelism between nouns and verbs is a deep discovery of contemporary linguistics, and it offers fascinating insights into our way of mentally organizing the world. In particular, objects and events alike are analyzed by the human mind as belonging to one of three categories: They may be singular and denote elementary entities of the relevant type (*a table*); they may be plural, referring to groups of such entities (*some tables*); or they may refer to things that are not viewed as having smallest entities (*water*). This three-way distinction is well known for objects, but it applies in rather similar form to events. It is a way or organizing the world that has far-reaching consequences for nouns and verbs, for spoken and sign language. It will have repercussions for adjectives and adverbs as well. As we will see, *adverbs are to verbs/events as adjectives are to nouns/objects.*

## 4.1 SINGULAR, PLURAL, MASS

English and many other languages draw a distinction between count nouns like *coin* and *politician,* which characterize clearly individuated entities, and mass nouns like *water, gold,* and *smoke,* which don't. The term 'count noun' suggests that the first type can be used in counting, as in *two coins* and *three politicians.* The term 'mass noun' indicates that the second type is used to refer to stuff. The distinction matters for the choice of determiners, words like *the, some, a,* and *every* (they are called 'determiners' because they further determine the reference of nouns). Some determiners like *the* and *some* are compatible with count and mass nouns alike, and so we can talk of *the politician, some politician,* but also of *the gold* and *some gold.* Other determiners are more discriminating: We can talk of *a politician* or *every politician* but not of *a gold* or *every gold.* On the other hand, mass nouns can be used without a determiner. One can say *I saw gold* or *I saw smoke in the kitchen,* but you cannot say *I saw politician* (with a determiner, the sentence becomes fine: *I saw a politician*). You can check that the same contrasts hold with *coin,* a count noun (e.g., one can speak of *a coin, every coin*), as opposed to *water,* a mass noun (it is usually odd to speak of *a water* or *every water*).

Many further facts depend on the count/mass distinction. Count nouns can appear in the plural (*a lot of coins*), but mass nouns cannot (one must say *a lot of gold,* not *a lot of golds*). *Many* must be followed by a plural count noun, whereas *much* must be followed by a singular mass noun, hence: *Here there are many coins,* but *Here there is much gold. A few* and *a little* work in the same way. I can say that *I have a few coins,* not that *I have a little coins.* By contrast, I can tell you that *I have a little gold* but not *a few gold.*

One way to think about it is that count nouns, unlike mass nouns, refer to things that have clearly identifiable minimal parts that satisfy the expression. For example: Give me some water. Unless I am a chemist with an atomic force microscope, I'll be hard-pressed to find a minimal part that still counts as water (even a drop of water can be divided into smaller droplets). From a naive perspective, it looks like I can always cut the pieces smaller and still get some water. By contrast, if you give me a coin and I cut it into eight bits, there is no way I can point to one of them and say that it's still a coin, so the coin qualifies as a minimal part. Similarly, a politician's hand or foot can't be called a politician. Mass nouns but not count nouns satisfy what is called the 'Divisibility test': from a naive perspective (which need not be the chemist's), any part of something that qualifies as *water* or *gold* still qualifies as *water* or *gold*. Count nouns fail the Divisibility test because they refer to things that have minimal parts to which the noun can be applied (any one coin or politician qualifies as a minimal part; if you divide them further, you have part of a coin or part of a politician, but it doesn't qualify as a coin or politician anymore).

Even some apparent exceptions end up proving the rule. If I tell you that *China got many golds in the Olympics*, you'll understand that it got many gold *medals*, and certainly medals are easy to individuate; a gold in the sense of a gold medal fails the Divisibility test, as do *coin* and *politician*. Similarly, if I ask you, *Got a smoke?*, I am not just asking for stuff you could blow in my face; more likely, I'm asking for a cigarette. Giving me half a cigarette wouldn't quite satisfy me, as I used a count noun that is indicative of clearly defined minimal parts. And if you order *a water* at a bar, you are likely asking for a *glass* (or a *bottle*) of it, which counts as the minimal part.

Because the count/mass distinction has to do with how we conceptualize the world ('are there clearly identifiable minimal parts'), it is constrained by objective properties of things. But sometimes the same thing can be conceptualized in two ways, depending on whether we think of it as having minimal parts or not. *Having change* is usually close in meaning to *having coins*, but *change* is mass (hence the absence of a determiner), whereas *coin* is count. Sometimes one and the same noun can be treated as count or mass, with subtle semantic nuances. If I have stones (the objects), then I also have stone (the stuff, as shown by the absence of a determiner with the singular). Similarly, if I have a rope (count noun, as shown by the use of *a*), I also have rope (mass noun). The reason English can go either way is that we can think of the individuality of a rope to be what matters (the fact that it has a beginning and an end and can be put to use as a unit), or we can view it as material that could be used for a variety of purposes—for instance, if we sell it in bulk and are just interested in being able to cut some rope for customers.

Sometimes the count version makes greater demands of unity and individuality than the mass version. If given a box of chocolates, I might quickly proceed to eat each chocolate in turn. Besides a possible indigestion, the result might be that I'll have chocolate on my face (mass), rather than *a* chocolate on my face (count): the count version refers in this case to neatly individualized pieces, whereas the mass version can apply to scattered chocolate parts.

Since count nouns refer to things that have minimal parts, we can easily count them, even if the context doesn't tell us what unit to use: The minimal parts are their own unit. So if I have two thin ropes totaling 60 meters but Ann has fifteen thick and short ones totaling 30 meters, she has more ropes than I do because she has fifteen and I have two. But it won't do to say that she has fifteen *rope*: We need the count noun, which refers to the rope conceptualized as having minimal parts (the individual ropes). If we provide an explicit unit, however, we can say that Ann has 30 *meters* of rope. And we can also say that I have more *rope* (rather than *ropes*) than she does because my total is 60 meters and hers is 30, and for *rope* it makes sense to take 'more' to mean 'a greater length of' (it might not matter if Ann's thick ropes are heavier than my thin ones). If I bought more stone than Ann did, total weight rather than total length might make more sense, or possibly total volume. On the other hand, if I bought more stones than Ann did, the number of individual stones rather than their cumulative weight or volume is what matters.

In sum, in English and other languages, nominal reference is structured by the distinction between count and mass terms, which has numerous grammatical repercussions but is grounded in how we conceptualize the world.

Besides its cognitive interest, the count/mass distinction occasionally matters in law. In 2020, a 22-page opinion of the U.S. Supreme Court entirely revolved around the count/mass distinction applied to *notice*, a noun which, like *stone, rope,* and *chocolate*, comes in a count and in a mass version (one can be given *notice to move out*, and one can be given *a notice to move out*). The story goes like this. In the United States, immigrants that would otherwise be deportable may be let off the hook if they have been continually present in the country for at least 10 years. But the law specifies that the clock stops as soon as "the alien is served a notice to appear" at a removal proceeding. After that point, the alien's presence in the country doesn't count toward the 10 years threshold any longer. An immigrant, Agusto Niz-Chavez, received such a notice before reaching this 10-year minimum, but in two separate installments: first with just the charges, then with just the date and location of the hearing. The Supreme Court ruled that this did not count as "a notice" and thus that the clock had not been stopped. Through the use of *a*, the law clearly employed a count noun, the court reasoned: The alien should be given "a notice to appear," not just "notice to appear." And as was the case for my use of "a chocolate" a few paragraphs back, the justices took the count version to come with a requirement of unity and individuality that ruled out scattered parts. In other words, "a notice to appear" should be made of a single document, not two separate ones. Thanks to the semantic peculiarities of the count noun, Niz-Chavez was given a second chance.[2]

## 4.2 MAKING IT VISIBLE: REPETITIONS IN SIGN LANGUAGE

Sign language makes use of the same categories as spoken language (singular/plural, count/mass), but with interesting twists. Once again, we will both confirm the validity of the categories we posited for spoken language and learn something new: in sign language, a plural and a mass noun may simultaneously carry a grammatical function (as in English) and serve as simplified pictures of what they refer to.

Let us go back to ASL. It doesn't quite work like English, because plural marking is optional. Thus one can say *I have seven book*, without the plural marking that would be obligatory in English. Nothing too surprising here: Several spoken languages make optional use of plurals, as is the case of Mandarin and Japanese for some nouns. In ASL, if one elects to use a plural, it can (in some cases) be realized by repeating the noun in different parts of signing space. This too needn't be too surprising, as some spoken languages also use repetition to express plurality. To give but one example, in Warlpiri, an Aboriginal language of Australia, the plural of *child* ('kurdu') is formed by repeating the noun ('kurdu-kurdu').[3] ASL repetition-based plurals often involve more iterations (e.g., three or more). But, in addition, the repetitions can't be realized in any old way. If a signer produces two clearly distinguishable occurrences of the sign *BOOK*, we won't get the meaning of *books*; rather, this will be understood to refer to two books. Similarly, signing *BOOK BOOK BOOK* with clear breaks will refer to three books. To express an indefinite quantity akin to *several books*, we must realize the repetitions without clear breaks between them. By making the individual repetitions hard to count, the signer sends the signal that an indefinite plurality is intended. This is called an 'unpunctuated repetition,' and it often involves at least three iterations. Conversely, *BOOK BOOK BOOK* signed with clear breaks is a 'punctuated repetition,' which refers to as many books as there are iterations—three in this case.[4]

ASL also has a distinction between count and mass nouns. Like English, it has different words for *a little* and *a few*, and they follow the English pattern: ASL *A-FEW* can precede count nouns like *BOOK*, while *A-LITTLE* can precede mass nouns like *WATER*. Some mass nouns (although not all) can also be realized with a repetition, but it's a different kind of repetition from what is seen in simple plurals. *Smoke* in the normal sense certainly refers to things that are conceptualized without minimal parts; in fact, one typically says in English that *There is much smoke in the kitchen*, not *There are many smokes in the kitchen*. The way the repetition is effected with ASL *SMOKE* is rather special: It is a continuous repetition that doesn't make it possible to discern any minimal parts (similar facts hold with ASL *SALT*, also a mass noun). In other words, it looks like the absence of minimal parts in the thing *SMOKE* refers to has consequences for the realization of the sign.

These repetitions come with another striking property. Sometimes, their arrangement forms a simplified picture of the denoted things or stuff. This extends an observation we already made about sign language loci, which can simultaneously be logical variables and iconic representations of what they denote. In the case of plurals, if I have a row of trophies (e.g., sports cups) in my office, I might just say that I have *TROPHY-rep-*____, with three or four unpunctuated iterations of the ASL word for *trophy*, signed on a horizontal line, represented as ____ (I use *-rep* to refer to unpunctuated repetitions). So we start from the dictionary form of *TROPHY*, which looks like this:

**Figure 4.2.1**
*The sign TROPHY in ASL*

To say that there are trophies arranged horizontally, the signer starts signing one *TROPHY* on his left, then he signs another occurrence in the middle and a last one on his right, all in a straight row and with no clear breaks between them, with the result that it is hard to count precisely how many iterations he has signed (this is an unpunctuated repetition [**AV4.2.1**]). This yields the meaning 'some trophies' arranged horizontally, rather than 'three trophies.' The horizontal repetition is illustrated in figure 4.2.2 (where *TROPHY-rep* was signed rather high).

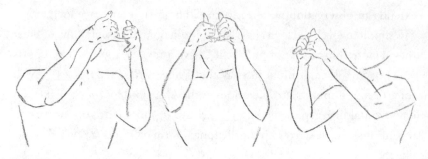

**Figure 4.2.2**

*TROPHY-rep in ASL, repetition on a line*

In case the three horizontal iterations are signed with pauses (hence punctuated repetitions that are easy to count), the meaning will be 'three trophies,'
horizontally arranged ([**AV4.2.2**]).

Now, if the signer wants to convey that some trophies are arranged as
a triangle, he starts on his left (a bit lower in this case), then he signs the
intermediate *TROPHY* high, and finally he signs the rightmost *TROPHY*
low, yielding a triangular representation: /\, (here too, it's important to sign
the three iterations without clear breaks, as an unpunctuated repetition
[**AV4.2.3**]).

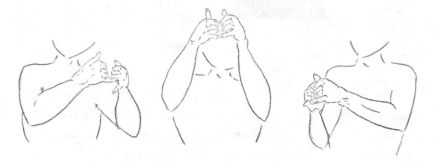

**Figure 4.2.3**

*TROPHY-rep in ASL, repetition as a triangle*

If instead the three triangle-shaped iterations are signed with pauses (hence punctuated repetitions that are easy to count), the meaning becomes 'three trophies,' arranged as a triangle ([**AV4.2.4**]).

Things don't end here. Signers can modulate the repetition to convey further meanings. For instance, if they want to signify that there were a lot of trophies, they can add a word like *many*, but they can also do without it, simply by producing more repetitions—say, five instead of three: The more repetitions, the larger the denoted quantity! As long as these repetitions are signed in an unpunctuated fashion, it won't be understood that there were five specific trophies, just that there were a lot of them.

Mass nouns also lead a dual life as grammatical expressions and as simplified pictures. Take *SMOKE*. In some cases, depending on how the repetition is realized and where it is produced, we may gain information about how much smoke there was and where it was. Thus, if our chemistry lab has two wings and there was smoke following a leak, we'll get very different meanings depending on whether the repeated version of *SMOKE* is signed throughout the area representing the lab or just in one wing. Doing so is optional: ASL also has the ability to use *SMOKE* without all this iconic information.

In sum, plurals and mass nouns in ASL behave like sign language loci in being simultaneously grammatical and iconic.

### 4.3 GRAMMAR MEETS ICONICITY

In our discussion of sign language pronouns in chapter 2 (section 2.7), we saw a more abstract case of plurals that lead a dual life as grammatical objects and as diagrams. As you may recall, standard plural pronouns are realized by pointing toward plural loci, which are circular areas representing groups. But signers may also elect to sign one circular area within another to represent, say, the set of students who came to class relative to the entire set of students. This yields a picture of sorts, but very diagram-like, as shown below. In fact, we were able to use our understanding of diagrams to infer that if the large area *ab* represented the entire group of students and the small area *a* represented the students who came to class, the area *b* had to refer to the students who *didn't* come to class.

MY STUDENT ☞ ⬭-ab MOST ☞ ⬭-a aCAME. ☞ ⬭-b b-STAY HOME

'Most of my students came to class. They [meaning: the students that didn't come to class] stayed home.' (ASL)

It was in the end a reasoning about diagrams that made it possible to say in ASL something like, *Most of my students came to class; they stayed home instead.* This makes no sense in English because *they* cannot mean *the students who didn't come* stayed home. But in the ASL sentence, once one had a large locus *ab* representing the students and a small locus *a* representing the students who came, a third locus *b* visually popped out, and it was easy to point toward it to refer to the students that *didn't* come.

Something analogous happens with repetition-based plurals, but now with genuine pictorial representations rather than diagrams. If I tell you in English, *My office has books; its cover is beautiful,* you won't really understand me, or you'll think that I misspoke and meant *their covers are beautiful.* But in ASL, when you sign the repetition-based plural for *book* as a row, or as a triangle, you create a simplified picture of the books, and you make some of them salient—namely, those that are at an edge: the leftmost and the rightmost ones in the row case, and also the top one in the case of the triangle. As a result, you can point toward an individual book representation and say that *its cover is beautiful*—and people will understand you. Similarly, if I say that I visited your apartment and saw *TROPHY-rep* (an unpunctuated and horizontal repetition of *TROPHY*), I can point toward the leftmost or rightmost iteration and my interlocutor will understand that I am referring to the leftmost or rightmost *thing* in the group. This wouldn't be surprising if we were dealing with genuine pictures. But what gets repeated isn't a pictorial representation: It is the conventional ASL word for *book* or *trophy*. In other words, the arrangement of the repetitions is pictorial, but each iteration is just a normal word.

I should add that in one respect ASL also departs from English, which may not use mass nouns in the plural unless different *types* of the relevant substance are intended (as in *I enjoy many wines*). Thus, in a very dirty street, it won't do to say *There are a few urines here* to mean that there are a few areas of urine, nor will it work to talk of *many urines* or *three urines* in this context. But in ASL, if three distinct areas are signed (each with a continuous repetition but with gaps between the areas), then the sentence makes sense with *A-FEW*, which normally must be followed by count nouns. In this case, by making pictorially clear what the minimal units are (the areas in question), it seems that the mass noun can be treated in the same way as a count noun. Still, I don't want to overemphasize this difference between sign language and spoken language: There are in fact spoken languages such as Yudja (a Tupi language spoken in Brazil) in which mass nouns can be preceded by words like *many* or *three*, provided the context makes salient certain concrete portions of the stuff denoted by the mass noun.[5] Maybe ASL uses iconicity to do precisely this.

## 4.4 THE NOUN/VERB ANALOGY: PLURALS VERSUS PLURACTIONALS

A key insight of contemporary semantics is that verbs are very much like nouns, with the difference that they characterize events rather than objects. So if you say that *it rained*, you assert that there was a raining event in our past. Similarly, *Robin ate* means that there was an eating event in our past, one whose agent was Robin.

The reason it's worth bothering with these convoluted paraphrases is that they bring out a beautiful finding: As we will now see, verbs display some of the same distinctions as nouns do. Events, just like objects, can be conceptualized as being count, mass, or plural. In other words, the nominal categories we discussed up to this point are far more abstract than you might initially have thought; they correspond to a kind of mental grammar that allows us to conceptualize and organize very diverse types of entities.

The depth of the noun/verb analogy can be seen in the fact that some languages mark plurals on verbs to indicate that there were several events of the relevant type. For instance, in Hausa (a language of southern Niger and northern Nigeria), the pluralized version of the verb *to call* can mean something like *to call repeatedly, to keep on calling*.[6] This is a 'pluractional' form because it refers to a plurality of events. It shouldn't be confused with plural marking on English verbs. If I tell you about my friends and say that *they are meeting nearby*, I have to make both the subject (*they*) and the verb plural, hence *are meeting* rather than *is meeting*. But here the verb just agrees with the subject and tells you that there are several individuals involved, not that there were several meetings (in this example, there is a single meeting event). If I tell you that *Robin gave away a lot of money*, English grammar doesn't tell you whether this was in a single event (all the money was given at once) or across several events, with various gifts being made at various times.

Just like Hausa, sign languages can have pluractionals. For instance, LSF and ASL can draw a distinction between singular and plural giving events. Earlier we saw that nominal plurals in sign language can be marked by repeating the noun. As for pluractionals, they are marked by . . . repeating the verb! This needn't be too surprising from the perspective of spoken language: Just like some mark plurals by repeating the noun, some mark pluractionals by repeating the verb—in fact, Hausa is one of them.[7] In LSF, the analogy between nominal plurals and verbal pluractionals is particularly transparent because repetition is used in both cases. While a single giving event can be described by just signing the verb for *give* once, if there were several giving events, one may sign the verb relatively quickly, without clear pauses; this is similar to the unpunctuated repetition we saw at work in nominal plurals.

The analogy runs even deeper. As we saw, some sign language plural nouns lead a dual life, as grammatical constructions comparable to English plurals and as simplified pictures of what they refer to. So, in ASL, the horizontal repetition of *TROPHY* was indicative of a row of trophies, but if the noun was repeated so as to form a triangle, it was understood that this represented a triangular arrangement of the trophies. Something very similar happens with sign language pluractionals. In our LSF example, if the repetitions of *give* are signed at an accelerating pace, one understands that the giving events took place more and more quickly; conversely, if the repetition is realized at a decelerating pace, one understands that the giving events happened more and more slowly. Just like repeated nouns are simultaneously plurals and pictorial representations of the denoted things, repeated verbs are simultaneously pluractionals and simplified animated representations of the denoted events.

## 4.5  COUNT/MASS VERSUS TELIC/ATELIC

When it comes to the singular/plural distinction, verbs are to events as nouns are to objects. But what about the count/mass distinction (*coin* versus *gold*), which structures nominal reference to things? It too turns out to have a counterpart in verbs. Let's recall the semantic property, divisibility, that distinguished mass nouns from count nouns. Give me some water—I can always (within limits) divide it into smaller parts that still count as water. Give me a coin—I can try to cut it into eight bits, but the attempt will immediately fail because none of the eight parts qualifies as a coin anymore. Strikingly, the same distinction is found in verbs. Suppose that, in a race, *Ann ran.* Take any subpart of this event and it will still be an event in which Ann ran. *Run* behaves in this respect like *water.* But now suppose that you say, near the finish line, *Ann arrived!* That means that there was an event that counts as Ann's arrival, maybe one that starts three meters before the line (call this point -3 meters) and ends right after the line. But subparts of this event need not count as an arrival anymore: Ann's running between -2 and -1 meter (counting from the finish line) is a running, but definitely not an arrival, as it doesn't include the finish line.

So *run*, like *water*, passes the Divisibility test, but *arrive*, like *coin*, fails it. In effect, *run* is a mass verb and *arrive* is a count verb. But linguists use a different terminology in this case. They say that verbs like *arrive* are 'telic,' which means that they specify that an intrinsic endpoint was reached ('telos' means 'end' or 'goal' in Ancient Greek). Correspondingly, verbs like *run* are 'atelic' because they don't come with an intrinsic endpoint. It is the existence of this endpoint that explains why telic verbs fail the Divisibility test: to count as an arrival, an event must include the finish line; but many of its subparts won't include it (as was the case for Ann running between two and one meter before the line).[8]

At this point, the distinction is really a logical one, but it turns out to have grammatical consequences, just as it did for nouns (as you'll recall, the count/mass distinction explained, for instance, why one can say a *coin* but not a *gold*). Specifically, the telic/atelic distinction has grammatical consequences for prepositions like *in* and *for* when they are used with a temporal meaning. In the examples we discussed, I can say that as part of the race *Ann ran for one hour*, but not that *she ran in an hour*. Atelic verbs go with *for*, not *in*. The opposite pattern is found with telic verbs: I can say that *Ann arrived at the finish line in five minutes*, not that *she arrived for five minutes*.

The same distinction is at work in verb after verb. It is natural to say that *Sam danced for three minutes*, although it would be odd to say that *Sam danced in three minutes*. The reason is that *dance* passes the Divisibility test: Any subpart of a dancing event still qualifies as a dancing event. By contrast, *Sam won the competition in three minutes* is a bit more natural than *Sam won the competition for three minutes*. The reason is that *win (the competition)* fails the Divisibility test: while winning is a process, what happened before victory doesn't count as a winning.

Th telic/atelic distinction also applies to very abstract verbs. During an exam, I could tell you that *Ann reflected for five minutes*, not that *she reflected in five minutes*. On the other hand, I can say that *she understood in five minutes*, not *for five minutes*. Why such a distinction? Let's apply the Divisibility test again. Take the event of Ann's reflecting: Reflection doesn't come with a natural endpoint, so any subpart of it still counts as an event in which Ann reflected. For this reason, *reflect* is atelic and thus behaves in the same way as *run* in our earlier example. This, in turn, explains why *reflect* goes with *for*, not *in*. Things are different with *understand*. The concept of understanding comes with a natural endpoint, that at which there was finally light (think of it as the 'finish line' of the understanding). And thus if there is an event that counts as Ann understanding something, subparts of it need not count as events of understanding (the beginning of the understanding process doesn't qualify, for instance). This explains why *understand* behaves like *arrive* in taking *in*, not *for*.

Since the evidence for the telic/atelic distinction is a bit indirect, it would be nice to find a more concrete trace of it. Once again, sign language can help. As we saw, the meaning of telic verbs specifies a natural endpoint, and this explains why they fail the Divisibility test. But in sign language, the endpoint is often made visible in the realization of the verb by way of sharp boundaries, a discovery made by the linguist Ronnie Wilbur.[9] For instance, *ARRIVE* involves one hand hitting the other—hence a sharp deceleration when the hitting occurs. Similarly, *WIN*, another telic verb, is signed with the fist of one hand closing as if taking something from the other hand, hence again a sharp deceleration and a clear boundary, as seen in figure 4.5.1.

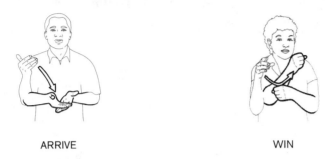

ARRIVE                                                      WIN

**Figure 4.5.1**
*Two telic verbs in ASL ([**AV4.5.1**]; [**AV4.5.2**])*

By contrast, ASL *RUN* (one of our atelic examples above) is realized as a repeated forward motion of one hand pulling the other, without a sharp boundary see figure 4.5.2). And *DANCE* (another atelic example) is realized by a repeated motion of an inverted V realized with two fingers (representing the legs, like this /\) above the palm of the other hand (representing the floor). Because of the repetition, there are no sharp boundaries here, either.

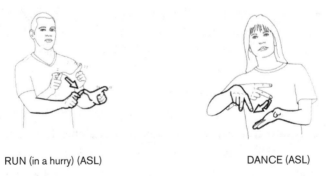

RUN (in a hurry) (ASL)                          DANCE (ASL)

**Figure 4.5.2**
*Two atelic verbs in ASL ([**AV4.5.3**]; [**AV4.5.4**])*

The same facts hold in other sign languages, and they even apply to abstract verbs. Take *understand*, one of our telic examples. In LSF, it is realized with three fingers forming a tripod that ends up closing on the forehead; the closure is realized quickly and thus displays a sharp boundary, see figure 4.5.3). By contrast, *reflect*, which is atelic, is realized by the repeated movement of the curved index finger toward the temple, so there is no sharp boundary here.

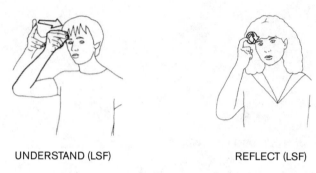

UNDERSTAND (LSF)                    REFLECT (LSF)

**Figure 4.5.3**
*A telic verb and an atelic verb in LSF ([**AV4.5.5**]; [**AV4.5.6**])*

Finally, as in our earlier cases, sign language doesn't just make visible some grammatical categories of language in general. It can also modulate them in rich iconic ways. So, for instance, the LSF verb for *reflect* can be modulated so that the movement starts slow and then becomes quick, and the meaning will be that the person reflected slowly at the beginning and then more quickly. And if the LSF verb for *understand* is realized slowly and then fast, the meaning will be that there was a difficult beginning and then an easier conclusion.[10]

You might conceivably have thought that there was something natural about the fact that ASL *ARRIVE* and *WIN* and LSF *UNDERSTAND* were signed with sharp boundaries. If so, you are not alone. This pattern is so intuitive that psychologists have shown that non-signers can 'guess' it, at least to some extent. Of course, non-signers can't be expected to guess the precise meaning of signs they have never seen before (this would only be possible if iconicity played an extremely strong role, which isn't generally case). But when given a choice between a telic and an atelic meaning, subjects often categorize the verb correctly. As an example, naive non-signers are shown the sign for *ARRIVE*, which is in fact telic, and then they are asked to guess: Does it mean *understand*, or does it mean *reflect*? They tend to go with the *understand* meaning, which is telic, rather than with the *reflect* meaning, which is atelic. In other words, among two equally incorrect meanings, they tend to choose the telic one for a telic sign. If instead they were shown the sign for *DANCE*, which is atelic, they would preferably go for the atelic meaning—namely, *reflect*.[11]

You may wonder why psychologists found it necessary to give their subjects a choice between two incorrect meanings. Suppose we had shown them the sign *ARRIVE*, and they had correctly picked the meaning *arrive*. There could have been two reasons for this choice: There might have been a subtle kind of iconicity in the sign, which was enough to guide the subjects' choice, or telicity might have been at the heart of the subjects' behavior. By giving them a choice between two equally incorrect meanings, we eliminate the first possibility: Subjects had to be guided by telicity, not iconicity (if iconicity nonetheless plays a role, it is of a far more abstract kind, one that represents the endpoint of telic actions by way of sharp boundaries).[12]

Remarkably, then, non-signers know *something* about sign language— namely, that sharp boundaries of signs tend to represent the endpoints of telic verbs. We will see in chapter 13 that this is not an isolated case: there are several further properties of sign language that non-signers know without realizing that they know them.

## 4.6 ADJECTIVES AND ADVERBS

Having seen that verbs are to events as nouns are to objects, can we say something about the meaning of adjectives and adverbs? These are expressions like *beautiful*, as in *This is a beautiful song*, or *beautifully* as in *Robin sang beautifully* (some complex expressions like *in a beautiful way* work like adverbs, and for this reason they are often called *adverbials*). Their form (*beautiful* versus *beautifully*) is already indicative of a connection between adjectives and adverbs. But the point can be made more forcefully: Adverbs modify (i.e., enrich) verbs in the same way that adjectives modify nouns. In fact, the noun/verb analogy was discovered when philosophers tried to understand the meaning of adverbs. They were led to conclude that an adverb provides additional information about the events denoted by a verb, in the same way that an adjective provides additional information about the objects denoted by a noun. The connection is so strong that some words, such as *early*, can equally be used as adverbs, as in *Robin arrived early*, and as adjectives, as in *Robin's early arrival was unexpected*.

So, adverbs can be thought of as adjectives that modify verbs. But what is the meaning of adjectives? In simple cases, it's fairly transparent. If I tell you that *Leonard Cohen is a Canadian singer*, all I mean is that he is Canadian and that he is a singer: *Canadian* just further specifies the kind of person that Cohen is. Similarly, if I tell you that *Leonard Cohen is a world-famous Canadian singer*, *famous* just adds one further specification—namely, that Cohen is a world-famous singer.

But sometimes one must be a bit more cautious in stating these paraphrases. *Someone is a world-famous Canadian singer* doesn't just mean that *someone is a world-famous singer, and someone is a Canadian* singer. The latter conjunction isn't very informative. Certainly, there are world-famous singers, and certainly there are Canadian singers. Nothing new there. By contrast, *someone is a world-famous Canadian singer* is true thanks to just a few individuals (such as Leonard Cohen, Céline Dion, and Justin Bieber). The reason the conjunction is so much less informative is that its two components can be made true by different individuals: There is no requirement that one and the same person should be a world-famous singer and a Canadian singer. By contrast, *someone is a world-famous Canadian singer* is true only if the following holds (where the underlined part is the contribution of *someone*):

<u>For some person x</u>, x is world-famous, and x is Canadian, and x is a singer.

The key, then, is that it must be one and the same individual x that has all these properties together. Unlike *Leonard Cohen*, which names a specific individual, *someone* is a quantifier: It counts (or 'quantifies') the number of objects that satisfy a certain property without regard to their identity. In the statement *someone is a Canadian singer*, it tells you that the set of Canadian singers is not null (i.e., that it contains at least one individual, but it needn't single out a specific person). That's the reason *someone is a Canadian singer* and *someone is a world-famous singer* can be made true by different individuals.

Somewhat surprisingly, even without any word like *someone*, the same pattern of inference is found with adverbs and more generally adverbials.[13] Suppose I am talking about a certain concert and say, *Leonard Cohen sang beautifully in French*. It certainly implies that *Leonard Cohen sang in French* and also that *Leonard Cohen sang beautifully*. But the latter two statements together don't entail the first one. To see this, suppose that during the relevant concert, Leonard Cohen sang beautifully in English, and he also sang in French, but not so beautifully (maybe he just didn't feel comfortable in French, which wasn't his native language). In that case, *he sang in French*, and *he sang beautifully*, but it definitely doesn't follow that *Leonard Cohen sang beautifully in French*. The noun/verb analogy suggests a reason: maybe we should analyze *Leonard Cohen sang* with an event equivalent of *someone*, and with a meaning akin to *At some past point, Leonard Cohen sang*, or to put it more explicitly:

> For some past event e, Leonard Cohen sang in e.

Here you can think of the underlined part as being the specific contribution of the past tense of *sing*, just like *for some person x* was the contribution of *someone* in our earlier example. It then makes sense to analyze *Leonard Cohen sang beautifully in French* as:

> For some past event e, Leonard Cohen sang in e, and e was in French, and e was beautiful.

This is certainly much more informative than the conjunction of *Leonard Cohen sang beautifully* and *Leonard Cohen sang in French*: This conjunction leaves open the possibility that Cohen sang beautifully and sang in French *on different occasions*. The analysis based on events explains why. To put it in somewhat pedantic terms, *Leonard Cohen sang beautifully* means that

> For some past event e, Leonard Cohen sang in e, and e was beautiful.

And similarly, *Leonard Cohen sang in French* means that

> For some past event e', Leonard Cohen sang in e', and e' was in French.

There is no guarantee that e and e′ are the same or, in other words, that one and the same event satisfies both properties. This is the reason the conjunction of these two claims doesn't give us the same meaning as *Leonard Cohen sang beautifully in French*.

This is, of course, precisely the pattern we saw at work in *someone is a world-famous Canadian singer*, which could not be equated with *someone is a world-famous singer and someone is a Canadian singer*. The only difference is that the event equivalent of *someone* is understood but not made explicit. For the rest, the logic is the same: adverbs are to events (and verbs) as adjectives are to objects (and nouns).

## 4.7 CONCLUSION

How does language organize reality? We now have a first shot at an answer. The most basic distinction is between objects and events. In simple cases, nouns characterize objects just like verbs characterize events. In each domain, we find the same abstract categories: Nouns can be count or mass, singular or plural. Verbs display related categories: Telic verbs resemble count nouns, atelic verbs resemble mass nouns, and there are even pluractional verbs, which refer to pluralities of events.

As was the case for pronouns, sign language makes use of the same categories as spoken language, but sometimes in a more transparent fashion. With nouns, sign language optionally realizes plurals by way of unpunctuated repetitions, and some mass nouns involve continuous repetitions. It also makes visible the endpoint of telic verbs by way of sharp boundaries in the sign, whereas atelic verbs lack these sharp boundaries—a property that can to some extent be guessed by non-signers. In addition, sign language sometimes goes beyond the resources of spoken language in adding an iconic component to these constructions so that the way the repetitions are realized provides information about the spatial or temporal arrangement of the denoted objects or events. Lastly, the noun/verb analogy immediately explains the striking similarity between adjectives and adverbs, which had motivated the object versus event comparison in the first place.

# 5 BEYOND THE HERE AND NOW I: FROM OBJECTS TO SITUATIONS

Animal calls almost always pertain to the here and now, with meanings akin to *there is a snake, there is a serious aerial alarm,* and so on. But part of what it means to be human is to be able to conceive of situations beyond the here and now, and to communicate such thoughts to others, as in: *I was alarmed; I will be alarmed; if I were alarmed, I would call you.* And we don't just talk about situations that did or will happen. We also talk about situations that are merely possible and even ones that we know to be entirely far-fetched. *It ain't necessarily so*—in George Gershwin's *Porgy and Bess*, this phrase was a way for one of the characters to cast doubt on the Bible's teachings, and it meant that not all possible situations that are compatible with what we know accord with the Bible: The Bible might be wrong. More assertively, NASA once stated that *if earth were the size of a nickel, the moon would be about as big as a coffee bean*: certainly, a true statement, but one that pertains to a situation we know to be . . . unreal.

How does language go beyond the here and now? Remarkably, it employs the same tools to refer to situations as it does to refer to objects, but under a different guise. Pronouns refer to salient objects, person indicates how they relate to the context, (e.g., *I* versus *he/she/it*), and descriptions (e.g., *the greatest philosopher*) pick out objects that satisfy certain conditions. All three categories (pronouns, person, descriptions) have rather precise counterparts that talk about situations.

## 5.1 SITUATIONS

In chapter 4, we saw that, in simple cases, verbs are to events as nouns are to objects. We will shortly discover that the object/event analogy runs even deeper, but we will also want to take a somewhat more abstract perspective. Robin's being American is not really an event but rather a state. And we will want to talk, more broadly, about all sorts of real or possible situations, be they present, future, or past. So, we will now replace the talk of *events* with a broader talk of *situations*.

This small step will already allow us to approach the meaning of temporal expressions, which talk about future or past situations, and modal expressions, which also talk about merely possible ones.[1] *Leonard will sing* can be taken to mean that for some future situation s, Leonard sings in s. *Leonard will be famous* means that for some future situation s, Leonard is famous in s. Here we are making use of a device, the word *some*, which we already discussed in connection with nouns and adjectives (and, less transparently, in connection with adverbs in chapter 4). In the statement *someone is a Canadian singer*, the quantifier *someone* tells you that for some (i.e., at least one) person x, x is a Canadian singer. Now, what does it mean that *Leonard will be famous*? It means that *at some future point, he will be famous*. The similarity between *some future point* and *someone* gives us a hint as to the correct analysis. When we wish to paraphrase the meaning of *will*, we replace *someone* with *some future situation*—hence, for some future situation s, Leonard is famous is s.

When we use verbs in the past tense, there is no separate word in English to express tense; rather, we use the ending *-ed* in regular verbs (*Leonard played beautifully*) or a modification of the verb in irregular ones, as in *Leonard sang*. But it's easy to make the past tense appear as a separate word. We just need to be emphatic, as in *Leonard did sing*, or to ask a question: *Did Leonard sing?* (Negation can do the trick, too: *Leonard didn't sing*.) We can then treat *did* (or *-ed*) by analogy with *will* in the previous paragraph. *Leonard sang* means that for some past situation s, Leonard Cohen sings in s, and similarly *Leonard was famous* means that for some past situation s, Leonard Cohen is famous in s.

Besides past and future situations, we can also talk about imagined ones, which may be conceivable or 'possible' (in the sense of being coherent) without being actual. *If Donald Trump were president right now, he would be at war with Iran*: This is a sentence about the present moment, but clearly not about the situation we are in; rather, it is about a merely conceivable one. Many other expressions allow us to talk about merely possible situations. If we are in a basement and start hearing some noise outside, I might tell you, *It might be raining*. Here too, everything is about the present moment, and I am still talking about situations, just conceivable ones (statements about conceivable or 'possible' situations are called *modal statements*, and correspondingly auxiliary verbs such as *might* and *must* are called *modal auxiliaries*).

Still, *it might be raining* has a more precise meaning than this. A fairly accurate paraphrase is that for some situation s compatible with my beliefs, it is raining in s. What does it mean that a situation s is compatible with my beliefs? Well, from my basement, even with my less-than-perfect knowledge, I can exclude some situations—that a warhead has hit my house, for instance, or that there was a huge earthquake, or that my basement has been submerged by seawater. On the other hand, there are other situations that are compatible with what I know—in some situations it is raining, or water is dripping in the kitchen. I am certainly not in a position to specify everything that's going on in the world, and yet there are a variety of situations that are compatible with my beliefs. What the sentence means is that in <u>some</u> of these situations, it is raining outside.

A couple of paragraphs back, I argued that the future tense *will* and the past tense *did* have in essence the same logic as *someone*: They are quantifiers, but instead of talking about people, they talk about future and past situations. Now the same conclusion extends to *might*. Our paraphrase of *it might be raining* was that for <u>some</u> situation s compatible with my beliefs, it is raining in s. This makes *might* yet another incarnation of *some*, one that talks about possible rather than real (future or past) situations. In other words, even though the auxiliary verb *might* has a completely different form and syntax from the quantifier *some*, it has a very similar meaning, just pertaining to situations, not objects. *Possibly* works very much like *might*. *It's possibly raining* says something rather weak, just like *it might be raining*, and so this too can be paraphrased as: *in some situation compatible with my beliefs, it is raining.*

So far I have tried to keep the discussion relatively simple by focusing on *some*, which takes different forms when we talk about individuals (*someone, some student, something*), about future or past situations (*will, did*), or about conceivable situations (*might*). But there are further quantifiers besides *some*. *Everyone sings* is more informative (i.e., logically stronger) than *someone sings* because the first sentence requires that for <u>each</u> person x, x sings, whereas the second just requires that for <u>at least one</u> person x, x sings. (The meaning of *some* may seem stronger than this, for reasons we'll explore in chapter 10. *Someone sings* sometimes suggests that not everyone does; still, it's no contradiction to say that *someone and in fact everyone sings*, which shows that the *at least one* meaning is available and, as we will later argue, primitive—it is the meaning we have in our mental dictionary.) Now *must* is to *might* as *everyone* is to *someone*. Still in my basement, I say, *It must be raining.* The claim is stronger than *it might be raining.* Instead of asserting that *in some situation compatible with my beliefs, it is raining*, my claim is that *in <u>every</u> situation compatible with my beliefs, it is raining* (here too, it is no contradiction to say that *it might and in fact it must be raining*; the former is definitely compatible with the latter.)[2]

*Necessarily* works very much like *must*. Referring back to Gershwin's song, *the Bible is necessarily true* means something like *the Bible must be true*, or in other words: *In all situations compatible with our beliefs, the Bible is true.* And so when Gershwin's character sang, *The things that you are liable to read in the Bible—it ain't necessarily so*, this meant that *not all situations compatible with our beliefs accord with the Bible:* The Bible might be wrong.

In sum, we have discovered an abstract logical structure that is uniform across apparently very different constructions such as *someone*, the future tense, the past tense, and *might*. And the analogy extends even further, since *must* and *necessarily* have the same logic as *every*. (Can we find analogues of *every* pertaining to past or future situations? Here the parallelism is, regretfully, a bit less neat. We need to say something like *it will <u>always</u> rain*, where the contribution of *always* is to claim that *every* future situation is one in which it is raining.)

## 5.2 TENSES AS PRONOUNS

As we just saw, quantifiers are a key device to talk about past or future situations, real or merely conceivable ones. Despite the difference in form, *will*, *did*, and *might* have the same kind of meaning as *some* (corresponding in essence to *some future situation, some past situation, some possible situation*), while *must* behaves like *every* (*every possible situation*). But this is only the tip of the iceberg. Several other nominal expressions have counterparts that make it possible to talk about situations. Since we saw that pronouns are essential to the expressive power of human language, I will start with pronoun-like expressions that refer to situations, not objects.

The existence of pronominal expressions that refer to situations was an important discovery of contemporary linguistics. In fact, the traditional view in logic and philosophy was that they should not exist. The idea, prima facie a reasonable one, was that language has far greater expressive resources to talk about objects than about situations. Granted, pronouns referring to *things* are ubiquitous, but it was thought that these don't have counterparts that talk about *situations*. And indeed, it's initially hard to see how equivalents of *it, he, she* could be found in the verbal domain. In fact, my discussion so far was compatible with the traditional philosophical view: I only discussed uses of *will, did, might*, and *must* that were akin to quantifiers (*some, every*), not to pronouns.

But appearances can be deceptive. After all, who could have initially guessed that *might* would display the behavior of *some* and *must* that of *every*? It took a theoretical leap to come to this conclusion. A similar leap will prove insightful when it comes to pronouns. As it turns out, tense and mood can play a role that is very similar to that of pronouns. Traditional logicians and philosophers were wrong, and language provides the same kinds of resources to talk about objects and situations—and these are very rich resources indeed.

To reach this conclusion, however, a bit of patience will be needed. We'll first have to take a closer look at the behavior of pronouns and then argue that each of their uses has a counterpart with tense (later, we'll extend this finding to mood).

Let's jump right in. Pronouns have four kinds of uses, depending on how they find their denotation. First, the context alone may suffice to provide this denotation. If someone sitting on a bench says, crying, *She left me*, we won't have difficulties understanding that *she* refers to the person's (former) partner. Second, a pronoun can play the same role as a repetition of its antecedent. *The president came and he fired me* means very much the same thing as *the president came and the president fired me*. Third, a pronoun may play the role of the variable *x* in *for every x, x + 1 is greater than x*. This happens when pronouns depend on quantifiers, as is the case in *every man knows that he is mortal*. This means, in essence, *for every man x, x knows that x is mortal* (and here a very different meaning would be obtained if we replaced the pronoun with its antecedent: *every man knows that every man is mortal* attributes to every man a knowledge about all men, not just about himself). Finally, in some cases a pronoun really has the meaning of a description. Suppose I say, <u>*Some*</u> *American woman will go to Mars. She will be famous.* That second sentence really means that <u>*the American woman who goes to Mars*</u> will be famous.

Remarkably, all four uses exist with tense.[3] To see a counterpart of the first use (denotation provided by the context), suppose an elderly author is asked to select a picture of himself for the back cover of his next book. Looking at one of the pictures, he says: *I was young*. This is easily understood to refer to the situation in which the picture was taken, and thus it means something like, *I was young* <u>*at the time made salient by the picture*</u>. Strikingly, the sentence is understood even in the absence of any linguistic antecedent, just like *she left me* could be understood without an explicit antecedent for *she*. In effect, the past tense of *was* behaves like *she* in being able to refer to something (a situation rather than an object) which is made salient by the context—in our case, by the picture (the elderly author could also have decided to say *I was young then*, and in fact *then* also plays the role of an additional, emphatic situation pronoun).

The import of the pronominal use is even more striking in negative sentences. Suppose now that the elderly author says, still talking about the picture: *I wasn't young*. This means rather transparently: *I wasn't young* <u>*at the time made salient by the picture*</u>. But if the past tense could only mean *there is some past time at which blah*, taking the negation into account, we would get an obvious falsehood: *There is no past time at which I was young* (and it won't really help to put the negation elsewhere; for instance, to say *There is some past time at which I wasn't young* is rather uninformative given that the speaker is elderly!). So there seem to be clear cases in which a tense, just like a pronoun, can get its denotation from the context.

Pronouns that behave like a repetition of their antecedent (the second use described above) also have counterparts that talk about situations. *I will leave next Monday. I will go to China.* This statement means pretty much the same thing as: *I will leave next Monday. I will go to China next Monday.* This is a case in which our original analysis of *will* as meaning *some future situation* is insufficient. It wouldn't do to paraphrase the second clause as *at some future point I will go to China.* The future point is next Monday, and this is correctly captured by taking the second *will* to have a meaning that repeats the meaning of the antecedent *next Monday.*

In other cases, tense can behave like a variable, just likes pronouns can (this was the third use I described above). *Whenever I go to Paris, I buy cheese* means in essence that *for every situation s in which I go to Paris, I buy cheese in s.* There is no particular time or situation that *buy* makes reference to in this case. Finally, there are cases in which tense plays the role of a description (this was the fourth use of pronouns). *Someday, I will visit China. I will eat Peking duck.* Here the second sentence doesn't mean that *Someday, I will eat Peking duck.* The initial discourse makes it clear that I will eat Peking duck while in China, whereas my attempted (and incorrect) paraphrase implies no such thing. Rather, the intended meaning of the original discourse is very much the same as: *Some day, I will visit China. When I visit China, I will eat Peking duck,* or in other words: *The future situation in which I visit China is one in which I will eat Peking duck.* The underlined expression is a description, and the conclusion is that just like pronouns, tenses can display the behavior of descriptions.

Alright, this was a lot of linguistic details, but let's step back to contemplate what we have discovered: All uses of pronouns have counterparts with tense. This motivates our conclusion that *tenses behave like pronouns that refer to situations.* Mission accomplished.

But wait—there is still a glitch. Didn't I set out to show a few pages back that *will* and *did* behave like *some*, not like pronouns? Truth be told, this was a bit of a simplification. *Will* and *did* can either behave like *some*, or like pronouns. But there is way to unify these two behaviors if we start from the pronominal use. As we saw, *Leonard will be famous* need not be about any specific moment and has a reading akin to: *For some future situation s, Leonard will be famous in s.* We can capture this reading by positing that there is an invisible expression akin to *for some situation* (a quantifier), which allows the tense to behave like a variable. So, our sentence can really be analyzed like this, where the underlined expression is just a logical variable—one of the standard uses of pronouns:

For some future situation s, Leonard is famous <u>in s</u>.

In fact, we already made an assumption of this kind when we discussed the (more narrow) category of events: We had analyzed *Leonard Cohen sang* as meaning something like, *For some past event e, Leonard Cohen sang in e.* Since situations are a more general category than events, it's rather natural that we should use this device (with an invisible *some*) more broadly.

### 5.3 MOODS AS PRONOUNS

Let's take one further step. So far our discussion has been restricted to actual situations, but imagined situations can also be denoted by pronouns of sorts. Grammarians don't call them tenses but moods. A pure case is the auxiliary *were* in some varieties of English, as in, *If I were rich, I would pay taxes.* In the first person, the verb *be* takes the form *am* in the present and *was* in the past tense. These are both in the indicative mood, which is used to refer to real situations as well as possible situations that are still open possibilities. When talking about situations that go against the facts and are thus merely imagined ('counterfactual situations'), we can use the subjunctive form, hence *were*. The difficulty in English is that in most cases, the subjunctive is conflated with the past tense, as in: *If I left tomorrow, I would fly to Berlin* (note that you can express very much the same meaning by saying, *If I were to leave tomorrow, I would fly to Berlin*). Here, the 'past' tense *left* doesn't have a past meaning at all, but it is used to indicate that it's impossible (or at least very unlikely) that I'll leave tomorrow. And many speakers can say just as well, *If I was rich, I would pay taxes.* A few lines back, I picked the version with *were* because it is one of the few cases in which the subjunctive isn't pronounced like the past tense. (In the main clause, *would* as in *would fly* and *would pay* is also a mood, called the conditional. It too turns out to indicate that the situations referred to are impossible or unlikely—otherwise one must use the indicative, as in, *If I get rich, I will pay taxes*. But for simplicity I'll set this fact aside in our discussion, focusing just on the *if*-clause, not on the main clause.)

In a way, it needn't come as a surprise that tenses and moods are so similar: They both serve to locate situations relative to the context, as being present, past, or future, and real, possible, or impossible (we will revisit this point in chapter 6). But for the moment, I wish to make a simpler point: Just like tenses, moods can behave like situation-denoting pronouns. And the argument is once again that moods can have the same uses as pronouns: They can refer to salient situations; they can function as a repetition of their antecedent, or as a variable, or as a description.[4] So let's consider these uses one at a time.

First step: moods that can refer to salient situations. Suppose I am looking at a high-end stereo in an electronics store and say, *My neighbors would kill me*. The sentence doesn't make reference to a real situation, since I am strongly suggesting an intention *not* to buy this stereo. So what situations does *would kill me* refer to? Those that were made salient by the extra-linguistic context: minimally different situations from the actual one, but in which I own the stereo and play it at home at a "satisfying" volume, thus prompting the neighbors to . . . well, retaliate. What is asserted is that *in those situations* my neighbors would kill me. This is thus a counterpart of the pronominal use we saw at work in the statement *she left me*: in the absence of any linguistic antecedent, the context was enough to make clear what the pronoun referred to.

Second step: moods that function as a repetition of their antecedent. These are common and very useful, as they save us the trouble of repeating an *if*-clause over long discourses. Take the following discourse: *If I were Rothschild, I would be rich. And I would pay lots of taxes.* It is clear that the second sentence makes reference to some counterfactual situations, but things are more precise: It means that *if I were Rothschild, I would pay lots of taxes*. Here the *if*-clause is in effect the antecedent of *would pay*, just like *the president* is the antecedent of *he* in the statement: *The president came, and he fired me.* In both cases, the pronominal expression (*he* or *would*, as the case may be) save us the trouble of repeating its antecedent (namely, the description *the president* or the *if*-clause *if I were Rothschild*).

A famous tune from the 1964 musical *Fiddler on the Roof* makes extensive use of this device to avoid repeating an *if*-clause. The main character, Tevye, a poor Jewish milkman, pauses to imagine what it would be like to be rich—and given his circumstances, this is clearly a counterfactual, hence *if I were a rich man*, in the subjunctive. The pronominal nature of mood comes in handy as well. In the lyrics below, each of the four underlined expressions refers back to the counterfactual situations introduced by the *if*-clause—*If I were a rich man*—and this stretches over 11 lines! Repeating the *if*-clause each time would have made the song impossibly convoluted, of course.[5]

**If I were a rich man**

( . . . )

I'd build a big tall house with rooms by the dozen
Right in the middle of the town
A fine tin roof with real wooden floors below
There would be one long staircase just going up
And one even longer coming down
And one more leading nowhere, just for show

I'd fill my yard with chicks and turkeys and geese and ducks
For the town to see and hear
And each loud "cheep" and "swaqwk" and "honk" and "quack"
Would land like a trumpet on the ear
As if to say "Here lives a wealthy man."

[AV5.3.1]

Coming back to our main point, let's take the third step: There are also cases in which mood plays the role of a variable that refers to possible situations. We saw above that if I say from my basement *It might be raining*, the meaning obtained is akin to, *In some situation compatible with my beliefs, it is raining*. Here *might* does the heavy lifting, and there is no further mood to speak of on the verb. But I can also express the same thing a bit differently; for instance, *It's possible that it's raining*, or just, *Maybe it's raining*. Now we have a normal (indicative) mood on *is*, and the meaning is still that *in some situation s compatible with my beliefs, it is raining in s*. The mood seems to be realizing this variable *s*, which doesn't refer to any situation in particular. This is rather similar to the use of *he* in *some man believes he made a mistake*, which means in essence, *for some man x, x believes that x made a mistake*, where *he* corresponds to the variable *x*.

Fourth and final step: There are cases in which mood plays the role of a description of sorts. *I might get rich. I would pay lots of taxes*. Here the second sentence needn't be about a real situation. Rather, it means something like, *In the (salient) situation in which I get rich, I will pay lots of taxes*. This pattern makes sense. We saw above that *I might get rich* can be analyzed as, *In some situation compatible with what I believe, I will get rich*. So the meaning of the sentence really involves an abstract version of *some*. But we also saw earlier that pronouns that depend on *some* can play the role of a description. For example: *Some American woman will go to Mars. She will be famous*. Here, *she* means, in essence, *the American woman who goes to Mars*. We find the very same pattern in our wealth-related example: The mood of the second sentence (*would pay*) serves to describe *the (salient) situation in which I get rich*.

Stepping back, we have reached a momentous conclusion: Tense and mood can be used as pronouns, with the difference that they refer to situations rather than to individuals. They allow us to talk about specific past or future situations, real or unreal ones. Each use of standard pronouns has a counterpart with tense and mood. The upshot is that despite initial appearances, language offers the same types of expressive means to talk about objects and situations. A striking consequence is that we have extraordinarily rich resources to talk about times and possibilities—contrary to the view that used to be dominant in philosophical and logical circles.

## 5.4  TEMPORAL PRONOUNS IN SIGN LANGUAGE

You might object that this argument is . . . well, a bit involved and abstract. After all, tense and mood look nothing like pronouns, and it took a rather indirect argument to show that they have pronominal uses. Couldn't I make my point more quickly by finding a language in which one and the same pronoun can be used to refer to objects and to situations?

ASL is such a language. The pointing sign can be used not just to refer to objects but also to locations and to situations, be they real or merely possible.[6] Like some spoken languages, such as Mandarin, ASL almost doesn't have tense or mood morphology (such as the auxiliaries *will/would* or the suffix *-ed* in English). But sometimes it can use the pointing sign to refer to situations just like English tense and mood do. In English, if I tell you, *Tomorrow it will rain and the day after tomorrow it will snow. Then I'll be happy*, it's hard to know what *then* and the future tense of *I'll be happy* refer to. Are they referencing tomorrow or the day after tomorrow? In some cases, these ambiguities may be avoided in ASL by adopting a different strategy: Associate a locus *a* with *tomorrow it will rain* and a locus *b* with *the day after tomorrow it will snow*. And instead of the word *then*, use a pointing sign toward locus *a* or toward locus *b*. If I point toward *a*, the meaning will be that *tomorrow* I'll be happy. Similarly, if I point toward *b*, the meaning will be that *the day after tomorrow* I'll be happy. Thus we have a striking result: The same pointing sign that can otherwise refer to objects can also refer to situations. (Pointing to situations in this way is by no means a common strategy. It is merely an option, which is particularly enlightening for the present discussion.)

In this case, the pronoun could be replaced with *tomorrow* (if the pointing was towards locus *a*) or *the day after tomorrow* (if it was toward *b*) without a change in meaning. This is the simplest use of pronouns I described above: The pronoun plays the same role as a repetition of its antecedent. In other cases, the pronoun plays the role of a description of situations. Discussing annual flu outbreaks, I say in English: *Sometimes I get infected, but sometimes I stay healthy*. Then I continue with: *Then I get to relax*. In such cases, it is not entirely explicit whether *then* refers to the situations in which I get infected (maybe I get to relax because of a sick leave?) or those in which I stay healthy (because I am freed of flu-related worries). The grammar of ASL allows for greater explicitness. One can associate locus *a* with *sometimes I get infected*, locus *b* with *sometimes I stay healthy*, and use a pointing sign toward *a* or *b*, depending on whether one wants to say that *in the situations in which I get infected*, *I get to relax*, or in *the situations in which I stay healthy*, *I get to relax*. In this case, the pronoun can be paraphrased by a description, and it certainly isn't equivalent to a repetition of its antecedent (we'd get a very different meaning if the end of the sentence were *sometimes I get to relax*). This is easily explained if the pointing sign can be used as a situation-denoting pronoun. *Sometimes I get infected* means very much the same thing as *for some situation x, I get infected in x*. And as we previously saw, pronouns that depend on *some* can play the same role as descriptions (e.g., *Some American woman will go to Mars. She [= the American woman who goes to Mars] will be famous*).

In sum, ASL strengthens our case for the existence of temporal pronouns, as the pointing sign can refer to moments in addition to individuals. This temporal use of pointing isn't restricted to ASL. Other sign languages behave in related ways. For instance, Chinese Sign Language (CSL) can do very much the same thing as ASL in the examples we discussed, using normal signing space (in front of the signer) to establish loci that refer to moments. But CSL also adds an interesting twist to the story. It can make use of a dedicated timeline to realize some signs (e.g., forward for the future, backward for the past). For instance, signing *in four years* involves a forward movement, whereas *four years ago* involves a backward movement. ASL and LSF can do something similar too, but CSL is special in sometimes establishing loci on this timeline. So a signer may establish a locus backward to refer to a past event, and then she has to rotate her body somewhat in order to point toward it![7]

Strikingly, then, in ASL and CSL, the pointing sign can behave not just like a pronoun that refers to individuals but also like one that refers to past, present, or future situations (including on a dedicated timeline in CSL). This provides a visible argument for our conclusion that human language has an abstract pronominal system that makes it possible to refer to objects and to situations in a rather uniform fashion.


### 5.5  MODAL PRONOUNS IN SIGN LANGUAGE

So far, I have only discussed cases in which sign language makes reference to real situations. In ASL, similar sentences can be constructed to refer to possible situations as well. Suppose I say in English: *If it rains tomorrow, it will be warm, and if it snows tomorrow, it will be cold. Then I'll be happy.* The same remark holds as for the earlier English example involving time and the word *then*. It's not entirely explicit what *then* refers to (the situations in which it will rain tomorrow or the situations in which it will snow tomorrow?). In ASL, one can once again lift the ambiguity by associating a locus *a* with *if it rains tomorrow* and a locus *b* with *if it snows tomorrow*. Instead of saying, *Then I'll be happy*, we can replace the word *then* with a pointing sign toward *a* to obtain the meaning *if it rains, I'll be happy*; similarly, we can point toward *b* to mean *if it snows, I'll be happy*. In this case, the pronoun plays the same role as a repetition of its antecedent, but it's a pronoun that refers to situations, not to objects.

We can also modify a bit our earlier flu-related example so that it refers to possible situations. Suppose I now say, *There was a flu outbreak. I might get infected, and I might stay healthy.* As in earlier examples with *might*, the first sentence asserts that *some situation compatible with my beliefs is one in which I get infected*, and similarly, the second sentence means that *some situation compatible with my beliefs is one in which I stay healthy*. Now let's add, *Then I'll get to relax.* We might want *then* to refer back to the situations in which I get infected, or to those in which I stay healthy—but here, too, the grammar of English is less than explicit. In ASL, one can associate a locus *a* to *infected* and a locus *b* to *healthy*. *Then* can be replaced with a pointing sign, but depending on whether one points toward locus *a* (= *IX-a*) or locus *b* (= *IX-b*), different meanings are obtained: *IX-a* refers to *the situations in which I get infected* and thus the meaning will be that I'll get to relax if I get infected. *IX-b* refers to *the situations in which I say healthy*, and the corresponding meaning will thus be that I'll get to relax if I remain healthy. In this case, the pointing sign plays the same role as a description of situations. Here, too, the conclusion is that the pointing sign behaves like a pronoun that refers to possible situations—and this comes on top of its uses to refer to objects and to real (past or future) situations.

What we learned from English was that language uses the same abstract resources to talk about objects and situations. Although tense and mood look nothing like pronouns, they have the same uses as *he, she*, or *it*. What sign language teaches us is that sometimes all these resources are realized by one and the same word—namely, the pointing sign. In other words, sign language clinches our case: sometimes the very same pronoun can refer to objects and to situations, be they real or merely possible.

## 5.6 CONCLUSION

We have discovered a rather extraordinary symmetry between the way language refers to objects and to situations. First, despite initial appearances, English has pronoun-like expressions to talk about real and possible situations, since tense and mood have all the uses that pronouns do. Second, in ASL one and the same pronoun—the pointing sign—may be used to refer to objects and, in some cases, to real or imaginary situations that would be referred to in English with tense and mood. Third, besides pronouns, language uses the same types of quantifiers to talk about objects and situations, but here too they take diverse forms: the situation counterparts of *something* are the words *sometimes* and *might*.

I started this chapter with a question: How does language go beyond the here and now? We have the beginning of an answer. Just like language uses the same kinds of categories (involving count and mass, singular and plural) in the verbal and in the nominal domain, it appears to recycle mechanisms of object reference to refer to situations. This applies to pronouns and to quantifiers alike. We will see in chapter 6 that the object/situation analogy runs even deeper.

# 6 BEYOND THE HERE AND NOW II: DESCRIBING AND CLASSIFYING OBJECTS AND SITUATIONS

## 6.1 PUZZLES WITH *IF*

*With ifs, one could put Paris in a bottle.* There is definitely some truth to this French saying (in the original: *Avec des si, on mettrait Paris en bouteille*), which is intended to highlight that someone's assumptions are far-fetched. In fact, NASA once helpfully stated that *if earth were the size of a nickel, the moon would be about as big as a coffee bean*—from which it follows, with impeccable scientific backing, that both would comfortably fit in a bottle, and Paris along with them. While there is a such a thing as making conditional assumptions that go too far, *if* and the conditional statements it expresses are essential to reasoning and argumentation. *Why did you honk in a silent zone?* asks the cop. *Because if I hadn't, the drowsy truck driver would have killed the pedestrian.* But what does *if* mean here?

Logicians traditionally took this sentence to mean something like: *In all possible situations in which I didn't honk, the pedestrian was killed.*[1] But just like *everyone came to the party* doesn't mean that everyone *in the entire world* came to the party but rather everyone *in a salient domain in the context*, so similarly logicians took *all possible situations* to make reference to all situations within a contextually specified domain. More generally, *if p, q* was taken to mean: Within a certain domain D, *all situations satisfying p satisfy q*. The first puzzle is that this analysis doesn't work well for human language. *If you hadn't honked but the pedestrian had moved, nobody would have been killed*, the cop could reply. It's ungenerous but true. This suggests that the initial analysis of *if* is incorrect, for the following reason: On the assumption that within the domain D *all situations satisfying p satisfy q*, it also follows, a fortiori, that within the domain D *all situations satisfying both p and p' satisfy q* (this is simply because the situations that satisfy both $p$ and $p'$ are a subset of those that satisfy $p$). But this is precisely the pattern of reasoning that fails in our example: *If I hadn't honked, the pedestrian would have died* (= *if p, q*), and yet *if I hadn't honked and the pedestrian had moved, he wouldn't have died* (= *if p and p', not q*). Something more subtle seems to be going on than the logician's analysis allows for.[2]

The French saying about *ifs* and bottles is echoed in another saying, originally in Yiddish but borrowed by other languages: *If my grandmother had balls, she'd be my grandfather* (in the original: *As di bubbe volt gehat beytsim, volt zi gevain mayn zaidah*). Or in a version that can more easily be mentioned in polite society: *If I had wheels, I'd be a wagon*. Besides the word *if*, mood plays a crucial role in these sayings. Try them in the indicative, and the result will be . . . awkward. *If I have wheels, I am a wagon* suggests that it is open whether or not I have wheels. When the condition involved is far-fetched or known to be false (i.e., 'counterfactual'), we must mark it as such with *had* rather than *have*. *Had* is the past tense of *have*, and yet in this case the meaning pertains to the present, not to the past. This is not just an idiosyncrasy of English grammar. In many languages, the present and past lead dual lives, marking situations as present or past but also as possible or far-fetched.

So what is the meaning of *if*? And why do *have* and *had* occasionally provide information about what is or isn't possible rather than just about what is present or past? A sweeping answer will come once we extend the approach developed in chapter 5. *If* will turn out to behave very much like the word *the* applied to a description of situations rather than of objects. And the nontemporal meaning of *have* and *had* will come out as a special case of a very general system by which objects and situations alike are classified as close or far from the speaker, with several further subdivisions depending on the domain and on the language.

We will thus set out to explore in greater detail the meaning of the word *the*, apply the findings to *if* and *when*, and then investigate how person, tense, and mood classify objects and situations by their distance to the speaker.

## 6.2 DEFINITE DESCRIPTIONS OF OBJECTS: THE MEANING OF *THE*

Besides pronouns (*she, he, I, you*) and quantifiers (*some, every*), language offers a convenient way to refer to objects: definite descriptions that involve the word *the*, as in *the winner*. In the context of a lottery, for instance, this description refers to whoever won or will win, even if that person's identity isn't determined yet. The only requirement is that it should be established that there is exactly one winner. If that requirement (called a presupposition) is not satisfied, the definite description *the winner* is just odd, as happens after a lottery with no winning ticket. It's just hard to determine whether the sentence *The winner is happy* is true or false in this case, since there is no winner to begin with. We will come back to the issue of presuppositions in chapter 11, but for the moment what matters is that this convenient device, the definite description, can single out by way of a property (such as *winning*) some object that one may not have direct acquaintance with.

*The* doesn't just apply to singular descriptions. In our lottery example, I could be speaking of *the winners* and pick out in this way the entire set of winners in the relevant situation. Similarly, if I say that *the winners in the room have been called to the podium,* the applies to the expression *winners in the room* and refers to the entire set of them. But *the* is even more versatile: It doesn't just apply to singulars and plurals, it also applies to mass nouns. If I say that *the beer in the room has been drunk,* the applies to the expression *beer in the room* and refers to the entire substance that was present but, alas, isn't present anymore.

In fact, in simple cases, *the* has a fairly straightforward meaning, where *the blah* refers to the maximal group of the denoted thing, whether it is mass (without minimal parts) or plural (with minimal parts). Things work like this: *Winners* is true of all the groups of winners, and *the winners* picks out the largest such group—hence all the winners in the relevant situation. *Beer* holds true of all portions of beer, and *the beer* picks out the largest such portion, hence all the beer in the relevant situation. By contrast with *winners,* the singular *winner* only holds true of individual winners, not of larger groups of them. But this immediately explains why the expression cannot be used unless there is exactly one winner. If there is none, there will be nothing to refer to; if there are several, there just isn't any largest group denoted by *the winner*, as each individual is a possible denotation, but none is larger than the others. The problem disappears if there is a single winner. By being the sole one, it also makes up the largest group of winners, so to speak. This explains why *the winner* comes with a presupposition that there should be exactly one winner.

In sum, a very simple analysis can explain the apparent diversity of uses of *the* with singulars, plurals, and mass nouns. That's a nice result, but there is still something slightly inaccurate about this picture. The problem is that *the boys* is predicted to mean essentially the same thing as *all boys*, since *the boys* is supposed to pick out the maximal set of boys in the relevant situation. In many cases, this is a reasonable approximation, but sometimes it won't quite do. Suppose that in a sixth-grade class, three boys raise their hands with what appears to be an urgent need. To call attention to the gravity of the situation, a girl says, *The boys need to go to the bathroom*. It will be clear that she is referring to the three boys who raised their hand. But if she says instead, *All boys need to go to the bathroom*, she will have referred, weirdly in this case, to the entire group of boys in the class.

Thus our initial analysis must be refined a bit. It looks like *the boys* really refers to the *most salient* boys in the relevant situation and picks the maximal set among those (in the case we just discussed, we still need this maximality condition: it's not possible to refer to just two of the three boys that raised their hand). In other words, *the boys need to go to the bathroom* just means that *the most salient boys*, those raising their hand, need to go to the bathroom. And it doesn't follow that *the boys in the first row need to go to the bathroom*: If no boy in the first row raised his hand, the most salient boys in the first row will be the entire row, and the original sentence certainly doesn't entail that all these individuals need to go to the bathroom. Thus, on closer consideration, *the boys* means something a bit different from *all boys*.[3]

This slight adjustment has welcome consequences for singular descriptions as well. If I own a little brown dog and my neighbors own a large black-and-white dog, I could tell you without any air of contradiction: *The dog has been attacked by the black-and-white dog*. Without reference to salience, we would be forced to conclude, absurdly, that there is exactly one dog in this situation (to explain why *the dog* can be used). But with salience, the problem disappears: *The dog* just requires that there is exactly one most salient dog in this situation—which makes sense. In this conversation, my dog is certainly more salient than all other dogs. In fact, I could complicate my example to make salience play a key role in the second description as well. Suppose I tell you, *The dog has just been attacked by the black-and-white dog—remember? The one that looks like the Obamas' dog.* The Obamas' dog, Bo, happened to be black-and-white,[4] so now there are two black-and-white dogs mentioned in this conversation: my neighbors' dog and the Obamas' dog. But the neighbors' dog is more salient, and thus *the black-and-white dog* has no trouble referring to it. Needless to say, what counts as 'more salient' lies in the eye of the beholder, and so the context plays a crucial role in establishing such salience hierarchies.

## 6.3  DEFINITE DESCRIPTIONS OF SITUATIONS: THE MEANING OF *WHEN* AND *IF*

This detour through definite descriptions has an immediate benefit: It will allow us to view *when-* and *if*-clauses as definite descriptions of situations and to account for some of their very subtle properties. In other words, *when* and *if* behave essentially as the word *the*, with the difference that they refer to real or merely possible situations rather than to objects.

Let's first consider *when*-clauses, which are easier because, in simple cases at least, they refer to real situations. *When Ann comes home, she brings her laundry.* Here the *when*-clause behaves very much like a plural definite description, yielding a meaning akin to, *In the situations in which Ann comes, she brings home her laundry* (it's unlikely that there is only one such situation). But if I say instead, *When Ann came home, we were away,* chances are that the intended meaning is that of a singular definite description, referring to a particular occasion on which Ann came home. Which occasion? Without further context, probably the *most recent* one—with no implication that there weren't earlier occasions when Ann came home as well. Here we observe the same kind of behavior we noted in connection with *the dog*: It need not refer to the one and only dog in the relevant situation but rather to the _most salient_ dog. With _when_-clauses, greatest salience is replaced with greatest temporal proximity, but for the rest the logic remains the same.

Strikingly, the same analysis can be applied to _if_-clauses. The word _if_ turns out to behave much like the word _the_ applied to a description of possible situations. Since it originally came as a big surprise to logicians that _if_ works in this way, let me first explain in greater detail what they expected.

The reason _if_ matters in logical reasoning is that it makes it possible, given the right circumstances, to acquire new information. Suppose that a scientific theory predicts that _if the water is heated to 100 degrees centigrade, it will boil,_ and that in addition we learn that in fact the water was heated to 100 degrees. We then acquire the new information that the water in fact boiled. This is undoubtedly useful in scientific and nonscientific life alike. This logical behavior is easily captured by a traditional analysis, according to which _if the water is heated to 100 degrees, it will boil_ means that within a certain domain, _every situation in which water is heated to 100 degrees is one in which it boils._ This will indeed guarantee that on learning that we are in a situation in which water was heated to 100 degrees, we can deduce that in that situation water will also boil.

The traditional logical analysis of _if_ also guarantees that you will still get boiling water if you heat it to 100 degrees and all sorts of further things happen. For instance, from our original conditional statement, it still follows that _if water is heated to 100 degrees and the lab manager is distracted, the water will boil._ This is definitely what we want for real scientific laws, and this is also what we expect in view of the traditional analysis: Certainly if (within a given domain) all water-heating situations are water-boiling situations, then a fortiori, all water-heating situations with a distracted manager are also water-boiling situations.

Alas, that's not quite how _if_ works in real language, as I mentioned at the outset. To reiterate my initial point, suppose I say, _If my parents come to visit tomorrow, I'll be delighted._ It certainly doesn't follow that _if my parents come to visit tomorrow and turn out to be sick, I will be delighted._ And more scientific-looking examples don't really work much better. _If I strike this_ *match, it will light* seems like a true enough statement. But it doesn't really follow that *if I dip this match in water and strike it, it will light!*

Now the pattern we just discussed might remind you of something. We saw before that *the boys need to go to the bathroom* doesn't entail *the boys sitting in the first row need to go to the bathroom,* precisely because *the boys* doesn't mean *all boys* but *the most salient boys.* Well, *if* behaves very much like *the* applied to situations, but the notion of salience needs to be adjusted. When I utter, *If I strike this match, it will light,* the situations that count as most salient are those that are *most similar* to the situation I am in. Let us now see how this explains the actual behavior of *if.*

The idea is that we are not interested in far-fetched situations but rather in situations that are as similar as possible to the one we are in. So, the statement *If my parents come to visit tomorrow, I'll be delighted* means something like, *In the most similar situations in which my parents come to visit tomorrow, I'll be delighted.* This seems right: The conditional sentence yields a prediction that I'll be delighted in case my parents come *and nothing out of the ordinary happens.* In this way, if my parents come but turn out to be sick, no prediction is made: Such a situation doesn't count as one of the most similar ones that satisfy the condition. In other words, we now correctly block the inference that *if my parents come to visit tomorrow and turn out to be sick, I'll be delighted.* The match-striking case is similar. When I say, *If I strike this match, it will light,* I am only committed to the claim that in the most similar situations in which I strike the match, it lights; certainly, the scenario in which I first dip the match in water is out of the ordinary, so my statement may have been entirely truthful while not making any predictions about the match-dipping case.

We saw before that what counts as 'more salient' is a highly context-dependent affair. Relatedly, there may be differences of opinion as to what counts as 'the most similar situations.' A nice illustration is this joke often told about the Clintons (and later recycled in a version pertaining to the Obamas):[5]

> The couple are driving along when they stop to get some gas, and it turns out that the attendant is a high-school boyfriend of Hillary's. As they're pulling

away, Bill says, *Just think—if you had married him, today you'd be a gas station attendant's wife.* Hillary shakes her head and says, *No, Bill, if I had married him, today he'd be president of the United States.*

For Bill, the most similar situations to the actual one are ones in which the fact that *Bill is president* is held constant. For Hillary, a more important fact is that *Hillary's husband is president,* so this is what should be held constant— and because of this minor disagreement, when using the very same conditional, they are actually talking about different conceivable situations. For Bill, the most similar situations in which Hillary marries a gas attendant are ones in which Bill is still president (and the gas attendant is not): Bill's presidential status is held constant. For Hillary, the most similar such situations are ones in which her husband (the gas attendant, not Bill) is president: Hillary's status as the First Lady is what is held constant.

Stepping back, we have now obtained an appealingly simple picture. Language has quantifiers, pronouns, and definite descriptions to talk about objects, and it uses the same logical tools to talk about situations. *When* can be seen as the form taken by *the* when it applies to real situations, while *if* is the form taken by *the* to talk about situations that include imaginary ones. Salience gets modulated a bit from one domain to the next: Temporal proximity plays a key role for *when*, whereas for *if*, it is similarity to the situation of utterance that matters (and for salience and similarity alike, context plays an important role). In sum, the logical behaviors of *the*, *when*, and *if* are all very similar.

Still, it would be nice to have direct evidence for the existence of an abstract *the* that applies in identical fashion to objects and situations. And you might expect that I'll turn once again to sign language to make the point. Alas, there is no word that cleanly corresponds to *the* in ASL or LSF, which makes the task a bit arduous. But in this case, a spoken language comes to the rescue: Marathi, an Indo-Aryan language spoken in India, uses almost the same construction to talk about objects and situations.[6] In order to say *The man who lives in your neighborhood is a writer*, a Marathi speaker can say something like, *The man who lives in your neighborhood, that man is a writer.*[7] *The* is pronounced *dzo*, and *that* is pronounced *to*. In the sentence, *If he studies, then he will pass, if* is pronounced as *dzar* and *then* is pronounced as *tar*. So the pattern is as follows: *dzo—to* when talking about objects, *dzar—tar* when talking about situations. The element *dz*, which is present in both *dzo* and *dzar*, seems to be a concrete realization of the abstract *the* that we postulated for more indirect reasons in English.

## 6.4 CLASSIFYING BY PROXIMITY: OBJECTS

At this point, I have said nothing about the distinction between *Ann is sick* and *Ann was sick*, or between *if Ann is sick right now, she'll stay home* and *if Ann was* (or *were*) *sick right now, she would stay home*. In these examples, *is* and *was* do double duty, just as *have* and *had* did in the examples discussed at the beginning of this chapter: When talking about real situations, *is* and *was* present them as being around the situation of utterance or before it (present versus past situations); when talking about possibly imagined situations, *is* and *was* situate those described by the *if*-clause as being reasonably similar to the situation of utterance or more far-fetched (i.e., very different from it). Depending on the speaker, the latter case will involve *was* or *were*, but in any event there are numerous cases across languages (such as French) in which the past tense does double duty to express both anteriority and remoteness in the realm of possibilities.

The fact that *is/was* and *have/had* can be used both as tenses (to talk about real situations) and as moods (to talk about imagined ones) should give us pause. It suggests that there is an interesting general notion at work here. As we will now see, our analogy between object talk and situation talk can be extended to this case. To get to this point, however, we'll need to take a closer look at systems of object classification in language. In a nutshell, languages often classify objects as being close or far from the speaker, and the present and past do something similar with respect to situations.

The distinction between *here* and *there*, or *this* and *that*, is often related to (real or metaphorical) proximity to the speaker. Further instances of a distinction between proximity and remoteness are easy to find. The clearest case is that of personal pronouns: *I* refers to the speaker, *he/she/it* to a non-speaker; *we* refers to a group that includes the speaker, *they* to a group that doesn't.

In some languages, definite descriptions give rise to the same distinctions as *we* versus *they*. Thus in Bulgarian, if a woman says that *the women have nice clothes* and intends to include herself in the description, the verb has to be marked as first-person plural, just as is the case when *we* is used in English.[8]

But in some languages, the classification gets more sophisticated. In Potawatomi, a Native American language of the United States (of the Algonquian family), there is a further distinction among third-person expressions. If two are used, one is typically marked as 'proximate,' which means that it refers to an object that is close to the center of attention and thus most salient (it is in a way psychologically close); the other is marked as 'obviative,' which means that it refers to a less salient object (it is psychologically more remote). For instance, in a Potawatomi equivalent of *I went for a walk and saw <u>a bear</u> chasing <u>an elk</u>*, one of the two underlined expressions (say, *bear*) will be marked as proximate and the other (say, *elk*) will be marked as obviative; the bear will in that case be the focus of interest.[9]

So, across languages, we have the following distinctions: near the speaker; far from the speaker; and further from (meaning less salient than) an object which is itself far from the speaker. In fact, another Algonquian language, Blackfoot, makes the classification even more sophisticated, with a distinction between the obviative and the *further* obviative, used to refer to an object that is less salient than one that counts as obviative. These four levels of proximity to the speaker can be represented in a simple diagram, with the speaker position on the right as shown below.

| further obviative | obviative | 3rd person | 1st person |
| still further away | further away | away from the speaker | near the speaker |

The speaker's perspective is the initial point of reference for these classifications. But as we saw in chapter 3, perspectival elements come in different varieties: English *I* depends on the actual speaker's perspective. Amharic and Zazaki first-person expressions, by contrast, are more liberal and can depend either on an actual or a reported perspective. Finally, logophoric expressions found in Ewe obligatorily depend on the perspective of a reported speech or thought act. So, in the end, we have rich means of classification of objects across languages: they can be situated in terms of their proximity to the speaker's perspective, and in addition, one sometimes has a choice between the perspective of the actual speaker and that of someone whose words or thoughts are reported.

## 6.5  CLASSIFYING BY PROXIMITY: TEMPORAL SITUATIONS

Strikingly, several of these abstract distinctions exist with tense and mood, at least with present and past tenses (future tense is a more complicated story, which I will leave aside).

Consider first distance in the past. We'll find a system reminiscent of the categories of object classification we just discussed: the distinction between present, past, and pluperfect serves to classify situations as being temporally close to the speaker, away from the speaker in the past, or even more remote than that (we'll see in a second that some languages go even further with a double pluperfect).

| double pluperfect<br>still further away in the past | pluperfect<br>further away in the past | past<br>in the past | present<br>near the speaker |
|---|---|---|---|

Closest to the speaker is the present, which may pertain to the very time of utterance, as in *Sam is sick*, or to a larger interval of time around it, as in *Robin smokes* (which refers to a habitual action). *Sam smoked* refers to a past situation, of course. But what is interesting is that we can also say *Sam had smoked*, using the tense known as the pluperfect, although this is a bit odd if uttered out of the blue. For it to work, we need a discourse that already talks about a past situation, as in: *Sam's mother entered the room. Sam had smoked.* Now things are clear: There is a past situation in which Sam's mother entered the room, and there is an *earlier* situation in which Sam smoked.

What the pluperfect does in this case is establish that the smoking situation is more remote than another past situation that was mentioned in the discourse. This might sound familiar because it resembles the type of system of classification we saw at work with objects, but now ordering by temporal proximity has replaced ordering by salience. The fact that the pluperfect is a past in the past, so to speak, is particularly clear in a language like Yiddish, in which one says literally *I have had said* for *I had said*: with one auxiliary, we have one level of anteriority; with two auxiliaries, we go even further in the past.[10]

In fact, there are languages in which the classification system goes even further, with a double pluperfect. Thus, in some varieties of German, you can say that *Sam had had smoked* in order to situate Sam's smoking relative to a past situation that was referred to using a pluperfect. For instance, suppose we wanted to say something like the following: *Before Sam left the house, his mother had not been happy: he had smoked.* Here, *he had smoked* makes reference to a situation that precedes that in which Sam's mother wasn't happy, so it would make sense to say that *he had had smoked.* Granted, English is a bit limited here, but some southern varieties of German say precisely something like this (in German, *er hatte geraucht gehabt*). You can visualize it as in the following diagram, with four temporal levels ordered with respect to each other.

| double pluperfect | pluperfect | past | present |
|---|---|---|---|
| Sam "had had" smoked | His mother had not been happy | Sam left the house | Now |

(The double pluperfect occasionally arises in literature as well. The great German writer Goethe once wrote of one of his characters that she '*had had hid herself* " [in the German original, *hatte sich versteckt gehabt*] to mean that she had hid herself before another salient moment that was itself referred to with the pluperfect.)[11]

Taken together, these distinctions look a lot like those we found with respect to object classification, but with a twist: Psychological proximity (i.e., salience) is replaced with temporal proximity. We will now take things one step further and extend this system to cases in which possible situations are classified in terms of how far-fetched they are.

### 6.6 CLASSIFYING BY PROXIMITY: MODAL SITUATIONS

As we saw before, *is* and *was* do double duty. When talking about real situations, *is* and *was* present them as being around the situation of utterance or before it—that's the temporal use we just discussed. When talking about merely possible situations, *is* and *was* classify them as reasonably similar to the situation of utterance or more far-fetched—this is a modal use. In effect, used as moods, the present and past tenses serve to classify situations by their similarity to the situation of utterance. We will thus extend our systems of classification with the following picture: Used as a mood, the present classifies situations as being close (i.e., reasonably similar) to the one we are in. The past used as a mood classifies them as more far-fetched and remote. And we'll see that the pluperfect can be used to classify situations as being even more remote.

| pluperfect as mood | past as mood | present as mood |
|---|---|---|
| more remote situations | remote situations | close situations |

◄────────────────────────────────────────────────────────────●

Since these moods are primarily seen with *if*, we first need to think about how descriptions of various kinds interact with these systems of classification. In our discussion of the words *the*, *when*, and *if*, we saw that abstract versions of *the* apply in similar ways to objects, to real situations, and to merely possible ones, with a twist: *The dog* picks out the *most salient* dog, *when Ann came home* picks out the *closest past situation* in which she did so, and *if my parents come to visit* picks out the *most similar situations* (to the one we are in) in which my parents visit. The same adjustment is needed when we classify situations: when we turn from tense to mood, temporal proximity is replaced with similarity to the situation we are in.

As I briefly mentioned, in Bulgarian, person marking can correspond to a definite description, with a woman using first-person plural marking to say, *The women have nice clothes*. The same thing arguably happens with *if*-clauses in English, except that the marking shows up within the *if*-clause: The mood on the verb tells us how the situations denoted by the *if*-clause are classified relative to the speech situation. To be concrete, suppose there is a tennis tournament tomorrow and you are a good player, and I tell you: *If you play tomorrow, you will win*. Here the indicative mood suggests that there is a reasonable chance you will play tomorrow. But suppose I say instead: *If you played tomorrow, you would win*. It is clear that the past tense on *played* doesn't have a temporal (past) meaning, since the action is to take place tomorrow. Rather, it refers to a more far-fetched situation and carries the implication that it's at a minimum unlikely that you will play tomorrow (you would get a similar effect saying, *If I were to play tomorrow, I would win*. Here, *were* in the first person is definitely not a past tense but rather a mood).

The contrast can be explained in terms of the distinctions we've seen up to this point.[12] In both examples, the *if*-clauses picks out the most similar situations (to the actual one) in which you play tomorrow. With *if you play tomorrow*, the indicative has the same kind of effect as the present and situates the relevant situations as close to the speaker—not temporally close, but rather close in the sense that they are fairly similar to the situation we are in. With *if you played tomorrow*, by contrast, these situations are presented as being further away and thus more far-fetched. The fact that the closest situations in which you play *still* count as far-fetched just means that we assume you won't play: an effort of imagination is needed to get to situations in which you do play.

From this perspective, it is no accident that it is often the same suffixes that serve to mark present tense and indicative mood. The present tense suffix *-s* appears in *John plays tennis* (present tense, he does so around the speech time) but also in *if John plays tomorrow* (indicative mood, the closest situations in which he plays tomorrow are not too far-fetched). By the same reasoning, it is no accident that in many languages, the past tense does double duty as a genuine tense and as a mood that marks remoteness. So the same suffix appears in *John played tennis* (past tense, he did so in the past) and in *if John played tomorrow* (counterfactual mood, the closest situations in which John plays tennis tomorrow are more far-fetched).

Of course, it is nice to be able to find some reason for the apparently capricious fact that *have/had, is/was, -s/-ed* can serve both as tenses and as moods. But there is still a gap in this analogy, since I have not displayed any mood comparable to the pluperfect, as in *John's mother entered the room. He had smoked.* With a bit of imagination, however, you can find pluperfects that function as moods. Suppose that you are a good tennis player but that you broke an arm. And now I tell you: *Too bad—if you had played tomorrow, you would have won.* Since the relevant action is situated tomorrow, it's clear that the pluperfect can't have a temporal meaning. What it does is classify the closest situations in which you play tomorrow as more remote (more far-fetched) than some other counterfactual situations, probably ones in which you didn't break an arm. So the sentence means something like, *If you didn't have a broken arm, and if you had played tomorrow, you would have won.* You can visualize it like this:

| pluperfect as mood | past as mood | present as mood |
|---|---|---|
| more far-fetched situations | counterfactual situations | possible situations |

◄─────────────────────────────────────────────────●

In the end, the picture we obtain for mood is eerily reminiscent of the one we saw with tense—and also with systems of object classification in Algonquian. (You might ask whether there are *double* pluperfects to refer to still more remote situations—and here I must confess that I don't know of studies of this phenomenon.)

There is one more thing to ask, however. Are there situation counterparts of the case in which an object can or must be classified with respect to a reported perspective, as happens with Zazaki and Amharic first-person pronouns or with Ewe logophoric pronouns? We don't have a full typology yet, but some facts definitely go in that direction. Russian and Hebrew present tenses mirror the liberal behavior of Zazaki and Amharic first-person pronouns. If in English I tell you that *a week ago, Robin told me that John is crying*, you'll think that my grammar is a bit odd. The word *was* is expected because *is* would have to refer to a period around the time of utterance. But in Russian or Hebrew, a similar sentence is entirely natural because the present tense can correspond to the perspective of a reported speech or thought event.[13]

Finally, we saw that Ewe logophoric pronouns *must* correspond to a reported perspective. Something similar happens with a certain mood in German (called the 'first subjunctive' or 'Konjunktiv I'). This mood can be used in indirect discourse. For example, *Robin believes that Maria be sick*, where *be* corresponds to this subjunctive form (which is entirely different from the English subjunctive). But just saying *Maria be sick* as an independent sentence won't work at all to mean that she is sick; rather, the reading obtained will be that <u>according to some people</u>, Maria is sick. The reason is that this subjunctive is a kind of 'logophoric mood' that is used to represent somebody else's perspective.[14]

## 6.7 CONCLUSION

We now have solutions to the puzzles we started out with. While the puzzles were about *if*, the solutions are broader and rely on two abstract semantic devices: definite descriptions and systems of classification. Both apply in rather similar ways to object talk and to situation talk.

Strikingly, the words *when* and *if* can be analyzed as the form taken by the word *the* when it describes real or imagined situations. The fact that *the* picks out objects that are *cognitively closest* (i.e., most salient) has counterparts with *when* and *if*, but with appropriately adjusted notions of proximity: *when* picks out the situations that are temporally closest, and *if* picks out those that are most similar to the situation of utterance.

The same kind of correspondence can be found in systems of classification. Objects as well as situations can be classified as close, far, further than an entity classified as far, or even further than *that*. While systems of object classification are not very rich in English, they definitely are in several Algonquian languages. On the other hand, English has a rich system of situation classification: the present, past, and pluperfect can be used to refer to situations that are more or less remote temporally (in the past) or more or less far-fetched in the realm of possibilities. In addition, objects and situations alike can be classified relative to the perspective of the actual speaker or to that of another person whose words or thoughts are reported. In particular, the Amharic or Zazaki first person, which can liberally depend on the speaker's or on another person's perspective, has a counterpart in the behavior of the Russian present tense; similarly, Ewe logophoric pronouns, which report the perspective of a non-speaker, have a counterpart in a German subjunctive.

In chapter 5, we saw that quantifiers and pronouns can apply, in different forms, to objects and to situations. This general analogy has now been extended to definite descriptions and to systems of classification. Strikingly, language has a very abstract system of reference that applies in comparable ways to objects, which are often easily perceptible, and to real and imagined situations, which need not be. This might be a reflex of a very fundamental way in which the human mind organizes the world. As a consequence, we have remarkably sophisticated means to represent and to reason about situations, including imagined ones.

# II  USING MEANING

*In previous chapters, we investigated some of the most important building blocks of meaning: pronouns; nouns and verbs; adjectives and adverbs;* the, if, *and* when; *and person, tense, and mood. We saw a beautiful architecture in which human meaning works by way of simple but abstract logical categories that are found in spoken and signed languages alike, and apply in nearly identical fashion to objects and events or situations. But none of this would be useful if, at the end of the day, we couldn't put the blocks together to convey information or, in other words, produce inferences.*

*In this part, we will see how language can put it all together. Since the task is complex, we first consider in chapter 7 an artificial case, that of Predicate Logic, which offers a precise language for science. In chapter 8, we turn to a simplified yet detailed exploration of how human language (in our case, English) can be seen as a completely formal logical language. And in chapter 9, we will see why human language is more expressive than standard logical languages. These three chapters explain how entailments are produced by language. But human language also differs from standard logical languages in having a richer typology of inferences: not just entailments but also implicatures (which are drawn by reasoning on the speaker's motives), presuppositions (preconditions on an utterance), and several others. This rich typology is the topic of chapters 10 and 11.*

*At the end of part II, we will have understood what kind of logical system human language is, and we will have reached the conclusion that it is more expressive than standard logical languages along two dimensions: the entailments it produces and the typology of inferences it gives rise to.*

# 7 LOGIC MACHINE I: PREDICATE LOGIC

## 7.1 FORMAL VERSUS NATURAL LANGUAGES

In the early days of artificial intelligence, Marvin Minsky, a pioneer of the field, allegedly assigned to an undergraduate student the following project: *Link a computer to a camera and get the computer to "describe what it saw."*[1] This was in 1966, and more than 50 years on, despite considerable research resources (including by teams at Google, Facebook, and the like), the problem is still a very hard one. Something similar happened in semantics. In the late 1960s, the philosopher and logician Richard Montague noticed that there was something odd about the logic textbook he was writing. The logical part was mathematically rigorous and explicit, and then the exercises asked the students to translate English sentences into logical formulas, but that part was entirely left to the student's and professor's intuition.[2] In other words, to determine whether a logical formula was the 'right' translation of an English sentence, students and professors alike had no choice but to introspect to see if the predicted truth conditions 'seemed right.' This was one of Montague's motivations for defining a new problem: to find a systematic way to translate English sentences into logical formulas and, eventually, to derive their precise truth conditions. Unlike Minsky, however, Montague had the good sense to assign the problem to himself rather than to an undergraduate. While he initially regarded the problem "as both rather easy and not very important,"[3] he spent years working on it and founded a field, formal semantics, some of whose results are described in this book.

From a traditional perspective, Montague's project was an odd one. To put it succinctly, language often seems to be a mess, one that's not amenable to the precision of formal logic. Earlier chapters showed how wrong this impression is, but there are still some reasons behind the traditional view. One of them is that language seems to be hopelessly ambiguous. Some ambiguities are innocuous enough. For instance, *tale* and *tail* are spelled differently but pronounced in the same way, hence an amusing exchange in *Alice in Wonderland*:

> "Mine is a long and a sad tale!" said the Mouse, turning to Alice, and sighing. "It is a long tail, certainly," said Alice.

In other cases, spelling doesn't help. In Charles Dickens's namesake novel, Oliver Twist endures unspeakable ill-treatment in a workhouse governed by a board of heartless gentlemen. As he is summoned by this governing body, Oliver is told to "bow to the board." At which point, "seeing no board but the table," he "fortunately bowed to that." Whether in the pronunciation or in writing, *board* is ambiguous between a flat piece of wood and a governing body. Still, from a theoretical standpoint, it doesn't seem too bad to posit that *board* can really stand for *board₁* or *board₂*, with two abstract words that happen to be pronounced in the same way. Unfortunately, other cases are far more worrisome because the ambiguity of the sentence can't be reduced to an ambiguity of individual words.

The Greek writer Diogenes Laertius (third century AD) had this to say about Socrates: *Once, when he was asked what was the virtue of a young man, he said, "To avoid excess in everything."* I received a similar-sounding (albeit unsourced) recommendation when growing up, from which I inferred that overindulging in chocolate and other delicacies was permissible as long as one also maintained moderation in at least *some* area. With a modicum of bad faith, I had interpreted *avoid excess in everything* as meaning that one should avoid the following: committing excesses in everything—which has the advantage of allowing for excesses in *some* things. Alas, this was not what was intended: the original recommendation, μηδὲν ἄγαν (meden agan), stood in the temple of Apollo in Delphi, Greece, and its literal meaning is unambiguous: *Nothing in excess.* In other words, *in everything, one should avoid excess.*

In English, the ambiguity of the intimation to *avoid excess in everything* is real, but it cannot be explained by an ambiguity of any of the individual words *avoid, excess,* or *everything.* This is not an isolated case. Groucho Marx famously recounted:[4]

> One morning I shot an elephant in my pajamas. How he got in my pajamas, I don't know.

The first sentence would normally be understood as: *I shot an elephant while I was in my pajamas.* The second sentence makes it clear that Groucho had something different in mind, namely: *I shot an elephant that was in my pajamas.* It certainly won't help to say that there are two kinds of pajamas, *pajamas₁* or *pajamas₂*. Rather, an ambiguity arises because *in my pajamas* could provide information about the speaker's state while shooting, or about the elephant's location while it was shot.

Logicians have long bemoaned the vagaries of language, of these and other varieties. Long ago they devised formal languages intended to avoid precisely these ambiguities, and their development in the early twentieth century led to rigorous logics that can formalize all of science—and gave rise to computer science. But here is a well-kept secret: English and other natural languages are *also* formal languages, and the ambiguities they give rise to are, on closer inspection, a sign of the exquisitely detailed logical syntax they have. Thanks to language, we are in effect logic machines.[5]

In this chapter, we explore the workings of a particularly important formal language, Predicate Logic. In chapter 8, we will extend the approach (against all odds!) to English, and then in chapter 9 we will see how much more expressive English is than Predicate Logic.

## 7.2 THE SYNTAX OF PREDICATE LOGIC: GETTING RID OF AMBIGUITIES

In mathematics, where precision really matters, one can get a true or a false statement depending on how *every* is understood to interact with *some. Some number follows every number.* Does this mean that *for every number x, for some number y, y follows x* (in other words, *for every number x, there is some number or other that follows it*)? This is true. Certainly x + 1 follows x, as do (in a looser sense of 'follows') x + 2, x + 3, and so on. Or does the sentence mean that *for some number y, for every number x, y follows x?* That would be false, as there is no greatest number (and also because the purported greatest number couldn't follow itself anyway!). Since such distinctions greatly matter in mathematics and more generally in science, formal logics were invented in which all statements are unambiguous.

The most common logic, called *Predicate Logic*, starts from statements of the form *5 = 3, 5 > 3, x = 3, x > y*, or for that matter *x + y = z* (or any other simple statements, really). These are the *elementary formulas*, which we may abbreviate abstractly as *A, B, C,* etc. But to make more sophisticated statements, we need to use these formulas to obtain more complex ones. This can be easily done thanks to negation (*not*), conjunction (*and*), and disjunction (*or*). They allow us to construct complex formulas such as *not 5 = 3, (5 = 3 and 5 > 3)*, and *(5 = 3 or 5 > 3)*. The first statement, with a negation, is true (because 5 isn't equal to 3). The second statement is false because its first component, 5 = 3, is false. And the third statement is true because its second component is true. We can form even more complex statements by combining *these* statements—for instance, *(not 5 = 3 and (5 = 3 or 5 > 3))*. All this can be summarized conveniently in two rules:

–Every elementary formula is a formula.
–If *A* and *B* are formulas, so are *not A, (A and B), (A or B)*.

The first rule goes without saying (but I mention it nonetheless because, for the time being, we are in the business of defining the language of science!). The second rule says that new formulas can be built out of 'old' ones by adding *not, and, or* as well as parentheses in the right places. Just as in a LEGO game, once you've built a formula, you can use it to build larger ones, and there is no limit to the size of what you can build in this way (in a LEGO game, the pieces get exhausted at some point, but with abstract symbols, you get to do what you want without end—if you have the required patience).

You might wonder why we need to put brackets around *(A and B)*, for instance. There are two related answers. One is that they keep track of the way the formulas are built—and this will greatly matter when we come to their meaning. The other answer is that without these brackets, we would have ambiguities just as bad as those we started out with! Take this formula, without brackets:

not 3 = 5 and 3 > 5

It could be read in two completely different ways. First, it could be taken to mean this, where *not* just applies to 3 = 5:

(not 3 = 5 and 3 > 5)

In other words, *3 isn't equal to 5* is true, and *3 is greater than 5* is true. This is obviously false because the second conjunct is. On the other hand, the formula could also be understood in another way:

not (3 = 5 and 3 > 5)

Now the claim denies the conjunction (i.e., the conjunctive statement) *3 = 5 and 3 > 5*. Negating this is definitely right, as it denies an obvious falsehood (since 3 isn't equal to 5, nor greater than 5). So, without the brackets, the formula is false on one reading, true on the other—a disaster if precision is of the essence. With brackets, clarity is enforced.

You may find these simple examples less than exciting, and for good reason: They only talk about particular things (here particular numbers) and have no way to make general statements, which are the essence of science. To express generality, we need quantifiers, expressions like *every number is such that* (or *all numbers are such that*, which essentially means the same thing), and *some number is such that* (or *there exists some number such that*, which is also the same thing). Since these are a mouthful, mathematicians invented special symbols: an upside-down *A* for *all*, written as ∀, and an inverted *E* for *there exists*, written as ∃. ∀*x blah* will thus be read as *for all things x, blah holds*, while ∃*x blah* will mean that *there exists a thing x such that blah holds*. Sometimes we'll make our lives easier by paraphrasing these in near-identical fashion—for instance, *for every thing x, blah holds*, and *for some thing x, blah holds*. So now we have to make our rules a bit more sophisticated, with the addition of the boldfaced parts, where $x$ could be any variable $(x, y, z, \ldots)$.

–Every elementary formula is a formula.

–If *x* is any variable and *A* and *B* are formulas, so are *not A, (A and B), (A or B)*, $\forall x\, A$, $\exists x\, A$.

(Typically, in $\forall x\, A$ and $\exists x\, A$, the formula *A* will contain the variable *x*, for otherwise the preceding quantifier won't do any semantic work—which is permissible but not very interesting.)

That's it—this in essence is all we need to have a logic for science. Now we can go back to our ambiguous sentence: *Some number follows every number*. It corresponds to two different statements that can be defined with this logic (I'll assume that the things that we are talking about are numbers, and more precisely, integers—that is, 0, 1, 2, . . .). We start from the elementary formula $y > x$, which corresponds to the loose sense of 'y follows x.' Certainly, $y > x$ is a formula *A*, so we can form from it $\exists y\, A$. And this entire thing is a formula, too, so we can form a new formula by adding to it $\forall x$:

$$\forall x\, \exists y\, y > x$$

Paraphrasing, this means that *for every number x, for some number y, y follows x*. That's true!

But we could also have decided to put the quantifiers in a different order: from $y > x$ we form $\forall x\, y > x$, and then we obtain:

$$\exists y\, \forall x\, y > x$$

This can be paraphrased as *for some number y, for every number x, y follows x*. That's definitely false! The point is that the two statements are now completely different in form, and there is no risk of confusion any longer: clarity has been regained.


## 7.3 THE SEMANTICS OF PREDICATE LOGIC: ADDING MEANING

So far I have only discussed the *form* of logical statements (their syntax). One can go rather far with form alone. The reason is that we can make use of inference rules—for instance, that from *(A and B)*, *A* follows, and *B* follows. There is an entire branch of logic (called proof theory) that devises rules that guarantee that from true statements we only obtain new ones that are equally true. But there is another way to approach the formal languages used in logic, one that makes them particularly similar to human language and also *justifies* the appropriate inference rules. The key is to endow these purely formal symbols with meaning—in other words, with a semantics. Providing such a semantics for some formal languages was a key contribution of Alfred Tarski in the 1930s, and it paved the way for the semantic analysis of natural languages by Montague and his followers starting in the 1970s.

Here as elsewhere in this book, we take the meaning of a sentence to be the conditions under which it is true. So assuming that the way the world is determines the truth value of elementary expressions (in our examples, they were all mathematical statements), we need a systematic procedure to find the truth value of all the complex sentences of the formal language (this effort will pay off later when we extend these methods to English as well). In other words, we'll take as given the truth values of elementary sentences, but we'll want a procedure that can derive from them the truth values of all sentences in the formal language, no matter how complex they may be. Since we won't make any special assumptions about the way the world is (we will consider all possible truth values for elementary expressions), we will in the end derive the truth conditions of complex sentences from the truth conditions of their elementary expressions.

But the task isn't quite trivial. While simple, our formal language contains infinitely many sentences. The reason is that from existing formulas, we can always obtain new ones by adding negations or quantifiers at the beginning, or by forming the conjunction or the disjunction of two of them (as in the LEGO game in which elementary pieces never run out). It wouldn't be illuminating to just list, by brute force, truth values for the entire language at once, since the point of complex formulas is precisely that their truth value can be deduced from that of their component parts. The question is how to do this.

The key idea is to associate a corresponding semantic rule with each rule by which the sentences were built. Take the complex sentence we discussed above:

not (3 = 5 and 3 > 5)

How did we determine its truth value? We took as given the truth values of the elementary formulas *3 = 5* and *3 > 5* (both false). From that, we computed the value of the conjunction *(3 = 5 and 3 > 5)* (still false!). And from that, we computed the value of the negative statement *not (3 = 5 and 3 > 5)* (true, because it is the negation of a false statement).

So all we need for this case are rules that specify how to derive the truth value of a conjunction and of a negation from the values of their immediate component parts. And these rules are very easy to specify:

If *A* and *B* are formulas,
*not A* is true just in case *A* is false.
*(A and B)* is true just in case *A* is true and *B* is true.
*(A or B)* is true just in case *A* is true or *B* is true or both.

I have added to the list a rule that interprets *(A or B)*. For it to be true, we just require that at least one of its component parts should be true, not that exactly one is. This is called the 'inclusive' *or* because it is true under these liberal conditions. If instead you want *(A or B)* to be true just in case *A* or *B* is true but not both, you are a proponent of the 'exclusive' *or*, which is not commonly used in logic but in some cases seems to exist in English, although a closer investigation (in chapter 10) will show that in this case the logician is right.

There is still something missing in our system: We haven't associated a semantic rule with the quantifiers. Take a statement such as $\forall x\, x \geq 0$. If we are talking about (positive) integers, this statement is true because it says that every object (here, every integer) is greater than or equal to 0. What this means is that *for every object, if we call it x, the statement $x \geq 0$ is true*. And similarly, for $\exists x\, x > 0$, it means that for at least one object, which we will call x, the statement *$x > 0$ is true*. In other words, at least one integer is greater than 0, which is certainly the case. So we can complete our semantics with the boldfaced parts (a more precise version can be found in the endnotes).[6]

If *x* **is any variable, and** if *A* and *B* are formulas (which could contain the variable *x*),

*not A* is true just in case *A* is false.

*(A and B)* is true just in case *A* is true and *B* is true.

*(A or B)* is true just in case *A* is true or *B* is true or both.

∀*x A* **is true just in case for every object *x*, *A* is true.**

∃*x A* **is true just in case for at least one object *x*, *A* is true.**

Since we may have to use several variables, it is understood that they will work in the same way as *x*. So, for instance, ∃*y A* is true just in case for at least one object, which we will call *y*, *A* is true. As mentioned at the outset, *A* will typically contain the variable *y*. For instance, *A* could be *y* > *1*, in which case the entire formula, ∃*y y* > *1*, means that at least one object is greater than 1—surely true if the objects we are talking about are the integers.

This way of doing things really gives us the results we want. Take the reading of *some number follows every number* on which the sentence means, falsely, that *there is a number that follows every number*. I suggested that it corresponds to the logical statement ∃*y* ∀*x y* > *x*. To derive what it means, we can note that it is of the form ∃*y A*, assuming we call *A* the statement ∀*x y* > *x*. So, applying the semantic rule for ∃*y*, we derive that the sentence is true just in case for at least one object *y*, ∀*x y* > *x* is true. But we still need to interpret *that* statement. Applying the rule for ∀*x*, we derive the meaning that for every object *x*, *y* > *x* is true. Putting the two parts together, the final meaning is:

for at least one object y, for every object x, *y* > *x* is true

Or to put it differently:

for at least one object y, for every object x, y is greater than x

While none of this is stylistically elegant, it's rather explicit and unlikely to cause ambiguities among mathematicians. Mission accomplished.

## 7.4 CONCLUSION

We saw toward the beginning of this chapter that, when scientific precision is of the essence, it won't do to say that *some number follows every number*, as this is just ambiguous. The beauty of Predicate Logic is that its formulas are entirely unambiguous: one must thus make a decision between $\forall x \, \exists y \, y > x$ (true—every number is followed by another number) and $\exists y \, \forall x \, y > x$ (false—there is no greatest number!).

While the problem of ambiguities is particularly acute when we use English to discuss math or science, it is pervasive in everyday talk as well. *Someone lies to everyone* is as ambiguous as our number-related example: It can mean that everyone is lied to by someone or other; or that there is someone, maybe a compulsive liar, who lies to everyone. If we could 'speak' in Predicate Logic, we would have to make a choice between two unambiguous formulas:

$\forall x \, \exists y \, y$ lies to x (everyone is lied to by someone or other)

$\exists y \, \forall x \, y$ lies to x (there is someone who lies to everyone)

But of course we speak in English and other natural languages, not in Predicate Logic—and the precision of the latter only highlights the ambiguity of the former.

Why is language so perverse, then? One might be tempted to throw in the towel and conclude that language is just badly designed and ill-suited to a formal analysis. But the opposite is true: English and other natural languages can be seen as formal languages too. They are just far more complex than Predicate Logic. Chapters 8 and 9 explain why this is, and what ambiguities can tell us about how meaning is constructed.

# 8 LOGIC MACHINE II: ENGLISH AS A FORMAL LANGUAGE

We shall now encounter an extraordinary instance of scientific chutzpah in the history of linguistics: Nowadays, human language is routinely treated as a formal language, with a rule-governed syntax and semantics. Once we understand how it works, we will see that the ambiguities we noted at the outset are not at all signs of a mediocre design but rather by-products of the highly systematic nature of language. There are sometimes two meanings because there are two ways to form sentences in the syntax.

The proposal to treat human languages as formal languages is associated with the names of Noam Chomsky and Richard Montague, two pioneers of contemporary linguistics. Chomsky applied this idea to the form (the syntax) of sentences, and Montague applied it to their meaning (semantics). That was the "rather easy" project that Montague had the good sense to assign to himself (rather than to an undergraduate, as mentioned in chapter 7), although the project turned out to be devilishly complex, but extraordinarily insightful. Chomsky and Montague disagreed about several things, but a key point of agreement—that human language can be treated as a formal language—is a cornerstone of contemporary linguistics.

## 8.1 ENGLISH AS A FORMAL LANGUAGE: SYNTAX

Unlike Predicate Logic, which is so simple that it can be defined by just a few rules, human language is very complicated indeed, so the best I can do is give you some simple examples of how it works. In Predicate Logic, everything was either an elementary formula or a logical word such as *not, and, or, something, everything*. Human language has many more categories and thus a more complex syntax. To focus on the simplest elements, in the statement *Kennedy died*, we already have a noun and a verb; we'll call this *Verb₁*, with the subscript *1* because it is combined with a single noun. Here *died* only takes a subject. but in *Robin admired Kennedy*, the verb takes both a subject (namely, *Robin*) and an object (*Kennedy*); we'll call this *Verb₂*, with the subscript *2* because it combines with two nouns. There is a third category of verbs, like *learned, claimed, believed*, which take both a noun and a *that*-clause, as in: *Robin learned that Kennedy died* (we'll call these verbs *Verb_that*). The name of the game is to specify rules that make it possible to construct correct English sentences and no impossible ones.

We can begin to define a toy grammar of English with just three rules that involve some abbreviations (in the prose, I'll initially underline the first letters to help). It will be neither perfect nor complete, but it will give you an idea of how the real grammar of English works.

**Syntax**

S → NP VP

VP → V₁, V₂ NP, V_that CP

CP → that S

The first rule says that a sentence S is made of a noun phrase NP, followed by a verb phrase VP. The term 'verb phrase' is used here to refer to a phrase that is built from a verb. This category is useful to capture the intuition that *died, admired Kennedy*, and *learned that Kennedy died* all play a similar function—namely, that of providing information about the subject. For the moment, all our noun phrases will just be proper names, but later we'll investigate further nominal types. So our first rule, S → NP VP, should be read as follows: 'A sentence can be made of a noun phrase followed by a verb phrase.'

The second rule just expands on what a verb phrase VP is: It is formed from a *die*-type verb alone, or from an *admire*-type verb followed by a noun, or from a *learn*-type verb followed by a complementizer phrase, which is another name for a *that*-clause. Instead of listing three separate rules, which would be cumbersome, we state a single one with commas separating the possible outputs of the rule. Finally, the category complementizer phrase, abbreviated as *CP*, is just made of the word *that* called a 'complementizer', followed by a sentence, as specified by the third rule (so a CP is really just a *that*-clause!).

We still need to put some concrete words behind these abstract categories. So we specify which words belong to which categories: *Robin* is an example of a noun phrase (NP), *died* of a $V_1$, *admired* of a $V_2$, and *learned* of a $V_{that}$. There are many further words in each category, of course (don't worry that some verbs, like *smoke*, can be used with one or two noun phrases, as in *Sam smokes* and *Sam smokes cigarettes*, because this just means that this verb can belong to several categories, although for simplicity I just discuss *Sam smokes*). So, besides the syntax proper, we need a mental dictionary that puts words under these categories. That's called the lexicon (*lexicon* just means 'dictionary' in Greek and Latin).

**Lexicon**

NP $\rightarrow$ Robin, Sam, Kennedy, Alex . . .

$V_1$ $\rightarrow$ smoked, died, worked, . . .

$V_2$ $\rightarrow$ admired, hated, loved, met, . . .

$V_{that}$ $\rightarrow$ learned, claimed, believed, . . .

It's time to see how these rules produce actual sentences. Take *Kennedy died*. It can be formed by applying the first rule, S $\rightarrow$ NP VP, followed by one that says that VP $\rightarrow V_1$, followed by appropriate choices of words for the noun phrase and verb. For *Robin admired Kennedy*, we keep the beginning (namely, S $\rightarrow$ N VP), but choose the rule VP $\rightarrow V_2$ for the verb phrase. For *Robin learned that Kennedy died*, we choose instead the rule VP $\rightarrow V_{that}$ CP. Then we use the rule CP $\rightarrow$ that S, and instead of doing things from scratch, we use our first sentence all over again to replace *S* with *Kennedy died*.

Saying all this in words is cumbersome, so linguists use instead a tree representation. At the top, you have an *S*, and immediately underneath it, the symbols corresponding to the way in which we expanded *S*. So the preceding (convoluted) paragraph can be summarized in the three tree diagrams below. .

**Syntactic trees**

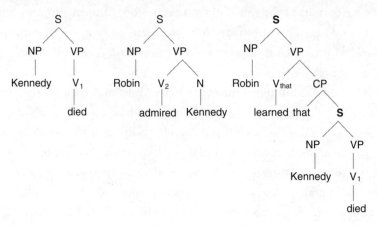

**Figure 8.1.1**

Our toy grammar is, of course, only a beginning, but it already has some nice properties. In particular, it puts words in the right order for English (rules would have to be tweaked for other languages). And it delineates possible from impossible sentences. For instance, our grammar produces (or 'generates,' as linguists say) the sentence *Kennedy died*, but not the impossible sentence *\*Died Kennedy*—linguists put a star in front of it to indicate that it's impossible and thus judged as being 'weird' by native speakers of English. Similarly, our grammar generates *Robin admired Kennedy* but not *\*Robin Kennedy admired*—all good.

But here I should pause to note that putting the words *Robin*, *admired*, *Kennedy* next to each other doesn't quite do justice to what the grammar does. Rather, the words *admired Kennedy* were put together to form a group, and then *Robin* was added to it. If we wanted to keep track of this information, we would need to write *[Robin [admired Kennedy]]*, and similarly, *[Robin [learned [that [Kennedy died]]]]*. Here I have put brackets around words that were produced as a unit in the diagrams above, and form subtrees of the entire tree. For instance, *admired Kennedy* was produced as a unit in the second tree by rewriting VP as $V_2$ N and then as *admired Kennedy*, so I put brackets around these two words: they correspond to a subtree within the larger tree that represents the entire sentence, namely this one:

```
        VP
       /  \
     V₂     N
      |     |
   admired Kennedy
```

Of course, unless you are a linguist, you won't go around writing or pronouncing square brackets. While they play the same role as the round brackets we used in Predicate Logic (as in *(A and B)*), the difference is that in human language they are not seen or pronounced. We will see that this lies at the source of many ambiguities.

We can easily enrich our toy grammar with *and* as well as *or*. *Not* comes with complications, so we'll use instead *it's not the case that*, which we'll treat as a unit; hence, *it's-not-the-case-that*. So our first rule can be enriched as follows, with the additions boldfaced:

S → NP VP, **S and S, S or S, it's-not-the-case-that S**

(English *not* is more complicated because it appears next to the verb, although its meaning behaves like that of *it's not the case that*.)

We will make one further enrichment to allow for certain adverbs, words like *here* and *yesterday*. They can be added to verb phrases, as in *Kennedy died here* or *Robin met Sam yesterday*. So the enriched version of our rule for verb phrases says that a VP can be expanded as a VP followed by an adverb, abbreviated as *Adv*. The enriched rule is the following, again with additions boldfaced, and we specify in a separate rule what kinds of objects qualify as adverbs.

VP → V₁,   V₂ NP,   V_{that} CP, **VP Adv**
**Adv → here, yesterday, once, . . .**

Putting all our rules together, we have the following mini-grammar (note that in the example below, I also treat *was murdered* as a unit, although it is made of two words).

**Syntax**
S    → NP VP, S and S, S or S, it's-not-the-case-that S
VP   → V₁, V₂ NP, V_{that} CP, VP Adv
CP   → that S

**Lexicon**

NP → Robin, Sam, Kennedy, Nixon, . . .

$V_1$ → smoked, died, worked, was-murdered, resigned, . . .

$V_2$ → admired, hated, loved, met, . . .

$V_{that}$ → learned, claimed, believed, . . .

Adv → here, once, yesterday, . . .

While this is a very simple-minded grammar, a key property of human language can be observed: It allows for the production of infinitely many sentences, just as was the case for Predicate Logic. The reason is that the grammar allows for some 'loops': cases in which the category $S$ is found under another $S$ in a syntactic tree. Whenever this happens, if you have built a structure with an S under another S (i.e., S . . . S), you can copy the S . . . S part another time to obtain a larger sentence (i.e., S . . . S . . . S), which is a property called 'recursion.' This is illustrated below in tree form:

**Recursion**

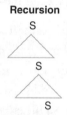

For instance, since there is an S under an S (both boldfaced in figure 8.1.1) in *[$_S$ **Robin learned that** [$_S$ Kennedy died]]* (where I've added a sub-scripted *S* to the groups that are of this category), you can also produce the sentence *[$_S$ Sam claimed that [$_S$ Robin learned that [$_S$ Kennedy died]]]*: We just duplicate, with different words, the structure corresponding to the boldfaced part. And of course we could keep going in this way, saying: *Alex believed that Sam claimed that Robin learned that Kennedy died.* Wordy for sure, but nonetheless a possible sentence in English, especially in comparison with random permutations of the words (e.g., *Believed Alex that . . .*).

Still, even in our toy grammar there isn't just one source of recursion. In a way that is directly reminiscent of our Predicate Logic, we can form *[S and S]*, but then we can also form *[S and [S and S]]* and also *[S and [S and [S and*

*S]]]*, and so on. In fact, our rules even predict that adverbials could in principle be iterated, as in *Robin smoked here*, *Robin smoked here once*, and *Robin smoked here once yesterday*. There are many sources of infinity in language.

## 8.2 ENGLISH AS A FORMAL LANGUAGE: SEMANTICS

What we just saw was the first bit of scientific chutzpah I announced, associated with Chomsky and his followers: the idea that the syntax of natural language can be treated as if it were a formal language. The second bit of scientific chutzpah is associated with Richard Montague, who proposed in 1970 that English could be treated as a formal language from the standpoint of its semantics as well. The development of this program didn't involve an undergraduate but several generations of researchers, and it is rather logic-heavy, but I'll give simple examples of how this goes. The gist of it is that the methods developed for Predicate Logic can be adapted to English grammar.

To illustrate, let's take a sample of rules developed above:

**Syntax**
S → NP VP, S and S, S or S, it's-not-the-case-that S
VP → $V_1$
**Lexicon**
N → Robin, Sam, Kennedy, Nixon, . . .
$V_1$ → smoked, died, worked, was-murdered, resigned, . . .

The key insight was that whenever some words are put together by a syntactic rule, we can associate truth conditions to them.

To begin with, we need to associate meanings with words. Intuitively enough, we will take the meaning (or 'denotation') of the noun *Nixon* to be the person Richard Nixon, and the meaning of *resigned* to be the set of people who resigned. To distinguish words from their denotations, we will use boldfacing, thus writing **Nixon** as standing for the person Nixon, **resigned** as standing for the set of people who resigned. This allows us to take care of the first rule, S → NP VP. Here, our only type of verb phrase involves *die*-type verbs, so all the relevant groups of words will have the form *[NP $V_1$]*, and it's clear that the rule should just specify that *[NP $V_1$]* is true just in case

**NP**, the person denoted by *NP*, belongs to the set **V₁**: *Nixon resigned* is true just in case **Nixon** belongs to **resigned**—or in other words, just in case the person Nixon is one of the people who resigned.

*[NP V₁]* is true just in case **NP** belongs to **V₁**.

(Alright, this is a simplification. As I argued in chapter 4, verbs are to events as nouns are to objects, and thus the meaning of a verb should be taken to be a set of events. But I am simplifying things in order to give you an idea of how the initial treatments of English as a formal language could work; contemporary treatments are more complex, and yield a meaning akin to: Nixon took part in one of the events of resigning.)

Note that I've put brackets around *[NP V₁]* because we want to associate meanings to the output of syntactic rules. It's not that brackets are part of English; rather, they are our way of keeping track of how the words were put together, and this matters to meaning—a point to which I will return below.

For the groups of words that include *and*, *or*, and *it's-not-the-case-that*, we can just recycle what we did for Predicate Logic. So you've already seen versions of these rules:

> *[it's-not-the-case-that S]* is true just in case *S* is false.
> *[S₁ and S₂]* is true just in case *S₁* is true and *S₂* is true.
> *[S₁ or S₂]* is true just in case *S₁* is true or *S₂* is true or both.

Once we have these rules, it's easy to compute mechanically the conditions under which arbitrarily complex sentences are true. Take the conjunction *Kennedy was murdered and Nixon resigned*. It has the structure *[S₁ and S₂]*, with *S₁* = *[Kennedy was-murdered]* and *S₂* = *[Nixon resigned]*. So our mental 'logic machine' can reason as follows (needless to say, this is an unconscious computation): *[S₁ and S₂]* is true just in case *S₁* is true and *S₂* is true. *S₁* = *[Kennedy was-murdered]* is true just in case Kennedy belongs to the set of people who were murdered. *S₂* = *[Nixon resigned]* is true just in case Nixon belongs to the set of people who resigned. Putting everything together, then, the entire sentence *[S₁ and S₂]* is true just in case Kennedy belongs to the set of people who were murdered and Nixon belongs to the set of people who resigned. Definitely true, and simple enough in this case.

But we could use the same simple rules to compute the meaning of far more complex sentences just as mechanically.

## 8.3 EXPLAINING STRUCTURAL AMBIGUITIES

Let's now modify our example slightly, swapping *Nixon* and *Kennedy* so that we get *Nixon was murdered and Kennedy resigned.* The result is of course false. So, by adding a negation, we obtain a true sentence:

It's not the case that Nixon was murdered and Kennedy resigned.

But wait—while this sentence is true on one reading, it is false on another. If you put a long pause after *murdered*, the negative expression just applies to the first part (namely, to *Nixon was murdered*), and since the second part is false, the entire sentence is false as well:

It's not the case that Nixon was murdered, and Kennedy resigned.

By contrast, if you understand the negative expression as applying to the conjunction we started out with, the result is true.

This is a case of structural ambiguity, which has nothing to do with the alleged vagueness of language. Rather, the ambiguity results from the fact that brackets are usually not pronounced (though we can sometimes use pauses to signal how words are grouped, thus producing some of the effects of brackets). In fact, this example is analogous to the ambiguity of the purely logical examples we discussed at the outset:

not 3 = 5 and 3 > 5

Brackets eliminate the ambiguity when we rewrite this either as *(not 3 = 5 and 3 > 5)* (where *not* just applies to 3 = 5—false!), or as *not (3 = 5 and 3 > 5)* (true!). But in human language, we don't really have the luxury of pronouncing brackets (although long pauses can help). Once this fact is taken into account, the ambiguity of our sentence makes perfects sense. The key is that there are two distinct ways of putting the sentence together.

One possibility is to first produce the conjunction *Nixon was murdered and Kennedy resigned*, and then apply a negation to it, producing a sentence with a structure of the form *[it's-not-the-case-that [S₁ and S₂]]*:

[it's-not-the-case-that [Nixon was-murdered and Kennedy resigned]]

Our semantic rules for negation and conjunction (at the end of section 8.2) tell us exactly how to interpret this: The entire sentence is true just in case *[Nixon was-murdered and Kennedy resigned]* is false—which is definitely the case. So on this reading, the entire sentence is true (when you add a long pause after *it's not the case that*, you help bring out the unity of *[Nixon was-murdered and Kennedy resigned]*, but without having to pronounce brackets).

But our initial sentence can also be put together in a different way, by first forming the negation of *Nixon was-murdered* and then using this structure, of the form *[it's-not-the-case-that $S_1$]*, to form a more complex sentence *[[it's-not-the-case-that $S_1$] and $S_2$]* (a long pause before *and* might help bring out this reading):

[[it's-not-the-case-that Nixon was-murdered] and Kennedy resigned]

Here, too, our rules tell us exactly how to compute the truth conditions: *[[it's-not-the-case-that $S_1$] and $S_2$]* is true just in case *[it's-not-the-case-that $S_1$]* is true, and $S_2$ is also true. But here $S_2$ is *Kennedy resigned*, a false sentence, so there is no way the entire sentence could be true.

While this example has a logical feel to it, many other cases of structural ambiguity arise in everyday talk. Take, for instance, *Robin learned that Kennedy died yesterday*. In the present context, many years after Kennedy's assassination, *yesterday* can't specify the time of the murder but only the time of the learning. But if the sentence had been uttered a day after the assassination, one would have gotten the other reading, that on which the murder rather than the learning took place 'yesterday.'

Why does this sentence allow for such different readings? This can be understood once we recall that meaning depends on the way words are put together, and that brackets are not pronounced. The key is that we can expand a verb phrase VP with an adverb, as we specified in section 8.1, in rules that are repeated below:

VP   →   **VP Adv**

**Adv**   →   here, once, yesterday, . . .

So we can apply this rule to the rightmost verb phrase, forming a group *[died yesterday]* in which *yesterday* provides further information about the murder. Or we can start from a group *[learned that Kennedy died]* and add the adverb to that group, with the result that *yesterday* provides information about the event in which it was learned that Kennedy died. Thus, the two meanings arise from two different ways of putting words together, as represented in the trees below.

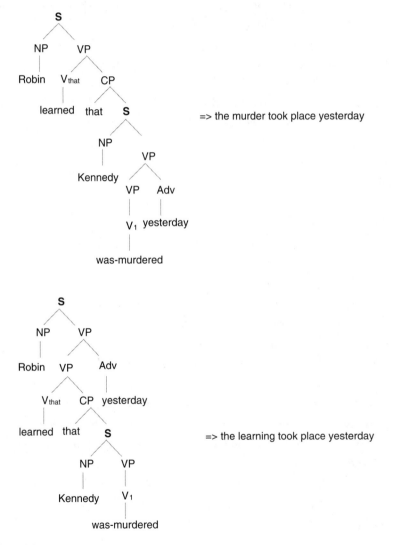

=> the murder took place yesterday

=> the learning took place yesterday

**Figure 8.3.1**
*Two ways to add an adverb*

(As hinted above, when linguists give semantic rules that correspond to these structures, they usually treat verbs as denoting sets of events, and make use of the analysis of adverbs briefly sketched in chapter 4, section 4.6. But this would take us too far afield.)

Here, too, we can to some extent use pauses to indicate what the intended grouping is. If we put a big break after *learned* and pronounce the rest as a unit, this will help bring out the reading on which the murder took place yesterday. The reason: In the first tree above (in figure 8.3.1), the words *that Kennedy was murdered yesterday* form a natural unit that corresponds to a subtree encoding how these words were put together. By adding a long pause before these words, we can highlight that they form a natural unit. In the second tree, these words don't form a natural unit: In order to find a subtree that has all these words, we need to also include *learned*. So the long pause after *learned* discourages this reading. (If you wish to bring out the second structure, maybe you can do so by pronouncing *learned that Kennedy was murdered*, followed by a long pause, followed by *yesterday*.)

In sum, meaning doesn't just depend on strings of words; it also depends on their structure or, to say it differently, on the way the words are put together. A further fact highlights the importance of this idea. Some words can be moved to the beginning of the sentence, sometimes with small adjustments in the process. So, from *I admire Kennedy*, you can form *Kennedy, I admire _* (I use _ to mark the original position of the moved element). Here a proper name is moved to the beginning of the sentence, but other groups of words can be moved as well. For instance, you can say, *Learn that Kennedy was murdered, Robin did _*. In this case, the entire verb phrase *learn that Kennedy was murdered* is moved to the beginning of the sentence without its tense, which remains in the original position (hence the insertion of the past tense auxiliary *did*). Similarly, you can say something like, *That Kennedy was murdered, Robin (just) learned _*. Here we moved a smaller group to the beginning of the sentence. But you cannot do this with sequences of words that do not form natural units. So, for instance, it won't do to say: *\*That Kennedy, Robin learned _ was murdered*. The reason is that there is no subtree that just contains *that Kennedy*: the smallest subtree that contains these words also contains *was murdered*.

These facts make it possible to probe further the reality of the grouping principles we posited. In the first tree above (in figure 8.3.1) but not in the second, *that Kennedy was murdered yesterday* forms a natural unit. So we predict that when we move these words to the beginning of the sentence, it stops being ambiguous. Why? Because only in the first structure is there a subtree (i.e., a natural unit) corresponding to *that Kennedy was murdered yesterday*. And this is indeed what we find: the following sentence only has the meaning on which the murder took place yesterday.

That Kennedy was murdered yesterday, Robin (just) learned _.

By contrast, if you move to the beginning of the sentence the group *learn that Kennedy was murdered* but now without the word *yesterday*, the structure has to be the second one rather than the first one, because the first one doesn't have a subtree corresponding to the words displaced. Here, too, this is what we find: the following sentence only has the reading (corresponding to the second structure) on which the learning happened yesterday.

Learn that Kennedy was murdered, Robin did __ yesterday.

And for the same reason, the following sentence is unambiguous as well (the learning took place yesterday) because *that Kennedy was murdered* forms a subtree in the second tree structure in figure 8.3.1 above, but not in the first.

That Kennedy was murdered, Robin learned __ yesterday.

Although brackets are not pronounced, the structure they encode makes itself felt in all sorts of indirect ways—not just as pauses, but in ambiguities, word movement, and also subtle interactions between ambiguities and word movement.

## 8.4   USING STRUCTURAL AMBIGUITIES

While structural ambiguities tell us something deep about how language works, they are also an endless source of amusement when newspaper copy editors let phrases with unintended meanings slide by. Linguists have made a specialty of collecting those for the edification of their students, and some are precisely of the type we discussed above. When a newspaper headline read *Killer sentenced to die for second time in 10 years,*[1] the words *for second time in 10 years* were intended to provide information about the sentencing, with the structure below:

[Killer [[sentenced to die] [for second time in 10 years]]]

But the title can be read with a different bracketing, where *for second time in 10 years* is attached to *die*, with the implication that the killer already died once and is sentenced to die another time:

[Killer sentenced to [die [for second time in 10 years]]]

Since newspapers don't print brackets any more than we pronounce them, ambiguities of structure can yield rather undesirable semantic ambiguities.

It is not too hard to see that how the English version of Socrates's recommendation ("Avoid excess in everything," mentioned at the beginning of chapter 7) could lend itself to a structural ambiguity as well. The reading I preferred was one on which *excess in everything* forms a natural unit and describes situations to be avoided; on this optimistic view, excess in *some* things is still allowed:

[You should [avoid [excess in everything]]]

The intended meaning was different—namely, that one should, in everything, avoid excess—the latter two words formed a natural unit:

[You should [[avoid excess] [in everything]]]

Similarly, the Groucho Marx joke mentioned at the beginning of chapter 7 illustrates a structural ambiguity as well:

One morning I shot an elephant in my pajamas. How he got into my pajamas, I don't know.

Here the point is that *in my pajamas*, just like *for second time in 10 years*, can be attached to different groups of words. The natural reading is that it tells you something about the action of shooting an elephant (the shooter was in his pajamas while doing so).

[I [[shot an elephant] [in my pajamas]]]

Groucho's meaning, however, is different, because *in my pajamas* provides further information about the elephant, and thus the intended structure is this one:

[I [shot an [[elephant] [in my pajamas]]]]

The same trick has been used in numerous other jokes, such as this one appearing on social media and featuring a picture of a stern dog owner telling her pet:[2]

The neighbor tells me you are chasing people on a bicycle.

To which the dog replies, unfazed:

He is lying. I don't even have a bicycle!

This is in a way the mirror image of the Groucho Marx joke. The pet owner intends a meaning on which *on a bicycle* tells you something about the dog's victims, with the following structure (*people on a bicycle* forms a natural unit):

. . . [you [are chasing [[people] [on a bicycle]]]]

But the dog cleverly interprets the sentence in a different way. For the dog, *on a bicycle* provides further information about the chasing, with the following structure:

. . . [you [[are chasing people] [on a bicycle]]]

This allows the dog to respond, with undeniable veracity, that he never did such a thing. Alas, with the brackets added, any hint of a joke disappears . . .


## 8.5  CONCLUSION

Structural ambiguities make an important point: Meaning is computed through structure. The main difference between human language and formal languages is not that human language doesn't have a precise syntax or a precise semantics. Rather, it is that it doesn't always wear its structure on its sleeve, so to speak. Standard formal languages were designed with brackets precisely to avoid the kind of structural ambiguities that are pervasive in human language. But once the structures of sentences are properly understood, we realize that the semantics that was developed for formal languages can be applied to human languages as well. In brief, it pays off to treat human language as a formal language. This is not to say that human language is identical to the very simple formal languages we started out with—human language is different and more expressive along several dimensions, as we will see in chapter 9.

# 9 LOGIC MACHINE III: THE EXPRESSIVE POWER OF HUMAN LANGUAGE

*On average, 2.3 people are infected by each infected person.* In March 2020, in various parts of the globe, this and related statements were on everyone's mind as they epitomized the exponential growth of contaminations by the coronavirus. This particular version referred to a model discussed in the *New York Times,*[1] but less precise statements were common as well: *Almost three new people will be infected by every sick person.* This meant, alas, that for every sick person, a *different* three individuals would be infected. Linguistically, however, this should give us pause, because in structurally analogous sentences a different meaning is obtained. For example: *Three antiviral drugs will be used by every hospital.* Here the more plausible reading is that the *same* three antiviral drugs will be used by every hospital. Sometimes common sense doesn't quite suffice to lift the ambiguity. *Someone loves everyone* can mean that everyone is loved by someone or other (possibly the more natural reading), but the sentence can also mean that there is a given person (one with unbounded love) who loves everybody. And yet English can convey these two very different messages in the same way.

We saw in chapter 8 that structural ambiguities are not a result of the unruly nature of human language, but rather follow from a key insight: Meaning is determined by structure. Because there are no brackets to tell you what the structure is, when you hear or read a sentence that could have been produced in two ways by the rules of grammar, several readings can arise. Still, some of the apparent flaws of language for scientific purposes are not yet covered by this observation. *Someone loves everyone* doesn't have the same consequences whether this is understood to mean that everyone is loved by someone or other, or that there is a given person (with unbounded love) who loves everybody. Predicate Logic, which was designed to avoid such ambiguities, represents these two meanings without ambiguity, as we saw in chapter 7. The more natural reading is that for every person x, for some person y, y loves x, and this can be represented as follows:

$$\forall x \; \exists y \; y \text{ loves } x$$

The 'unbounded love' reading is that for some person y, for every person x, y loves x:

$$\exists y \; \forall x \; y \text{ loves } x$$

In fact, one of the motivations I gave for using Predicate Logic in science was precisely to avoid these ambiguities. *Some integer follows every integer* can be understood in two entirely different ways, but the logical formulas ($\forall x \; \exists y$ y > x versus $\exists y \; \forall x$ y > x) are appropriately unambiguous.

There are numerous further cases in which language seems to be ambiguous in this way, and this has been a rich source of jokes across cultures. One goes like this:[2]

A man is robbed every five minutes in Boston. Poor guy.

The first sentence would normally be understood to mean that every five minutes, some man or other is robbed in Boston. But the addition of the second sentence makes it clear that the speaker understood this as meaning instead that one and the same person is robbed every five minutes.

This is the same kind of ambiguity we saw in the sentence *Someone loves everyone* (or *some integer follows every integer*), but our understanding of structural ambiguities gained in chapter 8 won't help in these cases. *Someone loves everyone* would seem to have the same structure as *Robin loves Sam*, and that sentence doesn't seem ambiguous. So it's unlikely that just grouping the words in the sentence differently will be of much help.

Why does English perversely choose to express in the same way meanings that are so different? Surprisingly, it turns out that the sentence *Someone loves everyone* (and others like it) has two abstract syntactic representations that correspond rather closely to those we would find in Predicate Logic. In one representation, *someone* is before *everyone*, and in the other, it's the other way around. Of course, what gets pronounced in both cases is just *Someone loves everyone*, so we must posit that people don't just group words in ways that are not encoded in the pronunciation (as was the case with structural ambiguities). Sometimes, they mentally move words around!

Now you may think that linguists are singularly lacking in imagination to posit that human language looks so much like Predicate Logic. This isn't an absurd criticism—some excellent linguists make it, too! But we will see that aping Predicate Logic isn't the motivation: there are completely independent reasons for coming to this thought-provoking conclusion.

Still, there are numerous differences between Predicate Logic and the logic of human language, and I will start this chapter with some of the most salient ones.

## 9.1 ENGLISH IS MORE EXPRESSIVE THAN PREDICATE LOGIC

While Predicate Logic suffices to formalize mathematics and science, there is a precise sense, studied by logicians, in which English is a more expressive language. Not at all because it is more emotional, or more human, or more vague—or at least that's not what I have in mind here, since my point is that English can be studied as a formal language. Rather, viewed in this way, English makes it possible to define truth conditions that just cannot be defined in Predicate Logic. I won't go through the detailed arguments, which require quite a bit of math, but I'll try to sketch the main idea.

The first difference is that Predicate Logic as defined in chapter 7 solely talks about individual objects by way of *something* and *everything*. Of course, English has close counterparts of these. But English can also talk about groups of objects by way of plurals, as we saw in earlier chapters. Sometimes the use of plurals doesn't add anything that couldn't be paraphrased without them. *Some people smoke*, for example, could be translated in Predicate Logic into something like *Some person smokes and some other person smokes*. But in other cases, the plural is essential, and logicians can prove that the meanings you can define with them genuinely go beyond what you could express without them. *Some scientists only cite one another,* for instance, makes essential use of plurals.[3] It claims that there is a group of scientists (without specifying its size) such that its members only cite members of the group—and this is not something that can be expressed in Predicate Logic. The intuitive reason human language is more expressive than Predicate Logic in this case is that the latter can only talk about individual objects whereas plurals make it possible to talk about *groups* of objects.

Of course, Predicate Logic has variables (the little $x$'s and $y$'s we found in some of our formulas), but as I argued in chapter 2, language has counterparts of these, too. One of the functions of pronouns, including pointing signs in sign language, is to make it possible to refer back to a quantifier, as in:

Every human being knows that he/she will die.

In logician's talk, this has a meaning akin to: *For every x that is a human being, x knows that x will die,* and we could make the formula even more explicit if we used the Predicate Logic we defined before. Still, we already discussed a second way in which human language goes beyond Predicate Logic, as it has variables (and also quantifiers) that specifically talk about situations rather than just objects (as I argued in chapter 5, tense and mood can play the role of situation-denoting pronouns). This is a sizable difference, as it makes it possible to talk about times and possibilities.

A third and striking difference is that the quantifiers of natural language go beyond those of Predicate Logic. In some cases, the difference is one of convenience, in the sense that we could find paraphrases in Predicate Logic of some of the quantifiers we find in language. For instance, besides *everything* and *something,* we obviously have the quantifier *nothing.* And although it's not a standard part of Predicate Logic, we can paraphrase it with some of the 'official' quantifiers: *I own nothing* can thus be paraphrased, with no elegance whatsoever, as *It's not the case that I own something.* Similarly, *I own at least two things* can be paraphrased, even less elegantly, as *There is something I own, and there is something else I own.* When you see the paraphrases, you immediately understand why human language makes use of shorter expressions to convey these notions!

In other cases, there is just no paraphrase at all that will do. The existence of these cases is of some interest, as it highlights the expressive power of human language. One case in point is the quantifier *most*. If I say that *I own most things*, there is no paraphrase with *some* and *every* (as well as negation, conjunction, disjunction) that will have the same truth conditions. Of course if there are just three things in the universe, saying that *I own most things* just amounts to saying that *I own at least two things*—and we saw that *this* can be paraphrased with the 'official' quantifiers of Predicate Logic. But in general, we don't know how many things there are in the universe, and so we would need a paraphrase that will work in all conceivable cases; this paraphrase doesn't exist within Predicate Logic. *Most things* isn't the only case in point. Other quantifiers that pertain to proportions (*one-third of the things, three-quarters of the things*, etc.) behave in the same way.

There is yet another respect in which natural language quantifiers differ from those of Predicate Logic: They are restricted by noun phrases. In fact, you might have been startled that I chose to talk about *everything* and *most things* in the preceding paragraph. We are usually interested in *which kinds* of things we are counting: *I know every senator. I have met most professors.* Here, too, the difference between Predicate Logic and human language is sometimes a matter of elegance. *I own a painting* can be paraphrased with the 'official' quantifiers of Predicate Logic as *for some x, x is a painting and I own x*. Not poetic for sure, but accurate enough. In other cases, however, the addition of restrictions really makes a difference. This is the case for *most stars*, which cannot be defined from *most things* combined with expressions like *x is a star*. For instance, it won't do to paraphrase the sentence *Most stars are bright* as:

For most x, x is a star and x is bright.

This means something completely different—namely, most things x are bright stars. And while I don't know whether *most stars are bright*, it can't be that *most x's are bright stars*: After all, there are lots and lots of atoms in the world, and they are not bright stars. In fact, each star is made of numerous atoms, which certainly aren't bright stars. So this particular paraphrase (*for most x, x is a star and x is bright*) won't do the job. Of course, my failure to find a paraphrase might just suggest that I wasn't clever enough; logicians tell us that something deeper is going on and that no paraphrase will do.[4]

## 9.2 EXTENDING THE LOGICAL APPROACH TO ENGLISH

If English has resources that go beyond Predicate Logic, should we conclude that logical methods are hopeless to analyze the meaning of real sentences? Not at all. We just need to adapt them in appropriate ways.

The first order of business is to ensure that our syntax can produce expressions like *every senator, some politician, most stars*. This isn't too difficult to achieve. These are all expressions that play the same grammatical role as proper names, and they belong to the larger category of noun phrases. *Every, some, most* are called determiners, or *D* for short, and *senator, politician, star* are of course nouns, or *N* for short. All we need, then, is to expand our earlier rule that said that a noun phrase (NP) is made of a proper name; we'll now add that it can also be made of a determiner *D* followed by a noun *N*, and voilà—we can mechanically produce statements such as *every senator resigned*, and *some politician admired Kennedy*, and so on. The proper names of our earlier examples will sometimes be replaced with more complex noun phrases.

NP → Robin, Sam, Kennedy, . . .
NP → D N
D   → every, some, most, . . .
N   → senator, politician, star, . . .

(If you are worried that our rules also produce statements like *most senator resigned*, with the final *s* missing on *senators*, you are entirely right: for simplicity, I blithely disregard this fact in the present discussion.)

The next step is to explain how these new expressions are interpreted. Here we will build on an insight developed in chapter 2 with the help of sign language data: Language has counterparts of the variables *x* and *y* of logic. These variables are often visible in sign language, and they are always invisible in English (as pronouns are ambiguous), but their effects can be felt nonetheless. So we'll take *every senator resigned* to be processed by the human mind as something like *[every senator]ₓ x resigned*. Once we have made this move, the sentence isn't too different from the logical formulas we discussed before, such as $\forall x \, x > 0$. All we need to do is adapt this logical rule, copied below, to the linguistic case.

$\forall x \, A$ is true just in case for every object $x$, $A$ is true.
$\exists x \, A$ is true just in case for at least one object $x$, $A$ is true.

The meaning we should get is that for every object (!) x which is a senator, *x resigned* is true. To deal with *[some senator]ₓ x resigned*, we just replace *every object* with *some object*. For some object x which is a senator, *x resigned* is true. These new rules will do the trick:

*[Every N]ₓ VP* is true just in case for every object x which is an *N*, *VP* is true.
*[Some N]ₓ VP* is true just in case for at least one object x which is an *N*, *VP* is true.
*[Most N]ₓ VP* is true just in case for more than half of the objects x which are *Ns*, *VP* is true.

Strikingly, this approach seamlessly extends to *most*. We can state a very similar-looking rule that will give the right meaning for *most senators resigned*. We get the result that it is true just in case for most objects x that are senators, *x resigned* is true—convoluted, but correct enough.

The upshot is that the program of treating English (and other human languages) as a formal language needn't be adversely affected by the observation that English has greater expressive power than Predicate Logic. Rather, we adapt and extend to English the methods that are traditionally used for Predicate Logic, and we discover in the process that human language (be it spoken or signed) is endowed with exquisitely detailed and expressive logical resources, ones that go beyond Predicate Logic.

### 9.3 LOGICAL FORM IN HUNGARIAN

We saw at the outset that English occasionally gives rise to some unfortunate ambiguities. *Someone loves everyone* can be interpreted in two very different ways. In logic, the problem is solved by using unambiguous formulas. *Some integer follows every integer* is as ambiguous as *Someone loves everyone*. It can wrongly claim that there is some number that follows every number, or it can rightly claim that every number is followed by some number or other. But Predicate Logic can only express unambiguous meanings. If you wish to express the statement that is false, you will use the following formula:

$\exists x\, \forall y\, x > y$
('there is a number that's greater than every number')

If you want to express the statement that is true, you will reverse the order of the quantifiers and use this formula instead:

$\forall y\, \exists x\, x > y$
('for every number, there's a number that's greater than it')

Surprisingly, natural language is sometimes much more similar to Predicate Logic than we might have thought. In some languages, such as Hungarian, the quantifiers sometimes appear roughly in the position that they would have if people were "speaking in Predicate Logic" (I say "sometimes" because I am just trying to give you a taste for rules that are in fact more complex). In English, if you say that *many people called every senator*, this is ambiguous: It could be that there is a group of many people who each called every senator, or it could be that for every senator, a (possibly different) large group called him or her. But in Hungarian, structure helps disambiguate. Turning from *call* to *love*, the following sentence only has the first kind of reading: There is one group of many men who each love everyone. It's important to note that in Hungarian, *sok ember*, meaning *many men*, is a subject form, whereas *mindenkit*, meaning *everyone*, is an object form—this is the kind of distinction we have in English with *he* versus *him*. So, despite a relatively free word order, it's clear that the men are doing the loving, so to speak.[5]

Sok     ember    mindenkit    szeret.
many    man      everyone     loves
(meaning: there are many men who love everyone)

Both the word order and the meaning are reminiscent of what we would find, especially if we formalize the Hungarian sentence like this:

[many men]$_x$ everyone$_y$ x loves y

Change the word order, however, and the meaning changes as well. The following sentence only has a version of the second reading, on which for everyone, a (possibly different) large group of men loves him or her (but as before, the men are doing the loving):

Mindenkit    sok    ember    szeret.
everyone    many    man    loves
(meaning: for everyone, there are many men who love him/her)

Here, too, the word order and meaning come close to a logic-like representation, which can be formalized like this:

everyone$_y$ [many men]$_x$ x loves y

The upshot is that *some* human languages can disambiguate the readings of quantifiers in something like the way Predicate Logic does. A syntactic representation in which the quantifiers appear in the position in which they are interpreted is often called a "Logical Form," and linguists sometimes say that Hungarian tends to "wear its Logical Form on its sleeve."

## 9.4  LOGICAL FORM IN ENGLISH

But if some languages are logically transparent in this way, why isn't English one of them? When one digs deeper, English turns out to resemble Hungarian, and thus Predicate Logic, but on a more abstract level: on some theories, speakers mentally move around certain expressions in order to obtain certain meanings, but this operation is neither heard nor seen.

While we already posited that sign language has visible indices that are invisible in English, the claim that there can be invisible word orders is admittedly a hard pill to swallow. But when we take a more global view of the patterns found in language, this hypothesis won't be as surprising as it initially looks.

The first thing to note is that it is sometimes possible to move words around. We already saw examples of precisely this type in chapter 8. Starting from the sentence *I will invite Sam*, I may decide to emphasize that Sam is the main topic, and to say:

Here it makes much intuitive sense to think that the word *Sam* has been moved from its usual position (which we mark as __ following the verb) to the beginning of the sentence. But this movement turns out to be very constrained. For instance, from *I will invite Robin and Sam*, you might think that I can say:

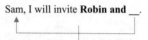

But the result is . . . incomprehensible. The movement seems to be blocked, hence the crossed line I have put on this example. It doesn't matter whether the movement originates in the second conjunct, as above, or in the first. The following attempt at movement is just as incomprehensible as the first one:

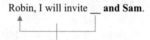

And things are no better if you replace *and* with *or*:

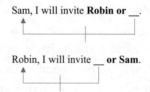

To describe these data, linguists came up with an evocative name. They say that some constructions, like conjunctions . . . *and* . . . and disjunctions

. . . *or* . . . are *islands to movement.* That is, expressions cannot be moved out of these constructions (I guess the idea was that words can't swim). The islands have been boldfaced in the four examples above: they are created by the conjunction and the disjunction.

Now this could all be a nice curiosity, but it turns out that movement is very common in English. For instance, to ask a question corresponding to the answer *I like Sam*, you could say:

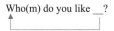

Here linguists have often posited that *who(m)* starts out as the object of *like* (as was briefly mentioned in section 3.5). First, this has the advantage of explaining why it can take the object form *whom* rather than *who*. Second, it is possible to say *You like who(m)?*—for instance, in case one hasn't heard a certain word when the speaker said *I like.* . . . Third, there are languages such as Japanese or Chinese in which the interrogative word always stays in its original position and others, such as French, where the movement is optional.

Mandarin Chinese:

Nǐ    xǐhuān   sheí?
you   like     who

French:

Tu    aimes    qui?
you   like     who

Qui   tu       aimes?
who   you      like

It's rather natural to think that English just represents the case in which the movement is obligatory. But if you add a further interrogative expression and thus make sure that the beginning of the sentence is somehow already 'too crowded,' you can form a perfectly natural (if complex) question in which *whom* does appear after *like*:

Who likes whom?

But what nails the case is that the same islands we saw in our initial examples apply to interrogative sentences as well. Take the following sentence:

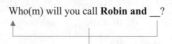

It's clear what it ought to mean: *Which individual x is such that you will call Robin and x?* But it's incomprehensible: movement is blocked by a syntactic island—namely, the conjunction—just as in the incomprehensible sentence *Sam, I will invite Robin and _.*

You'll get the same result if you replace *and* with *or*:

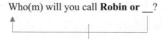

This ought to mean: *Which individual x is such that you will call Robin or x?* But once again the movement is blocked by a syntactic island. (You'll reach similar conclusions if you try to have the movement originate from the first element rather than from the second, be it in a conjunction or disjunction.)

With these observations in mind, we can go back to the case of quantifiers in English. What if they too could move to the beginning of the sentence but covertly (i.e., only in the minds of the speaker and addressee)? This would make English rather similar to Hungarian with respect to quantifier movement, just . . . in an invisible way! This was, after all, the way we already analyzed the relation between English and ASL in chapter 2: both have variables on pronouns, but ASL has them in a visible way whereas they must be inferred indirectly in English.

The view that there is invisible movement of the quantifiers in English makes a prediction: This movement should be disrupted by syntactic islands. And this seems to be correct. Let's for instance start from the sentence: *Some voter called every senator.* We will have two representations for it, reminiscent of Predicate Logic:

[some voter]$_x$ [every senator]$_y$ x called y

[every senator]$_y$ [some voter]$_x$ x called y

The first representation states that there is a voter (maybe an extraordinarily energetic activist) who called every senator. The second representation says, more boringly, that for every senator, there is at least one voter that called him or her.

But when the movement of *every senator* is blocked by an island, the sentence should become unambiguous. This is what we find. Take the sentence *Some voter called Kamala Harris and every senator*. It can only mean that *for some voter x* (a very energetic one), *x called Kamala Harris and every senator*. It cannot usually mean that *for every senator y, there is at least one voter x that called Kamala Harris and y* (with possibly different voters calling different senators). The reason is that the second reading would require that *every senator* move out of an island in order to appear to the left of *some voter*.

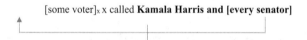

Things are no different if the syntactic island involves a disjunction rather than a conjunction. Take, for instance, the sentence *Some voter will call the White House or every senator*. It can only mean that *for some voter x, x will call the White House or every senator* (hence, if x doesn't call the White House, x has to call every senator!). It cannot mean, more boringly, that *for every senator y, there is at least one voter x that will call the White House or y*. This too can be explained by the fact that the island blocks the movement:

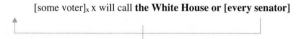

In sum, it's not just Hungarian that looks like Predicate Logic. English does too, but on a more abstract level of representation. And it's not that we arbitrarily decided, out of lack of imagination, that English had to look like

Predicate Logic. Rather, we were led to this conclusion by island constraints: They block both the overt movement of *who* and the covert movement of quantifiers. In the end, English looks considerably more logical than it did on initial inspection.

With some complications, the joke I mentioned at the beginning of this chapter works in the same way as *some voter called every senator*. The sentence was: *A man is robbed every five minutes*. It is naturally understood like this, with a different victim every five minutes:

[every five minutes] [a man] is robbed

But adding *Poor guy!* suggests that the other reading was intended, that one and the same man is robbed every five minutes:

[a man] [every five minutes] is robbed

Here, too, adding a semantic analysis is, unfortunately, a sure way to kill the joke.

## 9.5 THE DYNAMIC LOGIC OF LANGUAGE

As we saw with examples from spoken and from signed languages, variables lie at the heart of the logical engine of language. But they have something more to teach us: Language is only partly similar to Predicate Logic in its use of variables. Let me start with the similarities and then point out some differences.

We saw above how the meaning of *every senator resigned* can be computed: We add to the sentence some variables, which are invisible in English but can often be made visible in sign language, and we obtain:

[Every senator]$_x$ x resigned

The meaning, analyzed as before in terms of truth conditions, is that for every object x which is a senator, *x resigned* is true. This can easily be extended to more sophisticated cases, such as *every senator admires himself*. In ASL, *every senator* can introduce a locus x, and *himself* can point toward that locus. This wouldn't be a simple pointing (with the index ☞) because, in ASL as in English, when a pronoun is 'too close' to its antecedent, one must use a reflexive pronoun, realized in ASL with a pointing thumb 👍. So it's natural to take the Logical Form of this sentence to be something like the following:

[Every senator]$_x$ x admires himself$_x$

Here $x$ doesn't refer to anybody in particular, which is in fact the reason it is called a variable. But the rule we already applied before derives the appropriate meaning:

for every object x which is a senator, *x admires himself$_x$* is true

The same type of analysis could easily be applied to more complex examples, such as *Every senator thinks the president likes him*. Here *him* depends on *every senator*, and it's far enough from it that it takes the form of a normal pronoun rather than of a reflexive; otherwise, things work as in the sentence *Every senator admires himself*.

In these examples, $x$ is used as a kind of temporary name, one that only 'lives' during the evaluation of a sentence. The result is somewhat odd if you try to say

Every senator came. He gave a speech.

This much is expected given the analysis we developed: *He* has to be dependent on *every senator*, but the only way to obtain this result is to have a variable $x$ on *every senator* and to continue to use it in the next sentence. This doesn't fully work because the variable $x$ is only a temporary name, which gets its meaning (in particular the fact that it should denote senators) from the quantifier.

[Every senator]$_x$ x came. He$_x$ gave a speech.

Interestingly, however, when *every senator* is replaced with *some senator*, the result is far more natural:

Some senator came. He gave a speech.

Now this discourse is fine, and we must draw the conclusion that the variables introduced by certain quantifiers—in particular by *some*—are not so temporary after all. They make it possible to obtain the 'right' meaning in this configuration:

[Some senator]$_x$ x came. He$_x$ gave a speech.

In the 1980s, there were heated debates about these examples. They forced linguists and logicians to team up to propose a new logic, called 'dynamic logic,' in which existential quantifiers (such as *some senator*) introduce variables that remain available in later sentences; in linguistics, this idea was defended by two pioneers of the field, Hans Kamp and Irene Heim. Because the resulting systems involved some complications, quite a few researchers were resistant and proposed alternative accounts. For instance, it was suggested that *he* really corresponds to a description in disguise, akin to *the senator*. This was a reasonable idea, since there is no particular problem in interpreting the sequence: *Some senator came. The senator gave a speech.* In addition, it was correctly predicted on this approach that *some* and *every* would work differently. This is because the following discourse is somewhat odd:

Every senator came. The senator gave a speech.

The problem here is that there are too many senators to serve as the denotation of *the senator* in the second sentence. You should say instead *the senators*, with an *s*. And in fact when a plural is used in the second sentence, both the pronoun and the description become acceptable:

Every senator came. They / The senators gave speech.

Of course, the price to pay for this analysis is that you must treat *he* and *they* as descriptions, even though . . . well, they don't look like descriptions! So the debate about the correct logic to use for human language was rather subtle. Proponents of dynamic logic argued that pronouns really do behave like logical variables, as I suggested in chapter 2, but that one needed a new logic. Opponents replied that traditional logic was just fine, but that one needed a new analysis of pronouns: not variables, but descriptions.

The debate remained open for many years. But once again sign language offered a new argument. As we discussed before, a pronoun is typically realized by way of a pointing sign toward a locus that was previously introduced by a noun phrase. Such loci are the visible realization of logical variables, as we saw in chapter 2: *Sarkozy$_b$ told Obama$_a$ that he would win the election* can be realized in different ways depending on whether *he* refers to Sarkozy (introduced in position *b* on the signer's left) or to Obama (introduced in position *a* on the signer's right). In the first case, the pronoun is realized by a pointing sign toward *b*, ☞-b, and in the second case by a pointing sign toward *a*, ☞-a (as before, I write these as *IX-b* and *IX-a*, as one 'indexes' locus *b* or locus *a*).[6]

Strikingly, the same mechanism is at work across sentences when a pronoun depends on quantifiers meaning *a former senator* or *a current senator*. In English, if I say, *I know a former senator and a current senator. He is smart but he isn't*, the sentence will strike you as decidedly odd because you can't tell which senator is denoted by each pronoun. In ASL, the problem is easily solved: *a former senator* establishes, by way of pointing, a locus *a*; *a current senator* establishes a locus *b*. With this context, *IX-b SMART* means that the current senator is smart, while *IX-a NOT SMART* means that the former senator isn't.[7]

IX-1 KNOW [PAST SENATOR] IX-a. IX-1 KNOW [NOW SENATOR] IX-b.

IX-b SMART BUT IX-a NOT SMART.

'I know a former senator and I know a current senator.
He [= the current senator] is smart but he [= the former senator] is not smart.'

Besides the small advantage that ASL has in avoiding ambiguities in this case, this example makes a more momentous point: If loci are, as I argued, visible logical variables, then a variable can depend on a quantifier that appears in an earlier sentence. This strongly suggests that the dynamic view of natural language is correct. Analyzing pronouns as descriptions in disguise isn't the right answer; rather, pronouns are variables, but human language doesn't quite treat these as Predicate Logic would.

In the end, then, we haven't just treated human language as a formal language modeled after Predicate Logic. We had to go beyond Predicate

Logic along multiple dimensions. First, English has distinct variables to talk about objects and about situations. Second, English has plurals as well as quantifiers that don't exist in Predicate Logic—and sometimes can't even be defined within it. Finally, English pronouns can depend on some quantifiers that appear in an earlier sentence. In spoken language, the latter view was just one of the theories that made sense given the data; an alternative would have been to treat pronouns as descriptions in disguise. But in sign language, variables can be made overt by way of loci. And strikingly, they show that a pronoun can be visibly linked to a quantifier that appears in an earlier sentence by way of loci. In this way, sign language makes visible the dynamic logic of human language.

## 9.6  LOGIC IN GRAMMAR

The initial impression that language is hopelessly vague and unsystematic disappears once its structure and logic are investigated in greater detail.[8] But it's not just that grammar produces sophisticated meanings. Some aspects of grammar are directly dependent on the inferences that are drawn from a sentence; in other words, meaning sometimes determines grammar. In fact, some apparently grammatical properties can be viewed as ways to signal that certain inferences hold.

A case in point is a class of expressions called 'negative polarity items,' which were originally described as dependent on negative words (hence their name). Examples include the words *at all*, *ever*, and some uses of *any*. They are natural in negative sentences such as those in the first group below, and almost incomprehensible in positive sentences such as those in the second group below (hence the stars that precede them).

> Robin won't ever go to France.
> Robin won't help at all.
> Robin doesn't have any common sense.

> *Robin will ever go to France.
> *Robin will help at all.
> *Robin has any common sense.

Initially, it would seem that we are dealing with the same kind of phenomenon as grammatical agreement, the process by which a word modifies its form because it depends on another word: *My parents are French* is a grammatical sentence. *My parents is French* isn't grammatical, because *is* must depend on a subject that is singular, not plural. So *my parents* licenses the plural form *are* but not the singular form *is*. By similar reasoning, one might be tempted to think that *ever* and *at all* must be licensed by a negation. This would be a bit too narrow, however, as other negative expressions work in the same way: *none of your friends, none of my colleagues, nobody* can do the trick just as well.

> None of your friends will ever go to France.
> None of my colleagues will help at all.
> Nobody has any common sense.

> *One of your friends will ever go to France.
> *One of my colleagues will help at all.
> *Somebody has any common sense.

The initial idea, then, is that there are more agreement phenomena in language than one might have thought: Just like *are* agrees with *they* in *they are tired*, the expressions *ever*, *at all*, and *any* agree with negative expressions in the examples we just discussed. But this turns out to be a flawed idea, and the final explanation will be far more interesting. To see that the 'negative agreement' idea won't work in the end, notice that the same contrasts can be reproduced within sentences that contain no negative expression whatsoever. To start with, negation can be replaced with *I doubt that*, with the same effects:

> I doubt that Robin will ever go to France.
> I doubt that Robin will help at all.
> I doubt that Robin has any common sense.

Now you might think that *doubt* is just a more abstract negative word, and this is a reasonable idea. But things get really tricky when we turn to sentences with the word *every*. Keeping the beginning of the sentence constant, *ever* and other negative polarity items seem to be appropriate when they appear before the main verb, as in the first group below, but not when they appear after the verb, as in the second group below.

> Every student **who has ever been to France** speaks some French.
> Every student **who helped at all** got an A.
> Every professor **who has any common sense** supported my proposal.

> *Every student who speaks some French **has ever been to France**.
> *Every student who got an A **helped at all**.
> *Every professor who supported my proposal **has any common sense**.

The rule is that in these sentences with *every*, negative polarity items can appear within the noun phrase but not within the verb phrase. But no negative expression appears in these sentences. How should these contrasts be explained?

The correct statement of the rule involves inferential patterns. Let us start with negation. Its key inferential property is that it reverses patterns of informativity. Concretely, *Robin will go to Paris* is more informative than *Robin will go to France*, in the following sense: From the first sentence, I can infer the second, but not conversely (linguists say that the first sentence asymmetrically entails the second, so in essence, 'more informative' means 'asymmetrically entails'). Now add a negation and the opposite relation holds: *Robin won't go to France* is now more informative than (i.e., asymmetrically entails) *Robin won't go to Paris*. Certainly, from the first sentence I can infer that Robin won't go to Paris; on the other hand, from the second sentence, I cannot infer the first (maybe Robin will in fact go to France, just not to Paris). Writing entailment with arrows, we can see that negation reverses the direction of the arrows:

> Robin will go to Paris $\Rightarrow$ Robin will go to France
> Robin won't go to Paris $\Leftarrow$ Robin won't to France

Interestingly, negation isn't the only expression that reverses informativity (i.e., entailment arrows). Further expressions create environments that are negative-like in this sense. To start with a very simple case, *I doubt that* has the same effect as *not*: if I doubt that Robin will go to France, then a fortiori, I doubt that Robin will go to Paris.

I doubt that Robin will go to Paris  ⇐  I doubt that Robin will go to France

The same conclusion holds with *none*. Start with *none of your friends will go to France*. Replace *go to France* with *go to Paris* and the result is a less informative sentence: if none of your friends go to France, then none go to Paris, but not conversely.

None of your friends will go to Paris  ⇐  None of your friends will go to France

By contrast, *one of your friends ___* doesn't reverse informativity. *One of your friends will go to Paris* clearly entails *one of your friends will go to France*:

One of your friends will go to Paris  ⇒  One of your friends will go to France

At this point, *being a negative expression* and *reversing informativity* would seem to be synonymous. But when we consider further expressions, the informativity-related property is more general and characterizes precisely the environments in which *ever* and its kin are acceptable. This is striking when we consider *every*. Start from *every student who has been to France speaks good French*. Replace *has been to France* with the more specific expression *has been to Paris*: The result is less informative. In other words, *every student who has been to France speaks good French* entails *every student who has been to Paris speaks good French*, but the latter sentence doesn't entail the former. For instance, maybe the students who went to Paris had better language classes than those who went to other parts of France, so that in the end *every student who has been to Paris speaks good French*, but it's not true that *every student who has been to France speaks good French*.

Every [student **who has been to Paris**] speaks good French  ⇐
(noun phrase)
Every [student **who has been to France**] speaks good French
(noun phrase)

Here, *student who has been to France* is a noun phrase, and *speaks good French* is a verb phrase. And our result is that, in this type of sentence (starting with *every*), the environment of the noun phrase reverses informativity relations.[9]

But things are entirely different within the verb phrase. To make the comparison minimal, let's start with this sentence: *Every student who speaks good French has been to Paris*. Now *has been to Paris* is in the verb phrase. Let us replace it with the less specific expression *has been to France*. The result is less informative. If *every student who speaks good French has been to Paris*, it certainly follows that *every student who speaks good French has been to France*. But the converse needn't hold: Maybe some students with good language skills wanted to avoid Paris because of subway strikes, for instance. So the environment of the verb phrase doesn't reverse informativity, unlike the environment of the noun phrase.

Every student who speaks good French [**has been to Paris**] ⟹
(verb phrase)      ⟩
Every student who speaks good French [**has been to France**]
(verb phrase)

This leads us to a new hypothesis. Instead of being just licensed by negative expressions, as we originally thought, *negative polarity items are licensed in environments that reverse informativity*. Among these environments are negative ones, but there are others besides. They are negative-like only in the sense that they too reverse informativity. So we explain the subtle data we saw at the outset on the basis of a simple hypothesis, one that doesn't pertain to the precise words used (e.g., the presence of negative expressions) but rather to patterns of reasoning that are associated with certain positions.

The puzzling question is why grammar should care about inferences. This is still a matter of debate, but it seems clear that there is in this case a direct connection between reasoning and grammar; plainly put, grammar cares about reasoning. This was shown with great clarity in an experiment that started from the observation that . . . well, people are not so good at drawing inferences! In fact, you may have noticed that in the cases I discussed, assessing entailments required a bit of thought: Reasoning doesn't always come easily. If you ask experimental subjects whether *none of my friends will go to France* entails that *none of my friends will go to Paris*, some of them will make reasoning errors and say 'no.' But then you can seek to correlate their reasoning patterns with their assessment of sentences with *ever*. If there is a direct link between reasoning and grammar, you would expect that it is only *to the extent* that subjects endorse the entailment that they like the sentence with *ever*. The more they accept the inference (from . . . *go to France* to . . . *go to Paris*), the more they should accept *ever* in the same context. And this is exactly what was found, both in examples of this sort and in cases in which the entailment does not go through but people erroneously think that it does. In fact, one may sometimes *help* people draw correct but complex inferences by adding negative polarity items. Not only does grammar care about reasoning: sometimes, it can help us reason better.[10]

## 9.7 CONCLUSION

It might initially have seemed crazy, or presumptuous, to treat English and other human languages as formal languages. The vagaries of language seemed to make this a hopeless proposition. We saw in chapter 8 that some systematic ambiguities can be explained with a very simple hypothesis: English has a syntax that is as well defined as that of formal languages (such as Predicate Logic); its only limitation is that it doesn't use brackets to make explicit how sentences are constructed. Once this fact is taken into account, several semantic observations fall into place. We saw in this chapter that treating English as a formal language yields extraordinary insights. We are now in a position to say what kind of formal language it is and which logic it has. In particular, it is strictly more expressive than Predicate Logic, for instance, because it has quantifiers (such as *most*) that couldn't even be defined with Predicate Logic.

This enterprise seemed on the verge of collapsing because of our initial observation that the sentence *Someone loves everyone* displays an ambiguity which suggests that English is rather ill-designed. The absence of brackets couldn't on its own explain this ambiguity, which could be paraphrased with two word orders, as *everyone* may be interpreted after *someone* or before it. But an explanation suggested itself: Just like the word *whom* in *Whom did you invite?*, *everyone* might have the option of moving to the beginning of the sentence, just in an invisible fashion (but one that can be diagnosed by the fact that syntactic islands block the movement). This led to a remarkable conclusion: When we dig deeper and take into account the representations that are obtained with invisible movement (as in English) or visible movement (as in Hungarian), human language produces representations that look a lot like standard logic.

Still, there are some differences: The logic of natural language isn't just more expressive (for instance, because of *most*) than that of Predicate Logic; it is also more dynamic, in the sense that it offers more flexible ways for variables to depend on quantifiers, something that can be seen in sign language or inferred more indirectly in English.

Finally, our findings have consequences not just for meaning but also for grammar. Grammatical constraints on the distribution of *ever* and its kin (negative polarity items) turn out to be based on inferential patterns, and they might have to do with the fact that human language is designed as an exquisitely sophisticated logic machine: sometimes grammar might help us reason better.

# 10 NOT QUITE SAYING IT: FOCUS AND IMPLICATURES

On October 2, 1989, peaceful demonstrators are facing off with the East German police in a tense atmosphere. The demonstrators' goal? The democratization of communist East Germany. Their slogan? *We are the people* ('Wir sind das Volk'). The demonstrators' intent is clear: It is to stress that *WE*, not the police, are the people. On November 11, 1989, the Berlin Wall is torn down, and the West German newspaper *Bild Zeitung* runs this headline:

> 'We are the people,' they cry today. 'We are one people,' they will cry out tomorrow.
>
> 'Wir sind das Volk' rufen sie heute—'Wir sind ein Volk' rufen sie morgen.

In German, *a* and *one* are the same word: *ein*. Accenting makes all the difference. Accented *EIN* gets contrasted with *zwei* ('two'), and the numerical meaning is obtained: *We are one people, not two people.* The newspaper's title is prescient. On October 3, 1990, Germany is reunited, and the two German people become 'one' again.

The transition from 'We are the people' to 'We are one people' recapitulates the history of the democratic movement in the former East Germany. But it wasn't just the replacement of *das Volk* ('the people') with *ein Volk* ('one people') that made all the difference. The change in accenting made clear what the demonstrators were *rejecting*: WE, and not the police, are the people. We are ONE people, and not two.

This is a general fact about language: A considerable part of the information conveyed by a sentence stems from the alternatives it rejects. As we will now see, comparing what was said to what could have been said (but wasn't) is an essential and very common way of enriching the meaning of sentences.

## 10.1 WHAT IS SAID AND WHAT ISN'T

There is more to meaning than what is encoded in words. Sometimes one fills in the blanks by just relying on common sense, combined with one's understanding of the speaker's goals. There can be a considerable gap between the literal meaning of words and the information they convey to an appropriately cooperative audience.

A viral video made this point clear. In the "exact instructions" challenge, a father asks his two kids to write instructions to make a peanut butter and jelly sandwich (*why* one would want to make such a thing is a question many non-Americans might ask, but I will set this point aside). The son starts with some instructions that include this sequence: *Get some jelly. Rub it on the other half of the bread.* The father dutifully takes the jelly jar and proceeds to . . . rub the jar on the bread slice. Since *jelly* could refer to the stuff or to the jelly jar, that counts as a possible meaning—just not the one that was intended. Having learned from her little brother's mistake, the daughter sets out to make the written instructions "extremely specific," as she says, and orders her father to spread peanut butter on a piece of bread. Her next instruction reads: *Open the jelly jar. Squeeze it onto the other piece of bread.* At this point, the father takes the jelly jar, puts it horizontally on the bread, and squeezes the jar—after which his sandwich is made of a plastic jelly jar between two pieces of white bread. Here, too, he did as he was told—just not as the writer intended ([**AV10.1.1**]).

But meaning enrichment doesn't just proceed by adding a modicum of common sense to what the speaker said. Sometimes one gets a lot of information by reasoning about what the speaker *didn't* say. As the philosopher Paul Grice famously noted, a letter of recommendation won't land the student a job if it just says, *His command of English is excellent, and his attendance at tutorials has been regular.* While these are indeed qualities, the letter strongly suggests that the applicant is no good. Why? Because we understand that the professor is supposed to provide the *strongest* arguments she can find to hire the student; so if regular attendance is the student's best quality—well, he shouldn't be hired.

When we analyze sentences, we constantly compare them to alternatives that could have been uttered but weren't. Reasoning about alternatives is such an important part of language that there is a dedicated mechanism, called focus, to help reconstruct which alternatives should be taken into account. *WE are the people* evokes the alternative *YOU are the people*, and it indicates that the latter is rejected: accenting *WE* has the effect of rejecting the alternative that differs from the uttered sentence relative to the focused (i.e., accented) word.

Meaning as it is encoded in words is the purview of semantics in the strict sense. The additional inferences one draws on the speaker's intentions are the purview of pragmatics. The Ancient Greek etymologies are somewhat helpful: *semantikos* is 'significant' while *pragmatikos* means something like 'fit for action' (hence also the use of *pragmatic* to mean 'realistic,' as in *a pragmatic approach*). As we will see in this chapter, much information conveyed by utterances comes from pragmatics. Pragmatic enrichment is ubiquitous in language. The German demonstrators who chanted *WE are the people* were telling the police, *You are not the people*. The demonstrators who later changed the slogan to *We are ONE people* were telling East German authorities that the age of a divided Germany was over. In other cases, pragmatic enrichment can be harder to spot, and in some devious instances it may even allow one to mislead without a risk of being caught red-handed.

## 10.2 MOORE'S PARADOX

The first component of pragmatic reasoning is that speakers present themselves as believing what they assert (in addition, they often present themselves as *not* believing some salient alternatives, as we saw in our initial examples—we'll revisit them shortly). This might seem entirely obvious, but the distinction between the literal meaning of a sentence and the fact that the speaker believes it holds the key to an apparent paradox that has puzzled quite a few philosophers.

The problem was discovered by the philosopher G. E. Moore in 1942.[1] As he observed, it is decidedly odd to assert sentences like the following:

It's already past midnight but I don't believe that it is.

Now you might think that there is nothing puzzling about this statement; it is just a plain contradiction, as is found in the less interesting sentence that says:

I am 50 years old and I am not.

But there is a crucial a difference. If we put Moore's example in the third person, we get an entirely coherent sentence:

It's already past midnight but Moore doesn't believe that it is.

By contrast, *I am 50 years old and I am not* remains contradictory when stated in the third person—for instance, as *Moore is 50 years old and he is not*. Why should a sentence be a contradiction in the first but not in the third person? This is Moore's puzzle—which is usually called, a bit inaccurately, Moore's "paradox."

The solution is that Moore's sentence is not a semantic but a pragmatic contradiction. While there are situations that simultaneously make both conjuncts true, there is no belief state that makes it possible to sincerely utter the conjunction. In other words, it could be that both conjuncts are simultaneously true (this is the reason it's not a semantic contradiction—that is, one that arises from the literal meaning of words), but no speaker could coherently assert them at the same time (this is what makes it a pragmatic contradiction).

The reason is simple: People present themselves as believing what they say (whether they are in fact sincere is another issue; all we need is that they must appear to be). So we have a principle like this one:

If Moore asserts a sentence *S*, then Moore believes (or presents himself as believing) that *S*.

In addition, when we believe a conjunction, we certainly have to believe both conjuncts. So when Moore utters his famous sentence, we obtain two conclusions:

(i)  Moore believes the first conjunct: he believes that it is past midnight.
(ii)  He also believes the second conjunct: he believes that he doesn't believe that it's past midnight.

The last step in the reasoning is based on a kind of introspection principle. If I believe something, I believe that I believe it.[2] So Moore doesn't just believe that it's past midnight, he believes that he believes it. Summing up, Moore believes

that he believes that it is past midnight (from (i) above and introspection);
that he doesn't believe that it's past midnight (from (ii) above).

In other words, Moore presents himself as holding contradictory beliefs! This is the reason his sentence is so odd: no speakers could use it without presenting themselves as holding inconsistent beliefs.

When we restate Moore's sentence in the third person, the problem disappears. For instance, suppose I say:

It's past midnight but Moore doesn't believe it.

In this instance, no problem arises. I, the speaker, have a belief that it's past midnight (because I am supposed to believe the first conjunct) and also a belief that I believe that it's past midnight. I simultaneously have a belief that Moore doesn't believe that it's past midnight—and there is nothing inconsistent at all in my position.

In the usual sense, a 'paradox' is any statement whose logical status is not well understood. But as we will see in chapter 16, a paradox in the precise sense is something different: It is a statement that cannot coherently be assigned the value *true* or the value *false*. This is not what is going on in Moore's 'puzzle.' Rather, Moore's sentence is a pragmatic contradiction— that is, a statement that cannot be coherently uttered by any speaker.

### 10.3  THE FORM AND MEANING OF FOCUS

Many cases of pragmatic enrichment are not just due, as in Moore's 'paradox,' to the assumption that the speaker believes what she says, but also that she *doesn't* believe salient alternatives she could have decided to utter but didn't. This was why Grice's unfortunate student had little chance of getting the job, despite having a recommendation that only mentioned positive qualities (*excellent English, regular attendance*). The problem was that the letter *failed* to mention even greater qualities. By assuming that the writer was appropriately cooperative, the reader could infer that the applicant didn't have these qualities. In this case, then, we used the assumption that the writer was in a sense maximally informative (hence the falsity of salient alternatives), whereas to deal with Moore's sentence we relied on the assumption that the speaker was sincere.

As we saw, pronunciation may help identify the rejected alternatives: *WE are the people*, with accent on *we*, tells the addressee that the salient alternative to be rejected is of the form *x are the people*. In the context of a demonstration, *x* would naturally be taken to be *the police*. This is the mechanism of focus: The speaker highlights an expression that needs to be replaced to obtain the relevant alternatives. And in all cases the asserted sentence is somehow contrasted with one or several of the alternatives—often because they are rejected.

A relatively recent internet meme vividly illustrated the importance of focus. It was based on the correct observation that, depending on which word is focused, one gets seven different meaning for the following sentence: *I didn't say she stole my money.*[3] This is sometimes presented as an argument that English is a weird language. But that's not at all the right conclusion. What it really shows is that focus greatly matters to meaning, in a regular and predictable fashion: in each case, focusing a word evokes an alternative that is rejected. Let's start with the case in which *didn't* is focused:

I *DIDN'T* say she stole my money.

This just rejects an alternative with *did*, and so all we have is a reinforcement of the negation.

The other cases are based on the fact that if we reject a sentence of the form *It's not the case that blah . . .* well, that's usually because we accept that *blah* (to put it in logician's talk, if you reject *not p*, you usually accept *p*!). This will yield the desired results. Let's see why.

First, _I didn't say she stole my money_, with emphasis on _I_. This rejects an alternative obtained by replacing _I_ with _x_ (for _x_ ≠ _I_). So, we reject _x didn't say she stole my money_, and hence we accept that _x said she stole my money_. In other words, I didn't say she stole my money, but someone else did.

Next, _I didn't SAY she stole my money_. Here we accept something like, _I implied she stole my money_. In other words, I didn't SAY she stole my money, but I implied it.

The last four cases work in similar fashion:

_I didn't say SHE stole my money_. We accept _I said x stole my money_ (for _x_ ≠ _she_), hence I didn't say SHE stole my money, but (I said that) someone did.

_I didn't say she STOLE my money_. Here, we accept _I said she did x to my money_, where _x_ is something other than stealing. So: I didn't say she STOLE my money, but (I said that) she still did something to it—maybe she borrowed it.

_I didn't say she stole MY money_. Now we accept _I said she stole x's money_ (with _x's_ ≠ _my_), hence the meaning, I didn't say she stole MY money, but she did steal someone's money.

_I didn't say she stole my MONEY_. Here we accept _I said she stole my x_ (with _x_ ≠ _money_). So I didn't say she stole my MONEY, but she did steal something from me.

So successful was this meme that it reached a team of scientists, who used a version of it in an experiment (with _never_ replacing _didn't_).[4] They were studying the brain regions that control vocal pitch, which is itself raised in each focused word. To do so, they needed to get their subjects to systematically vary vocal pitch on different parts of a sentence. The internet meme was the ideal test case, as each difference in vocal pitch gave rise to a completely natural and easily understandable example.

Besides higher pitch, focus is marked in English by greater loudness and duration. You might wonder how sign language marks focus in the absence of sound. The details depend on the sign language under study, but in ASL several strategies are simultaneously used (along others): longer duration as in English, greater sign amplitude (which might be a signed counterpart of increased loudness), and also eyebrow raising.[5] This is one of many cases in which facial expressions in general and eyebrows in particular play a crucial role in sign language.

Eyebrow raising might have a particularly interesting evolutionary history, and it is one of the rare cases in which we might have an idea of when a grammatical marker arose. The reason is that, according to researchers, archaic humans that lived as little as 125,000 to 300,000 years ago had a huge brow ridge that made vertical movement of the eyebrows more limited.[6] Eyebrow raising might thus be a relatively recent innovation (to see how recent it is, remember that humans diverged from chimpanzees and bonobos about 6 million years ago). The authors of the study speculate that it was its use in social communication that led to the development of eyebrow raising in more recent times. Whether linguistic communication in general and gestural/signed communication in particular was crucial, we do not know—in fact, the relative role of gestural/signed and spoken communication in human evolution is a matter of debate. Still, it is interesting to note that eyebrow raising is also used as a gesture in spoken language (using 'gesture' in an extended sense, one that includes movements of the face, not just movements of the hands). You may want to give it a try for yourself in *I didn't say SHE stole my money*: it might not be out of place to raise your eyebrows as you put focus on *she*.

I should add that there are also further strategies to mark focus. Some spoken languages, such as Catalan, Spanish, or Russian, can mark focus by moving the target expression to a special position, and some sign languages (including ASL) do this, too. This is yet another area in which the typology of sign languages resembles that of spoken languages.

To go back to English, in the cases mentioned so far, the contrasting alternatives evoked by focus were left implicit (although they were easily reconstructed). But sometimes the contrasting alternative is explicitly mentioned, as if I say:

Ann introduced your parents to me, and then she introduced you to me.

Here it is natural to highlight *you* by pronouncing it with emphasis (i.e., with an accent). Why? Because it contrasts with an alternative that was mentioned earlier, and *you* is the only part of the sentence that is new. Highlighting it suggests, correctly, that the first sentence was of the form *Ann introduced x to me*. If you put the accent on *she* instead, the result is decidedly odd, because it suggests, wrongly, that the contrastive sentence was of the form *x introduced you to me*.

This phenomenon is found in other cases as well. If I ask you, *Who should Ann introduce to us?*, a natural answer will be, *Anne should introduce ROBIN to us*, with emphasis on *ROBIN*. Why? Because the question asks for answers of the form *Ann should introduce x to us*, and thus *x* is where the action is, so to speak. If you focus *Ann* instead, and thus answer, *ANN should introduce Robin to us*, the result will once again be odd because it suggests, wrongly, that the question was of the form: *Who should introduce Robin to us?*

Focus is so central to language that some words are specifically designed to provide information about the alternatives that are evoked. *Only* is one such word. Suppose I tell you:

I only drink WINE.

The effect of *only* is to deny alternatives of the form *I drink x*—so probably not beer, for instance. But suppose that instead I say:

I only DRINK wine.

The inference is different here—maybe that I don't make wine. Similarly, suppose I tell you:

I only drink RED wine.

Now the effect of *only* combined with the emphasis on *red* is to deny alternatives of the form *I drink x wine*—so probably I don't drink white wine.

### 10.4 FOCUS IN PUBLIC COMMUNICATION

Focus doesn't just matter to scientists and language nerds. We saw at the outset the implications of the focus on the first word in *WE are the people* as used by East German demonstrators in 1989. There are several further striking cases in history.

**Figure 10.4.1**
*World War I recruitment posters: United Kingdom (left), United States (right)*

The United Kingdom and the United States made a clever use of focus in their recruitment efforts during World War I, with posters that read, *Your country needs YOU* (depicting the British secretary of state for war, 1914) or *I want YOU for U.S. Army* (depicting Uncle Sam, 1917; see figure 10.4.1). A natural reaction when told that one's country needs soldiers is to think of all the *other* people that could enlist. The focused *YOU* (in large font) in the posters, combined with a pointing gesture and a stern eye gaze, were designed to discourage this convenient thought: in particular, Uncle Sam hinted not so subtly that he wasn't currently thinking of the others but specifically of the person reading the poster.

The difference in emphasis sometimes reflects social conflicts. In the years following 2013, a series of protests were organized in the United States after numerous deaths of unarmed African Americans following police actions or while in police custody. The movement used the hashtag and name *Black Lives Matter*. The reason was that the situation had called into question whether, for American institutions, the lives of African Americans matter. And given the situation, it seemed urgent to reaffirm that black lives do in fact matter, and thus the focus was on *matter:* what was rejected was the view that black lives do not matter.

But opponents of the movement replied with their own slogan, *All Lives Matter*, pronounced with an accent on *all*. It was rhetorically impactful because it implied that *Black Lives Matter* was an answer to the question *Which lives matter?* rather than an answer to the question *Do black lives matter?*, as was no doubt intended. And if the question is *Which lives matter?* and someone says *All lives matter*, while someone else says *Black lives matter*, the first person will appear to have the upper hand. By wrongly suggesting that the focus was on *black* rather than on *matter*, the opponents of the movement changed the intended meaning of the slogan.[7]

This was not without consequence. A poll was conducted in 2015, whose wording was the following:[8]

> Which statement is closest to your own—black lives matter or all lives matter? Or does neither statement reflect your point of view?

Of likely US voters, 78 percent answered that *all lives matter*, 11 percent that *black lives matter*. But it is clear that the disjunction *black lives matter or all lives matter* strongly invites the interpretation on which the underlying question is *Which lives matter?*, as the opponents of the movement had hoped, rather than *Do black lives matter or do black lives not matter?*, which was the question that prompted the movement in the first place. When it comes to focus, context *really* plays a role—and the focus of the question in the poll helped bring out a meaning that was not the intended one in the *Black Lives Matter* movement.

Focus can thus have far-reaching consequences because it helps reconstruct the implicit question that people are trying to address and which alternatives are being excluded. In this way, changing the placement of focus can sometimes radically change the meaning of an utterance.

## 10.5  SCALAR IMPLICATURES

While focus is a very effective way of highlighting important alternatives, we don't need focus to reason about what the speaker *could* have said but didn't. In fact, in the case of Grice's letter of recommendation for a job applicant, we didn't need any focus to get the reasoning going. By comparing the qualities mentioned to the greater ones that could have been mentioned but weren't, the reader had no difficulty inferring that the job applicant was no good. Such inferences are called *implicatures*.

We already saw primitive examples of implicatures in our discussion of primate calls in chapter 1. For instance, we had observed in our discussion of Titi monkeys that the A-call was primarily used when there were urgent non-ground threats, while the B-call was used in very diverse situations and was thus plausibly a general alert call. But the puzzle was why an eagle-related sequence of calls systematically started with A-calls, not B-calls: After all, if an eagle is present, a general alert ought to be licensed. The answer we explored was based on the Informativity Principle: If you can say something more informative and true, do so! Since the A-call is clearly more informative than the completely underspecified B-call, when there is an eagle and thus it is appropriate to use the A-call, it ought to be used.

In monkeys, the Informativity Principle might just be automatic. There is no evidence at this point that monkeys reason about what the speaker could have said but didn't. Things are different in the case of Grice's letter: we need to be acutely aware of what is expected in a letter of recommendation to infer from the words used (*Smith's command of English is excellent, and his attendance at tutorials has been regular*) that the applicant is no good.

Because none of Grice's words carried negative implications while the entire letter definitely did, it was transparent that pragmatic reasoning was needed to supplement semantic meaning. But other cases are far less obvious. A case in point is the little word *or*, which has given rise to endless debates in the history of logic. They can be summarized in three words: *inclusive or exclusive*? Logicians usually take *or* to be inclusive (as we did in chapter 7): *A or B* is true if *A* is true or *B* is true or both are, which thus includes the possibility that *A and B* is true. But in English and other languages, it often looks like *or* is exclusive: *A or B* is true if *A* is true but not *B*, or if *B* is true but not *A*; this excludes the possibility that *A and B* is true, and thus *A or B* entails 'not both.' For instance, if I tell you that *I'll invite Robin or Sam*, you'll infer that I'll invite one or the other but not both.

*So what's the big deal?* you might ask. Logicians are logicians, not linguists—maybe English *or* is just exclusive. The trouble is that there are many cases in which one needs to posit that *or* is inclusive. First, it's no contradiction to say that *I'll invite Robin or Sam—I might even invite them both*. But if *or* had an exclusive ('not both') component, this should definitely come out as a contradiction—which isn't right. Second, there are cases in which the inclusive meaning is the only one available. Suppose I tell you:

Every person who invites Robin or Sam will have a pleasant time.

It's rather difficult to understand this as meaning *every person who invites Robin or Sam but not both will have a pleasant time*. In other words, my original sentence commits me to the prediction that you'll have a pleasant time if you invite both. Furthermore, this inference follows from the words I used, not from independent facts about the world: If Robin and Sam can't stand each other, it might well be that inviting both is a recipe for disaster, but my sentence still commits me to the prediction that if you invite them both you'll have a pleasant time. Similarly, suppose I tell you:

I doubt I'll invite Robin or Sam.

This statement doesn't just exclude a scenario in which I invite Robin alone or Sam alone—it also excludes one in which I invite them both. But to get the latter inference, *or* has to be inclusive.

For a long time, the standard view was that *or* is ambiguous: It can be inclusive, and it can be exclusive. But what we just observed with *every person* and *doubt* is that this isn't quite right. In these cases, unless you pronounce *or* in a special way (with a strong focus[9]), you won't get the exclusive meaning. On the ambiguity view, this comes a surprise.

A more elegant theory has become the consensus among linguists, one that doesn't need to posit that *or* is ambiguous. And it crucially involves reasoning with alternatives. The basic idea is that *or* has an inclusive reading (so the logicians were right after all!), but it automatically evokes *and* (in the cases we'll consider, we'll deal with *both . . . and*, which is often clearer). Thus if I tell you *I'll invite Robin or Sam*, my utterance automatically evokes an alternative obtained by replacing *or* with *and*—to wit, *I'll invite both Robin and Sam*. But now the situation is similar to that of the recommendation letter. The sentence with *and* is more informative than the one with *or*, in the sense (used in section 9.6) that it asymmetrically entails it. Remember that *or* is inclusive, so if I invite Robin and Sam, it certainly follows that I invite Robin or Sam— meaning Robin or Sam *or both*—while of course the converse doesn't hold (the version with *or* doesn't entail the version with *and*). Now speakers usually try to be as informative as possible. So if the speaker is in a position to assert the sentence with *and* rather than the less informative sentence with *or*, the speaker should go for *and*. This also means that if the speaker *didn't* choose this more informative statement, she probably didn't believe it to be true—either because she lacked information or because she knew the sentence with *and* to be false. Since the statement pertained to the speaker's own decisions (*I'll invite Robin or Sam*), it's unlikely that the speaker lacked information, and so the speaker probably intends not to invite both Robin and Sam.

In this way, we can have our cake and eat it, too: *A or B* is inclusive, but pragmatic reasoning is responsible for the 'not both' inference (i.e., not both A and B) that makes *or* seem exclusive. Because the words *and* and *or* evoke each other but have different levels of informativity (with *both A and B* being more informative than *A or B*), linguists have called <or, and> a 'scale,' and correspondingly, the implicatures triggered by these terms are called 'scalar implicatures.'

There are several benefits to this analysis. One is that context should play an important role in triggering implicatures. In the case we just discussed, *I'll invite Robin or Sam*, it seemed implausible that the speaker would lack information about her own intentions. But things are different in other examples. Suppose I am looking for a job and tell you, rather confidently:

I'll get an offer from Google or Amazon.

Being optimistic, I certainly don't want to exclude the possibility that I'll get an offer from both, so in this case we just get the inference that the speaker isn't in a position to assert that he will get an offer from both. That seems right.

There are also cases in which the implicature-based analysis explains facts that are genuinely surprising for proponents of an exclusive meaning of *or*. Suppose I tell you:

I hope to visit Madrid or Rome.

All an exclusive *or* can give us is a meaning akin to *I hope to visit only one of these two cities* (i.e., *I hope to do the following: visit Madrid or Rome but not both*). But that's not the meaning that comes to mind. If you are like me, you'd be delighted to visit both Madrid and Rome. Rather, the natural meaning is that I hope to visit at least one, and I don't have the more ambitious hope that I'll be able to visit both. This is exactly what we get by negating the alternative *I hope to visit Madrid and Rome*. In other words, the meaning we find is correctly explained with a scalar implicature that denies the entire sentence with *hope . . . and . . .* , as shown here:

Literal meaning:    I hope to visit Madrid or Rome.
Scalar implicature:   It's not the case I hope to visit both Madrid and Rome.

An exclusive *or* meaning would predict something incorrect—namely, *I hope to visit [Madrid or Rome but not both]*. In this case, implicatures achieve a result we couldn't obtain without them.

Once you start looking for scalar implicatures, they turn up everywhere. In chapter 5, we analyzed in some detail the meaning of *everyone* and *someone*. *Everyone sings* requires that for each person x, x sings, whereas *someone sings* just requires that for at least one person x, x sings. But this was only a partial truth: When implicatures are taken into account, *someone sings* suggests that *everyone sings* is false. The reason is that, as soon as there are people in the first place, *everyone sings* is more informative than (i.e., asymmetrically entails) *someone sings*.[10] So uttering the less informative statement triggers an implicature that the more informative one is false, hence a meaning akin to *someone but not everyone sings*. We had further argued that *must* is to *might* as *everyone* is to *someone*. So, if I say (from my basement) that *it must be raining*, the claim is stronger than *it might be raining*: Instead of asserting that *in some situation compatible with my beliefs, it is raining*, my claim is that *in every situation compatible with my beliefs, it is raining*. But here, too, the analysis of *might* was only a half truth. *It might be raining* triggers the implicature that I can't assert *it must be raining*, hence there is a possibility *but not certainty* that it is raining. In fact, in chapter 1, I had briefly mentioned an example involving the word *possible*. If I tell you that *it is possible that Russia influenced the 2016 election*, you will normally infer that I don't take this to be a certainty. Here, too, the original sentence triggers an implicature. *It is certain that Russia influenced the 2016 election* would have been a more informative sentence to utter, hence if I did not choose it, chances are it was because I took it to be false.

Things can get more subtle. If I tell you that *most of my friends are honest*, you will infer that not all are. While it could in principle be that *most* means 'a majority but not all,' you can quickly check that this is the wrong explanation: It is no contradiction to say that <u>most and in fact all of my friends are honest</u> (but this ought to be a contradiction if *not all* were a hardwired part of the meaning). Rather, the 'not all' inference is an implicature: The sentence with *most* evokes another one with *all*, and the latter is more informative (if all my friends are honest, then certainly a majority of them are, but not conversely). From the fact that I didn't utter the more informative statement, you infer that it is likely false—hence *not all* my friends are honest.

But here comes the subtle part. If I tell you instead that *most of us are honest, and some of us are smart*, you still get the 'not all' inference for the first clause—hence *not all of us are honest*. But for the second clause (*some of us are smart*), you won't just get the inference that *not all of us are smart*. Rather, the implication is that only a minority among us are smart. Why? Because *some* doesn't just compete with *all*, but sometimes it also competes with *most*. Hence, you infer that it is not the case that *most of us are smart*—in other words, only a minority of us are. In this case, we have a scale with three members:

<some, most, all>

Asserting a simple sentence with *most* triggers an implicature *(most but) not all*, and similarly *some* can yield *(some but) not most*.

While our initial examples involved logical words like *or, some,* and *most,* implicatures can be found with numerous other expressions, such as adverbs. Charles-Joseph, Prince de Ligne, a near-contemporary of Casanova (and also a notorious womanizer), was once asked by his wife on his return from a long voyage: *Have you been faithful to me?* To which he apparently replied: *Often.*[11] Without literally incriminating himself, de Ligne made clear that he hadn't *always* been faithful to his wife (and furthermore, that he considered faithfulness to be a problem best tackled one day at a time); here the implicature is triggered by the adverb *often,* which forms a scale with *always.*

Adjectives can trigger implicatures as well. If you just returned from a movie and tell me, *It was nice,* I'll probably infer that it wasn't great. But here too, this isn't because *nice* is incompatible with *great,* as you could say without contradiction, *The movie was nice—it was even great!* Rather, from your use of *nice,* I infer that you decided not to use a more positive term, such as *great,* and I conclude that this is probably because you didn't like the movie that much. Similarly, if you tell me, *I liked it,* I will probably infer that you didn't *love* it. Scalar implicatures are ubiquitous and an essential source of meaning enrichment.

## 10.6 NEGATIVE-LIKE ENVIRONMENTS

We saw above that with *doubt,* the word *or* is inclusive: *I doubt I'll invite Robin or Sam* rejects, among others, scenarios in which both Robin and Sam are invited, hence the meaning of *or* must be inclusive in this case. On the view that *or* is ambiguously inclusive or exclusive, this would come as a complete surprise. Can the scalar implicature analysis provide a more satisfactory answer?

It can, and the key lies in issues of informativity, already discussed in section 9.6. Let's see why. When I utter *I'll invite Robin and Sam,* the sentence I picked is more informative than (i.e., it entails) the alternative with *or,* so of course you don't get an implicature (since there is no way to infer that the speaker could have uttered something more informative). Now, in the presence of *doubt,* and more generally of negative expressions, patterns of informativity are reversed, as we saw in the case of negative polarity items in section 9.6. *I doubt I'll invite Robin or Sam* is now *more* informative than the alternative with *and* (if it's unlikely that I invite Robin or Sam, certainly it's even more unlikely that I'll invite them both). So, of course, no implicature is triggered by the sentence with *or*.

I'll invite Robin or Sam  ⇐  I'll invite both Robin and Sam
I doubt I'll invite Robin or Sam  ⇒  I doubt I'll invite both Robin and Sam

The consideration of informativity relations immediately explains why *or* has its unadorned inclusive meaning after *I doubt that.* In this case, uttering the same sentence with the disjunction *Robin or Sam* replaced with the conjunction *both Robin and Sam* would yield a less informative sentence. But an implicature only arises when we consider *more* informative sentences, which the speaker could have decided to utter but didn't. So there can be no implicature in this case.

In sum, we've seen that environments that reverse informativity have two effects. First, they license negative polarity items such as *ever*, as we saw in section 9.6. Second, they remove implicatures that are computed in positive environments. Further examples bear this out. Let us consider again some negative-like environments that license *ever*:

None of your friends **will ever go to France**.
Every student **who has ever been to France** speaks good French.

The boldfaced environment after *none of your friends* reverses informativity. As a result, if *or* appears in that environment, it has its unadorned inclusive meaning: No implicature is obtained. For instance, the statement that *none of your friends will go to Paris or Lyons* certainly excludes cases in which one of the friends goes both to Paris and Lyons; in other words, what's denied is that they'll go to Paris or Lyons or both (i.e., the inclusive meaning of *or*).

Similarly, we saw before that the boldfaced environment after *Every student* reverses informativity. To say that *x has been to Paris* is more informative than *x has been to France*, but *every student who has been to France speaks good French* is more informative than *every student who has been to Paris speaks good French*. This explains why the word *or* displays an unadorned inclusive behavior in the following sentence with *every*:

Every person who invites Robin or Sam will have a pleasant time.

This is as expected because the sentence with *or* is more informative than the sentence with *and*. If *every person who invites Robin or Sam* (or possibly both!) *will have a pleasant time*, then a fortiori, *every person who invites both Robin and Sam will have a pleasant time*. The entailment obtained is thus the following:

Every person who invites Robin or Sam will have a pleasant time ⇒
Every person who invites both Robin and Sam will have a pleasant time

Here, too, since the sentence with *or* is more informative than its alternative, there is no way an implicature could be computed. This explains why *or* has once again its unadorned inclusive meaning.

This entire analysis has an unexpected benefit as well: It predicts the appearance of new implicatures in negative-like environments. The reason is simple. In the context of *I doubt . . .* and *every person who . . .* , informativity relations are reversed, and thus a sentence with *and* is less informative than a sentence with *or*. We used this fact to explain why *or* doesn't trigger an implicature here. But another consequence is that *and* ought to trigger an implicature, to the effect that the sentence with *or* couldn't be sincerely asserted. This is exactly right: *I doubt I'll invite both Robin and Sam* suggests that I think I'll invite one of them. Why? As noted above, the informativity relation is like this:

I doubt I'll invite Robin or Sam   ⇒   I doubt I'll invite both Robin and Sam

Now we reason, by way of an implicature, that the more informative alternative is false—hence *it's not the case that I doubt I'll invite Robin or Sam*. In other words, *I think I'll invite Robin or Sam*. This is a striking result: Our theory of scalar implicatures was motivated by the behavior of *or*. But it can be very smoothly applied to *and* when it appears in negative environments.

As you may also expect, we obtain new implicatures in further environments that reverse informativity, such as this one:

Every person **who invites both Robin and Sam** will have a pleasant time.

As we saw a paragraph back, the speaker could have uttered something more informative by replacing *and* with *or*. By reasoning that this more informative statement was likely false, we get: *Not every person who invites Robin or Sam will have a pleasant time.* In other words, some people who invite one but not both won't have a pleasant time. That too seems right.

The same reasoning applies to numerous other cases. In 2019, after a Democratic Congressman supported President Trump's funding request for a border wall with Mexico, the left-wing economist Paul Krugman tweeted the following reaction (*GOP*, for 'Grand Old Party,' is a familiar name of the Republican party):

Quite a few Congressmen are dumb as rocks. Not all of them GOP.

Strictly speaking, the *not all* sentence is true in case none of the dumb members of Congress are from the GOP. Still, this sentence carries an implicature that some of them are Republicans. Why? Because of an implicature. The *not all* sentence is less informative than an alternative with *none*, and by reasoning that this more informative statement is false, you'll infer that *some of them* (= not none of them) *are from the GOP*. In fact, you might get a stronger inference still—namely, that *many of them are from the GOP*. That's because *not many of them are from the GOP* is more informative than *not all of them are from the GOP* (e.g., *not many* might mean 'less than 50 percent,' whereas 'not all' just means 'less than 100 percent'). By inferring that the more informative statement with *not many* is false, you get that *many of them are from the GOP*. In other words, the inferences we just discussed (*some of them are from the GOP, many of them are from the GOP*) neatly follow from the theory of implicatures once we notice that the alternatives on the right (in the examples below) are more informative than the uttered sentence on the left, hence the inference that these alternatives on the right are likely false:

Not all of them are from the GOP   $\Leftarrow$   None of them are from the GOP
Not all of them are from the GOP   $\Leftarrow$   Not many of them are from the GOP

In sum, implicatures are a very powerful and general way of enriching meaning. They explain rather elegantly why *or* can be inclusive and yet have exclusive-like uses (because of pragmatic enrichment). They also provide a host of new explanations and predictions that yield genuine insights into how meaning works. The main message is of course that there is more to meaning than what is encoded in words: reasoning about the speaker's intentions can play a considerable role in the information conveyed by an utterance.

## 10.7 WHEN CHILDREN ARE MORE 'LOGICAL' THAN ADULTS

Psychologists who investigated children's understanding of logical words were faced with an apparent paradox. On the one hand, children ages 5 through 9 already speak extremely well and have acquired most aspects of meaning. On the other hand, they also differ from adults when it comes to understanding words like *might, some,* and *or.*

How do we know? It's not quite possible to directly ask your typical five-year-old what they take the meaning of *or* to be. But psycholinguists have developed indirect ways of finding out. One strategy is to ask a child to reward or punish a puppet depending on whether it's saying true or false things (besides making the task fun, using the puppet has the advantage that the child doesn't have to contradict an adult, which psycholinguists seem to think poses special problems). In this way, it's possible to probe how children understand the conditions under which sentences are true or false.

And the results are sometimes surprising. In a famous experiment conducted by the psychologist Ira Noveck, the children were shown two open boxes, one with a parrot only and the other with a parrot and a bear.[12] Then the experimenter displayed a covered box and said:

> A friend of mine gave me this box and said *all I know is that whatever is inside this box looks like what's inside this box* [the experimenter points to the open box with a parrot and bear] *or what's inside this box* [the experimenter points to the box that only contains a parrot].

The scenario was set up to ensure that we know for sure that there is a parrot in the covered box, although we don't know whether there is a bear in it. Then the children were asked whether sentences such as the following were appropriate:

> There might be a parrot in the box.

Adults tend to reject this, as you probably do. Your reaction might go like this: What do you mean there *might* be a parrot in the box? There *must* be one, since both of the boxes that were shown contain a parrot. If instead you are asked about the sentence *There might be a bear in the box*, everything changes and the sentence is acceptable. Five-, seven-, and nine-year-olds tend to accept the bear sentence, just like adults do. But here comes the surprising part: unlike adults, they also accept the parrot sentence.

Similarly, adults tend to reject the following sentence:

Some elephants have trunks.

Here, too, your kneejerk reaction might be: What do you mean *some* elephants have trunks? *All* do! But children seem to be happy with the sentence.

What is going on? The first thing to notice is that children behave like good logicians whereas adults don't. The literal or 'logical' meaning of *some elephants have trunks* is just that there are elephants that have trunks—and this is compatible with all of them having trunks (that's the reason it's no contradiction to say that *some and in fact all elephants have trunks*). In fact, this was precisely the meaning we defined for *some* in the logical analysis of chapter 9, when we posited that *some senator resigned* is true just in case for at least one object x that is a senator, *x resigned* is true. Similarly, the logical meaning of *there might be a parrot in the box* is just that there is at least a possibility of parrot presence in the box—which doesn't preclude this from being a known fact (here, too, this basic meaning explains why it's not contradictory to say that *there might be a parrot in the box—in fact, there must be one*). Adults are bad logicians in this case: they reject sentences that ought to be impeccable in view of the situation!

But there is a second thing to notice: The reason adults reject these sentences is that they compute an implicature. *Might* competes with *must*, and thus from this statement, *There might be a parrot in the box*, we infer that this isn't a necessity. This inference runs counter to what is known in the situation, and so we reject the sentence. Similarly, *some* competes with *all*, and as a result, from *some elephants have trunks*, we derive the implicature that *not all elephants have trunks*. This implicature is obviously false, so we reject the sentence. The reason children seem to be more logical than adults is simply that they fail to compute scalar implicatures.

This phenomenon is fairly general and applies to *or*, which motivated our initial discussion of scalar implicatures. As an example, in a different experiment conducted by another group, subjects are shown a story in which four boys can choose a variety of toys, and each ends up choosing a skateboard and bike. Subjects are then asked to accept or reject this sentence:

Every boy chose a skateboard or a bike.

Adults reject this sentence because they compute an implicature to the effect that *not every boy chose a skateboard and a bike*—which is false in this case. But quite a few children tend to accept the sentence.[13] The reason is that they fail to compute the implicature.

What is the source of this phenomenon? The debate is still ongoing, but it might be related to the construction of alternatives. It can be established in other experiments that children know that under-informative statements are suboptimal. Specifically, when they are given an explicit choice between the *or* and the *and* sentence in this case, they go for the optimally informative one—namely, the sentence with *and*. But if they are just given an under-informative sentence with *or*, they seem to have trouble computing the alternative with *and*, hence they fail to realize that it would have been a more appropriate thing to say.[14] In other words, they know that one should be maximally informative, but they seem to have difficulty constructing the right alternatives for the sentences they hear.

In sum, implicatures don't just make it possible to analyze the behavior of *or* and other scalar expressions in adult language. They provide fascinating new insights into the development of child language and explain the apparent paradox that children sometimes seem to be more 'logical' than adults.

### 10.8 IMPLICATURES TAKE TIME

There is another result that shows how fruitful implicatures can be: They turn out to explain the time course of online interpretation in adults. The idea is this: Enriching the inclusive meaning of *or* with a *not both* implicature should take time, because implicatures are superimposed on top of the literal meaning (and they involve some reasoning). So, if we have sufficiently precise measures of response times, it should be possible to show that subjects that compute implicatures respond more slowly than subjects that don't.

This is exactly what researchers found. Remember the sentence we discussed above:

Some elephants have trunks.

Most adults would reject this sentence, but some might accept it. What is the difference between them? The first group computes an implicature, to the effect that some *but not all* elephants have trunks—an obvious falsehood. The second group doesn't compute an implicature and for this reason takes the sentence to be true. Strikingly, the second group is faster than the first.[15] It can be shown by testing simpler true and false sentences (ones that have nothing to do with implicatures) that this isn't just because responding 'true' takes less time than responding 'false.' Rather, the group that responds 'true' is faster *because* it doesn't compute an implicature.

This result also leads to the expectation that subjects should take the sentence to be true more often if they are forced to answer very quickly. In a properly designed time-limited task, they won't have time to compute the implicature, and this will leave them with the literal meaning of the sentence and hence a true claim. This prediction too was borne out. In other words, implicatures take time—and the theory introduced in this chapter can thus explain fine-grained properties of the online interpretation of sentences.

## 10.9 MISLEADING WITH IMPLICATURES

Implicatures have more practical consequences as well. The fact that adults so readily draw inferences about *what was not said (but could have been)* turns out to be very important when one wants to mislead. What better way to do so than to imply something without stating it? This limits the risk of being caught red-handed, as one can always hide behind the literal meaning, while denying any implicature that may have been drawn.

The linguist Laurence R. Horn discusses a startling episode recounted by the *New York Times*.[16] Before February 1981, the Spanish government negotiated to have Picasso's masterpiece *Guernica* repatriated from New York to Spain after the death of dictator Franco, as specified in Picasso's will. A key issue, however, was to demonstrate that "the Spanish government had in fact paid Picasso to paint the mural in 1937 for the Paris International Exhibition." But there was a glitch: The person who had the archives that proved this demanded $2 million to cede them. The Spanish diplomat working on the case managed to get photocopies of the documents and proceeded to show them to the Paris lawyer named by Picasso to execute his will. This happened to be Roland Dumas, who would later become a minister of foreign affairs and would come to be known as a cunning diplomat himself. Upon seeing the documents, Dumas said:

> "This changes everything." He then asked casually: "You of course have the originals?"
> The Spanish envoy replied: "Not all of them."

This was enough to convince Dumas. The reply was literally true, since the Spaniard had none of the originals. But his reply carried the implicature that he had *most* of them, which was enough to outwit Dumas.

Implicatures can save in trials as well. The following exchange went all the way to the U.S. Supreme Court.[17] Samuel Bronston was a movie producer with activities in Europe, and after his firm filed for bankruptcy protection, he was questioned under oath at the creditors' committee meeting about overseas assets.

> "Q. Do you have any bank accounts in Swiss banks, Mr. Bronston?"
> "A. No, sir."
> "Q. Have you ever?"
> "A. The company had an account there for about six months, in Zurich."

Alas, it was later discovered that Bronston had in fact held a personal account in Geneva. He was convicted for perjury, since his answer implied that he had no such bank account.

The case went all the way to the Supreme Court, which decided otherwise: In 1973, it unanimously sided with Bronston. Why? His answer was misleading all right, but he had said nothing that he believed to be false. While he was being interrogated, he didn't hold bank accounts in Swiss banks any longer, so his first answer was truthful. His second answer (*The company had an account there*) strongly suggested that he himself had not held an account in a Swiss bank in the past. In view of the question (*Have you ever?*), replying that *the company had* implicated that he himself hadn't, for if so this would have been a more useful answer to provide. This was entirely misleading, but what he literally said—that the company had held a Swiss account—was truthful. Thanks to this highly misleading implicature, Bronston was able to avoid a perjury conviction—or rather, to have it annulled after it reached the Supreme Court. The precedent still stands and is known as the 'literal truth' rule. Sometimes implicatures save . . . from conviction.

### 10.10 CONCLUSION

*We are the people ('Wir sind das Volk'). We are one people ('Wir sind ein Volk').* These rallying cries epitomize the peaceful German revolution of 1989–1990, not just through their literal meaning, but also through their implicatures: They evoke alternatives that they powerfully reject. *We are the people, not you, the police. We are one people, not two.* In speech, these alternatives are naturally evoked by focusing the crucial words: *WE are the people. We are ONE people.* To paraphrase them even more explicitly, we can use the word *only*, whose function is precisely to say something about alternatives: *Only WE are the people. We are only ONE people.*

But implicatures are pervasive in far more mundane situations. They are a prime tool of pragmatic enrichment, one that is ubiquitous in language. Scalar implicatures offer a powerful analysis of multiple constructions that would be mysterious without them. We motivated them by an analysis of the word *or*, but they had far broader repercussions. It was by no means trivial to decompose the exclusive use of *or* into an inclusive *or* (the only meaning there is, according to this analysis), combined with an implicature that the alternative with *and* is false. This correctly predicted cases in which *or* can or cannot be enriched by an implicature: Implicatures can only enrich meaning, so in environments that reverse informativity, using *or* is already the most informative choice one can make and no implicature arises. But this also gave rise to an entirely new analysis of *and* in such environments. Because a sentence with *and* is, in this case, less informative than one with *or*, we predicted new implicatures. For this reason, *I doubt I'll invite both Robin and Sam* leads to the inference that *I think I'll invite Robin or Sam*—and further subtle facts followed as well.

There were further benefits to the analysis of implicatures: It gave a striking explanation for the surprising fact that children appear to be more 'logical' than adults (it's just that they don't compute implicatures), and also that certain interpretations of *might* and *or* take more time than others (because it takes time to compute an implicature). The concept of implicature has thus had far-reaching repercussions for our understanding of language. It has practical consequences as well: If one wishes to mislead while maintaining plausible deniability, implicatures are a weapon of choice. That's because implicatures, unlike literal meaning, are an optional and hence easily deniable component of what is said.

Stepping back, implicatures make a broader scientific point. Sometimes the best theory is one that 'divides and conquers,' postulating two modules (literal meaning and implicatures) to account for what seemed to be a unitary phenomenon (the meaning of *or*). The test of this theory lies in its ability to explain numerous further linguistic facts (such as the meaning of *and* in negative environments), but also in psychological data of a completely different nature: The effects of the two modules can be teased apart in language acquisition (young children can have literal meaning without scalar implicatures) and also in online processing by adults (computing implicatures takes time). In other words, the division between literal meaning and implicatures has palpable psychological reality and provides insights into the organization of meaning in the human mind (we will see in chapter 14 that this division has consequences for gestures as well).

# 11 NOT AT ISSUE: PRESUPPOSITIONS, SUPPLEMENTS, AND EXPRESSIVES

In 2017, a real-life online poll asked:

Will Barack Obama ever see real punishment for his crimes?

Now whatever you may think of Barack Obama, this is not a neutral question: It presupposes that Barack Obama committed some crimes. A consequence is that whether the respondents choose *yes* or *no*, they will have tacitly accepted the presupposition that Barack Obama did in fact commit crimes—something that most people wouldn't grant.

Things can get more devious. As lawyers well know, some questions are loaded:

Have you stopped mistreating your lover?

Here, too, the unfortunate defendant can neither answer *yes* nor *no* without granting the existence of the lover and the fact that the lover was mistreated by the defendant.

The expressions responsible for this nefarious semantic behavior are many, but they have something in common: They are presented as not being at issue (i.e., as not being open to debate), hence their ability to commit the unfortunate respondents to claims they might prefer to reject. More specifically, the reason our two questions are anything but neutral is that they contain presuppositions, components of meaning that are presented as being taken for granted. *His crimes* presupposes that the relevant person, here Obama, did in fact commit crimes. The same effect would be obtained with the description *the crimes he committed*. *Your lover* presupposes that the addressee has a lover. *His crimes* and *your lover* are instances of definite descriptions, a simpler example of which is *the winner*, already discussed in chapter 6. They have in common that they presuppose that the nominal expression is true of exactly one thing (or more precisely of exactly one maximal thing, as we argued for the plural *the winners* in section 6.2). So if I ask after a lottery, *Is the winner happy?*, I thereby presuppose that exactly one person picked the winning number. But there are presuppositions besides definite descriptions: *x stopped mistreating y* presupposes that x used to mistreat y (in order to stop doing something, you have to have been doing it), hence the unfortunate defendant's quandary.

Presuppositions are ubiquitous in language, and they make it possible to smuggle in claims that the addressee cannot easily challenge. Their use and abuse to bias readers of polls seems to be alive and well. In 2019, some groups received an invitation to take "Donald Trump's official impeachment poll," and two of the questions read as follows:

> Are you against these baseless impeachment proceedings?
> Do you believe that Democrats will continue with baseless impeachment pro-
> ceedings as long as President Trump is in office?

If you were in favor of impeachment, your desire to answer *no* to the first question was certainly diminished by the presupposition that the proceedings were baseless (here the culprit is not the word *the* but *these*). As for the second question, it presupposed that the Democrats were engaged in baseless impeachment proceedings. Here the culprit is not *stop* but *continue* (*Have you continued to mistreat your lover?* asks a different question from *Have you stopped mistreating your lover?*, but it triggers the same presupposition).

These ploys are by no means a recent invention. Fallacies resulting from presuppositions have a long history and were already known in the fourth century BC in Greece. Eubulides of Miletus famously discussed the question, *Have you lost your horns?* Whether you reply *yes* or *no*, you will have granted that you used to have horns. Some presuppositions are more momentous. A popular Christian slogan is: *Jesus saves*. The New Testament has more specific statements, such as this one:

If you declare with your mouth, "Jesus is Lord," and believe in your heart that God raised him from the dead, you will be saved. (Romans 10:4–15)

When you read *you will be saved* in this context, you are told two things at once: First, that you are in grave danger (presumably because of your sins); second, that this condition can be alleviated (thanks to your belief in Jesus). These two components of meaning don't have the same status. It is *presupposed* that you are danger, and it is *asserted* that this can be remedied. Presuppositions are presented as being uncontroversial; assertions are what is at issue. Just like *yes* and *no*, questions target the at issue component but preserve the presuppositions. *Will I be saved?* As soon as you ask the question, you have accepted the presupposition that you are in fact in danger. And whether the answer is *yes* or *no*, the presupposition remains the same—namely, that you are in need of salvation, and this part is presented as obvious.

The remarkable fact, then, is that language doesn't just convey information about the world: It simultaneously tells you what the status of this information is and, in particular, whether it should be at issue or not. This may help us concentrate on the main point of an utterance; occasionally, this may also trick us into committing to assumptions we would prefer to reject (since presuppositions are typically preserved by a *yes* as well as by a *no* answer). As we will see, presuppositions are a prime example of a content that is not at issue, but there are others: language offers remarkably subtle ways to present contents as being off the table for discussion.

## 11.1 WHAT PRESUPPOSITIONS ARE

What is a presupposition? It is a component of meaning that is presented as being already settled and thus redundant (i.e., uninformative). Given the assumptions of the conversation, disregarding or 'erasing' this component should make no difference at all. So if I tell you that *John knows that he is incompetent*, I am presupposing and thus presenting as already settled that John *is* incompetent. And I am calling your attention instead to the fact that he correctly believes that he is incompetent. As a result, the question

*Does John know that he is incompetent?* still presents John's incompetence as a settled fact and just asks whether he has an awareness of it.

Presuppositions radically differ from more standard components of meaning such as (asserted, at issue) entailments. If I tell you that *Robin lives in France*, it certainly follows that *Robin lives in the European Union*. But if I negate the original sentence, the entailment disappears: *Robin doesn't live in France* certainly doesn't entail that *Robin lives in the European Union*—the negation suspends any such commitment and leaves open that Robin might live in Canada or in the UK, for instance. Things are very different with presuppositions: *Ann knows that Robin lives in France* gives rise to the inference (a presupposition!) that *Robin lives in France*. But *Ann doesn't know that Robin lives in France* still carries the inference, despite the negation. As a result, if I tell you that *the guy we just hired doesn't know that he is incompetent*, I am not merely denying the conjunction of *the guy we just hired is incompetent, and (correctly) believes that he is*.[1] Rather, I am presupposing that this guy is incompetent and denying that he believes that he is.

There are many further linguistic environments in which entailments disappear but presuppositions are preserved. Questions are a case in point. If I ask, *Does Robin live in France?*, there is no inference that Robin lives in the European Union. On the other hand, in the question *Does John know that he is incompetent?*, the inference is preserved that he is in fact incompetent. *Will Jesus save me?* similarly preserves the inference that I am in grave danger. The same remark extends to questions like *Did you understand her?* In this case, the inference that the person talked about is female is once again preserved.

Presuppositions are preserved in many further environments from which entailments disappear. *Maybe Robin lives in France* doesn't entail that *Robin lives in the European Union*. *Maybe* removes the entailment. But here, too, presuppositions are preserved: *Maybe John knows he is incompetent* leaves little doubt about his incompetence. *Maybe Jesus will save me* similarly presupposes that I am in danger. Things can get more surprising. *None of the guys we hired comes from France* doesn't tell you much about where they do come from, and certainly implies nothing about their relation to the European Union. Given its negative meaning, *none* removes the entailment. But strikingly, in the same environment, presuppositions are preserved, and in a particularly strong form. *None of the guys we hired knows that he is incompetent* yields, despite the negative word *none*, a strong inference that each the of guys in question is in fact incompetent.

Going back to the online poll I mentioned at the outset, we now see why its question was loaded. Asking *Will Barack Obama be punished for his crimes?* presupposes that he committed several crimes, owing to the possessive description *his crimes* (an instance of a definite description). That's why either answer—*yes* or *no*—will commit the respondent to the presupposition. *Have you stopped mistreating your lover?* presupposes that the addressee has a lover (again because of the possessive description, *your lover* in this case) and that this unfortunate person was mistreated. This is because *you stopped doing x* presupposes that you did x before. *Did you stop smoking?* presupposes that you smoked, and *Did you stop mistreating x?* presupposes that you mistreated x. Similarly, *Are you against these baseless impeachment proceedings?* presupposes that the proceedings in question are in fact baseless, because of the description *these*. *Will the Democrats continue with baseless impeachment proceedings?* (or the more complex version that appeared in the "official impeachment poll") presupposes that the Democrats are engaged in baseless proceedings. This is because of the word *continue*. *Will you continue to smoke?* presupposes that you currently smoke, and similarly *Will the Democrats continue with baseless impeachments proceedings?* presupposes that they are currently engaged in baseless impeachment proceedings. There are multiple ways for questions to be loaded because there are multiple words that trigger presuppositions.

The fact that presuppositions are presented as trivial can be exploited to humorous effect. Building on President Ronald Reagan's reputation as someone who didn't read much, the writer Gore Vidal once quipped:

> The Reagan Library burned down and both books were lost—including the one Reagan had not finished coloring.[2]

*Both* is a presupposition trigger: *Did you lose both of your books?* strongly suggests that you only have two, unlike the less loaded (but more pedestrian) question: *Did you have just two books and did you lose them?* Vidal's quip presents as established that Reagan had only two books. But that's not all: Just like *the crimes Obama committed* presupposes that Obama did commit crimes, *the book Reagan had not finished coloring* presupposes that there was exactly one book Reagan had not finished coloring, which in turn presupposes that this was a coloring book. (To top it off, there is a less direct suggestion that the other book too was of the same type, for otherwise why bother to refer to the first one in such a convoluted fashion?) What makes the joke, of course, is that the presuppositions are presented as already settled and thus self-evident. The content would be considerably less interesting if Gore Vidal had said instead: *The Reagan Library contained two books; it burned down and both were lost.*

A Soviet story from the 1970s went like this:[3]

> A proud Jewish grandmother is asked how old her two grandsons are. "Well, the doctor is five," she replies, "and the engineer will be two next month."

What makes the joke is that the grandmother is presupposing that the five-year-old is a future doctor and the two-year-old is a future engineer (of course, omitting 'future' contributes to the joke as well). You'll fully kill the joke if you say instead: *Well, one will be a doctor and he is five, and the other will be an engineer and he will be two next month.*

Just like presuppositions are presented as being already settled, the at issue component of sentences is presented as being nontrivial and informative (= the opposite of settled). This is the reason the following discourse is odd:

> Ann is in southern Italy. She is in Italy.

The second sentence makes a contribution that ought to be at issue, but this contribution is entirely redundant in view of the first sentence, which makes the discourse weird.

This nontriviality condition may seem like a subtle condition, but we already saw a version of it in . . . chimpanzees! We called it the Economy Principle ('Do not state the obvious!'). In chapter 1 (section 1.9), we discussed a field experiment with a fake snake. Primatologists noticed that when the target chimpanzee could determine that its audience had seen the snake, it produced fewer *hoos* (the snake-related call) than when the audience hadn't seen the threat. In effect, chimpanzees don't seem to go around uttering trivialities: it's not worth producing a *hoo* if its content is trivial.

Going back to humans, this condition of informativeness can also be exploited to humorous effect. Another Soviet story goes like this:[4]

> The Jewish boy comes home from school and says, "Ma, our psychologist says I have the Oedipus complex!" "Never mind," says the mother stroking the boy's head. "The important thing is that you love your mother!"

Since by definition the Oedipus complex implies that the boy loves his mother, the last sentence would be an odd thing to say if the mother knew what the complex is all about. Her answer shows that her understanding of the concept is rather hazy, although her practice certainly doesn't contradict it.


## 11.2 WEAK AND STRONG PRESUPPOSITIONS

While presuppositions are presented as being uncontroversial, in some cases there is a bit of room for maneuver. Given a sufficiently clear context, you can to some extent understand *stop smoking* without a presupposition. For instance, no presupposition is perceptible in the following example: *I notice that Ann keeps chewing on her pencil. Did she recently stop smoking?* Here the question is really *whether* Ann smoked and recently stopped, with no inference that she in fact smoked before.

But some presupposition are more demanding. If no person wearing a tie is visible or somehow salient, it is decidedly odd to ask (with an accent on *you*):

> Will YOU wear a tie too?

The question presupposes that somebody besides the addressee wears a tie, and it asks whether the addressee will do so as well. This is certainly not a way of asking whether two individuals, including the addressee, will wear ties.

The way *too* works involves focus (already discussed with different examples in chapter 10): *Will YOU wear a tie too?* presupposes that an alternative of the form *x will wear a tie* is true.[5] This would be a natural thing to say in a discourse like this one:

I will wear a tie. Will YOU wear a tie too?

If you stress *wear* instead, the meaning changes. Now the presupposition will be that an alternative of the form *you will x a tie* is true. This would be a natural thing to say in a different discourse:

I am told you intend to buy a tie. But will you WEAR a tie too?

*Too* can have powerful effects. In October 2017, the hashtag #MeToo spread on Twitter to denounce sexual harassment and sexual assault. The *Washington Post* poignantly recounts how the movement grew out of Tarana Burke's work:[6]

In Alabama, Burke worked at an organization that ran a youth camp. There was a girl there—Burke publicly calls her Heaven when she tells this story—who clung to her. "People would call her trouble," Burke said. "And she was trouble, because she was a survivor." Heaven was about 13 years old.

One day, Heaven wanted to talk to Burke privately. She began to tell Burke about the sexual violence she had survived. "I was not ready," Burke said. "When she disclosed, I rejected her." She sent her to someone else.

"She never came back to camp," Burke said. To this day, she doesn't know what happened to Heaven.

The guilt Burke felt became a refrain, a repeated question: "Why couldn't you just say 'me too?'"

In the original context, *me too* would have been a simple and powerful signal that the speaker had also been a victim of sexual violence. As a hashtag, this is powerful for a slightly different reason: *Me too* makes it clear that victims of sexual violence are now salient in the public discourse. Sexual violence must be the topic so that it can be understood what property *me too* refers to: *I am a victim of sexual violence too*. But in addition, *too* requires that the victims themselves should be salient. And giving the victims a voice was indeed one of the goals of the movement.

Some striking uses of *too* can be found in less serious contexts. In the following story, *too* is not just the last word but also the punchline:[7]

A Rabbi prays to God: "Why, Lord?" he cries out. "Why did this have to happen? How could my son, my only son, destroy me like this? My—my only son—he converted to Christianity!" And a great voice booms down from the heavens: "Yours, too?"

Although the last sentence is a question, it presents quite a bit of information as presupposed—namely, that the voice has a son, and that this son converted to Christianity. The reader only needs to connect the dots to infer that the Rabbi is not quite talking to the God he thinks, but rather to the God of the New Testament.

Another word with strong presuppositional requirements is *again*. *Are you in China again?* is no way of asking whether the addressee has been in China before and is there right now. Rather, it presupposes that the addressee was in China but stopped being there, and it asks whether the addressee is currently in China. Because the presupposition is so strong, using *again* can help convey that certain facts are not only true but also so uncontroversial that they go without saying. Political slogans have often made use of this device. Several examples popped up in U.S. presidential campaigns over the years:[8]

1932: Happy Days Are Here Again—Democratic candidate Franklin D. Roosevelt
1980: Let's Make America Great Again—Republican candidate Ronald Reagan
2004: Let America Be America Again—Democratic candidate John Kerry
2016: Make America Great Again!—Republican candidate Donald Trump
2016: Make America Sane Again—Libertarian candidate Gary Johnson

Roosevelt's 1932 slogan took for granted (not so controversially after the 1929 crisis) that happy days had been present earlier and had vanished. Reagan's 1980 slogan and Trump's 2016 version of it both took for granted that America had been great before and had stopped being so. John Kerry's 2004 slogan, for its part, took for granted that America had stopped being America, presumably during George Bush's first term. And the unofficial slogan of Gary Johnson's libertarian campaign was that America had been sane but had stopped, possibly around the time it nominated Donald Trump as the Republican candidate.

Some strong presuppositions are also triggered by pronouns. In fact, we already saw an example of this in chapter 2. *She is approaching* presupposes that the person denoted is female and asserts that she is approaching. The presupposition is strongly preserved in the question, *Is she approaching?* This is a very different question from *Is this a woman approaching?*, which asks whether (rather than presupposes that) the denoted person is a woman. We also discovered in chapter 2 a strong similarity between gender specifications of English pronouns and height specifications of sign language pronouns, and these too trigger presuppositions. In English, if I say *I didn't understand her*, what is denied is that there was understanding on my part, not that the person I am talking about is female, as is expected since the latter component is presupposed. In ASL or LSF, if one signs an equivalent of *I didn't understand ↗*, with a pronoun pointing upward, it will be presupposed that the person referred to is tall (or important or powerful), and what will be denied is that the signer understood the person. In this case as in others, the preservation of presuppositions in negative sentences is one of their characteristic properties.

The presuppositions of gender features can be used to powerful rhetorical effect. At the height of the coronavirus epidemic in March 2020, *New York Magazine* ran an article entitled:[9]

The Leader of the Free World Gives a Speech, and She Nails It.

The article was about German Chancellor Angela Merkel, who combined empathy and clarity in a speech that quickly went viral. Many readers might have thought that *the leader of the free world* referred to the then U.S. president, Donald Trump. The use of *she* showed that the journalist took the leader of the free world to be a woman, Chancellor Merkel, and furthermore, it presented this fact as being entirely uncontroversial and thus obvious.

## 11.3 PRESUPPOSITIONS AND LINGUISTIC CONTEXT

At this point, it might look like presuppositions don't interact much with the details of the sentences they appear in. In questions as well as with *not* and *maybe*, presuppositions are preserved, unlike entailments. But when we dig deeper, things get more interesting: Presuppositions sometimes genuinely interact with the logical structure of sentences. As we saw before, it is odd to ask *Will YOU wear a tie too?* unless it is established that some salient person is wearing a tie. But there is no such requirement in the following more complex sentence:

If I ever wear a tie, will YOU wear a tie too?

It is certainly not established in this context that I will in fact wear a tie, or else the *if*-clause would be idle. Rather, the *if*-clause itself (rather than the extra-linguistic situation) provides the appropriate context for the presupposition triggered at the end of the sentence.

The same behavior is displayed by possessive descriptions. *Will John quarrel with his wife?* presupposes that John has a wife. But if we add an appropriate *if*-clause, this presupposition doesn't show up anymore:

If John ever gets married, will he quarrel with his wife?

The presupposition triggered at the end of the sentence doesn't have to be satisfied in the initial context of the conversation; rather, it is satisfied by the *if*-clause itself.

This provides a clue about what presuppositions are. You might initially have thought that they are just meaning components that must already be established in the nonlinguistic context: They are thus redundant (i.e., obvious) in view of that context. This was indeed the case in our simpler examples (e.g., *Will YOU wear a tie too?*). Here, the fact that *somebody besides the addressee will wear a tie* was presented as obvious (for instance because of the speaker's conspicuous tie). But as soon as we consider more complex sentences, we find cases in which presuppositions are not preestablished in the nonlinguistic context; rather, a presuppositional expression may be made acceptable by what appears in its immediately linguistic environment, as in the sentence, *If I ever wear a tie, will YOU wear a tie too?* Here it just isn't presented as obvious that *somebody besides the addressee will wear a tie*, as the sentence leaves this entirely open. However, this proposition is in fact redundant when it comes after the *if*-clause: the underlined component below feels uninformative because it adds nothing to the content of the *if*-clause.

If I ever wear a tie, <u>somebody besides you will wear a tie</u> and. . . .

Importantly, then, presuppositions are meaning components that are presented as redundant in view of the context *combined* with the preceding linguistic environment.

Somewhat paradoxically, learning that a bit of information is redundant may be very informative about what the speaker takes for granted. We saw examples of this with the #MeToo hashtag and also with political slogans using *again*. But other examples crucially involve the linguistic environment:

If John ever gets married, will he quarrel with his husband?

The presupposition triggered by *his husband* is that John has a husband, but here too this couldn't be obvious in view of the extra-linguistic context (because, if so, the *if*-clause would be idle). Rather, *John has a husband* is presented as obvious in view of the context combined with the linguistic environment—namely, the *if*-clause. Thus, the speaker presents as uncontroversial the statement:

If John gets married, he will have a husband.

In other words, the speaker presents as established that John is gay.

Here, too, you can think about it like this: In the initial sentence, the contribution made by the presupposition (underlined below) should be redundant in view of the words that precede it:

If John gets married, <u>John will have a husband</u> and he will quarrel with his husband.

What would it take to make the underlined words redundant in view of what precedes it? Precisely an assumption that *if John gets married, he will have a husband.*

The same phenomenon can be found with *too*:

If Trump Jr. met with a Russian lawyer, did Trump Sr. too violate the law?

If no other person has been mentioned in the discourse, this strongly suggests that for Trump Jr. to have met with a Russian lawyer would have counted as a violation of the law. Why do we draw such an inference? Earlier, we saw that the question *Will YOU wear a tie too?* presupposes that someone salient besides the addressee will wear a tie. In similar fashion, *Did Trump Sr. too violate the law?* presupposes that someone salient besides Trump Sr. violated the law. In view of the *if*-clause, this salient person must be Trump Jr. As a result, the sentence can be unpacked as follows, with the underlined component presented as redundant in this linguistic context:

> If Trump Jr. met with a Russian lawyer, <u>Trump Jr. violated the law</u> and Trump Sr. violated the law.

Since the underlined part must make an uninformative (i.e., redundant) contribution in view of what precedes, it must be obvious that *if Trump Jr. met with a Russian lawyer, Trump Jr. violated the law.* The word *too* makes all the difference: if we drop it, the resulting sentence might *ask* whether meeting with a Russian lawyer counted as a crime (and could implicate Trump Sr.), rather than taking this for granted:

> If Trump Jr. met with a Russian lawyer, did Trump Sr. violate the law?

The simple idea that presuppositions are meaning components that are presented as redundant explains a lot of their behavior. *Our senator stopped taking bribes* presupposes that our senator took bribes because of the verb *stop*, which is similar to the example we discussed at the beginning of this chapter (*Have you stopped mistreating your lover?*). But in the same way, *Each of our senators has stopped taking bribes* presupposes that each of them used to take bribes, as can be seen by applying the question test:

> Did each of our senators stop taking bribes?
> *Inference:* Each of our senators took bribes before.

Why does the question trigger this inference about each of the senators? In effect, the question asks whether the following holds, with the presupposition underlined:

> Each of our senators <u>took bribes</u> and stopped.

The underlined part is presented as redundant given what precedes it, so the speaker takes for granted that *each of our senators took bribes.*

In sum, presuppositions give rise to a calculus of redundancy that turns out to be very informative. By presenting something as presupposed, we don't just convey it, we also present it as being already settled and uncontroversial—which is the reason our interlocutors can be put in a difficult position if they'd rather not accept the presupposition in question.

## 11.4 SUPPLEMENTS

There are more ways than one to put a defendant in a difficult position. *Did you stop mistreating your lover?* presupposed that the addressee was guilty of abuse, and as a result both a *yes* and *no* answer committed the addressee to this assumption. But similar results can be obtained with a very different construction:

> Did John Doe, who you mistreated, press charges?

Here, too, the question is anything but neutral, and answering with a *yes* or *no* will yield the impression that the addressee did in fact mistreat John Doe. A more neutral way of asking the question would be: *Did you mistreat John Doe, and did he press charges?* Here a 'no' answer is entirely compatible with a denial that the addressee mistreated John Doe in the first place.

In this case, the question is a loaded one because of the relative clause *who you mistreated*. It is called a <u>*non-restrictive relative clause*</u> because it doesn't further specify the reference of *John Doe*. This sharply contrasts with the case of *restrictive* relative clauses. For example: *The employee who you mistreated pressed charges*. Here the relative clause is crucial to identify the reference of the description. In other words, it further restricts the meaning of *employee*, and for this reason it's not preceded by the long pause that you can have in our John Doe example.

There are further differences between the two constructions. Restrictive *who* can be omitted, but non-restrictive *who* cannot be: I can say that *the employee you mistreated pressed charges* but not *John Doe, you mistreated, pressed charges*. Similarly, in some standard dialects of English, restrictive *who* can be replaced with *that* when it introduces a restrictive relative clause but not when it introduces a non-restrictive one. For example, one can say *the employee that you mistreated pressed charges* but not *John Doe, that you mistreated, pressed charges*.

Conversely, having a long pause helps bring out the non-restrictive reading. It can be further enhanced by adding *by the way*, which highlights the fact that the relative clause doesn't play a role in identifying the referent of the noun phrase. So, if I tell you that *the employee, who by the way you mistreated, pressed charges*, the relative clause is non-restrictive: the sentence presupposes that there is a single salient employee, and it adds in passing that you mistreated this unfortunate person.

Initially, it might look like non-restrictive relative clauses trigger presuppositions. *Does this guy know that he is incompetent?* presupposes that the relevant person is incompetent and asks about his beliefs. *Does this guy, who is incompetent, have an awareness of it?* Here the facts are rather similar, and they clearly contrast with a less loaded question formed with *and*: *Is this guy incompetent, and does he have an awareness of it?* But on closer inspection, there are two important differences between presuppositional expressions and non-restrictive relative clauses, which are said to contribute 'supplements,' not presuppositions. The first difference is that presuppositions are typically redundant whereas supplements are not. This can be seen in the following discourse:

John Doe and Mary Doe are both incompetent.

*Possible continuation:*  Does John know that he is?
*Odd continuation:*  Does John, who is, have an awareness of it?

The first sentence of the discourse clearly entails that John Does is incompetent. Adding this as a presupposition (triggered by the verb *know*) to the following sentence is entirely natural. But adding it as a supplement (i.e., by way of a non-restrictive relative clause) is decidedly odd. It sounds as if we are unnecessarily repeating something that was already established. This is a more general fact: unlike presuppositions, supplements should not be redundant.

The second difference is that supplements are just odd in certain negative contexts in which presuppositions are fine. If I tell you that *not one senator regrets underestimating the threat*, you'll infer that senators in fact underestimated the threat. But it's rather odd to utter the following sentence (I'll put a star * in front of it to indicate that it's odd):

> *Not one senator, who by the way underestimated the threat, got infected with the coronavirus.

If you drop *not*, the sentence becomes acceptable again:

> One senator, who by the way underestimated the threat, got infected with the coronavirus.

So non-restrictive relative clauses seem to genuinely dislike being in certain types of negative environments, unlike presuppositions.

I hasten to add that when they modify a proper name or a definite description, non-restrictive relative clauses are acceptable in negative environments, but their content is not targeted by the negation, as in this May 2016 excerpt taken from the *USA Today* website:[10]

> George Clooney, who played Batman, feels confident that America won't elect Trump, who thinks he's Batman.

Despite the negation, it is clear that the writer implied that Trump thought he was Batman (for good measure, a link was added to a CNN story entitled: '*I am Batman,' Trump tells boy on helicopter ride*).

In sum, presuppositions can smuggle in information that is not easily targeted by negation and other expressions, but they are not alone in this nefarious behavior. Non-restrictive relative clauses can smuggle in information as well. Unlike presuppositions, however, they are not presented as being redundant. Quite the opposite. They have to make a nonredundant contribution. And they are genuinely a different kind of beast from presuppositions, as shown by the fact that they dislike appearing in certain negative environments.

## 11.5 EXPRESSIVES

Besides presuppositions and supplements, another class of expressions makes contributions that are hard to deny. They are called expressives, and many of them are slurs. Among the more innocuous ones, the French are occasionally called *Frogs*, possibly because they are supposed to eat frogs' legs (they occasionally do). No matter what the origin of the term is, it has clear nonculinary implications: In a 1974 movie adaptation of Agatha Christie's *Murder on the Orient-Express*, a British woman observes detective Poirot after he sneezed, and exclaims: "What a funny little man!" To which her companion, a British colonel played by Sean Connery, replies: "Obviously a Frog." The colonel's intention isn't just to characterize Poirot's nationality, but also to insult the French in general, and Poirot along with them. (As it happens, Poirot is Belgian, so the *real* insult might just be that he is being mistaken for a Frenchman). Similarly, *Some Frogs oppose Brexit* suggests that the speaker doesn't like the French—and of course that the speaker thinks they are against Brexit. Now, let us add a negative expression, or put the sentence in a question:

> I doubt any Frogs oppose Brexit.
> Do any Frogs oppose Brexit?

The inference that the French oppose Brexit disappears, which is expected in view of the meaning of negative expressions and of questions. But what definitely does not disappear is the inference that the speaker dislikes the French.

There are many expressions that behave in this way. During and after World War I, the derogatory term *Boche* appeared in French and in English to refer to Germans. While the term is a bit incongruous today, asking whether *any Boches oppose Brexit* will be a telltale sign that the speaker doesn't like Germans (and might be especially old-fashioned too!). Innumerable ethnic slurs that are common in the English language behave in the same way. They provide specific information about the speaker's attitudes and are also offensive by the mere fact of being used.

Unlike supplements, expressives can appear in all sorts of negative environments. A non-restrictive relative clause was decidedly odd when combined with *not one senator*, but *Frog* can without difficulty appear in such environments:

> Not one senator will hire any Frog.

Slurs also differ from presuppositional expressions. For one thing, presuppositions are not offensive in anything like the way slurs are. *Does Robin know that I hate the French?* presupposes that I am prejudiced, but this doesn't cause offense in the way that a slur does. Slurs also differ from presuppositions in the way they interact with the linguistic context. As we saw a few paragraphs back, presuppositions are just meaning components that are presented as trivial in view of the preceding linguistic context. Thus, *Will Ann stop smoking?* presupposes that Ann smoked. But there is no such presupposition in the sentence: *If Ann smokes, will she stop smoking?* This is because the *Ann smokes* component of the question *Will she stop smoking?* is guaranteed to be redundant thanks to the *if*-clause, and as a result no additional requirements are imposed by the entire sentence: The presupposition has been absorbed by the *if*-clause. Slurs are different, however, as can be seen here:

> If I really hated the French, I wouldn't hire a Frog.

*If I really hated the French* should suffice to make the slur component of *a Frog* uninformative (and this is in fact what happens in comparable examples involving presuppositions—for example, *If I really hated the French, Robin would know that I do*). But this is still not enough to absorb the offensiveness: in slurs, this component seems to be inherited by the sentence no matter how complex and irrespective of components that could make it uninformative.

In the case of presuppositions and supplements, there are ways to defuse the information that is smuggled in. *Will Barack Obama ever see real punishment for his crimes?* It's not too hard to reply: *Well, I don't think he did commit crimes.* And the same rejoinder will work if a supplement is used instead: *Will Barack Obama, who committed multiple crimes, ever see real punishment?* With expressives, things are harder, especially with slurs. As soon as they are used, an offense is caused. More devious ways must be found to avoid the damage—as in this story, in which the insult *Schwein* (*swine* in German) is cleverly reinterpreted:[11]

> A little Jew in Hitler's Germany brushes by a Nazi officer, knocking him off balance. "Schwein" roars the Nazi, clicking his heels imperiously. To which the Jew, undaunted, makes a low bow and replies, "Cohen. Pleased to meet you."

The precise analysis of expressives can have far-reaching repercussions. In 2019, several soccer games in France had to be interrupted because supporters chanted songs with derogatory terms referring to gay people (one case involved the slur *pédé* ['faggot']). One of the supporters' lawyers argued that this measure was excessive:[12]

> In criminal law, what is prohibited is to insult a group of people because of their sexual orientation. But this isn't the case here, as the chants in question do not target the sexual orientation of a particular person. In general, the chants are about the Football League.

This didn't hold much sway,[13] and for good reason: Whoever the target of the term may be, the term that was used expressed a derogatory attitude toward gay people in general. The same holds of the term *Frog* as applied to French people. If I say that *this Frenchman is terrible*, I just denigrate the particular person I am referring to. If I say instead that *this Frog is terrible*, I denigrate French people in general. The term *Frog* is usually amusing. But when it comes to real slurs, they are anything but.

## 11.6 CONCLUSION

While presuppositions, supplements, and expressives display subtly different behaviors, they have something in common: They are not presented as the main point of an utterance, and this allows them to smuggle in information that cannot easily be targeted by negation, questions, and other logical expressions. Say any of the following:

> Does John know that he is incompetent?
> Will you hire John, who is incompetent?
> Will you hire a Frog?

While these are all questions, there is something that they do not call into question—namely, that John is incompetent or that the speaker doesn't like the French.

This is the reason presuppositions, supplements, and expressives can all be used to ask highly loaded questions. For the same reason, negation alone won't defuse the unwanted inferences. Using an expressive, a parliamentarian says about the president: *The country should get rid of this pig-headed fool!* The speaker asks him to show respect and to take it back. The parliamentarian could reply: *Okay, I take it back—the country shouldn't get rid of this pig-headed fool!* This won't quite satisfy the speaker because the insult is preserved in the negative sentence. Similarly, using a supplement, the parliamentarian could say: *The country should get rid of the president, who is behaving like a crook.* It won't quite address the speaker's admonition to say: *Okay, I take it back—the country shouldn't get rid of the president, who is behaving like a crook!* Here it is the supplement that is preserved in the negative statement. And similarly, suppose the offending sentence is: *The president should stop behaving as a crook.* Taking it back by just adding a negation (*the president shouldn't stop behaving as a crook!*) won't work either, this time because the presupposition is preserved.

So someone who disagrees with these meaning components will have to do something a bit more complex to defuse them than just adding a negation. In other words, these are cases in which one must disrupt the normal course of a conversation to avoid tacitly granting points that one disagrees with. While this is relatively easy to do with presuppositions and supplements, things are trickier with slurs: their mere occurrence suffices to cause offense, which is an excellent reason . . . not to use them, as many a parent has tried to argue.

# III  EXTENDING MEANING

*Having studied meaning in spoken and signed languages, we will now go on more adventurous explorations and investigate the meaning of nonstandard forms such as gestures and even music. This is the realm of 'Super Semantics,' the study of meaning beyond standard linguistic forms.*

*We already saw some of its applications to primate communication in chapter 1. In this part, we start from an uncontroversially linguistic phenomenon— the existence of rich mechanisms of iconic enrichment in sign language. It raises a question: Could it be that, along some dimensions at least, sign language is more expressive than spoken language? This is a natural thought because sign language has the same kind of logical structure as spoken language and richer means of iconic enrichment. But one might object that the comparison is unfair to spoken language: Sign language with iconicity ought to be compared to speech with gestures rather to speech alone. This consideration makes it necessary to study in some detail the ways in which gestures enrich words. It will lead us to an exploration of a rich typology that nicely dovetails with the inferential types we uncovered in earlier chapters. But gestures will also bring new insights into this typology. When words are fully replaced with some made-up gestures and even visual animations, the human mind divides their informational contribution on the fly among the rich typology we saw in earlier chapters. In other words, our mind has a meaning engine that can effortlessly apply to a variety of nonconventional forms.*

*The exploration of iconicity in gestures will naturally lead us to a more abstract form of iconicity—that found in music. We will revisit the perennial question of the meaning of music. We will discover that music has a systematic meaning, although it is in some ways far more abstract than that of words and is produced with very different means.*

# 12 ICONICITY REVISITED: SIGN WITH ICONICITY VERSUS SPEECH WITH GESTURES

## 12.1 THE IMPORTANCE OF GESTURES

It takes good signing skills to walk around while signing with one hand and holding one's smartphone with the other—a scene I evoked when we first discussed sign language in chapter 2. But of course, the action makes perfect sense. If you are a signer and want to talk on Skype or WhatsApp while walking, that's what you have to do. Hearing people often do something considerably weirder when they talk on the phone: They gesture and gesture while speaking and make all sorts of facial expressions as well—but their interlocutors catch none of those because the connection is audio only. You may have been struck by people that seem to be gesturing to themselves as they walk on the street. As you get closer, you realize that they have earphones on and are in the middle of an animated phone conversation. There's nothing wrong with them. They just can't repress the gestures.

This should give us pause: Gestures and facial expressions are so intimately connected to language that we can hardly speak without them, even if our interlocutors can't see them. Removing gestures can come at a cost, especially when intonation can't compensate. Writing without gestures and especially facial expressions can lead to serious misunderstandings. That's one reason why emoticons were invented. With punctuation marks, they produce iconic representations of facial expressions—for instance, :-) for a smiley face (which one should read with one's head tilted to the left). Social media makes heavy use of them to compensate for the absence of facial expressions. On Twitter, someone had this to say about Sci-Hub, a website that gives free and often illegal access to millions of scientific articles without regard to copyright:

I'm a librarian, so I'd never use Sci-Hub! ;-)

Without the emoticon ;-), which represents a wink, one would certainly understand that the librarian disapproves of Sci-Hub. The emoticon changes everything. Since the wink signals irony, the meaning is inverted, and we understand that the librarian is probably a Sci-Hub user but can't really write it in so many words on social media.

Emojis take emoticons one step further, with more realistic and diverse graphic representations: A smiling face is represented as ☺ and a wink as ☺. Emojis can also represent all sorts of gestures that would be hard to encode with punctuation marks, such as the thumbs-up gesture 👍. But there are many further important gestures, some of them strongly associated with some cultures. The Italian 'what do you want' gesture is realized with the fingertips of one hand held together, upright (it's also called the 'tulip' gesture because of its shape). It is so prevalent that it was probably borrowed by Italian Sign Language (LIS), where a sign with the same form is used as a grammatical marker of questions. In 2018, several petitions circulated online to ask that this gesture be made an emoji[1]—and at last, in 2020, it became one: 🤌.

Emojis are so interwoven with the written language that Chinese speakers are routinely offered emojis alongside characters when they type text in their computers and smartphones. So to enter the character for the Mandarin word for *good*, one may type *hao* using a Latin script transcription, at which point the computer offers some choices: The first one is the corresponding character —namely, 好, but the next choice is an emoji, 👌. Further character possibilities (which can also be pronounced as *hao*) only appear later. Emojis are also routinely integrated with normal words in English-language apps, especially when they try to predict what is the next 'word' one might want to use.

Emojis have become so prominent that, going full circle, some of them have been borrowed as gestures. In an episode of a Chinese series in which a somewhat inhibited lawyer finally falls in love with a client's sister, the male character asks right at the start of the relationship: *You're giving me a like?* The silent answer starts with a nod, followed by two gestures.[2]

**Figure 12.1.1**

It is clear from the context that this answer is a gestural rendition of 💪👍: The flexed muscle emoji extols the lawyer's strength, and the thumbs-up emoji expresses approval. Both emojis have gestural origins—and are here borrowed back into the gestural system.

Setting emojis aside for the moment, gestures have important theoretical ramifications for the comparison between signed and spoken languages. Sign languages have often been mischaracterized as being less expressive or sophisticated than spoken languages, but as we saw throughout this book, nothing could be further from the truth: Sign languages have the same types of grammatical and expressive resources as spoken languages. Sometimes, they even reveal logical structures that are covert in spoken language, as we saw in the case of variables (they are covert in spoken language but often visible in sign language, as discussed in chapter 2). Furthermore, sign languages make use of rich iconic resources *on top of* their sophisticated grammar. In particular, the form of a word can be modulated (i.e., modified) to resemble what it denotes. Thus, in the ASL sentence for *My group grew*, the verb *GROW* can be realized with broader endpoints to evoke a larger growth, and it can also be realized more rapidly to evoke a faster growth. In rare cases, this can be done in English, too. If you say that *the talk was loooong*, your interlocutor will understand that it was very long, because the length of the vowel gives an idea of the length of the talk. But as we saw before, means of iconic enrichment are far more diverse in sign language. From this perspective, then, spoken language looks like an iconically challenged version of sign language: while it has the same kinds of logical resources, it is devoid of many of its means of iconic enrichment.

This is where gestures come into the picture. Maybe our conclusion about spoken language is too hasty. It would make good sense to compare sign language with iconicity to speech with gestures rather than to speech alone. Could it be, then, that speech with gestures is a good match for sign with iconicity? Think of *grow* in English. *Sam has grown* can mean that Sam has grown *a lot* if the speaker adds to *grow* a gesture representing the person's height. For instance, like this:

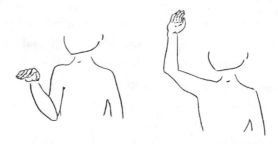

**Figure 12.1.2**

Similarly, if I tell you that *I caught a fish*, I may produce with *fish* a gesture indicating how large it was, as so:

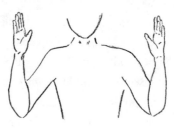

**Figure 12.1.3**

Unlike the thumbs-up gesture 👍, these are not primarily conventional. The gesture is a simplified pictorial representation of the person's height or of the fish's size, and thus they have an iconic character reminiscent of iconic modulations in sign language.

So, is sign with iconicity really the same thing as speech with gestures? While the debate is open, I'll argue that the answer is *no*, or rather *not quite*. But to understand why, we will need to see how gestures fit in the typology of inferences that we discovered in earlier chapters. The short of it is that iconic modulations of signs, as in *GROW* and *loooong*, can make standard at issue (i.e., assertive) contributions. By contrast, gestures that modify speech have a parasitic status and are not normally used with an at issue meaning. This is why there is in the end a systematic difference between sign with iconicity and speech with gestures—or so I will argue.

While our investigation of gestures is motivated by the comparison between speech and sign, it will lead to a surprising discovery: Depending on whether they accompany, follow, or replace words, gestures fall rather neatly in the typology of inferences we uncovered in chapter 11 (presuppositions and supplements will play a central role in our discussion). This is our first step toward a linguistic analysis of apparently nonlinguistic phenomena; there will be more in later chapters.

### 12.2 ICONIC MODULATIONS

As we noted, *loooong* means something like *very long*, and thus it makes a standard, at issue contribution. If I ask you, *Was the talk loooong?*, I am in effect *asking* whether it was very long. And there is no inference that it was in fact long, as would be the case if I used a presupposition or a supplement, as in: *Did you know the talk would be long?* (clear inference that the talk was long), or *Did you attend the talk, which was long?* (same inference).

Now the behavior of *loooong* resembles that of ASL *GROW*, which can be modulated in more interesting ways. To remind you, the sign looks like this, with the two hands initially forming a sphere, and then moving away from each other:

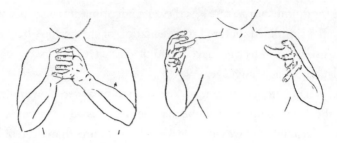

**Figure 12.2.1**

While this is a conventional word that one has to learn, it can be modulated to yield different meanings. The iconic rules go like this: *The faster the movement of the hands, the faster the growth process. The bigger the sphere* [formed by the final position of the hands], *the larger the final size of the group*. And just as is the case with English *loooong*, the iconic modulation makes an at issue contribution. In ASL, there are multiple cases of such iconic (and at issue) modulations, including in the realization of repetition-based plurals discussed in Section 4.2 (the number and arrangement of the repetitions provides information about the number and arrangement of the denoted objects), and in the realization of repetition-based pluractionals mentioned in Section 4.4 (the number and speed of the repetitions indicates how the action was performed).

The upshot is that in English and ASL alike, iconic modulations make full-fledged, at issue contributions. However, English is iconically challenged in this area, simply because the vocal modality is more limited in its iconic potential than the gestural/signed modality (of course, if you wish to evoke sounds, the vocal modality will be at an advantage, but that's not such a common occurrence).

The question, then, is whether English has comparable resources to ASL when we reintroduce gestures into the picture. The answer will be 'not quite.' The reason, as we will now see, is that gestures do not typically make at issue meaning contributions; rather, depending on their timing, they trigger presuppositions or supplements.

## 12.3  CO-SPEECH GESTURES TRIGGER PRESUPPOSITIONS

Suppose that little Robin tells you the following, with a slapping gesture co-occurring with *punish* (*co* means *with* in Latin, which is why these gestures are called *co-speech gestures*; the picture appears right above the expression it co-occurs with, and the latter is boldfaced):[3]

I am going to **punish** my enemy.

Clearly, you'll get an inference from this gesture—namely, that little Robin intends to punish the enemy in question by slapping him or her. The effect might initially seem rather similar to that obtained with the explicit adverbial expression *like this*, where *this* refers to slapping action:

I am going to punish my enemy like **this**.

Here, *like this* means the same thing as *by slapping him/her*. But does our initial sentence, with the slapping gesture co-occurring with the verb, really have the same meaning?

Not quite. There is a subtle difference between the two constructions, which can be perceived if little Francis asks little Robin one of the following questions:

Are you going to **punish** your enemy?

Are you going to punish your enemy like **this**?

The first question leaves open whether there will be a punishment, but there is something that it takes for granted—namely, that the punishment in question would involve a slapping-like action. In other words, it takes for granted that:

If you punish your enemy, slapping will be involved.

The *like this* question assumes nothing of the sort (although it does suggest that some punishment or other is likely). Why such a difference?

There is nothing too surprising about the meaning of the expression *like this*. *This* can refer to an object (such as a table) or to an action, if one is made sufficiently salient. In our case, *this* refers to the action depicted by the gesture. Thus the meaning contribution of *like this* is expected, as it behaves in the same way as other adverbials, such as *with your fists*, *physically*, and so on. These expressions make at issue contributions, and so does *like this*.

What is surprising, on the other hand, is that despite the question, the gesture co-occurring with *punish* triggers a conditional inference. This inference turns out to be a presupposition. As we saw in chapter 11, presuppositions interact in a peculiar way with questions, negations, and the word *maybe*. The statements *Did Ann stop smoking?*, *Ann didn't stop smoking*, and *Maybe Ann stopped smoking* all suggest that Ann smoked before. Inferences triggered by co-speech gestures interact in similar ways with these contexts; the only difference is that the inference itself is more complicated because it is conditional in nature, as we saw above ('if you punish your enemy, slapping will be involved'). But once we take this difference into account, co-speech gestures behave like *stop smoking*. The following sentences, respectively, deny and evoke the possibility that there will be punishment, but they both take for granted that *if a punishment is exerted, slapping will be involved*.

I won't **punish** my enemy.

Maybe I will **punish** my enemy.

Facial expressions behave in this respect like manual gestures: They trigger conditionalized presuppositions. Suppose someone utters the following sentence, with a disgusted facial expression accompanying the thought of *skiing with my parents*:

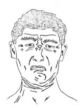

I'll go **[skiing with my parents]**.

It won't be hard to infer that the speaker finds this prospect repulsive: Skiing with his parents is presented as somehow disgusting. If you put this in a question, or add a negation or the word *maybe*, the result will be the same as with the manual gestures we discussed. That is, we obtain an inference that if the speaker were to go skiing with his parents, disgust would be involved.

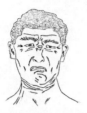

I won't go **[skiing with my parents]**.

You can perform the test: The same inference is obtained if the speaker says instead *Maybe I'll go **skiing with my parents***, with a disgusted expression co-occurring with the boldfaced words. Thus, the disgusted facial expression triggers a presupposition, although a more complex one (due to the conditional) than *stop smoking*.

Disgusted facial expressions have another advantage: They make it possible to test a counterpart of co-speech gestures in sign language. Using manual gestures as co-sign gestures is usually difficult because the hands are already occupied by the signing! Sometimes the same problem arises with the face, as facial expressions can play an essential grammatical role in sign language (for instance, in ASL, yes-no questions can be marked by raising one's eyebrows, and as we briefly saw in section 10.3, this can serve to mark focus as well). Still, there are *also* facial expressions that are not grammatical. In particular, one can test the behavior in sign language of disgusted facial expressions of the sort we just discussed in English. And lo and behold, in ASL at least, some behave like their English counterparts and trigger conditionalized presuppositions as well.

Some co-speech 'gestures' can take a very unusual form. The linguists Robert Pasternak and Lyn Tieu performed an experiment to compare the behavior of standard co-speech gestures with noises co-occurring with spoken words and with emojis surrounding some words.[4] On the face of it, these look nothing like gestures, and yet they display the characteristic semantic behavior of co-speech gestures by triggering conditionalized presuppositions. In one example, the sound of an explosion was artificially added to *assassinate his target*:

BOOOOOOOOOOOM
The soldier will    [**assassinate his target**].
[**AV12.3.1**]

The effect is unmistakable: One gets the inference that the soldier will assassinate his target *via an explosion*. What is particularly interesting is the negative case:

BOOOOOOOOOOOM
The soldier will not    [**assassinate his target**].
[**AV12.3.2**]

Despite the negation, subjects obtained a conditionalized presupposition to the effect that *if the soldier were to assassinate his target, he would do so via explosion*. The explosion sound really seems to behave like a vocal gesture of sorts—although one that isn't produced by the speaker's mouth, which is occupied with . . . words. Here, too, this presupposition disappears if instead you use a *like this* expression (just as was the case above with *punish my enemy like this*):

The solder will not assassinate his target like this: BOOOOOOOOOOOM.
[**AV12.3.3**]

Pasternak and Tieu also showed that some emojis display the behavior of co-speech gestures (I say 'some' because there is a lot of ongoing research on the semantics of emojis, and they certainly have a diverse behavior). Here the experiment had to involve written words, of course. What they did to maximally imitate the behavior of a gesture co-occurring with a word was to have two emojis surrounding the target expression; this may not be the most natural use of emojis, but it is a good first step to build a bridge between the analysis of co-speech gestures and emojis. So, subjects saw sentences like the following, where *step out of the classroom* was surrounded with a toilet emoji.

The student will 🚽 step out of the classroom 🚽.

The effect was clear: the sentence was understood to mean that the student in question will step out of the classroom *to go to the bathroom*.

Here, too, the crucial effect arose in the negative case:

The student will not 🚽 step out of the classroom 🚽.

Despite the negation, subjects drew the inference that if the student were to step out of the classroom, it would be to use the toilet. This is exactly the kind of conditionalized presupposition we saw with co-speech gestures, facial expressions, and even sounds in our earlier examples. In other words, some emojis genuinely seem to function like co-speech gestures (and there will no doubt be a lot more fine-grained research on this uber-cool topic in the coming years).[5]

## 12.4   POST-SPEECH GESTURES TRIGGER SUPPLEMENTS

Since the freedom of iconic modulations can't be obtained with co-speech gestures, maybe we will get more promising results by putting gestures after the words they modify—thus using 'post-speech gestures' *(post* means *after* in Latin, which is why this terminology was chosen). Suppose little Robin once again utters some fighting words, but now with a post-speech gesture instead of a co-speech one. In the example below, the dash (—) indicates a pause between the last word and the gesture.

I will punish my enemy –          .

As in the case of co-speech gestures, the inference is that the punishment will involve a slapping. But when we add a negation, the similarity with co-speech gestures ends. In the previous section, we saw that the co-speech gesture with *won't* triggers the inference that *if I were to punish my enemy, slapping would be involved*:

I won't **punish** my enemy.

But when we try the same trick with post-speech gestures . . . it fails! The sentence is just odd (hence the star in front of it):

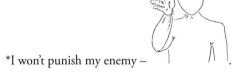

*I won't punish my enemy – .

At this point, you might recall that we already encountered a construction that doesn't like to be in certain negative contexts: non-restrictive relative clauses. Thus, it is odd to say: *Not one senator, who by the way underestimated the threat, got infected with the coronavirus.*

If we drop the negation, the sentence becomes impeccable. You can think of the post-speech gesture as having the same behavior as a nonrestrictive relative clause, for instance: *which will involve slapping him.* So little Robin could have said with the same kind of effect: *I will punish my enemy, which will involve slapping him.* But if you add a negation, the result becomes decidedly odd:

*I won't punish my enemy, which will involve slapping him.

Post-speech facial expressions turn out to behave in the same way, although a bit of reflection is required to see this. Adding a disgusted facial expression to the same positive sentence as before yields an unmistakable inference: the teenager who utters the sentences finds the prospect of going skiing with his parents disgusting.

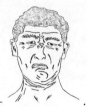

I'll go skiing with my parents – .

What happens when we add a negation? Unlike what happened in the case of the post-speech manual gesture, the result isn't odd anymore:

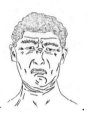

I won't go skiing with my parents – .

But the meaning (or at least one salient meaning) entirely changes. The facial expression doesn't convey information about skiing with one's parents, as was the case with our earlier example involving a co-speech facial expression:

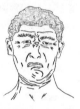

I won't go **[skiing with my parents]**.

The meaning obtained with the post-speech facial expression is (or at least can be) entirely different. It's not skiing with one's parents that entails disgust. Rather, it is the fact that the speaker *won't* go skiing with his parents that is presented as negative. In other words, the speaker would *love* to go skiing and is unhappy that he won't get to do so. And this ends up confirming the fact that post-speech facial expressions behave like non-restrictive relative clauses, which don't like to modify expressions that are in negative context. But if the entire sentence is modified instead, no problem at all arises, as can be seen here (the entire sentence contains a negation, but isn't itself *in* a negative environment):

I won't go skiing with my parents, which is a bummer.

So the upshot is that post-speech facial expressions also seem to behave like non-restrictive relative clauses.

As in our previous discussions, facial expressions are a very useful bridge between gestures in speech and in sign. And here, too, in ASL at least, disgusted post-sign facial expressions seem to display the behavior of non-restrictive relative clauses, with the same kind of difference between co-sign and post-sign facial expressions.

The conclusion is that post-speech and post-sign gestures and facial expressions display a rather uniform behavior, and this shows that gestures, too, have a grammar—in this case, the grammar of non-restrictive relative clauses. But there is also another lesson to be drawn from this investigation. We saw in chapter 11 that non-restrictive relative clauses trigger supplements and thus are not at issue. This means that post-speech gestures too will be a poor replacement for iconic modulations of signs, which *can* be at issue. In other words, our investigation has uncovered an interesting grammatical behavior but not a way of genuinely emulating iconic modulations with gestures.[6]

## 12.5   PRO-SPEECH GESTURES CAN BE AT ISSUE . . . BUT THEY ARE NOT WORDS

At this point, we have tried, and failed, to fully imitate the iconic modulation we saw in ASL *GROW*. Producing an overly long vowel in *loooong* seems to yield the same kind of effect, with a meaning contribution that is at issue. But modulations of this kind are severely limited in speech. Adding gestures would seem to solve the problem, except that this introduces peculiarities of its own. The meaning contributions of co-speech gesture are not at issue; rather, they behave like presuppositions, and those of post-speech gestures behave like non-restrictive relative clauses, hence they too fail to be at issue.

One last option I haven't discussed is to have gestures fully replace words and be 'pro-speech gestures' (*pro* in Latin can mean *replacing*, hence the terminology, and just like a pronoun replaces a noun, a pro-speech gesture replaces a spoken expression). Initially, things seem to work: Using a slapping gesture as a verb, we get a meaning similar to *slap*. When we add negation, we just negate this meaning, without the usual phenomena surrounding presuppositions and supplements, which remain unaffected by negation.

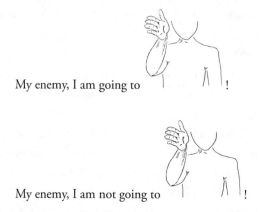

My enemy, I am going to                        !

My enemy, I am not going to                        !

So far, so good. Except that we haven't done at all the same thing as what signers can do with *GROW*. The reasons is that *GROW* is a conventional word and only the modulation is iconic. By contrast, there is no conventional word left in a pro-speech gesture! And what you can express in pure gestures is . . . well, severely limited. To give but two examples: In LSF, there are cases in which one can modulate the meaning of *UNDERSTAND* or *REFLECT* by altering the speed with which part of the sign is realized (to indicate a quick or difficult understanding process or reflection). How are you going to represent this in gestures? In this case, the power of sign language is that it starts from a conventional and very abstract verb and iconically modulates it to obtain a slightly different meaning. There is no way we can do something similar with pro-speech gestures.

## 12.6 CONCLUSION

Because of the rich iconic resources that come on top of its sophisticated grammar, sign language seems to be, along some dimensions, more expressive than spoken language. I asked at the beginning of this chapter whether the initial comparison between sign and speech might not have been unfair to speech. Because of the visual modality, sign has greater iconic resources than speech, and thus to restore equality one needs to compare sign with iconicity to speech with gestures. What we have discovered is that even when we do so, systematic differences arguably remain.

The key observation is that signs can often be modulated in highly iconic ways, as we saw with ASL *GROW* but also with LSF *UNDERSTAND* and *REFLECT*. And iconic modulations in these cases seem to be free to make at issue contributions, just as is the case of the iconic lengthening of the vowel in *loooong* in English. By contrast, when we add gestures to spoken words, they do not make an at issue contribution: Co-speech gestures are presuppositional, while post-speech gestures contribute supplements, just like non-restrictive relative clauses. So they won't quite deliver the same result as iconic modulations. To obtain meanings that are at issue, we need to use pro-speech gestures instead. But these are not conventional words, hence they can't express abstract notions like *understand* or *reflect*. To express the same thing as iconic modulations in sign language, we will often need to resort to complex paraphrases in speech combined with gestures. So, in the end, speech with gestures *isn't* really equal to sign with iconicity. While sign language has the same logical resources as spoken language, it can combine them with iconic contributions in significantly different ways from spoken language.

In the course of these investigations, we also made another discovery. Depending on their status and timing, iconic enrichments of spoken words (notably gestures) make at issue contributions, or trigger presuppositions, or behave like non-restrictive relative clauses. Disgusted facial expressions in English seem to pattern in the same way as co-speech and post-speech gestures, depending on their timing. And the same facts extend to disgusted facial expressions in ASL. In other words, there are gestures in sign language as well, but their behavior is easiest to study when they take the form of facial expressions—and when this is the case, they pattern just like co- and post-speech gestures in English.

In spoken language and sign language alike, then, we have uncovered a sophisticated typology of gestural meanings, with subtly different behaviors depending on whether the gestures co-occur with the words they modify, follow them, or fully replace them (this typology is illustrated below on the case of gestures enriching English sentences). Not only do gestures enhance human communication: their meanings fall under more general rules of human language.

| | Co-speech gestures | Post-speech gestures | Iconic modulations | Pro-speech gestures |
|---|---|---|---|---|
| Positive examples | 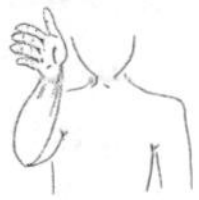 I will **punish** my enemy. | I will punish my enemy 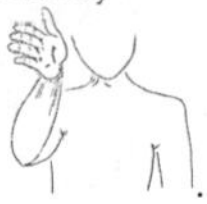 – . | The talk was loooooong. | My enemy, I am going to 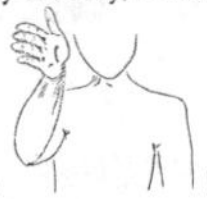 ! |
| Negative examples | 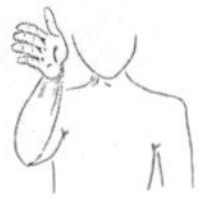 I won't **punish** my enemy. | *I won't punish my enemy 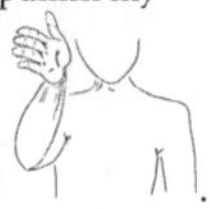 – . | The talk wasn't loooooong. | My enemy, I am not going to  ! |
| Meaning | presuppositions | supplements | at issue | at issue |

Figure 12.6.1

*Typology of iconic enrichments*

# 13 GRAMMAR IN GESTURES

Gestures clearly have a meaning. But could they have a grammar, too? Nothing as sophisticated as spoken and sign language grammar, to be sure. Still, there are extraordinarily interesting traces of a proto-grammar in gestures, one that is reminiscent of sign language. In fact, when tested with appropriate means, non-signers arguably know certain aspects of sign language grammar, although they don't know that they know them, and their knowledge is, of course, very limited.[1]

We saw in chapter 12 that gestural meanings fit neatly within categories developed for words. In most cases, gestures were parasitic on words and complemented them by co-occurring with them (co-speech gestures) or by following them (post-speech gestures); in the latter case, they behaved very much like non-restrictive relative clauses. But we saw in passing that sometimes gestures can fully replace words (pro-speech gestures). While this may not be a common way of talking, the resulting hybrids are extraordinarily interesting, as they make it possible to investigate the grammatical and semantic behavior of pure gestures, independent of the parasitic status they usually have relative to spoken words. The results are striking: as we will see in this chapter, pure gestures have a proto-grammar (and we will see in chapter 14 that they also have more sophisticated meanings than one might have thought).

## 13.1  HOMESIGNERS

There are further reasons to be interested in gestures, especially ones that fully replace words. Historically, sign languages often emerge from home signs, the communicative gestures used by deaf individuals who do not have access to a sign language but need to communicate with their hearing environment. We saw an instance of sign language grammar gradually developing from home signs in section 2.1. Successive generations of deaf children increasingly decomposed *roll down* into two signs when describing an unfortunate cat who, having swallowed a bowling ball, goes down a street "in a wobbling, rolling manner." Importantly, however, this development occurred as a full sign language emerged. By contrast, home signs are not full-fledged sign languages, and communication between homesigners and their friends and relatives is often limited. Still, it is remarkable that homesigners tend to 'invent' properties of mature sign languages despite not having any contact with them.

One example will make this concrete. As we saw in chapter 4, ASL can realize plurals by repeating a noun in different parts of signing space. But repetitions can be realized in two ways: They can be punctuated, with clear interruptions between them, or they can be unpunctuated, without clear breaks between the repetitions, with individual units that are hard to separate and to count. The two constructions have different meanings. Punctuated repetitions correspond to precise numbers, such as 'three books,' if three clearly delineated occurrences of *BOOK* are produced. Unpunctuated repetitions roughly correspond to plurals: Three unpunctuated repetitions of *BOOK* mean something like 'several books' (usually at least three). Remarkably, some homesigners from Nicaragua 'invented' essentially the same system, despite having no access at all to a sign language.[2] In an experimental study of four Nicaraguan homesigners, repetitions were used with differentiated meanings: Three iterations of a gesture representing a cup were regularly used to represent three cups. By contrast, unpunctuated repetitions could be used to represent any plural number, and they seemed to have a meaning akin to 'several.'

Could it be that the homesigners learned these grammatical devices from their hearing family and friends? Maybe on occasion. But one case was investigated in which a homesigner seemed to have invented these devices. Psycholinguists simultaneously studied a seven-year-old (deaf) homesigner and his 27-year-old hearing mother. To express numerical quantities in gestures, the mother only used explicit numbers expressed with fingers (one finger for *1*, two for *2*, etc.). But the son had the full range of number-marking devices found in adult homesigners (and also in ASL): He used punctuated repetitions to represent a precise number of objects and unpunctuated repetitions to express unspecific plurality. In other words, he seemed to have invented one part of the grammar of mature sign languages.

Pointing is another grammatical device of sign language that is used by homesigners. We saw in chapter 2 that sign language pointing isn't restricted to physically present people or objects. Rather, arbitrary positions in signing space can be established to refer to entities that are not present. As I argued, these are a visible realization of the cognitively real (but hidden) variables that disambiguate pronoun meaning in English, so that *Sarkozy$_x$ told Obama$_y$ that **he**$_x$ would win the election* is a representation on which *he* refers to Sarkozy. In LSF, *x* can be a position on the left, *y* can be a position on the right, and **he**$_x$ can be realized by pointing toward the left. This sophisticated system is already seen in homesigners, at least to some extent. As an example, psycholinguists showed homesigners from Nicaragua stills from a scene of a Charlie Chaplin movie, and asked them to describe the situation using their home signs.[3] Clearly, none of the characters were physically present in the situation, but the homesigners still used locations in space and pointing gestures to realize pronominal-like constructions. In other words, they seemed to have developed a system similar to loci in mature sign languages.

But there is more. As part of the same experiment, some hearing speakers of Spanish were asked to describe the same descriptions with gestures only. In effect, they were asked to invent a system of 'home signs' on the fly, probably with little prior experience of purely gestural communication (although they certainly had experience with co-speech gestures). Strikingly, they too turned out to use positions in space (loci) to represent non-present objects and pointing to express pronominal-like constructions.

We will now see that we can reach the same conclusion by considering hybrids of spoken words and gestures. In fact, even if you are not a signer, you may intuitively know some nontrivial properties of sign language, but without knowing that you know them. (Don't infer from this that learning a sign language is easy: you should expect to face the same kinds of difficulties as in learning any new language!)

## 13.2 GESTURAL GRAMMAR: POINTING AND AGREEMENT VERBS

To bring out your unconscious knowledge of a 'gestural grammar,' we will zero in on pro-speech gestures—that is, gestures that fully replace some words and must thus carry some of their grammatical functions. How do these gestures do it?

Let us start with loci, positions in signing space that are arguably the overt realization of variables. Remarkably, you can make use of them in English, although some tricks are needed to bring them to light. In sign language, an antecedent introduces a locus, and a pronoun is realized by pointing toward that locus. But spoken words can't be associated with spatial positions on their own. The first trick will be to use a co-speech gesture to establish the locus; below, I'll be using flat open hands, palms up, to introduce the loci. So, in the examples we'll discuss, 🖐-right will be an open (right) hand on the right, palm up; 🖐-left will be an open (left) hand on the left, palm up (these 'palm up' gestures could also be used rather naturally in a different context when you say something like *on the one hand . . . on the other hand*). The gestures will be transcribed above the words they co-occur with. Having established some loci by way of co-speech gestures, we'll be able to retrieve them by way of pointing, now used as a pro-speech gesture to fully replace a pronoun. It might help to produce a little onomatopoeia with the pointing gesture so as to avoid having an awkward silence in the sentence, but that's not so crucial. Here, then, is an example of what we can do in this way:

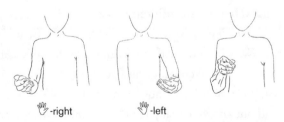

🖐-right          🖐-left

Whenever I can hire [a mathematician] or [a sociologist], I pick ☞-right

*A mathematician* is pronounced with an open hand on the right; *a sociologist* is pronounced with an open hand on the left. And instead of saying *I pick him*, you articulate the words *I pick*, but then replace *him* with the pointing gesture toward the right (optionally adding a little meaningless sound or onomatopoeia—such as *prh*—to avoid an awkward silence at the end of the sentence).

The result is crystal clear: The sentence means that *whenever I can hire a mathematician or a sociologist, I pick the mathematician*. You might think that the pointing gesture is just a code for a word, but that's rather unlikely. Certainly, pointing on its own couldn't encode *mathematician*. Maybe it could encode *him*. But notice that if you replace the pointing gesture with *him* (without any pointing at the end of the sentence), the result is incomprehensible: there are two possible antecedents, *a mathematician* and *a sociologist*, and *him* doesn't tell you at all which antecedent is meant!

In sum, in this case, we successfully used loci reminiscent of sign language in spoken language—with the help of co-speech and pro-speech gestures. In fact, our example already shows that there can be two third-person loci in the same sentence; it is clear that if you replaced the pointing gesture toward the right with a pointing gesture toward the left (i.e., if you replaced *pick* ☞*-right* with *pick* ☞*-left*), the meaning would be radically altered, and one would understand that whenever possible I hire the sociologist, not the mathematician.

Admittedly, the pointing system we've just used wasn't something entirely new to you (even independently of what you read in previous chapters!). Co-speech pointing is pervasive, as when I tell you, *Give me this*, pointing to a piece of chocolate. Still, in our example the pointing is used differently, to replace a word rather than to accompany one. And the gestural loci we introduced are certainly uncommon, as we imported devices from sign language into speech by introducing loci through co-speech pointing, and retrieving them by way of pro-speech pointing. Nonetheless, the meaning of the sentences was easy to discern.

It's one thing to show that gestures, even uncommon ones, can be understood, and quite another to show that their behavior is governed by rules. So, do these pointing signs obey grammatical constraints? In sign language, we noted that not anything goes. In particular, arbitrary loci should not be used to refer to people that are physically present in the conversation. Instead, you should directly point toward them. The same constraint seems to be at work with gestural pointing. First, let's start with a gestural example modeled after sign language: A locus on the right will refer to Mary, while one on the left will refer to John, even though neither of them is present in the conversation. A pointing sign toward the right at the end of the sentence will naturally be understood to refer to Mary. So far, nothing surprising.

🖐-right        🖐-left

Tomorrow the boss will have a conversation with   [Mary] and with   [John]. And you know who the company will promote? 👉-right

But now, let's replace *Mary* with *you*. Now, the resulting English sentence is a bit odd:

🖐-right        🖐-left

Tomorrow the boss will have a conversation with   [you] and with   [John]. And you know who the company will promote? 👉-right

What is a bit awkward is that we are pointing toward an arbitrary locus to refer to the addressee. This is dispreferred—which comes close to an observation we made in passing about sign language in section 2.3: Arbitrary loci are normally used only in case the denoted person isn't physically present. Of course, the problem disappears if you refer to the addressee with the correct locus—namely, the addressee's own position (for consistency, both the 'palm up' gesture co-occurring with *you* and the pointing index should target the addressee). This will make the sentence natural again.

Can we go further in importing parts of sign language grammar into English gestures? Sign language has some agreement verbs that start and/or end in positions corresponding to the subject or object. We briefly saw an example in section 2.3: In LSF, *I tell you* is realized by a hand movement that connects the signer to the addressee, while if a locus for Sarkozy is established on the left and a locus for Obama is on the right, the same movement realized from left (= Sarkozy) to right (= Obama) means that *Sarkozy tells Obama*. . . .

As it happens, ASL *TELL* works like its LSF counterpart, except that for ASL *TELL*, only the end of the movement can be modulated in this way, as seen in the examples below.[4]

I tell you:

I tell him/her:

**Figure 13.2.2**
*Agreeing forms of TELL ('I tell you,' 'I tell him/her') in ASL*

Interestingly, there are gestures that work very much like ASL *TELL*. In fact, we already saw one in a different context: It was the gesture for *slap*.[5] While one can produce it in a neutral fashion, in front of the speaker, it's also possible to modulate it in a way that's reminiscent of sign language. So, for instance, I could utter the following sentence while targeting an imaginary position on the right to represent the addressee's brother; you'll understand that I am talking, aggressively, of slapping this unfortunate individual.

Your brother, I am going to

(You may notice that it's also possible to use a neutral version of the gesture, oriented toward the addressee; that's probably because the position in front of the speaker is the easiest to articulate and so doesn't count as grammatically marked.)

Importantly, targeting the position on the right is only possible if the object (the person slapped) is in third-person form. If the speaker is facing the addressee but targets a position on the right to represent a slapping action, the result is decidedly odd:

*You, I am going to          .

Here we have no choice but to target the position in front of the speaker, corresponding to the addressee; so I'd have to say the following:

You, I am going to          .

In other words, the lateral position is reserved for the third person.

You can check that this is not a unique case. Try a punching or a shooting gesture (a metaphorical one, of course!), and they will behave in the same way. And if you are understandably tired of so much violence, you can try instead a gesture representing an action of sending kisses to somebody. The second-person versions, which target the addressee, appear in the top row below. To remind you that they are second person, -2 appears at the end of the transcription (e.g., *SHOOT-2*). The third-person versions, oriented toward the right, appears in the second row (with -3 at the end—e.g., *SHOOT-3*). Try these for yourself and you'll see that it's odd to use the third-person forms to talk about a second-person object.

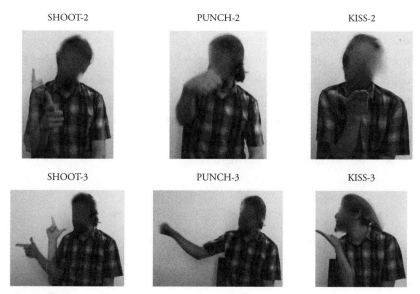

| SHOOT-2 | PUNCH-2 | KISS-2 |
|---------|---------|--------|
| SHOOT-3 | PUNCH-3 | KISS-3 |

**Figure 13.2.6**
*Gestural verbs with second- and third-person object agreement*

Things get even more interesting: There is some evidence that these modulations genuinely display the behavior of grammatical markers. We briefly saw related cases in section 2.5, where in English, when a verb phrase is copied to fill a gap in cases of ellipsis, one can selectively ignore some grammatical markers that appear in the antecedent. Take the sentence *Mary admires herself and I do too.* The second clause is naturally understood to mean that *I admire myself.* This means that *admires herself* must be copied with modifications: The third-person and the feminine markers must be disregarded. In other words, while the content of the example below is presumably obtained by copying *admires herself,* the *her* component can be omitted from the copying (which is the reason it's crossed out).

What is pronounced:   Mary admires herself and I do too.
What is understood:   Mary admires herself but I do too admire ~~herself~~.

The same facts can be reproduced in sign language, both with normal pronouns and with agreement verbs. This is not surprising in view of our earlier observation that these really behave like grammatical elements. So, for instance, if you say in ASL something like, *Your brother, I will give_right money to, but you I won't,* the verb *give_right* is an agreement verb that targets a position on the right. Despite this, the clause with ellipsis can disregard this third-person marker, just like *I do too* can disregard the third-person (and feminine) nature of *herself.*

With this detour through ASL, we can test whether the same grammatical rule applies to gestures. And lo and behold, it does! Let's add a clause with ellipsis to our earlier third-person example:

Your brother, I am going to , and then you too.

The last clause means in essence *you too I am going to slap.* If the missing verb phrase after *too* were obtained by just copying its antecedent from the first one, we would reconstruct the following for the second sentence, with a slapping gesture to the side rather than toward the interlocutor:

. . . and then you too I am going to .

But we already saw that this is rather odd because this construction refers to the addressee by pointing to the position on the right—which is reserved for third persons. So the verb phrase is only partly copied: The person marking of the gestural verb is disregarded in this case, just as it was in our ASL example or in our English example with *herself.* In fact, the result on gestures is one of the relatively few cases in which experimental methods were brought to bear on gestural grammar: a significant difference was found in subjects' acceptance of the sentence with ellipsis (fairly acceptable) and the sentence with the mismatched slapping targeting a position on the right to talk about the addressee (less acceptable).

Importantly, the third-person marking of our gestural verbs is not borrowed from English. Unlike their ASL counterparts, English verbs never display agreement with their object (for instance, the verb never takes a different form for *I admire/admired/will admire him*, or *her*, or *them*). But all the gestural verbs we discussed targeted a different locus corresponding to their object—for instance, the person slapped in our preceding example. So, in this respect, gestural verbs behave like ASL rather than English verbs.

We have thus reached a striking conclusion: Although there are no object markers on English verbs, we can 'import' them from ASL into English (thanks to gestural verbs), and naive subjects can infer that these object markers behave in some respects like their ASL counterparts. In other words, there exists a gestural grammar that fits well with more general properties of language: it resembles ASL grammar in allowing for object agreement; and it resembles both ASL and English grammar in allowing agreement markers to be disregarded under ellipsis.

The analogy with sign language cuts deeper. We saw in section 2.5 that loci are simultaneously grammatical objects and simplified pictures of what they denote. The same observation seems to carry over to gestural loci. Suppose that I am talking to an interlocutor of normal height whose brother is very tall, however. If, in a somewhat violent mood, I say (shamefully):

Your giant brother, I am going to        , and then you too.

You'll understand that I am threatening to slap the tall brother. Because of his height, it's rather natural to modulate the slapping gesture so that it targets a high position. To avoid complicating the discussion, I have used a neutral gesture in front of the signer, which is equally appropriate for a third-person and for a second-person object (remember that it's only the lateral position that is restricted to third person). So that bit won't cause any problem when we get to the second clause, with ellipsis. But now another problem arises: my interlocutor is of normal height, so using a high slapping gesture is inappropriate to refer to him or her (you can do the experiment for yourself—with an imaginary interlocutor).

The explanation of this phenomenon is that the 'high' specification of the slapping gesture can be disregarded under ellipsis, just like third-person markers were in earlier examples. But this was precisely the observation we made in section 2.5 when we noted that in LSF the word *SELF* could be modulated to point upward if it referred to a tall individual. So, when talking about a tall person, the equivalent of *he likes himself* involved a word *SELF^{high}* pointing upward. But we had also noted that this property could be disregarded under ellipsis in the same way as grammatical markers: Adding *he doesn't* to refer to a short person could then mean that *the short person doesn't like himself*, and the 'high' component of *SELF^{high}* could easily be disregarded in the process. In other words, it looks like gestural loci, just like sign language loci, lead a dual life as iconic and as grammatical elements.

### 13.3 GESTURAL GRAMMAR: NOUNS

In our discussion of nouns and verbs in chapter 4, we noted a striking rule for forming plurals in ASL: To refer to a plurality of books, one can repeat *BOOK* in different parts of signing space. Furthermore, there was a distinction between two kinds of repetitions, which a Nicaraguan homesigner seemed to have no trouble inventing. If the repetitions are punctuated and thus easy to distinguish and count, they refer to a precise number of objects (corresponding to the number of iterations). If the repetitions are unpunctuated and thus hard to delineate and count, they refer to a vague number. But we had also observed that the arrangement of the repetitions could convey iconic information. Thus the repetition of *BOOK* on the horizontal plane was indicative of a row of books, but if the noun was repeated so as to form a triangular shape, it was understood that the books formed a triangle. As we will now see, all these observations can be replicated in English gestures.

Instead of talking about books, which are a bit hard to represent in gestures, we'll talk about crosses, with this gesture:

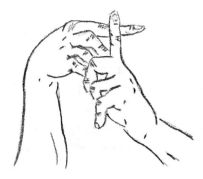

**Figure 13.3.1**
*A gesture representing a cross*

And we'll repeat it in various parts of gestural space, writing ✚ ✚ ✚ (with separating spaces) for three punctuated repetitions and ✚_✚_✚ (with dashes) for unpunctuated repetitions ([**AV13.3.1**]). Now suppose you are taking part in a treasure hunt in churches, and I have information that might help you find the treasure. I could tell you this:

If you enter a room and you see ✚ ✚ ✚, you have reached the prize.

With the crosses horizontally arranged, and clearly separated, the meaning is clear: If you enter a room and you see three horizontal crosses, you'll have reached your goal. But if instead I produce the crosses in an unpunctuated fashion, the result is slightly different:

If you enter a room and you see ✚_✚_✚, you have reached the prize.

The message now says something a bit different—namely, that if you enter a room and see some horizontal crosses, you'll have reached the prize (no commitment as to how many are needed—this remains vague).

We could also do something more complicated and arrange the cross gestures as a triangle. The punctuated version, with clear spaces, will now look like this:

If you enter a room and you see ✛ ✛ ✛, you have reached the prize.

Now the gesture provides information about the precise number but also the arrangement of the crosses: there should be three of them, and they should form a triangle.

Arguably, we can keep the shape but lose the precision of the number if we realize the cross gesture as an unpunctuated repetition:

If you enter a room and you see ✛ – ✛, you have reached the prize.

Now it's harder to get information about the precise number of crosses, while we still retain something about the intended shape that they form.

The upshot is that we can, to some extent, replicate in gestures both the distinction between punctuated and unpunctuated repetitions and the fact that these can come with a strong iconic component.

We had seen in our discussion of ASL that mass nouns too can be repeated, but typically in a continuous fashion. For instance, if our chemistry lab has two wings and there was smoke in the lab following a leak, we'll get very different meanings depending on whether the repeated version of *SMOKE* is signed throughout the area representing the lab or just in one wing. Can something similar be achieved with gestures? Quite possibly. In the next sentence, we use a moving open hand, palm down, to represent some disgusting substance; given the context, it might help to have the gesture produced with a disgusted facial expression, as shown.

There was a leak coming from the upstairs neighbor's bathroom, so when I got

home, I saw          .

If the hand movement is continuously repeated over a large area, we will understand that there was a large puddle of a disgusting substance (here the continuous movement differs for an unpunctuated repetition in that the iterations aren't just hard to count—they are presented as uncountable). But the shape of the area can easily be modulated in highly iconic ways to give an idea of what the speaker saw. In ASL, one can also modulate mass nouns in such a way as to represent several areas of the relevant substance. That's something you can do with the English gesture as well: make three discontinuous and clearly separable hand movements (so that it is now only within each area that the movement is continuous), and it will be understood that there were three puddles of the disgusting substance.

The conclusion is that punctuated, unpunctuated, and continuous repetitions all seem to be devices that you can use with pro-speech gestures, and each variety comes with its own meaning, reminiscent of similar devices in sign language grammar.

## 13.4 GESTURAL GRAMMAR: VERBS

We have now seen examples of gestural nouns and gestural verbs. As I argued in chapter 4, there is a general analogy between nouns and verbs, but it is particularly striking when it comes to pluralities. Just like plural nouns refer to pluralities of objects, pluractional verbs refer to pluralities of events. Furthermore, in ASL and LSF, pluractionals can be expressed by repeating a verb, just like nouns can be pluralized by way of repetition. And verbal repetitions too can be iconic: If the verb *GIVE* is signed at an accelerating pace, one understands that the giving events also took place at this accelerating pace, and conversely if the repetition is realized at a decelerating pace (one understands that the giving events happened more and more slowly). Something similar can be achieved with gestural verbs (i.e., verb-replacing gestures). Let's again use the gesture for *slap*, but let's repeat it three times, with pauses in between:

(The slapping gesture is realized three times, separated by pauses.)

My opponent, I am going to          .

The meaning is rather clear: The speaker intends to slap his opponent three times. But the repetition can also be realized without pauses, in an unpunctuated fashion that makes it hard to count the iterations. In that case, the meaning changes and becomes something like: *My opponent, I am going to slap several times*. But we can do more: If the repetition starts slow and then accelerates, it will probably be understood that the speaker's intention is to slap his unfortunate opponent in this particular way. In other words, repetition of a gestural verb can yield a pluractional reading, and just as was the case in sign language, the repetition can be modulated in a highly iconic fashion.

In chapter 4 (section 4.5), we saw that there is even more grammatical structure to verbs. Telic verbs have a natural endpoint, and their duration is measured with *in* (e.g., *Ann understood in five minutes*). Atelic verbs don't have a natural endpoint, and their duration is measured with *for* (e.g., *Ann reflected for five minutes*). The distinction between telic and atelic verbs is important across languages, but in addition it is overtly realized in the form of many sign language verbs. The endpoint of telic verbs is often made visible by way of sharp boundaries. As it turns out, this is something non-signers seem to know. I mentioned before (in section 4.5) that, given the right experimental conditions, they can correctly guess the telicity of sign language verbs they've never seen before. But we can go further and insert gestural verbs in English sentences to show that one can arguably analyze them on the fly as being telic or atelic.

Here is a way to do it. The speaker represents an action of skydiving with his or her hand circling downward. In the first rendition, the end of the movement is just the right hand slowing down in midair—and thus no sharp boundaries are made visible. In the second rendition, the left hand is added to represent the ground, and the right hand rapidly decelerates as it hits the left hand. So, is *for* or *in* more natural in the sentences that follow?

When skydiving tomorrow, you will _____ five minutes.

[**AV13.4.1**]

When skydiving tomorrow, you will _____ five minutes.

[**AV13.4.2**]

If you are like me and people I've talked to, you'll prefer to use the word *for* in the case without sharp boundaries and the word *in* when sharp boundaries are added. There is an easy explanation for this intuition. You understand that the version with sharp boundaries is a telic verb, meaning something like *reach the ground*. Being telic, the gestural verb wants to come with *in*, not *for*. On the other hand, the gesture without sharp boundaries is atelic and means something like *circle down*. As a result, it wants to be accompanied by *for* rather than *in*.

The upshot is that non-signers seem to 'know' a property of sign language grammar—namely, how the telic/atelic distinction can be marked by way of sharp boundaries. But of course they don't know that they know it—and it is only in very peculiar situations, with hybrids of words and gestures, that their knowledge can be brought to light.

## 13.5 GESTURAL GRAMMAR: CONTEXT SHIFT

Gestural grammar extends even beyond nouns and verbs. In chapter 3, we saw that sign language arguably makes visible an operation of 'context shift' that was originally posited for spoken languages such as Zazaki. In this language, we postulated the presence of an unpronounced word *C* that shifts the context, and we extended this view to ASL and LSF. In an ASL sentence such as *John told Mary C **I give you a-car***, the unpronounced word *C* causes *I* and *you* to be evaluated with respect to John's perspective, and thus *I* refers to John while *you* refers to Mary. In ASL and LSF, context shift is visibly realized by an operation called Role Shift, in which the signer shifts his or her body to adopt the position of the character whose thoughts or words are reported: The boldfaced words ***I give you a-car*** are realized from this shifted position. The unpronounced word *C* of Zazaki is thus realized by way of a body shift in sign languages.

But there was an additional twist to the sign language data—namely, that Role Shift can be used outside indirect discourse. If I am talking about an angry person associated with locus *a*, I could use an English strategy and say:

IX-a WALK-AWAY.

The meaning here is that he walked away (as before, *IX-a* is a pointing sign toward locus *a*, referring to the angry person). Alternatively, I could apply Role Shift after the initial pointing sign and say the following (with the unpronounced word *C* realized by Role Shift on the boldfaced words):

IX-a C **1-WALK-AWAY**.

Here ***1-WALK-AWAY*** is a first-person version of 'walk away,' but the overall meaning is just that the angry person associated with locus *a* walked away. By performing a body shift and adopting that person's position to sign *1-WALK-AWAY*, I make the description more vivid, as if I were embodying that person's action.

Do the same facts extend to gestures? They seem to, as is suggested by the following dialogue. Let's start with Role Shift used to report some words (here 🖐-right is the palm up gesture used to introduce a position on the right while uttering *little Robin*, and similarly 🖐-left introduces a position on the left while uttering *little Francis*).

-right          -left

I was standing next to [little Robin] and [little Francis], and I was holding a really yummy chocolate bar. And I asked: Who wants it? And so of course

-right                                    -left

[little Robin] goes:            . And [little Francis] goes:         .

[AV13.5.1]

Let's unpack this a bit. We start by introducing a locus for little Robin on the right and a locus for little Francis on the left. Then we represent Robin's gestural answer 'me!' by way of Role Shift—that is, the speaker shifts his body to adopt Robin's position on the right and points toward himself. Then he shifts again to adopt Francis's position on the left and again points toward himself. We have two gestural analogues of Role Shift, once on the right and once on the left.

But we can go further and display cases in which the speaker adopts the perspective of a character to display their actions. Let's continue the preceding discourse by once again making use of the slapping gesture whose grammar we investigated in earlier paragraphs.

-right          -left

Next thing I know,    [little Robin] turns to  [Francis] and                    . And so

-left

[Francis]            .

[AV13.5.1]

Let's unpack this as well. We keep the same two loci as before, with the Robin-locus on the right and the Francis-locus on the left. To represent Robin's (objectionable) action, the speaker shifts toward the right preceded by a palm up gesture toward Robin's position (thus adopting Robin's perspective) and performs a slapping gesture toward the Francis-locus. As in earlier cases, this gesture targets the locus corresponding to its object, so this is as desired. But what is striking is that the gesture is performed from a displaced position corresponding to Robin's perspective. Francis's (equally objectionable) response is represented by shifting toward the Francis-locus (on the left), and realizing a punching gesture that targets the Robin-locus. It is clear that these rotations, which are reminiscent of sign language Role Shift, do not serve to represent thoughts or words but rather the point of origin of (violent) actions.

The result is that both varieties of Role Shift seem to have counterparts in gestures. One can shift one's body to adopt the perspective of a character to represent their utterances or thoughts, or to represent their actions.

### 13.6 CONCLUSION

Stepping back, there are several properties of sign language grammar that you knew without realizing that you did (unless you are a signer!). Of course, you didn't have conscious knowledge of these rules, but when we create the right mixes of words and gestures, you have some inkling of the way in which sign language pronouns, nouns, and verbs work, and this even extends to context shift (realized as Role Shift). This is all the more remarkable since some of the gestural constructions we saw were definitely *recherché*, not gestures you'd often come across in daily conversations. None of this will allow you to learn sign language without extensive experience or training, of course, just as is the case for any language. But it's nonetheless striking that, in some cases at least, non-signers are able to apply to gestures some properties of sign language grammar (the extent to which this is possible is still under investigation and this research program is at its inception).

Noam Chomsky famously argued that we humans have innate knowledge of abstract rules of language, which he called 'Universal Grammar' (their nature and extent is still a matter of heated debate). Could it be that the reason non-signers intuitively know some sign language constructions is that, in the visual modality, Universal Grammar also determines the specific realization of some grammatical elements such as pronouns or plurals? Or are there cognitive reasons (ones that may be nongrammatical in nature) that explain why we are able to discover these properties on the fly?

It is too early to tell, and the debate promises to be fascinating. But our ability to discover these properties on the fly can help explain why home-signers can 'invent' properties of mature sign languages, or for that matter why mature sign languages tend to have quite a few grammatical properties in common. These properties might in some way be part of our 'language instinct' (to use a phrase coined by the psychologist Steven Pinker).

# 14  MEANING IN GESTURES

Human language has an exquisitely articulated typology of inferences, each with a characteristic linguistic behavior. You might think that words need to encode an awful lot of information to produce the panoply of inferences we discovered in earlier chapters, from entailments to expressives through implicatures, presuppositions, and supplements. But something far more surprising is happening: the human mind is endowed with the ability to divide new content on the fly among the various slots of this typology.

The argument comes from iconic gestures, especially ones that are rare and unlikely to have been seen before. We typically understand them by virtue of their iconic properties (the fact that their shape resembles what they refer to). We already caught a glimpse of their behavior when they function as co-speech and post-speech gestures. But taking into account their broader behavior, they make a more radical point: We can neatly divide their informational content among familiar slots of the inferential typology, and we can often do so upon first exposure. In other words, the human mind is endowed with a semantic engine that can systematically divide the content of new gestures among standard entailments, implicatures, presuppositions, supplements, and possibly even expressives.

The case of co-speech gestures, discussed in chapter 12, is rather special. Co-speech gestures arguably trigger presuppositions of a special, conditionalized kind, and their contribution is certainly due to the fact that they co-occur with words and are somehow parasitic on them. In this chapter, we will investigate gestures that have their own time slot, especially pro-speech gestures, which fully replace some words instead of accompanying them. We saw in chapter 12 that they typically make at issue contributions, which is unsurprising since they must fulfill the function of standard words. But this doesn't imply that their meaning contribution is *limited* to at issue information. As we will now see, they can make use of the entire typology of inferences unearthed in earlier chapters.

Besides displaying our semantic engine in action, these findings will suggest that gestures are in some way first-class citizens of language. Their meaning contribution is not at all an unstructured whole; rather, it gets conceptually divided among various inferential types. We will reach an even more surprising conclusion: In several cases, we can obtain similar results if we replace gestures with little visual animations. For practical reasons, we can't use these visual animations in daily communication, but they can be inserted in written sentences in an experimental setting. Remarkably, here too their content can be divided on the fly among established slots of the inferential typology.

## 14.1 THE INFERENTIAL TYPOLOGY OF LANGUAGE

Let me start by recapitulating the various inferential types we saw in earlier chapters. Besides standard, at issue entailments (e.g., from *Robin lives in France* to *Robin lives in the European Union*), we saw four further types of inferences.

Implicatures are derived by comparing what the speaker said to what she could have said. So a statement with *some* invites the inference that the corresponding statement with *all* is false:

Implicatures:   Some of my friends are honest.
⇒ not all are

Presuppositions are different: They are preconditions that must be met for a statement to be meaningful, and they are supposed to be trivial (i.e., redundant and uninformative) in view of the context and linguistic environment. Thus *x takes care of his computer* presupposes that *x has a computer*.

Presuppositions:   Does Sally take care of her computer?
⇒ Sally has a computer

Non-restrictive relative clauses trigger yet another meaning type—supplements. Unlike presuppositions, supplements are typically nontrivial, but like presuppositions, they remain unaffected by various logical words. In particular, they are not typically targeted by questions. Supplements also differ from presuppositions in having a more restricted distribution—for instance, they don't like to appear right after certain negative words (hence the * in the second sentence, already discussed in section 11.4).

Supplements:   Will you hire John, who is incompetent?
⇒ John is incompetent
*Not one senator, who by the way underestimated the threat, got infected with the coronavirus.

Expressives behave in many respects like supplements, and they too fail to be targeted by questions; they differ in not having the restricted distribution of supplements. And yet they can't quite be analyzed as presuppositions either, as we argued in section 11.5:

Expressives:   Will you hire a Frog?
⇒ the speaker doesn't like French people

So that's the typology we've uncovered. Let's now see how it can be reproduced with gestures.

## 14.2 GESTURAL SUPPLEMENTS

For supplements, we already saw the main results from a different perspective, when we argued in chapter 12 that speech with gestures isn't quite equivalent to sign with iconicity because iconic modulations are often at issue, whereas co- and post-speech gestures are not. In particular, we saw that post-speech gestures share the semantic behavior of non-restrictive relative clauses in being sometimes resistant to negative contexts; as before, I use a dash (—) in the examples that follow to indicate that there is a pause between the word and the gesture:

*I won't punish my enemy – .
*I won't punish my enemy, which will involve slapping him.

But it's worth going beyond these initial observations. A consequence of this similarity is that post-speech gestures, just like other supplements, are not at issue. For instance, we saw that questions typically do not target non-restrictive relative clauses:

Did John Doe, who you mistreated, press charges?

Here it is asked whether John Doe pressed charges, not whether the addressee mistreated John Doe; that this was indeed the case is established by the sentence. The same facts can be observed if we put post-speech gestures in questions. Suppose little Robin asks another child the following:

Will you punish your enemy –  ?

The effect would be rather similar if little Robin used a non-restrictive relative clause:

Will you punish your enemy, which will involve slapping him?

In both cases, what is asked is whether a punishment will take place, and the sentence takes as established that any punishment will involve some slapping. Things are very different in conjunctions:

Will you punish your enemy, and will this involve slapping him?

Now both parts are equally the target of the question.

Post-speech gestures are quite special, of course, as their timing makes them very similar to non-restrictive relative clauses. But as we will now see, pro-speech gestures make use of further slots of the inferential typology. Specifically, in addition to their at issue meaning, pro-speech gestures can contribute implicatures, presuppositions, and even expressive meanings.

## 14.3 GESTURAL IMPLICATURES

In some cases, the existence of further inferential types in gestures is expected by current theories. Consider the case of scalar implicatures. *Some of my friends are honest* triggers the implicature that *not all are* because *some* competes with *all*, which is more informative. Had the speaker taken the statement with *all* to be true, she ought to have used it. The logic of competition is very general—so much so that we even applied it to some primate calls in chapter 1. So, if a gesture evokes a more informative one, given the right environment, an implicature should be triggered.

This indeed happens, and here is a case in point (the first gesture represents a complete turning of a steering wheel and the second a partial one):

Last week you showed that you can . Now to get out of the parking space, you should .

The first gesture is understood to mean something like *turn the wheel completely*, and the second gesture something like *turn the wheel*. But what is striking is that the meaning of the second gesture is enriched to mean *turn the wheel but not completely*. This makes sense if it is understood to be contrasted with the more informative gesture that appears in the first sentence.

But wait—haven't I been too quick in this reasoning? Maybe something simpler is going on. The second gesture could mean *turn the wheel precisely as shown*, and since only a partial turning is depicted, this would immediately explain the inference that the addressee shouldn't turn the wheel completely. While reasonable, this alternative hypothesis won't quite do. The reason is that it predicts that when we negate the smaller gesture, as in the following sentence, we just mean that *the addressee shouldn't turn the wheel precisely as shown*.

After you've gotten out of the parking space, you shouldn't .

However, that's not what the sentence is most likely to mean. Rather, it suggests that the addressee shouldn't turn the wheel at all. This implies that the gesture means something like *turn the wheel*, rather than *turn the wheel precisely as shown*. But now let's go back to our initial positive example. We need to explain why the *turn the wheel* meaning is somehow enriched to *turn the wheel but not completely*. And that's where implicatures come into the picture: The small gesture means *turn the wheel*, the large gesture means *turn the wheel completely*, and so using the former suggests that the latter is false. This is a gestural implicature, and it helps derive the correct meaning in the end—namely, *turn the wheel but not completely*.

When we discussed implicatures with words, we saw that some new ones arise in negative environments. So, if I tell you that *not all of my friends are dishonest*, you'll certainly infer that at least some are.[1] The reason is that you compare the sentence I uttered to a more informative alternative—namely, that *not one of my friends is dishonest*. You reason that I probably didn't make this stronger statement because it's false—and so you infer that at least one of my friends is dishonest. Something similar happens when gestures appear in negative environments—for instance, this one:

After you've gotten out of the parking space, you shouldn't .

Here you'll infer that you shouldn't turn the wheel completely, but you should still probably turn the wheel. This implicature is derived, as always, by comparing my statement with a more informative one it evokes, to the effect that you just shouldn't turn the wheel (i.e., you shouldn't turn it at all):

You shouldn't .

You then infer that I avoided this stronger statement because it is false, and conclude that you should turn the wheel (just not completely).[2]

In fact, the same reasoning could have been made with the gesture-free sentence: *You shouldn't turn the wheel completely.* Certainly, I could have decided to say, more briefly, *You shouldn't turn the wheel.* Furthermore, this would have been more informative. By inferring that I didn't say this because it would have been false, you derive the inference that you should turn the wheel: same causes, same consequences.

But isn't this similarity too much of a good thing? It suggests an objection: Maybe the strong gesture is just understood as a code for *turn the wheel completely.* If so, there isn't much of linguistic interest in the gestures. Rather, we first translate them into words, and then these words behave as they always do—triggering implicatures or any other sort of inferences.

It's very unlikely that this is all that's going on, however. The reason is that a gesture often conveys information that would get lost in a translation in words. Depending on how I realize the *turn wheel* gesture, I can convey information about the precise size of the wheel; I can change my grip to provide information about its thickness, and I can even provide information about its position (low, high, somewhat to the side, etc.). It genuinely looks like the gesture is a mini-animation that represents the denoted action and the objects involved, with geometric information that would be almost impossible to convey in words. But if gestures are genuinely interpreted as mini-animations, it is all the more striking that they simultaneously display a highly linguistic behavior and, in particular, can trigger implicatures.

## 14.4 GESTURAL PRESUPPOSITIONS

We can use the same *turn wheel* gesture to make another point—namely, that pro-speech gestures can trigger presuppositions. This part is more surprising because it doesn't follow from what we discussed earlier (nor from contemporary linguistics, really) that presuppositions should be triggered on the fly from things that aren't words to begin with (as mentioned, I set aside the rather special case of co-speech gestures, discussed in chapter 12).

But to see an example of precisely this, suppose that Jake and Lily are watching their four children ride bumper cars at the carnival. Each bumper car has two seats, and as one of the bumper cars nears a bend in the track, Jake asks:

Will Sally ?
⇒ Sally is in the driver's seat

If you witness the conversation, you'll certainly infer (as experimental subjects did) that Sally is in the driver's seat. This is because the *turn wheel* gesture triggers a presupposition—namely, that Sally is next to a wheel. And it is because it is a presupposition that it gets inherited by the question, just as in our initial example, *Does Sally take care of her computer?*

You might recall that presuppositions are not the only type of inferences that get inherited by questions. Supplements do, too, as in *Did John Doe, who you mistreated, press charges?* (this strongly implies that you mistreated John Doe). But supplements are awkward in certain negative environments, and this is definitely not the case with our *turn wheel* gesture:

Sally won't .
⇒ Sally is in the driver's seat

None of our children will .
⇒ each child is in the driver's seat

Furthermore, the inferences we get in these cases are very similar to those obtained with standard presuppositions. *Sally doesn't take care of her computer* still conveys the information that Sally has a computer (despite the negation!), just like our negative *turn wheel* example triggers the inference that Sally is in the driver's seat. *None of my male students takes care of his computer* presupposes that each of my male students has a computer. In the same way, the *none* version of our *turn wheel* example triggers the inference that each child is in the driver's seat (and thus they are in different bumper cars).

I already made the point that it's unlikely that the *turn wheel* gesture is just a code for the words 'turn the wheel,' as the gesture conveys detailed iconic information that the English expression is silent about. This point can be made vividly with more complicated gestures as well. Suppose I visit someone's apartment and say the following:

The light bulb in that room, are you going to ?

If my hand rotates with the kind of movement needed to unscrew a bulb, the meaning will be entirely clear. But you won't just get a meaning akin to *Are you going to unscrew that light bulb?* For starters, my gesture triggers a presupposition to the effect that the bulb is positioned high: This is just not a gesture I would use to talk about a desk lamp, for instance. While my question asks whether my interlocutor will unscrew the bulb, it takes for granted that the bulb is positioned high, as befits a presupposition. And it's easy to modulate the gesture to modify the positional information conveyed: If the gesture requires a greater arm extension, I will convey that the bulb is positioned *very* high. If my arm has to reach far to the side, this too will convey presupposed information about the location of the bulb.

The upshot is that presuppositions are not just a property of words. We can easily create gestures that trigger presuppositions, and some of these gestures are very uncommon indeed (how often do you go around gesturing about light bulbs?). At the end of this chapter, we will go one step further and argue that even visual animations can trigger presuppositions.

## 14.5 GESTURAL EXPRESSIVES

In view of human nature, it is unsurprising that some gestures are used with a derogatory meaning. I won't display them here to avoid causing offense, but to be concrete: A supposedly effeminate hand gesture is used in some cultures to refer in a derogatory fashion to gay men; different hand or arm gestures can be used to refer in a derogatory fashion to some handicapped people; and gestures representing elongated eyes derogate people of Asian descent. What is relevant for our purposes is that these gestures pattern, down to the details, with the expressives we discussed in chapter 11.

*Will you hire a Frog?* is not a way of asking whether you hate the French and will hire one of them. This much is common between expressives and presuppositions. But there are differences as well. For starters, *Frog* causes offense in a way that a question involving a presupposition does not, as in: *Does Robin know that I hate the French?* But expressives also differ from presuppositions in how they interact with the linguistic context. As we saw previously, presuppositions must normally be redundant in view of the preceding discourse:

> If Ann used to smoke, she has stopped.

Here there is no need to assume that Ann in fact used to smoke because in view of the *if*-clause, the 'used to smoke' component of *stop smoking* is certain to be redundant (and in fact, it does sound atrociously redundant to say: *If Ann used to smoke, she used to smoke and . . .*). But expressives are not so easily satisfied, as we saw:

> If I really hated the French, I wouldn't hire a Frog.

You might expect that the derogatory component of *Frog* is trivial in view of the *if*-clause, but this doesn't suffice to 'absorbe' the offensiveness, and we still conclude that the speaker is in fact prejudiced against the French. In other words, the *used to smoke* component is 'filtered' by the *if*-clause in our first example, but the *hate the French* component of *Frog* is not filtered in the second sentence.

Remarkably, the very same behavior is found with the derogatory gestures I mentioned above. First, each of them causes offense in a way that presuppositions don't. Second, if you replace *the French* with *people of Asian descent* and then continue with a derogatory gesture referring to this group, the effect will be the same as in our *Frog* example: The speaker will have given away his or her prejudice by using such a term. Unlike a presupposition, whose content can be filtered, the derogatory content of these gestures is inherited by the sentence as a whole and gives away the speaker's prejudice.

The upshot is that it is not just supplements, implicatures, and presuppositions that can be realized with purely gestural means. Expressives too can be produced in gestures, and in gestures as in words, they can cause offense and inflict harm.

## 14.6 FROM GESTURES TO VISUAL ANIMATIONS

There are two conclusions we could draw from these gestural data (they needn't be mutually exclusive). One is that gestures are fully integrated with spoken language and have a far more semantic structure than meets the eye. This dovetails with the conclusions of chapter 13, where we saw that gestures have a grammar of their own, which shares some nontrivial properties with sign language grammar (although sign languages are of course incomparably more sophisticated than gestures). If we step back and consider our closest relatives, bonobos and chimpanzees, the integration between gestures and speech needn't be surprising: As we saw in chapter 1, ape communication is notoriously multimodal, with both calls (e.g., the snake alarm call *hoo*) and gestures (e.g., the chimpanzee reaching gesture that indicates a desire to acquire an object). Finding that gestures play an important role in speech might in the end be just what we expect from this broader perspective.

But there is a second conclusion we could draw—namely, that we can create new iconic forms (whether gestural or not) at will, and that their informational content will be immediately divided among familiar slots of the inferential typology of language. In some cases, this result is unsurprising. Think of implicatures: As soon as a sentence competes with a more informative one, an implicature can be triggered. It is because *some* evokes *all* that the sentence *Some of my friends are honest* triggers an implicature that not all are. That a gesture can evoke another gesture is rather unsurprising, and thus the presence of gestural implicatures is just what we expect on theoretical grounds.

This conclusion extends beyond gestures. Give me any representation that evokes a more informative one, put it in a sentence, and it will trigger an implicature. Do I really mean *any*? Yes, if the result is reasonably natural. This point was recently made by psycholinguists who embedded visual animations in written sentences and tested subjects to see if these animations triggered implicatures.[3] Sure enough, they did, as in this example, where images popped onto the screen between words.

John the alien has been training on the punching bag at the gym. At last week's workout, John had a lot of energy. He was able to ▨. This week, John will ▨.

The subjects of the experiment understood the sentence with the multiple flashes to mean that *John was able to punch a lot*. By contrast, the last sentence, with the single flash, was understood to mean that *John will punch, but not a lot*. When further tests were performed, this was shown to be the result of an implicature. In other contexts, the single flash just means *to punch*, but here it competes with an animation that means *to punch a lot*, and this triggers the expected implicature.

While it is fun to create sentences with visual animations replacing words, the results shouldn't be too surprising. Given how implicatures work, it's hard to see how they could fail to extend to these cases. But the other inferential types we discussed are not the result of such clear rules. Take presuppositions. For the longest time, the standard view in linguistics was that they are an arbitrary property of words. On this view, there is no general rule that makes it possible to predict that the information conveyed by *x stops smoking* is divided into a presupposition that x smoked and an assertion that x doesn't now smoke. One could imagine just as well that both components were at issue, or that *x doesn't now smoke* was presupposed while *x smoked before* was at issue. In other words, even after you have learned that *x stops smoking* conveys the information that x smoked and doesn't now smoke, you must *still* learn how this informational content is divided between the presuppositional and the at issue component: English makes the 'smoked' component presupposed and the 'doesn't now smoke' part at issue, although in principle, things could be different in other languages.

But, as a matter of fact, things don't seem to be different in other languages, which casts doubt on this account. French has two words for *stop*, *arrêter* and *cesser* (which is etymologically related to *cease*), and both words behave exactly like their counterpart *stop*. Nor is this just a property of European languages: Counterparts of *stop* display the same behavior in Swahili (spoken in the African Great Lakes region and an official language of several eastern African countries) as well as in Guaraní (an indigenous language of South American and an official language of Paraguay).[4] So there seems to be a rule by which we can somehow divide the informational content of an expression into a presuppositional and an at issue component. In fact, our example with the *turn wheel* gesture, which presupposes the presence of a wheel in front of the agent, gives a separate argument for the same conclusion. Certainly, you understand the informational content of the gesture by virtue of its iconicity (i.e., the fact that it resembles the action it denotes). But some kind of unconscious rule seems to tell you that part of the informational content—to wit, the presence of the wheel—is presupposed. It seems that just like implicatures, presuppositions are produced by a general rule, which has no difficulty applying to new cases.

Maybe you think that the *turn wheel* gesture is so common as to be part of the English vocabulary. I have my doubts, and I tried to make sure that the other presuppositional gesture I discussed, pertaining to a light bulb being unscrewed from the ceiling, is even more uncommon. You still had no trouble inferring that part of the information—namely, the fact that the bulb is positioned high—is presupposed. But with animations, we can do something more radical: We can investigate examples that you couldn't possibly have seen before, for the simple reason that people just don't go around talking in visual animations. And lo and behold, visual animations trigger presuppositions just like gestures do—even really odd visual animations that were *designed* to be ones that the subjects couldn't have seen in any linguistic context.

Here is an amusing text that was tested with experimental means:

Aliens are green. But when they are in a meditative state, their antennae are blue. There is a meditation session in progress on the first floor of a business firm. Bill is watching the union representative and says: Will the union representative's antenna 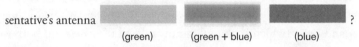 ?

(green)    (green + blue)    (blue)

[**AV14.6.1**]

Subjects saw a video with written words and, in lieu of a verb, an animation displaying a gradual change from green to blue. The question was thus interpreted as, *Will the union representative's antenna turn from green to blue?* The alien-related context was of course intended to facilitate the creation of a novel and very far-fetched animation. Still, the subjects treated the animation as presupposing that the antenna was initially green, and thus that the union representative was not initially meditating. Specifically, despite the fact that the visual change from green to blue appeared in a question, subjects drew the inference that the antenna was initially green, and they treated this meaning component as a presupposition. The at issue component (i.e., what the question was about) was whether there would be a transition to blue. Other tests and examples confirmed this conclusion: the fact that the antenna was initially green was treated as presupposed.

### 14.7  CONCLUSION

Language comes with an exquisitely sophisticated typology of inferences, which includes at issue entailments, presuppositions, implicatures, supplements, and expressives. Remarkably, all inferential types can be triggered with gestures and sometimes even visual animations that one may not have seen before. This supports the radical conclusion I outlined above: It's not just implicatures that are produced by a productive meaning engine. Rather, this seems to be the general case: We have access to rules that allow us to divide on the fly any new informational content among familiar slots of this sophisticated inferential typology (expressives are at this point a potential exception because the gestural examples I used seemed to have a conventional character). In the general case, it doesn't matter how unusual these new meanings are, or how they are expressed: we have no trouble generating presuppositions from visual animations that talk about aliens with antennae that change colors when they are in a meditative state.

The conclusion is that there is far less arbitrariness in the behavior of words than you might have thought. When we first encountered the rich inferential typology of language, we could have concluded that humans need to memorize how any word divides its meaning among the various slots of this typology. But our detour through gestures and visual animations suggests otherwise. We can effect this division without effort and on the fly, including for new 'words' we might encounter for the first time, such as gestures and visual animations. The challenge for current research is to uncover the sources of this rather extraordinary behavior.

# 15 MEANING IN MUSIC

## 15.1 THE METAMORPHOSES OF A SUNRISE

The composer Richard Strauss (1864–1949) did not write easy classical music, but in his time, he was a celebrity. His notoriety came in handy when U.S. forces occupied his native Bavaria at the end of the Second World War. As the New Yorker critic Alex Ross tells the initial story:[1]

> The G.I.s had intended to commandeer [Strauss's] house as a temporary headquarters. After listening to Strauss play excerpts from [his opera] "Rosenkavalier" at the piano, they let him be, and moved on to another destination.

Today, I am not sure Richard Strauss would be able to convince American soldiers of his importance by playing excerpts from *Rosenkavalier*. And yet his music is world famous, although people don't always know its origins. This is in large part thanks to the opening of his piece *Thus Spoke Zarathustra*, which has been used in innumerable shows, films, and TV commercials. Most famously, it was featured at the beginning of Stanley Kubrick's movie *2001: A Space Odyssey*, with something close to Strauss's intentions, to evoke the appearance of a sun behind a planet (Strauss's beginning was entitled *Sunrise*, so that's close enough). But Strauss's tune was also used at the beginning of Elvis Presley's concerts in the 1970s, to announce the appearance of . . . the King (a sun of sorts). The Strauss tune had even more diverse adventures in TV commercials, where it served to announce the dawn of new adventures in cooking (thanks to a line of oils and butters),[2] the advent of wholesome well-being as a glass of fruit probiotics was being drunk,[3] or the prospect of imbibed bliss as customers eyed a particular brand of beer in a supermarket.[4] Not to mention a liberation of sorts in a commercial for diapers that displayed the expressive faces of defecating babies (the ad got a prize, and one suspects that Strauss played a role in it).[5]

Most listeners would have been hard-pressed to put a name on the tune, so it's not the Richard Strauss brand that's responsible for this celebrity. And Kubrick aside, these shows and commercials had nothing to do with a sunrise. Yet the music greatly contributed to the meaning of all these scenes, highlighting that they represented, from a certain perspective at least, events of momentous significance. How could Strauss's tune serve to evoke a sunrise, the King of Rock and Roll taking the stage, wholesome well-being through probiotics, imbibed bliss though beer, and a baby's rapture through bowel movements? This is the puzzle posed by musical meaning: Its effects are hard to deny, yet its content is hard to discern. But as we will now see, music semantics might offer an answer.[6] (One disclaimer: This area of research is recent, and here I will only discuss a few examples from Western classical music, which of course doesn't do justice to the diversity of human musical experience.[7])

### 15.2  MEANING IN MUSIC—REALLY?

What does music mean? This might seem a bit like asking, What is the meaning of life? You don't expect people who start with this to say something particularly clear or concrete. Despite the risks, I would like to take the question literally. After all, we saw in earlier chapters that semantics can illuminate some aspects of gestures, so why not music?

Maybe that's a bit rash, however. It's not hard to think that gestures convey information by resembling certain things or actions. Music seems far more abstract, and thus the first order of business is to show that music does convey information about the world rather than just about itself (the information may be about a fictional world, of course, just like language can serve to tell imagined stories). I will then explain how music can do such a thing.

Usually one takes the meaning of music to entirely lie in the emotions it evokes in the listener. It is uncontroversial that music bears a special relation to human emotions. But reducing the meaning of music to emotions doesn't do it justice. Music can trigger all sorts of inferences about the extra-musical world. They turn out to be very abstract inferences (i.e., ones that can pertain to extremely diverse situations), which is why many people think that music has no meaning in that sense. But there is an important difference between an abstract meaning and no meaning at all. It is because music has meaning that the Strauss tune could radically affect the significance of all sorts of scenes it accompanied. But it is because this meaning is abstract that these scenes could be so diverse and could have little to do with Strauss's original goal of evoking a sunrise.

To see a much simpler case of an abstract representation, let's think about three little columns, which I'll label as A, B, and C.

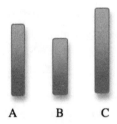

Figure 15.2.1

It's hard to say what, if anything, these columns represent. But if I tell you that they represent people, you can start treating them as highly simplified pictures, and they will immediately convey some information. For instance, if I ask you which of the following situations is best represented by my three columns, you might think that the columns are a better representation of Situation 1, on the left, than of the other situations.

Situation 1    Situation 2    Situation 3

**Figure 15.2.2**

Why? You probably thought along the following lines. First, the left-to-right order of the columns should reflect that of the individuals. Second, the relative heights of the columns should also reflect that of the individuals. Both conditions are satisfied in Situation 1. The leftmost individual, the boy, is intermediate in height between the second individual, the doctor, and the third one, the businesswoman; this is exactly what we find in the columns as well. By contrast, in Situation 2, if the left-to-right order of the columns is preserved, the first (leftmost) column must represent the doctor, the second column must represent the boy, and the third column the businesswoman. But then the ordering by height of the columns is not preserved: The first column is intermediate in height between the other two, but its denotation, the doctor, isn't. Of course, the columns don't have to represent people— they could equally represent trees or skyscrapers or any number of other things that can be ordered by height; this is the sense in which the meaning of this diagrammatic representation is abstract.

When you start animating geometric shapes, their representational potential only becomes greater. In the 1940s, the psychologists Fritz Heider and Marianne Simmel conducted a series of famous experiments in which geometric shapes moved in ways that violated intuitive physics but were consistent with the behavior of animate agents.[8] So, for instance, a big triangle could pursue a small one, and then a circle, with the apparent aim of getting rid of them ([**AV15.2.1**]). Or a triangle could start destroying a large rectangle, again with less than benevolent intentions. Surely these geometric shapes didn't resemble animate agents we know, but their movements did, with the result that the experimental subjects had no trouble assigning goals and even personalities to mere geometric shapes. As we will see, something similar happens in music.[9]

## 15.3 BERNSTEIN'S CHALLENGE

The idea that music conveys information about the extra-musical world is admittedly a nonstandard view. The great American composer and conductor Leonard Bernstein gave a radically different answer to the question *What does music mean?* This was part of a series of delightful televisions programs, the Young People's Concerts, which made music history. In concerts filmed from Carnegie Hall and then Lincoln Center, Bernstein explained music in simple yet detailed terms for an audience of children and accompanying parents, with illustrations played by the New York Philharmonic under his direction.[10]

When Bernstein discussed the meaning of music, he started with a famous tune from Rossini's *William Tell* Overture.

**Figure 15.3.1**
*A theme from Rossini's William Tell Overture ([**AV15.3.1**])*

"You will understand, I am sure, what my little daughter Jamie said when I played it for her," Bernstein commented. "She said, 'That's the Lone Ranger song, Hi-ho Silver! Cowboys and bandits and horses and the Wild West.'" But then Bernstein added:

> Well, it can't mean the Wild West for the simple reason that it was written by a man who never heard of the Wild West. He was an Italian named Rossini. We may think his music means horses and cowboys because we've been told so by the movies and television shows. But actually, Rossini wrote the music as an overture to the opera William Tell, which is about people in Switzerland—and that's pretty far from the Wild West. Everybody knows the

story of William Tell, the man who had to shoot an apple off his little son's head with a bow and arrow. You might, then, think that the music is supposed to be about William Tell and Switzerland instead of about cowboys. But it isn't that either. It's not about William Tell, or cowboys, or lampshades, or rockets, or anything like that which can be put down in words.[11]

Bernstein concluded that the real meaning of music is "the way it makes you feel when you hear it. ( . . . ) We don't have to know everything about sharps and flats and chords to understand music. If it tells us something—not a story or a picture, but a feeling—if it makes us change inside, then we are understanding it. That's all there is to it. Because those feelings belong to the music. They're not extra, like the stories and pictures we talked about before; they're not outside the music. They're what music is about."[12]

What was so persuasive about Bernstein's case—besides the notorious brilliance of the maestro—was that he discussed in detail some musical examples that seem to tell a concrete story, only to show that an alternative story would fit the music just as well ([**AV15.3.2**]). To make his point, Bernstein had the New York Philharmonic play a piece to illustrate an elaborate story he told about Superman:

> In the middle of a big city stands an enormous jail, full of prisoners. It's midnight and they're all asleep except for one who can't sleep because he's innocent; he was put in jail unjustly. He spends the whole night practicing on his kazoo while the other prisoners snore all around him. But this kazoo-playing prisoner has a friend who is going to come tonight and rescue him—Superman![13]

The music turns out to have been written by none other than Richard Strauss. This particular excerpt had nothing to do with a sunrise, as it was from a different piece written with the explicit intention of evoking a story. Except that the story wasn't about Superman, of course. As Bernstein told his young audience, it was in fact about Don Quixote, "a foolish old man" who "has read too many books about knighthood and conquering armies for beautiful ladies" and finally "decides he is a marvelous knight himself." And as Bernstein showed in detail, Strauss's music was just as good a fit for a story about Superman charging into prison to free a friend as one about Don Quixote departing to conquer the world.

In a way, TV commercials did to Richard Strauss's Sunrise what Bernstein did to the composer's *Don Quixote*: They showed that the music could be made to fit scenes that had nothing to do with the composer's original intentions. This, then, is Bernstein's challenge: If music has meaning, how come it can be made to fit stories that apparently have nothing in common? Doesn't this flexibility suggest that music has no meaning at all, or just one that reduces to the emotions it evokes in the listener?

Against this skepticism, I'll argue that music has a meaning, albeit a very abstract one. But before we get there, we must address Bernstein's challenge and show that music genuinely triggers inferences about a music-external reality.

### 15.4  FROM SOUND TO MUSIC

When we hear a car engine becoming louder, we infer one of two things: It is producing sound with increasing energy, or it is approaching. Perception in general and auditory perception in particular are designed to trigger inferences about their causal sources. After all, that's what perception is for, to give us information about our environment.

Now it has been suggested that musical meaning works in a similar way, but with imagined sources—objects that play in some respects the same role as the causal sources of sounds.[14] Of course, we can draw inferences about the real sources of the music: the pianist, the violinists, maybe even the conductor. But that's not what musical meaning is all about. For Bernstein's daughter, the beginning of the William Tell Overture triggered inferences about a bunch of cowboys riding horses—although being Bernstein's daughter, she certainly was in no doubt as to the real source of the music, which might have been her father's own piano or orchestra. Properties of the music help the listener draw inferences about these objects. The fast tempo of Rossini's Overture evokes a fast-paced movement (of the cowboys, for instance); a crescendo (i.e., an increasing loudness) might mean that the movement is gaining energy or drawing nearer. So the main idea is that musical meaning consists in applying to extra-musical objects (such as Jamie's cowboys, what I'll call the 'denoted objects') some inferences that we draw on the sources of the music: they may be inferred to be fast because of the musical tempo, and to be gaining energy or approaching because of the crescendo.

More surprisingly perhaps, we can take whichever situation satisfies these inferences to be something the music can be true of. In this way, we will eventually extend to music our truth-based approach to meaning. To achieve this result, we will have to interpret some but not all acoustic properties of the music. If we interpreted them all, we would end up with inferences about the real sources of the music (such as the instruments), whereas we are after something more abstract—among others, music can be used to evoke entirely silent events, as with Strauss's Sunrise. As for Jamie, when she takes the Rossini William Tell Overture to evoke cowboys pursuing bandits, she can certainly infer that they do so at great speed because the music has a fast tempo, but she can't attribute all the properties of the music (such as the violin sound) to the denoted objects, or else she'd identify them with musicians of the New York Philharmonic.

A further example might help. In various musical styles, including classical music, one can announce the end of a piece by various means, such as gradually diminishing the loudness ('playing *decrescendo*,' literally 'decreasing,' with the Italian terminology used in classical music) and diminishing the speed (*rallentando*, or 'slowing down'). One could take these to be purely conventional signals whose function must be learned by repeated exposure to certain musical styles. But there is an alternative view: These might be inferential mechanisms that are lifted from normal auditory cognition. A car engine becomes less loud because it's moving away or because it's losing energy. Either property could be appropriate to signal an ending. In the first case, the sound source is gradually disappearing in the distance, while in the second, it's gradually dying out. (This doesn't mean every piece has to end in these ways, just that they are particularly natural ways to end a piece. Sometimes the ending is triumphant and goal-driven, with a final *fortissimo*, literally, 'very loud.') What about speed? Someone is approaching in the corridor, but we can't see who it is. Their pace gradually slows down—this might be an indication that the person is about to stop. The same thing happens in music: by gradually slowing down the tempo, you can suggest that the piece is nearing an end.

A radical version of this hypothesis was explored by the music scientists Peter Desain and Henkjan Honing, who argued that the way in which one typically slows down at the end of a piece follows laws of movement within a physical model with a braking force.[15] This final slowdown is so important that it has a special name, the 'final *ritard*,' and it must be realized with great care to convey the appropriate impression (*ritard* is short for Italian *ritardando*, 'slowing down'). To show that this slowdown follows laws of movement, the scientists constructed a crank-activated music machine with a brake. Letting the machine slow down on its own created a perfectly convincing final *ritard*;[16] the video they made is particularly striking, as it shows that the braking force alone suffices to create a correctly realized *ritard*.

**Figure 15.4.1**
*Honing's "final ritard machine"* ([**AV15.4.1**])

We can push this line of thought further. Think of a rope spinning. The faster it spins, the higher the frequency of the sound produced. Conversely, as the rope slows down, it will start producing lower-frequency sounds. This leads us to expect that in music, if you want to create a really conclusive ending, it might be good to finish downward, because this will evoke a sound source dying out. That's not too hard to test. Many classical pieces end with identical chords (i.e., identical sequences of simultaneous notes) played at different heights, one or several octaves apart. When the last chord is higher than the preceding one, the effect is less conclusive (we'll discuss some examples later). So, this too seems to be an inferential mechanism that music has lifted from normal auditory cognition.

Still, not every inference is lifted from normal auditory experience. In an excerpt of classical music, a certain note, the tonic, counts as more central than others—a kind of attraction point, to which one expects to return.[17] The note in question depends on the 'key' the excerpt is in—that is, the implicit scale it is written with (some scales start with C, others start with G, etc.). The tonic is the first note of the scale. To keep things simple, let's focus for the moment on the scale of C major; it is obtained on a piano by pressing the white keys in sequence, starting from a C and ending on the next C to its right. C is the tonic, and correspondingly the chord CEG (called the C chord, with C, E, and G played at the same time) is the most stable chord in that key. Music theorists have an explanation for why this is: E and G are acoustically contained as harmonics within C, but we can set this point aside and just take for granted that CEG is the most stable chord in C major. There is a hierarchy of stability among chords—for instance, the G chord GBD is fairly stable as well, but less so than the C chord CEG. Now in classical pieces, an ending is signaled by a sequence (called a 'cadence') that gradually reaches the most stable chord, typically with a path that moves from a chord constructed from G (fairly stable) to one constructed from C (maximally stable). Again, you might think that this way of signaling the end is purely conventional, but another way of looking at it is that the stability of the chords is interpreted in terms of the stability of the denoted objects: an object that is in a completely stable position is more likely to have reached repose than one that is in an unstable position.

In fact, this notion of stability is put to further uses in classical music. If a composer wishes to signal a temporary rest, the composer may use a sequence that ends in the G chord (GBD) rather than the C chord: by ending on a stable but not maximally stable chord, a signal is given that the denoted object is stopping, but only temporarily.

### 15.5 REVISITING STRAUSS'S SUNRISE

With this background in mind, we can revisit Richard Strauss's hit, the introduction of *Thus Spoke Zarathustra*. Strauss's intention was to evoke a sunrise, and the beginning of the melody could not be simpler: in the key of C major, a C, followed by a higher G, followed by a higher C. Now this may not represent precisely a sunrise, but it's not hard to infer that something is developing and possibly rising, with the rise in frequency associated with a rise in space. This is combined with another inferential means lifted from normal auditory cognition: the C G C sequence is played with increasing loudness (*crescendo*). This is, of course, a very effective way of evoking something that is gaining energy.

But things are more subtle. The C G C sequence is just the very beginning of the first phrase, soon followed by another, symmetric one, which also starts with C G C. In figure 15.5.1, I have aligned these two phrases (or rather a simplified piano transcription) with the visuals of the opening of Kubrick's film, which features a sun (initially just a yellow dot) gradually appearing behind a planet. The first half of the sun appears as the first C G C sequence is heard, and the second half appears as the second C G C sequences is heard.

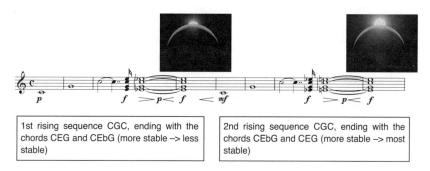

**Figure 15.5.1**
*Opening sequence of Stanley Kubrick's 2001: A Space Odyssey ([AV15.5.1])*

Still, the two C G C sequences are not quite identical. The first one ends with two chords constructed from C. One is CEG; as I mentioned above, it is the most stable chord in the key of C major, and it is in fact called the C major chord ([AV15.5.2]). But by lowering the E by a halftone, you get another chord constructed from C—namely, CE♭G (E♭ is E flat—that is, half a tone below E [AV15.5.3]). In this context, it is less stable than CEG, and it is also intrinsically a bit less consonant or harmonious (CE♭G is called the C minor chord; we come back to minor scales later).[18] So, as the first half of the sun appears, we hear C G C, C major chord (very stable), C minor chord (a bit less stable). When the second half of the sun appears, the beginning is the same, but the order of the chords is reversed: C G C, C minor (the less stable chord first), C major (the more stable chord second). In the C chords, E and Eb appear in the highest voice, which matters because that's what we tend to hear most (it's always easier to hear the highest voice).

If you listen to the music, you'll get a strong impression that there is a development in two parts, with a brief retreat at the end of the first part (not quite represented in Kubrick's visuals—it's as if the sun stopped midway, which isn't something you see) and a more assertive development in the second part.

Certainly, the melodic movement alone plays a role in these impressions. If you just pay attention to the highest notes heard, which are the most salient, you start on C, go up to G, then to C, then to E (because in the chord CGE, the E is repeated at the top and is thus the highest note), then to E♭ (because in the chord CE♭G, E♭ is repeated at the top). And the melodic movement is the same the second time around, with E E♭ replaced with E♭ E—hence no retreat at all and pure upward movement.

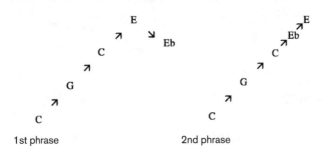

Figure 15.5.2

So, the melodic path traced by the highest notes serves to evoke something: a rise with a brief retreat at the end of the first phrase, a rise with no retreat at all in the second phrase. You can check that the general melodic direction alone can be powerfully evocative by playing a radical simplification of the music in which every note is a C, played at different pitch heights (i.e., at different octaves), with the same melodic movement as above: an upward movement followed by a small downward movement, then an upward movement without downward movement ([**AV15.5.4**]). You'll clearly perceive an impression of retreat at the end of the first phrase (in fact, it's magnified because the interval between the successive Cs is greater than that between the notes that actually appear in the music).

But that's not all. The impression of a retreat as the end of the first phrase of the original Strauss piece probably has to do with the C major–C minor sequence, from more stable to less stable, and the more assertive impression of the second phrase comes from the opposite movement: Instead of ending on the less stable chord, we end on the more stable one. Importantly, the stability of chords is not an inferential mechanism lifted from normal auditory cognition because there are no chords in the extra-musical world, and what counts as 'stable' depends on the scale (and gives rise to some variation across musical genres and cultures). This inferential device is thus essentially musical, but it arguably plays a key role in the evocative force of Strauss's hit.

In sum, diverse inferential means conspire to yield the effect of a development in two parts with a retreat at the end of the first one. This is consistent with the perception of the beginning of a sunrise (maybe with a pause in the development, corresponding to the retreat at the end of the first phrase). But the meaning of the music is so general that it could be made consistent with innumerable other situations as well: the entry of the King of Rock and Roll, the advent of wholesome well-being through probiotics, or imbibed bliss though beer (not to mention a baby's rapture through bowel movements).

One of the more amusing uses of the music can be found in the 2008 animated film *WALL-E*, whose pitch was that in "the distant future, a small waste-collecting robot inadvertently embarks on a space journey that will ultimately decide the fate of mankind."[19] Humans have become so reliant on robots, so obese, and so complacent that getting to their feet requires extreme effort. But, at a crucial moment, the spaceship captain literally rises to the occasion, and at that point you see him gradually rising to his feet with the opening bars of Strauss's Zarathustra playing in the background. After the first phrase he is on his feet; after the second he has the steering wheel in hand. And the music works beautifully, evoking a heroic rise and an event of historic proportion ([**AV15.5.5**]).

We are now in a position to explain why Strauss's tune can enhance such different scenes. As diverse as they may be, they have something in common: the slow development of an important event (for the beholder) with a striking climax. That's the key about music semantics: It is genuinely abstract because very diverse sequences of events are compatible with a given musical excerpt (just like our diagrammatic representation with the three columns could be true of very diverse situations involving objects ordered by size). It is tempting to infer that the idea of a music semantics is a nonstarter. But this would be a mistake. There is an important difference between an abstract (i.e., an underspecified) semantics and no semantics at all. This was the point we saw earlier with our little columns representing individuals, or with Heider and Simmel's abstract animations, which had no difficulty evoking animate agents.

### 15.6 MUSICAL INFERENCES FROM NORMAL AUDITORY COGNITION I: FREQUENCY

Admittedly, Strauss's Sunrise can be put to *very* diverse uses, so you might wonder whether something more specific can be conveyed by music. While music is and will remain abstract, it has diverse ways of conveying information about the world, some lifted from normal auditory cognition, some more specifically musical in nature. Let us see in greater detail how they work.

In nature, the frequency (i.e., pitch) of an animal call gives a good indication of the animal's size: The lower the frequency, the bigger the animal (the term *pitch* is often used in a musical context while *frequency* is used in a physical context, but for present purposes, the two are interchangeable). This is such an important source of inference that some birds and mammals extend their vocal tract in order to make themselves sound bigger and more imposing than they are.

The French composer Camille Saint-Saëns wrote for the enjoyment of his friends a musical composition called *The Carnival of the Animals*, in which each piece evoked a different animal. Amusingly, for the elephant, he picked a tune evocative of a waltz (having a dancing elephant was part of the joke, of course). But how could a waltz be made to evoke an elephant, of all things? The trick was that the melody was played by a double bass, which sufficed to evoke a very large animal. You can assess the effect by listening to an electronic (MIDI) version of the beginning of the piece ([**AV15.6.1**]) and immediately comparing it with a nearly identical one in which the pitch level has been raised (by three octaves, [**AV15.6.2**]). The effect is entirely lost and, if anything, the second version is evocative of a very small animal—maybe a small bird even.

This inference about size is routinely used in music, both operatic and instrumental. You may have seen the Commendatore scene in Mozart's *Don Giovanni*. The Commendatore, who was killed by Don Giovanni at the beginning of the opera, reappears at the end in the form of a statue. He invites Don Giovanni to have dinner with him—and to follow him to his grave. One of the reasons the Commendatore is so imposing is that his voice is that of a bass, with a low pitch; the talking statue would probably be less imposing with a soprano (high-pitched) voiced ([**AV15.6.3**]).

In normal auditory cognition, frequency (i.e., pitch) doesn't just indicate how large a sound source is. Once the source has been identified, the sound frequency provides information about its state: Higher frequency corresponds to more events per time unit (e.g., more turns per time unit for a rope spinning faster and faster) and hence to a more excited (and possibly a more constricted) source. As was mentioned previously, the faster a rope spins, the higher the frequency of the sound produced; conversely, as the rope slows down, it starts producing lower-frequency sounds. You can find this effect in old vinyl records. If you artificially slow them down, they distort melodies toward lower frequencies. So, if a composer wishes to send the signal that things are naturally coming to an end, it might help to lower the frequency. In particular, the end of a piece sounds a bit more conclusive when the last chord is lower in frequency than the preceding one, as I mentioned earlier. This can be easily tested, as there are numerous pieces in which the last chord is identical to the preceding one (as it involves the same notes) but is lower by one octave or more. It's not hard to rewrite these endings by doing the opposite and finishing upward rather than downward. For instance, we can start from the conclusion of a Chopin Nocturne (Op. 9 No. 2), which ends downward ([AV15.6.4]), and raise the final chord by three octaves so that it ends upward instead ([AV15.6.5]). Nothing terrible happens, the result is still well-formed music, but the effect is arguably less conclusive, as one might expect.

## 15.7  MUSICAL INFERENCES FROM NORMAL AUDITORY COGNITION II: LOUDNESS AND SPEED

Just focusing on frequency (i.e., pitch), we already see that musical inferences can be complex: Lower frequency may be indicative of a larger object, but when the object is known, the frequency may go down because the object is slowing down. Another case of ambiguity pertains to loudness. Take again the case of the car engine you hear in the distance, with the noise becoming louder. One possible inference is that the car is approaching. Another is that the car isn't approaching but that its engine is becoming more active. Both effects can be found in music (sometimes ambiguously). In his First Symphony (third movement), Gustav Mahler recycled a children's song, Brother John (originally, *Frère Jacques* in French; *Bruder Jakob* in Mahler's German). The melody is announced by timpani drums giving the beat, and the intention is to evoke a funeral procession: The tempo is slow and majestic, the register is low, played by a double bass, and the melody is written in a minor scale (apparently a common version of the song in nineteenth-century Austria, with less assertive chords than the major version). The timpani start with a crescendo, and this may suggest that the denoted object is gaining energy or that it is approaching ([AV15.7.1]). But if you artificially manipulate the crescendo to increase the effect, the result is unmistakable: you will strongly get the impression of a procession approaching ([AV15.7.2]).

Objects evoked by the music may be construed as animate, and in opera this is the only reasonable interpretation when it comes to singers (this interpretation is often possible as well in instrumental music, but opera is rather unambiguous in this respect). Correspondingly, loudness and frequency gain further interpretive possibilities. Take the case of a repetition. If you repeat something you've said before, you may want to say it louder in order to make it sound more authoritative or urgent, and you may produce it with a higher pitch if you are getting more tense or excited. The same effect can be found in music. In the Commendatore scene in *Don Giovanni*, there is a particularly poignant moment when the Commendatore, having extended his invitation, intimates to Don Giovanni: 'Answer me! Answer me!' (in Italian, *Rispondimi! Rispondimi!*). The same melodic line is repeated but one tone higher, and louder, with a very strong dramatic effect ([**AV15.7.3**]).

Going back to more mundane properties, the speed of discrete sound events provides an indication about the speed with which their source is producing them. A carpenter hammering nails will produce slower sounds as his action slows down. The same inferential mechanism can be used in music. Saint-Saëns made comical use of it in his *Carnival of the Animals* when he sought to evoke tortoises. He started from a popular dance tune of the time, the French *Can-Can*, and had his musicians play it in a radically slowed down fashion. Of course the music (without the title) will in no way suffice to evoke tortoises, but it sure will evoke something really slow ([**AV15.7.4**]).

Sometimes the effect is more subtle. To represent kangaroos, Saint-Saëns had the piano play a series of short notes separated by short pauses. This evokes a succession of brief events separated by interruptions. In the context of Saint-Saëns's piece, these sequences evoke kangaroo jumps: For each jump, the ground is hit, hence a brief note, and then the kangaroo rebounds, hence a brief pause. While the music alone isn't specific enough to describe kangaroos, it has no difficulty evoking little jumps ([**AV15.7.5**]).

At this point, it's worth stepping back to contemplate what we have uncovered. Frequency (pitch) can provide an indication about the size of the denoted object. When the object is known, frequency changes can further provide an indication of how energetic or excited the object is. For its part, loudness can provide information about how energetic or excited the object is, or how far away it is. And the speed of musical events can also provide an indication of the speed of what happens to the denoted object.

We can go a bit further and consider the inferences obtained when these inferential means are combined. A diminishing loudness (a *decrescendo*) may indicate that the sound source is losing energy or that it is moving away. On its own, this effect is ambiguous. But now let's add to it a diminishing speed. There is no reason a source that is moving away should give the impression of becoming slower: The sound level but not the speed should be affected. By contrast, a source that is gradually losing energy is expected to become both softer and slower (think of someone who is extremely tired or sick, and how they will often speak more slowly and more softly). So, just with these two simple parameters, speed and loudness, we can make a prediction about musical meaning: if the music simultaneously decreases in speed and in loudness, the most salient interpretation should be that the denoted object is dying out; if only the loudness is decreased, the denoted object may be understood to be moving away.

The last notes of Mahler's Frère Jacques make it possible to test this prediction, as it involves a repetition with a reduction in loudness. In a standard version, it could be interpreted in terms of an object moving away or gradually dying out ([**AV15.7.6**]). But if the music is manipulated so that the speed is gradually reduced as well, the 'moving away' interpretation becomes less likely, and the 'dying out' interpretation becomes more salient ([**AV15.7.7**]).

## 15.8  MUSICAL INFERENCES FROM HARMONY

At this point, you might have reason to wonder whether specifically musical properties give rise to inferences about the extra-musical world. Granted, you might think that music recycles some inferential mechanisms of normal auditory cognition to produce semantic effects. But music isn't just about loudness, speed, and frequency; it wouldn't be *music* if it didn't involve different degrees on a scale and chords. Can these produce meaning, too?

We saw some examples when we discussed the effect of minor and major chords in Strauss's Zarathustra, or of the conclusive effect of the C major chord to signal that a point of maximal repose has been reached. These inferences were triggered because, relative to a key, chords come with different degrees of stability or consonance. As I mentioned previously, in the C major scale (obtained by starting from C and just playing on the white keys of a piano), the chord CEG ([**AV15.5.2**]) is maximally stable. A separate effect is that chords may, irrespective of the musical context, sound more or less consonant or dissonant. For instance, CG played together sounds consonant ([**AV15.8.1**]). By contrast, simultaneously playing CC# ([**AV15.8.2**]) or CF# ([**AV15.8.3**]) sounds really dissonant. This observation can be made more general because the same intervals played from different starting points yield the same effects: CC# is an interval of a halftone, and C#D, the same interval, is equally dissonant, as is GG# or G#A. CF# is a three-tone interval (called a 'tritone'), and it too is usually thought to sound very dissonant. In the early eighteenth century, these three-tone intervals were sometimes called 'the devil in music,' with the clear implication that they had to be avoided! They were gradually tamed in later music, but they created an unmistakable effect of musical tension and instability.

Musical dissonances can produce powerful semantic effects. Saint-Saëns's tortoises provide an amusing example. The composer's main trick was to evoke these animals by way of a radically slowed-down version of the French Can-Can. But that's not the end of the story. There's a point at which the orchestra plays a terribly dissonant chord that includes G#A (with a halftone interval; [**AV15.8.4**]). And what's the effect? The tortoises appear to trip. In other words, the perceptual imbalance created by a dissonant chord is interpreted in terms of a *physical* imbalance on the part of the tortoises. If you remove the dissonance by replacing the G#s with As, so that the halftone interval is eliminated, the impression that the tortoises are tripping disappears as well ([**AV15.8.5**]).

Often the semantic effects are more subtle: A dissonance may be interpreted in terms of emotional rather than physical instability. The soundtrack of Alfred Hitchcock's *Psycho* makes extensive use of this mechanism, thanks to the wonderful music written by Bernard Herrmann. Toward the beginning of the film, the main character, a secretary, embezzles $40,000 from her employer's client and goes on the run in her car, only to see her boss at a traffic light; he immediately spots her. The script says that the secretary "watches the entire exchange with a look of stony horror on her face"— superbly realized in the film ([**AV15.8.6**]). But Herrmann's music is also extraordinarily evocative of the secretary's horror: Here the denoted object corresponds closely to the secretary's feelings. The rhythm plays a role, but the dissonances are crucial ([**AV15.8.7**]). This can be assessed by rewriting the music without the dissonances, following standard rules of composition. When the dissonances are removed, the impression of anguish subsides (see Arthur Bonetto's modifications: [**AV15.8.8**] [= G minor without dissonances]; [**AV15.8.9**] [= closer to the original harmony]).

Not every harmonic inference is due to differences of harmonic stability (as in our discussion of the C major chord) or to differences of consonance (as in our discussion of Saint-Saëns's tortoises or of Hitchcock's *Psycho*). Some further inferences arguably derive from the key a piece is in and pertain to the environments the objects find themselves in. The musical source of this phenomenon is that harmonic space is subdivided into different regions, corresponding to different keys, with relations of proximity among them. The key of C major is obtained from the C major scale, played by pressing in sequence the white keys on a piano: C D E F G A B C. The notes produced by the black keys can be given two names (with no difference for present purposes): They are sharp (notated #) relative to the immediately lower note, and flat (notated ♭) relative to the immediately higher note. For instance, the black note between C and D can be designated as C# (C sharp) or D♭ (D flat).

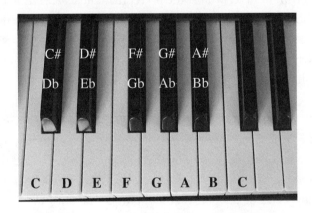

**Figure 15.8.1**

If you write a tune with just the white notes, you will have a melody in C, or in the key of C, as musicians say (more precisely, this is called the key of C major, to distinguish it from the key of C minor scale, which has different intervals between the degrees of the scale). Importantly, the intervals between the notes are not uniform within a scale: All involve a whole tone, except for E F and B C, which each involve a halftone only, as is depicted below (if one used instead a scale with whole tones only, all intervals would be the same and it would be harder to keep track of where the tonic—that is, the first degree—is).

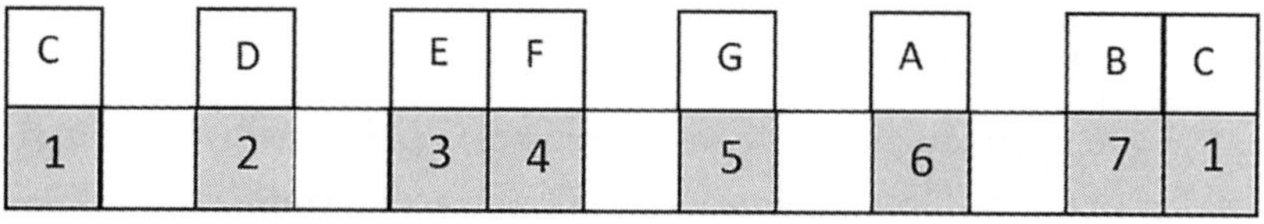

| C | | D | | E | F | | G | | A | | B | C |
|---|---|---|---|---|---|---|---|---|---|---|---|---|
| 1 | | 2 | | 3 | 4 | | 5 | | 6 | | 7 | 1 |

**Figure 15.8.2**
*The scale of C major*

You can obtain a scale that sounds the same but starts from a different point if you play the G scale instead. But for that scale to be isomorphic to that of C major (i.e., for it to display the same sequence of intervals), you must ensure that you preserve the same intervals: whole tones everywhere except between the third and fourth degree (E and F in C major), and again between the seventh and eighth degree (B and C in C major). Thus, if you start from G, the sequence that sounds homologous to the C scale has an F# instead of F: G A B C D E F# G (that's because there must just be a halftone between the seventh and the eighth degree).

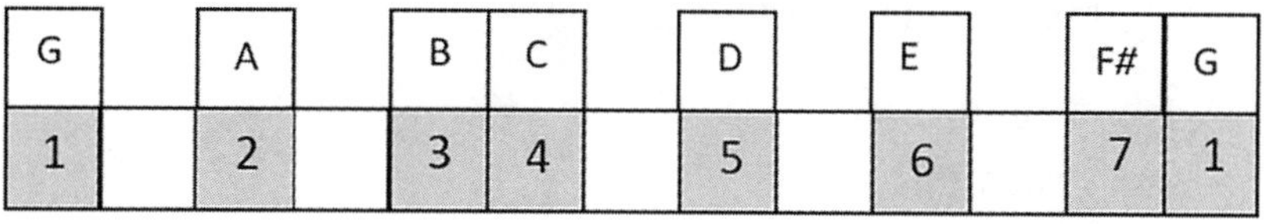

| G | | A | | B | C | | D | | E | | F# | G |
|---|---|---|---|---|---|---|---|---|---|---|---|---|
| 1 | | 2 | | 3 | 4 | | 5 | | 6 | | 7 | 1 |

**Figure 15.8.3**
*The scale of G major*

Simplifying quite a bit, music written in C is 'close' to music written in G because you only need to change one note, F, to go from one to the other. On the other hand, if you start from A, more changes are needed: A B C# D E F# G# A.

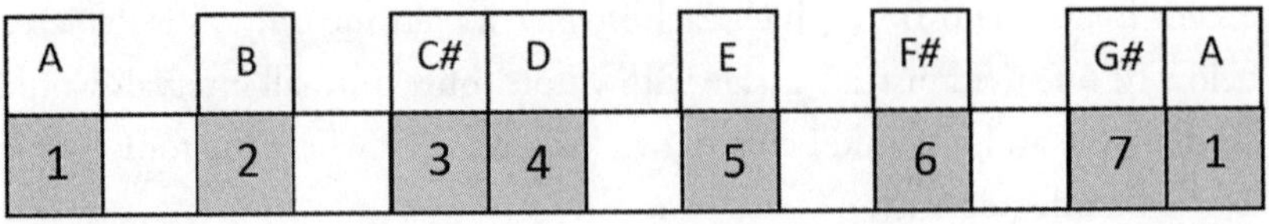

| A | B | C# | D | E | F# | G# | A |
|---|---|----|---|---|----|----|---|
| 1 | 2 | 3 | 4 | 5 | 6 | 7 | 1 |

**Figure 15.8.4**
*The scale of A major*

If you listen to a piece written in the key of C and then a tune written in the key of G, you'll get the impression that you are moving somewhere else but somewhere nearby: a vague impression for sure, but still one that can be exploited to convey semantic information.

Saint-Saëns arguably made use of precisely this when he sought to evoke a swan. This beautiful piece (the only part of the Carnival of the Animals that he publicized within his lifetime) starts with an undulating piano accompaniment evocative of ripples on a pond. Enter the cello, whose melodic line is intended to evoke the majestic movement of a swan. But at some point the music is written in a new key. The effect is subtle but evocative: One gets the impression that the swan is moving to a new environment, maybe a new part of the pond with a different quality of light ([**AV15.8.10**]). It is possible to rewrite the music without this change of key, and the result can be quite melodious, but it lacks this subtle impression that we are suddenly experiencing a new landscape (see Arthur Bonetto's modifications, in two versions: [**AV15.8.11**] [**AV15.8.12**]).

### 15.9   MUSICAL TRUTH

Stepping back, it looks like music can trigger inferences by two general means. On the one hand, it can recycle some inferential mechanisms of normal auditory cognition. On the other hand, specifically musical properties such as harmonic stability, consonance and dissonance, and changes of key can produce inferences as well. These inferences are very general or abstract, but as we saw at the outset with the example of the three columns denoting three individuals, there is a considerable difference between an under-specified semantics (compatible with diverse situations) and no semantics at all.

I initially defined semantics as the study of truth conditions. But so far I have only discussed *inferences* triggered by music. Can music be true of something? Yes, and this might sound like a provocative idea. But on reflection, it is less shocking than it seems. Think again of the three columns I introduced in section 15.2. It made sense to posit that they can represent three objects just in case their left-to-right order is correctly represented in the picture and their ordering by height is preserved as well: the picture need not be precise at all (it's highly schematic, after all), but since column C is the highest, followed by column A, followed by column B, the same ordering should be found in their denotations.

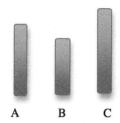

A    B    C

**Figure 15.9.1**

So any group of three objects that preserves the left-to-right order and their ordering by height can be taken to make this iconic representation 'true.' Why couldn't we extend the same line of reasoning to music?

To make things concrete, take a series of three musical events. To keep things really simple, let's discuss an ascending melody C—G—C (with the second C higher than the first one), as at the beginning of Strauss's Zarathustra, and let's take it to be realized *crescendo* (i.e., with increasing loudness). We'll greatly depart from Strauss in considering just this three-note sequence, but that's for the sake of simplicity. We'll take the three notes to represent three events undergone by the denoted object. For instance, we could consider a sunrise, with a first event in which the sun hasn't appeared yet, a second in which it's gradually moving up, and a third event in which the sun has reached its peak and isn't visibly moving anymore. Or we could consider a sunset with three events as well: first, the sun is entirely visible, barely moving; then it gradually disappears; then it is invisible.

Intuitively, our crescendo C—G—C fits much better with a sunrise than with a sunset (there's a reason Richard Strauss used this three-note sequence to evoke a sunrise rather than a sunset!). If you sense a distinction between situations that fit the music and ones that don't, you have, under a different name, a distinction between situations the music is 'true' and 'false' of. But why would the crescendo C—G—C sequence be true of a sunrise and false of a sunset? There are several reasons, including the rise in frequency, which is indicative of an increase in perceived energy (and possibly even of height). But to keep things maximally simple, we'll just consider three properties of our three-note sequence: ordering in time, loudness, and stability. (We also make the assumption that in the key of C, C is more stable than G, which is a bit of an extension since before I talked about chords rather than notes being more or less stable in a key.)

Preserving the ordering in time yields the same kind of effect as preserving the left-right order of the columns: C—G—C can be 'true' of a series of three events only if the first C can denote the first, G the second, and the last C the third. So, for the sunrise, the denotation relations can only be these:

| C | G | C |
|---|---|---|
| ↓ | ↓ | ↓ |
| invisible sun | rising sun | sun at its climax |

As we saw, loudness can provide information about the level of energy of the denoted object or about its distance from the observer. Certainly, a sunrise gives the impression of a rising level of energy so that a property of our three-note sequence (the rise in loudness) is properly interpreted in the sunrise situation. Finally, we want the relative stability of the notes in the

C G C sequence to be preserved. Since we are in the scale of C, C is the most stable note. So we just want the first and last events to be more stable than the intermediate event (and possibly at the same level of stability as each other). This too is properly interpreted in the sunrise situation in which the sun appears to move in the event corresponding to the intermediate note, whereas there is apparent immobility at each extreme: The 'more stable—less stable—more stable' pattern is properly interpreted. In sum, ordering in time, loudness, and stability are all preserved in this interpretation, so we can take our three-note sequence to be 'true' of a sunrise, just like our initial three-column representation was true of some sequences of objects. (This is but a toy model, of course; in a real analysis, many more musical properties would be taken into account.)

But why isn't a sunset just as good an interpretation of our C G C sequence? Among the properties we are considering, the key is the crescendo: It would be implausible for the rising loudness to be interpreted by a sunset. Initially, the sun is entirely visible, barely moving; then it gradually disappears; then it is entirely invisible. There is greater stability at the beginning and at the end than in the middle, so the ordering by stability of the notes is correctly interpreted. But the increasing loudness isn't correctly interpreted: there is no sense in which the sun seems to 'gain energy' or move closer to the observer as it sets.

| C | G | C |
|---|---|---|
| ↓ | ↓ | ↓ |
| whole sun | sun disappearing | invisible sun |

So, already with this extremely rudimentary model, we have a notion of musical truth. Furthermore, the music can be true of entirely silent events: Nothing in our discussion hinges on the claim that the sun is making audible noises! This is a welcome result. Music is regularly used to evoke silent events (Saint-Saëns even had a piece on an aquarium), and in fact the principles of interpretation we posited don't require at all that the denoted objects should be sound-producing.

Now you might think that this is all too much of a good thing. Granted, the C G C sequence *could* be interpreted in terms of a sunrise. But isn't this far too concrete? It is, and our toy semantic analysis predicts precisely this because our principles of interpretation are so general that numerous sequences of events will make the music 'true.' To see this, let's now consider a different silent object: a boat, which may be approaching the harbor where we are located or departing from it.

For this boat approaching, let us take its movement to involve three events. Initially, the boat is at a near-standstill in the distance; then it moves toward the shore; finally, it ends up immobile again, moored in the harbor. Respecting temporal order, the three notes can denote these three events:

| C | G | C |
|---|---|---|
| ↓ | ↓ | ↓ |
| boat in the distance | boat approaching | boat in the harbor |

Just as was the case in the 'sunrise' interpretation, the second event involves motion and is thus less stable than the first and last events, where the boat is at a standstill. This means that the relative stability of the three notes is correctly interpreted. But what about the increasing loudness of the music? It doesn't make much sense to posit that the boat is gaining energy as it nears the shore; if anything, it might be expected to slow down. But because of the ambiguity of loudness, the *crescendo* movement can also be interpreted in terms of the denoted object approaching the observer. In other words, the three-note *crescendo* sequence can be interpreted as a sunrise but also as a boat approaching.

Can it also be true of a boat slowly departing? Probably not, because the crescendo wouldn't be properly interpreted, as the boat neither appears to gain energy nor to approach the observer. In the end, music conveys information, but a very abstract kind of information, just as was the case for the three columns we started our discussion with.

We can now say more precisely in what sense these representations are abstract: Our three columns represent lots of diverse sequences of objects (as long as their left-right order and their ordering by height was preserved). Similarly, our three-note sequence can be true of a sunset, of a boat approaching, and countless other very different sequences of events.

This is as it should be. It would be absurd to take music to have as concrete a meaning as words or full-fledged pictures. But from this it doesn't follow that music doesn't have any meaning at all. Maybe it is *because* this meaning is so abstract that it can be so universal and can speak to very diverse human experiences.

## 15.10 EMOTIONS

The meaning of music is traditionally viewed in terms of emotions. But these emotions have been nearly absent from our discussion. What is their real role in music semantics?

We already saw that Bernard Herrmann's music for the Hitchcock film *Psycho* evoked anguish thanks to its dissonances as well as its rhythm. This isn't surprising from our perspective: music triggers inferences about the denoted objects, and a dissonance can suggest that these are physically imbalanced (Saint-Saëns's faltering tortoises) or emotionally imbalanced (Hitchcock's embezzler).

Music is routinely used to evoke internal feelings of the denoted objects (or rather individuals), especially in film music and in opera. *Simon Boccanegra*, an opera by Giuseppe Verdi, makes this point in a particularly poignant fashion. Simon is a former pirate who has been elected Doge (leader) of the Italian city of Genoa, but following a complicated course of events, he has been poisoned. True to operatic form, he sings his condition. He appears on the stage, faltering, and sings:

> '. . . My head is burning . . . I feel a dreadful fire creeping through my veins . . .'
> '. . . M'ardon le tempia . . . un'atra vampa sento serpeggiar per le vene . . .'

But much of the action is in the music: Each pause between the words (represented by . . . above) is made of a rising and then decreasing melodic sequence by halftones (i.e., by dissonant intervals). Each powerfully evokes a cycle in the unfortunate character's discomfort.

**Figure 15.10.1**

Verdi–Simon Boccanegra, act III, scene 3 (partial score: Simon and violins) ([**AV15.10.1**])
"My head is burning, I feel a dreadful fire creeping through my veins."

Sometimes the emotional implications of a piece can be modified by more systematic changes than just adding or removing a dissonance. Among musicians, a well-known trick to change the emotional character of a piece is to rewrite it with a structurally different scale. The two most famous scale types (also called 'modes') in classical music are the major and the minor scale. As mentioned before, the major scale corresponds to music written with the standard scale of C, starting on C and just pressing the white keys on a piano; because you start with C, this one is the C major scale. You can start on any other note, but you need to make adjustments to ensure that the intervals are kept the same as in the C major scale. The interval between the third and fourth note, and that between the seventh and eight note, should be a halftone rather than a whole tone. By contrast, the minor mode is obtained by writing music with a scale that has different intervals. Start from A and only press the white keys, and you get a version of the A minor scale (I say 'a version' because commonly the G is replaced with a G#; we can disregard this here).

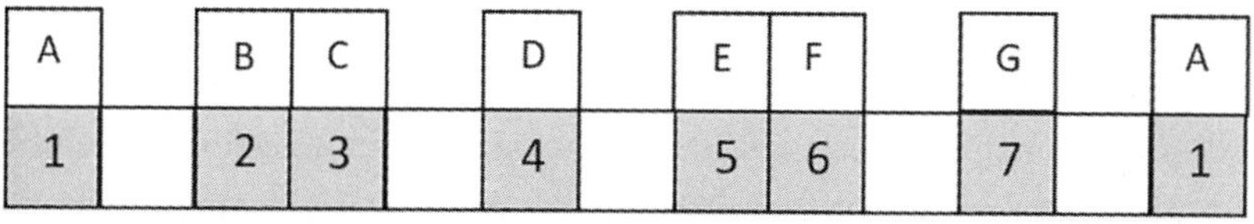

| A | | B | C | | D | | E | F | | G | | A |
|---|---|---|---|---|---|---|---|---|---|---|---|---|
| 1 | | 2 | 3 | | 4 | | 5 | 6 | | 7 | | 1 |

**Figure 15.10.2**
*The scale of A minor*

As in the major scale, there are two intervals that are just halftones, but they are not in the same positions: They appear between the second and third notes, and between the fifth and sixth notes. By contrast, in the major scale, the halftone intervals appear between the third and fourth notes (E and F) and between seventh and last note (B and C).

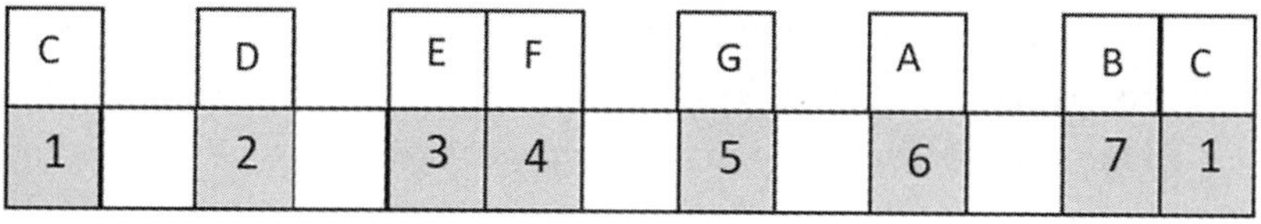

| C | | D | | E | F | | G | | A | | B | C |
|---|---|---|---|---|---|---|---|---|---|---|---|---|
| 1 | | 2 | | 3 | 4 | | 5 | | 6 | | 7 | 1 |

**Figure 15.10.3**
*The scale of C major*

To get a minor scale starting from C, you need to press some black keys, as indicated here:

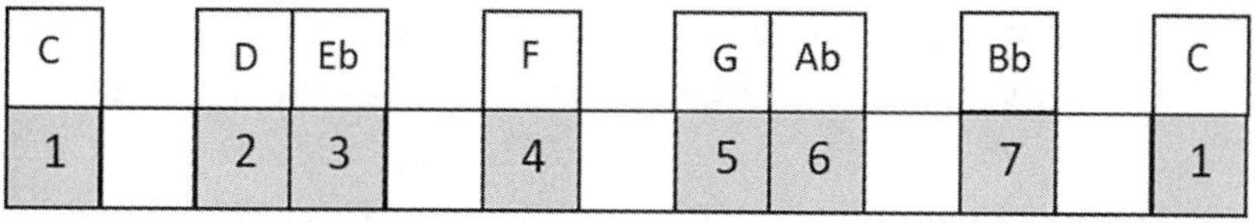

| C | | D | Eb | | F | | G | Ab | | Bb | | C |
|---|---|---|----|---|---|---|---|----|---|----|---|---|
| 1 | | 2 | 3 | | 4 | | 5 | 6 | | 7 | | 1 |

**Figure 15.10.4**
*The scale of C minor*

Now one common observation is that pieces written in the major mode sound more assertive or happy than pieces written in minor mode. (One possible reason is that the tonic chord is a bit more consonant in major than in minor; this tonic chord is CEG in C major and CE♭G in C minor.[20])

In fact, we already saw this trick at work in a great piece—in Mahler's use of the children's song Frère Jacques to evoke a funeral procession. Instead of using the major version of the song, he used a minor version, which fits the mournfulness of a funeral procession ([**AV15.10.2**]). If you rewrite the music in major mode, there is indeed something more assertive and happier about it, and the funeral effect gets a bit lost ([**AV15.10.3**]).

But that's not all. Usually, happy people act more quickly than sad ones, and sometimes they speak in a higher tone too, possibly out of excitement. Mahler's Frère Jacques didn't sound sad just because of the minor mode; it's also slow, and low in frequency. If we modify both properties and keep the major version, we can completely reverse the emotional meaning of the piece and obtain instead something that sounds very happy. As examples, one can consider a major version, two and a half times as fast ([**AV15.10.4**]); a major version, two octaves up ([**AV15.10.5**]); and a major version, two octaves up, two and a half times as fast ([**AV15.10.6**]).

In the examples discussed so far, things are fairly simple: By way of dissonances or of the minor mode, the music evokes certain emotions of the denoted 'objects,' corresponding to Simon Boccanegra or to the members of a funeral procession. But there are more subtle cases in which the music seems to tell us, the perceivers, how *we* should feel about a scene. In fact, in Verdi's opera, before Simon feels the effect of the poison, he drinks it. As he does so, and before he can feel any of its effects, the music tells us in no uncertain terms that something unsettling is happening: The music initially moves by halftones, only to then jump by a three-tone-interval (this is precisely the tritone interval that was called 'devil in the music'). And when Simon drinks the poison, the note produced is completely unexpected: After the note F gets iterated four times, we would expect a fifth iteration—and we have a completely unexpected note instead (A♭). Fate has changed its course.

**Figure 15.10.5**
*Verdi–Simon Boccanegra, act II, scene 8* ([**AV15.10.7**])

The emotions that are depicted in this way are not Simon's, but arguably our own. We can make sense of this if we extend a bit our understanding of what the denoted objects are: they need not just correspond to external objects taking part in various events, but they may correspond to *experienced* objects and events.

Switches between major and minor are ubiquitous in music to suggest changes of emotions and atmosphere, including when it is really the perceiver's emotions that matter. A powerful example is found in Puccini's *Madama Butterfly*, set in Japan in 1904. The beginning of the story centers around Pinkerton, a U.S. naval officer who is about to marry a fifteen-year-old Japanese girl that he will soon abandon for an American wife, causing endless suffering in the process. Before he expounds his carefree philosophy of life to the U.S. consul Sharpless, the orchestra intones "The Star-Spangled Banner," which will characterize Pinkerton throughout (it was officially in use by the U.S. Navy at the time and only became the U.S. national anthem in 1931). Effective but not subtle, one might say. But after two bars, assertive and in major mode, the melody changes and turns to minor. And this second phrase recurs as a counterpoint to Pinkerton's arrogant optimism. One can venture that this phrase is not associated with Pinkerton but arguably with the perceiver's experience of the situation, one in which Pinkerton's actions will sow grief and tragedy.

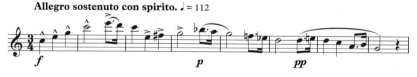

**Figure 15.10.6**
Puccini, Madama Butterly–'Star-Spangled Banner' theme (simplified score, A. Bonetto)
([**AV15.10.8**])

In sum, there is something true about the old idea that music bears a special relation to emotions. But this does not contradict our analysis of the meaning of music in terms of inferences about denoted objects. For starters, these objects may be human characters, as routinely happens in opera, and when this is the case it is only natural that music should depict their emotions. But in addition, if the denoted objects can be experienced objects rather than just objective ones, it makes much sense to map some properties of the music—such as stability, consonance and dissonance, major or minor—to the emotions that *we* have as we experience the events undergone by the objects.

Still, reducing the meaning of music to emotions doesn't do it justice. Music can trigger powerful inferences about the state and actions of the denoted objects, including when these inferences have nothing to do with emotions. These are abstract inferences, to be sure, satisfied by very diverse objects and events. But there is an important distinction between an abstract meaning and no meaning at all, or for that matter a meaning that reduces to emotions.

### 15.11 CONCLUSION

It is time to go back to Bernstein's challenge. His conclusion was that the meaning of music is "the way it makes you feel when you hear it." And his main argument was that music has no referential (nonemotional) meaning at all, because even 'referential' music such as Strauss's *Don Quixote* can be made to fit equally well a made-up story about Superman.

But let's think about this argument once again. Applied to the three columns we discussed before, it would go like this: "You are telling me that these columns represent three individuals of different heights. I don't buy it. They could just as well represent three skyscrapers of different heights. So they don't represent anything at all!" You wouldn't be too convinced. The mistake, you would think, is to claim that the three columns represent three *individuals*. That's far too concrete. Instead, the three columns should be taken to represent three things of different heights, arranged from left to right, be they individuals, skyscrapers, trees, or any reasonably elongated things you may care to imagine. These are different types of objects, but they still share some properties: they are thin, and their relative heights and left-to-right order are correctly represented by the columns.

The answer to Bernstein's argument is the same: Yes, the Don Quixote story and the Superman story are very different, and we'll grant that both can be made to fit the music. But this is because they share key structural properties, precisely the ones that are encoded by the music. To see this, it's worth putting Bernstein's two interpretations side by side.

| Don Quixote interpretation | Superman interpretation | Salient musical passage |
|---|---|---|
| **Context:** Don Quixote is a foolish old man who has read too many books about knighthood and decides he is a marvelous knight himself. Sancho Panza is his devoted servant.<br>[**AV15.11.1** 5:17] | **Context:** An innocent man can't sleep in a prison where he was put unjustly. He spends his night playing the kazoo while other prisoners snore. But his friend Superman is coming to rescue him.<br>[**AV15.11.1** 0:28] | |
| Don Quixote departs on his horse to conquer the world.<br>[**AV15.11.1** 5:36] | Superman comes charging along through the alley on his motorcycle.<br>[**AV15.11.1** 1:08] |  |
| We hear Sancho chuckling to himself.<br>[**AV15.11.1** 5:45] | Superman whistles his secret whistle (in the woodwinds) so the prisoner will know he's coming.<br>[**AV15.11.1** 1:20] |  |
| They see a flock of sheep in the field going *baa-baa*.<br>[**AV15.11.1** 6:03] | Superman hears all the prisoners snoring away peacefully in the dead silence of night.<br>[**AV15.11.1** 1:28] |  |
| A shepherd is playing on his pipe.<br>[**AV15.11.1** 6:16] | Superman hears his imprisoned friend playing his kazoo over the snoring, which gets louder as he gets nearer.<br>[**AV15.11.1** 1:50] |  |

**Figure 15.11.1**

*Bernstein's two interpretations of Strauss's Don Quixote, Variation II*

| Don Quixote interpretation | Superman interpretation | Salient musical passage |
|---|---|---|
| Don Quixote charges at the sheep, taking them to be an army. [**AV15.11.1** 6:27] | Superman charges into the prison yard and bops the guard over the head, done in the orchestra with a loud bang in the percussion. [**AV15.11.1** 2:14] |  |
| The sheep run off in all directions baaing wildly. [**AV15.11.1** 6:40] | The kazoo stops playing, and with all the snoring still going on, Superman grabs his friend and carries him away on his motorcycle. [**AV15.11.1** 2:22] The snoring gets farther and farther away, until we don't hear it anymore. [**AV15.11.1** 2:37] | |
| Don Quixote is convinced he has done a truly knightly deed, and is he proud! [**AV15.11.1** 6:45] | Our hero at last reaches freedom! [**AV15.11.1** 2:50] |  |

**Figure 15.11.1** *(continued)*

Strikingly, some key structural elements remain constant across the two interpretations, with only small modifications. In Bernstein's retelling, Don Quixote departing to conquer the world on his horse becomes Superman charging along on his motorcycle; in both cases, we are dealing with a heroic figure launching a conquest (when one analyzes the score, one can see that the enthusiastic character of the departure is due in part to a rising melodic movement). The sheep of the Don Quixote story become prisoners snoring in the Superman interpretation; in both cases, the music evokes a somewhat chaotic group (in part due to the use of very dissonant chords). The shepherd playing on his pipe becomes an innocent prisoner playing his kazoo. Here, too, the structural analogy should be clear. And the triumphant ending represents in one case Don Quixote's heroic pride and, in the other, Superman and his friend's conquest of freedom. The only salient structural difference between the two stories is that Sancho Panza has no counterpart in Bernstein's Superman story. This is because Bernstein reinterprets Sancho Panza's chuckling as Superman whistling his secret tune—a point of departure alright, but admittedly a fairly minor one.[21]

| Don Quixote interpretation | Superman interpretation |
| --- | --- |
| Don Quixote on his horse + Sancho Panza chuckling | Superman on his motorcycle + Superman whistling |
| Sheep going baa-baa | Prisoners snoring |
| Shepherd playing on his pipe, with the sound becoming louder as Don Quixote comes nearer | Innocent prisoner playing his kazoo, with the sound becoming louder as Don Quixote comes nearer |
| Don Quixote charges the sheep | Superman charges into the prison |
| Don Quixote is proud of his knightly deed | Superman and his friend reach freedom |

If anything, then, Bernstein's retelling supports the idea that music has a meaning beyond the emotions it evokes. Because this meaning is abstract, the music doesn't tell us whether it is talking about Don Quixote, or Superman, or countless other stories that share the same structural properties. In this, Bernstein is exactly right, and it would be foolish to think that music can tell *concrete* stories. But it doesn't follow that music has no meaning at all, or a meaning that is reducible to the emotions it evokes. Emotions do matter to the meaning of music, as we saw above, but they don't exhaust it. Rather, music tells abstract stories, applicable to lots of *very* diverse situations, from Don Quixote to Superman, with many things in between—but stories nonetheless.

# EPILOGUE: THE LIMITS OF TRUTH

*From primate calls to human language, gestures, and music, we have analyzed meaning in terms of truth, with the motto: To know the meaning of a sentence (or of an animal call, or even of a musical piece) is to know under what conditions it is true. In the last two chapters of this book, we explore one of the deepest challenges to this program: paradoxes, which appear to defy the very idea of truth conditions. They are cases in which we just cannot coherently assign any truth value to a sentence. One of the simplest and most difficult examples is the Liar's paradox, which can be stated as follows:* This very sentence is not true. *If it is true, the sentence ought to be false; but if it is false, what it says is . . . true, so it should be true, not false. We are stumped.*

*The solution is to posit that there are more truth values than meets the eye: not just* true *and* false, *but also* indeterminate *(i.e., neither true nor false). This will make it possible to integrate paradoxical sentences to the present enterprise. More general lessons will be gained as well: Paradoxes are just one type of sentences that are 'ungrounded' because they do not depend on facts about the world. But there are further ungrounded statements, in particular ones that can be assigned a standard truth value, but in a way that seems entirely arbitrary. Such is the case with the statement:* This very sentence is true. *It can be assigned any value one wishes: true, false, or even indeterminate (neither true nor false). As we will see, then, paradoxes are a serious challenge to semantics, but also a source of insight into the nature of truth.*

# 16 THE LIMITS OF TRUTH I: THE RIDDLE OF PARADOXES

## 16.1 LIARS

Epimenides was a sixth-century BC philosopher and prophet who was of the opinion that Zeus, the major Greek god, was immortal. This went against the dominant opinion in Crete, and thus Epimenides was quoted as saying the following (a sentence we will call *E* for Epimenides):

> (E) All Cretans are liars.

The reason Epimenides felt compelled to challenge Cretan opinions was that he himself was Cretan. But, as a result, his statement made a claim about Epimenides himself. And if, simplifying somewhat, we take a liar to be someone who *always* lies, the statement E pertained to lots of statements, including E itself. With an unfortunate consequence for Epimenides (who probably didn't intend this): E couldn't be true. For if it were, then all Cretans, including Epimenides himself, should always lie, and thus E should be false.

This state of affairs struck people as being paradoxical, and in fact this is sometimes called the 'Epimenides paradox.' But this obscures an important distinction: A paradoxical sentence ('paradox' for short) is one that cannot coherently be assigned the value *true*, nor the value *false* (I will discuss real cases shortly). But, at this point, nothing rules out the possibility that Epimenides's statement is false. To ensure that it is, just find some Cretan—for instance, Epimenides's mother—who at some point uttered a true statement. She won't qualify as a liar on our demanding understanding of the term (someone who *always* lies), and so certainly it will be false that *all Cretans are liars*.

So, in this case, Epimenides's statement is self-defeating (as it couldn't be true), but it needn't be paradoxical (as it could well be false). However, a far more serious problem is reported by a later Greek philosopher, Eubulides, who lived in the fourth century BC. It is raised by the following sentence (again we will give it a name, L):

(L) I am lying right now.

Or, if you prefer to avoid any reference to what the speaker is doing, it can be stated as follows:

(L*) This very sentence is false.

These are called 'Liar' sentences ('Liars' for short). And they raise some of the hardest problems for semantics, to the point that one can argue that with such statements we reach the very limits of semantics, and certainly of semantic intuitions.

To see what the problem is, suppose that the Liar sentence is true. We'll reason about L*, but things are similar for L. If L* is true, then the sentence it refers to—namely, L* itself—must be false. That's not a possibility—this was in fact what made Epimenides's statement self-defeating. But unlike the Epimenides situation, we also cannot coherently assign this sentence the value *false*. The reason is that if L* is false, this suffices to make the content of L* (what is says) true. So, if L* is false, L* is true—this case too is impossible. The upshot is that L* can neither be true nor false.

This is the hallmark of a genuinely paradoxical statement: It cannot coherently be assigned the value *true* nor the value *false*. (This is very different from a contradiction, such as saying, *It is and isn't raining*, which is always false—and doesn't give logicians headaches the way paradoxes do. Similarly Moore's 'paradox,' discussed in section 10.2, wasn't a paradox in the precise sense, but rather a pragmatic contradiction.)

## 16.2 TARSKI'S CHALLENGE

The Polish logician Alfred Tarski is one of the grandparents of formal semantics. In 1933, he showed in detail how to define truth for a language, as we did for Predicate Logic in chapter 7 and for a small part of English in chapter 8.[1] His own endeavor was limited to artificial languages, and it was left to others (notably the American philosopher and logician Richard Montague) to extend this program to natural languages. But Tarski's construction came with a warning: A sufficiently rich language should not be allowed to contain a word meaning *true*, for fear that it would also be able to produce sentences akin to: *This very sentence is not true*. Since Tarski's goal was to define truth for formal languages, this was an interesting result, not a real worry: it just suggested that truth for a formal language can only be defined in another language.

In Tarski's time, the idea that English could be treated as a formal language wasn't particularly plausible. But after Noam Chomsky treated the syntax of English as a formal language, and Montague extended this idea to semantics, the challenge became considerably more pressing. The difficulty is that English *does* contain words such as *true* and *false*, and we have no trouble understanding them and using them in all sorts of sentences, including self-referential ones.

Is there a way to address Tarski's challenge and thus to define truth for a language that contains the words *true* and *false*? There is, and even a beautiful one, but it will take a bit of reasoning to get there.

## 16.3 VARIETIES OF PARADOXES

Lest you think that there is just one paradox, the Liar, I first want to discuss a few others. What they have in common is that they are 'ungrounded,' in the sense that they talk about something that cannot be reduced to (non-semantic) facts about the world.

The simplest way to be ungrounded is to be self-referential. We can simplify our task a bit by giving names to sentences, but as was the case above, you can replace them with expressions like *this very sentence* or even *the sentence appearing on line x of page n* for appropriate choices of $x$ and $n$. So, the Liar can just be represented like this:

(L**) L** is false.

But sometimes the self-reference is less direct, as when two sentences each talk about the other:

(L1) L2 is true.
(L2) L1 is false.

Here, L1 doesn't directly talk about its own truth, and neither does L2. But L1 talks about the truth of L2, and L2 talks about the truth of L1, so indirectly L1 talks about its own truth. The circularity is particularly obvious if we use arrows to point from one sentence to the one it refers to:

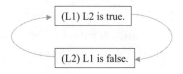

In this case, the indirect self-reference is enough to create a paradox: We cannot coherently assign any truth value to this pair of sentences. Suppose L1 is true. Then what it says is true, so L2 must true. But this entails that L1 is false! So L1 cannot be true. Can L1 be false, then? If so, contrary to what L1 says, L2 must be false. Since L2 claims that L1 is false, L2's falsity implies that L1 is true. So, if L1 is false . . . L1 is true. This too cannot be. We have once again run into a paradox.

### 16.4 WHY ARE THERE PARADOXES?

Now you might think that self-reference is such an odd phenomenon that we should just rule it out or forget about it. But that's not quite the right diagnosis. For starters, there are all sorts of self-referential statements that are logically unproblematic. Some are routinely used to make commitments:

I hereby promise to abide by the contract.
I hereby certify that I have read the terms and conditions.

In these sentences, *hereby* refers to the very sentence it appears in, but certainly we wouldn't want to excise these statements from ordinary language.

Other sentences make reference to their own form, truly or falsely:

This very sentence contains six words.
This very sentence contains three words.

You only need to count the words to see that the first sentence is true and the second one is false. And there is really no reason either sentence should get a logician exercised.

Furthermore, even some sentences that talk about their own truth value are fairly unproblematic to a logician. Take any sentence that starts with *two plus two equals five and.* . . . Add any self-referential content you wish to the end of the sentence; it won't matter. The reason is that the beginning of the conjunction is clearly false, which guarantees that no matter what comes after, the result will be false as well. In particular, the following sentence should be ruled false, not paradoxical:

Two plus two equals five and this very sentence is false.

In sum, getting rid of all cases of self-reference would be overkill. Many such cases are entirely innocuous and clear. But in addition, prohibiting self-reference won't suffice to solve our problem. That's because there are families of paradoxes that arise in infinite series of sentences without self-reference. Here is a case in point (it's often called a 'Yablo series' or 'Yablo's paradox,' in reference to the philosopher Stephen Yablo, who discovered this phenomenon).

(1) Every sentence on line 2 or after is false.
(2) Every sentence on line 3 or after is false.
. . .
(k) Every sentence on line k+1 or after is false.
(k+1) Every sentence on line k+2 or after is false.
. . .

Each sentence talks about sentences lower down in the list (as is displayed below with arrows), saying that they are all false; but no sentence talks about itself.

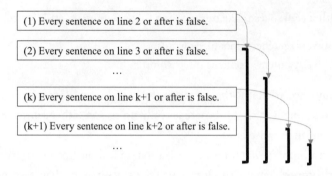

(1) Every sentence on line 2 or after is false.

(2) Every sentence on line 3 or after is false.

...

(k) Every sentence on line k+1 or after is false.

(k+1) Every sentence on line k+2 or after is false.

...

Why does a paradox arise? Let's first suppose that some sentence in the series is true—say, the sentence on line k. Then sentences on line k+1, k+2, k+3 . . . are all false, as sentence k claims. But that cannot be. The reason is that this would make true what sentence k+1 says, as its content is precisely that the sentences on line k+2, k+3, and so on are all false. Since our choice of k was arbitrary, the conclusion is that it can't be that any sentence in the series is true.

The only other possibility, then, is that all sentences in the series are false. But this too cannot be: If all the sentences are false, what each says is exactly right, so all should be . . . true, not false! Since it can't be that some sentence in the series is true, and it also can't be that they are all false, we have a paradox once again, and without any self-reference.

The upshot is that the source of paradoxes isn't self-reference per se but something more general: the fact that the truth of some sentences is ungrounded, in the sense that it cannot be reduced to independent facts about the world. All the paradoxical cases we saw were of this type. *This very sentence contains six words* has a content that can be reduced to certain facts about the world—namely, how many words are printed in a certain part of a piece of paper (or of a screen). And the conjunction *two plus two equals five and this sentence is false* was also unproblematic because the first conjunct pertained to the (mathematical) world, which was enough to refute the entire conjunction. By contrast, sentences that talk about themselves, or series of sentences that only talk about one another, run the risk of being ungrounded.

## 16.5 BEYOND TRUTH AND FALSITY

Now that we have seen how diverse paradoxes are, can we find a way to deal with them? It doesn't seem promising to treat them as being true, or as being false, so we might as well bite the bullet and introduce a third truth value. We'll call it # (a symbol often called 'hash'), and we'll take this to be the value of statements that are neither true nor false. For reasons I'll come to shortly, I'll often call it the 'indeterminate' truth value, with the intuition that in this case it just cannot be determined whether the statement is true or false.

This is not the end of the story, however. If elementary sentences can be indeterminate (i.e., neither true nor false), this unfortunate condition could in principle infect all sentences that are constructed out of them. So we need to go back to *all* meaning rules—for instance, those for negation, *and*, and *or*, and say how they are to deal with clauses that have the value #. Earlier (in chapter 7), we saw very simple semantic rules for logical words:

not *A* is true just in case *A* is false.
*(A and B)* is true just in case *A* is true and *B* is true.
*(A or B)* is true just in case *A* is true or *B* is true or both.

At the time, we just specified under what conditions these sentences are true; specifying when they are false would have been overkill, since if a sentence isn't true, well, it must be false! Or so we thought: Paradoxes show that this isn't correct, as we now have a third truth value (namely, #). So we must extend our earlier rules to the case in which the formulas *A* or *B* have the value #.

One very useful rule of thumb is to take # (the indeterminate value) to mean that we can't determine whether the sentence has the value *true* or the value *false*—we just can't tell. This suggests a cautious way of extending the meaning rules for our connectives. We want to ensure that if at any point we gain more information about the status of a formula we took to be indeterminate, this won't force us to revise any assignment of *true* and *false*, although it could, of course, have the desirable effect that a formula that was initially indeterminate may gain a normal truth value.

Let's put this in practice. If *A* is true, then of course *not A* is false, and conversely if *A* is false, *not A* is true. If *A* is indeterminate, we just can't tell if it's true or false, and the same applies to *not A*. So the correct semantic rule for negation goes like this:

> *not A* is true just in case *A* is false;
> *not A* is false just in case *A* is true.

Note that we now specify the conditions under which *A* is true and the conditions under which it is false. You might object that we have three cases to define, not two, since sentences can be true, false, or indeterminate. But it's enough to take care of two cases out of three—for instance, truth and falsity: the third case, #, will follow by elimination (a sentence must have some truth value, so if it is neither true nor false, well, it's indeterminate!). In this case, we can thus infer from these two lines that *not A* is indeterminate just in case it is neither true nor false (i.e., just in case *A* is indeterminate).

Let's turn to *(A and B)*. Certainly, for it to be true, both *A* and *B* must be true. For it to be false, it's enough that one of *A* or *B* is false. The other member of the pair could be anything it wants to be, including indeterminate, and it won't affect the result. For instance, if *A* is false and *B* is indeterminate, no matter what the eventual value of *B* turns out to be, the conjunction can be determined to be false. So, this gives us this rule:

> *(A and B)* is true just in case *A* is true and *B* is true.
> *(A and B)* is false just in case *A* is false or *B* is false (or both).

The fact that we picked a cautious rule plays out in the following way (and that will matter in chapter 17): If we assigned the value *false* to *(A and B)* because *A* is false while *B* is indeterminate, and we gain new information, learning that *B* is true in the end, this won't affect the value we assigned to the conjunction. That's because our rule was designed to take into account our uncertainty about *B* and thus to remain valid if we learned something more about *B*. This is a general fact: whenever we have assigned a standard value (true or false) with our cautious rules, this value will remain correct after we discover that some sentences we took to be indeterminate are in fact true or false.

The rule for *or* is deduced in the same way. Since we are, as before, dealing with inclusive disjunction (= *A or B or both)*, it's enough to know that at least one of $A$ and $B$ is true to ascertain that the disjunction is. To ensure that it's false, we must make sure that both are false; if either one is indeterminate, there's a chance that it is true and thus we can't tell for sure that the disjunction is false.

> *(A or B)* is true just in case $A$ is true or $B$ is true (or both).
> *(A or B)* is false just in case $A$ is false and $B$ is false.

The cautious rule of thumb we adopted can be applied to all sorts of logical words. The upshot is that it's not too hard to transition from a system that has two truth values to one that has three. And this means that we finally have a solution to the problem raised by paradoxes: they are neither true nor false but have the value #, and although this does require serious adjustments to the meaning of logical words, the changes are manageable.

### 16.6 TRUTH-TELLERS

More oddities pop up when we consider further ungrounded statements, defined (as above) as ones whose truth value cannot be reduced to (non-semantic) facts about the world. Besides Liars, there are Truth-tellers, sentences that assert their own truth. Here, too, they can be expressed in various ways:

> (T) I am saying the truth right now.
> (T*) This very sentence is true.
> (T**) T** is true.

Now you might think that these statements look paradoxical, but on closer inspection they are not. It is possible to coherently assign to them the value *true* or the value *false* (you can check—no incoherence follows from either choice). The problem is different: The choice between the two truth values seems to be entirely arbitrary! So, for instance, if T is true, what it says should be true as well . . . and so T should be true. Nothing wrong with that. On the other hand, if T is false, what it says should be false . . . and since its content is that T is true, yes, it is indeed false. Nothing wrong with that, either. But how are we going to choose, then? Since the Truth-teller only talks about its own truth, it doesn't seem that facts about the world can be of any help to determine its truth value. This is the sense in which the meaning of the Truth-teller is ungrounded. (In fact, now that we have three truth values, not two, we can check that we can also give the Truth-teller the indeterminate truth value #. If so, we can't tell whether this statement is true or false, and thus the claim that it is true is itself infected by the same indeterminacy.)

Just as Liars come in many varieties, so do Truth-tellers. Each of the next two statements, T1 and T2, talks about the other, so neither is directly self-referential.

(T1) T2 is true.
(T2) T1 is true.

If both T1 and T2 are true, then of course what they each assert is true and no problem ensues. If both are false, what each asserts is false, and no problem arises, either. Here, too, the choice of a truth value seems arbitrary—it is not derived from facts about the world. (On the other hand, not anything goes. For instance, it couldn't be that T1 is true and T2 is false. Since T2 claims that T1 is true, if T1 is true, so is T2.)

We saw before that the real source of paradoxes is not self-reference but the more general notion of ungroundedness. One way to be ungrounded is to be (directly or indirectly) self-referential, but another way is to have an infinite series of sentences that each talk about later sentences in the series. And, as you might have guessed, such infinite series can give rise to Truth-tellers as well. Just replace 'false' with 'true' in our infinite Liar, and you get this:

(1) Every sentence on line 2 or after is true.
(2) Every sentence on line 3 or after is true.
. . .
(k) Every sentence on line k+1 or after is true.
. . .

It is clear that no problem of coherence arises if all sentences in the series are true. But no problem will arise either if all are false! Each sentence claims that the following sentences are all true, and this is false—so each sentence is indeed false. Here, too, the choice between treating all the sentences as true or treating them all as false seems to be arbitrary.

## 16.7 EMPIRICAL LIARS

Does one *really* need to care about such arcane examples as *This very sentence is false*, not to mention the more complicated cases I just discussed? It's certainly *very* reasonable to disregard ungrounded sentences when one is interested in meaning phenomena, especially since many of the facts we discussed earlier in this book are already complicated enough as they are. In fact, this is the usual practice in linguistics, where paradoxes are typically left . . . for later! Still, this raises a kind of philosophical question: Can we neatly delineate which sentences are ungrounded and which are not? As it turns out, this cannot be achieved on purely formal or a priori grounds. The reason is that whether a sentence is paradoxical or not may depend on all sorts of empirical facts. Suppose we witness the following exchange in a political debate (where we'll take 'half' to mean 'exactly half'):

> Trump: Half of what Clinton says in this debate is false.
> Clinton: Everything Trump says in this debate is false.

Not an inconceivable exchange, I would think. And in most cases, it wouldn't get logicians exercised, at least not for logical reasons. For instance, if Trump uttered 100 sentences and 30 are true, Clinton is wrong. And if Clinton uttered 100 sentences and 80 are true, then Trump is wrong. But if we are really unlucky, we won't be able to come to a conclusion at all. Think about the following situation (admittedly an unlikely one!):

**The headache situation:** Clinton uttered 50 false statements, 49 true ones, and the one above. So, in the end, Trump's statement is true just in case Clinton's reply is true. While Trump may not realize it, it amounts to: *Clinton's reply is true*. Now suppose that in the rest of the debate Trump just utters 99 statements, which are all false, plus the quoted claim about Clinton. So really Clinton's claim is true just in case Trump's claim about her is false, and so it amounts to: *Trump's statement is false*.

What happens in this situation is that because of the distribution of truths and falsities in the rest of the debate, Trump's statement really claims that Clinton's statement is true, while Clinton's statement asserts that Trump's is false. This is tantamount to a case of indirect self-reference we discussed above:

(L1) L2 is true.
(L2) L1 is false.

There was no way to assign truth or falsity to these statements: they were paradoxical, and so are Trump's and Clinton's claims in the headache situation.

In fact, there is an older example that makes the same point, and it is none other than Epimenides's blanket statement about Cretans:

(E) All Cretans are liars.

What I told you at the outset was that this isn't a paradox because in standard situations, it is very easy to determine the truth value of this statement, even understood (with self-reference) as: *All Cretans, including I, always lie* (it's enough to find one Cretan that says one true thing to refute the claim). But in this case as well, we can find a headache situation in which the sentence ends up being paradoxical. If Epimenides is right about all Cretans other than himself (they always lie!), and all the other statements he himself makes are false, then we end up with this quandary:

If E is true, then E itself (as statement produced by the always-lying Epimenides) must be false.
On the other hand, if E is false, it confirms that every Cretan (including Epimenides) always lies; but since this is just what E asserts, E is true.

In the end, then, Epimenides's statement is a great example of an empirical Liar; it is a statement that is paradoxical in some empirical situations but not in others. Still, we don't need to resort to such complicated cases to find sentences that are paradoxical in some conditions but not in others. Here is a case in point:

(EL) It's raining and this very sentence is false.

If it's not raining, we can tell that EL (again an empirical Liar) is false because its first conjunct is. But if it is raining, the sentence is true just in case its second conjunct is, and we are back where we started: it is true just in case it is false, which means that it is paradoxical.

The same reasoning makes it possible to produce Empirical Truth-tellers, which are sentences that behave like the Truth-teller in some circumstances but not in others.

(ET) It's raining and this very sentence is true.

If it's not raining, ET is false because its first conjunct is. But if it is raining, ET is true just in case its second conjunct is, and we are back to a standard Truth-teller.

The upshot is that one can't decide once and for all which sentences are paradoxical (or truth-teller-like) and should thus be excised from semantic investigations: some sentences are perfectly innocuous in some states of affairs, but they become paradoxical (or truth-teller-like) in some headache situations.

## 16.8  CONCLUSION

Paradoxes are a genuine challenge to semantics. Throughout this book, our approach to meaning was based on truth conditions, but paradoxes can neither be true nor false. This is no cause for despair, however: the natural solution is to add a third truth value (#, or 'indeterminate') corresponding to *neither true nor false*. This requires a revision of the semantic rules we posited in earlier chapters, but it is in principle feasible.

Why are there paradoxes in the first place? The source of our predicament initially seemed to lie in self-reference, as in the statement, *This very sentence is false*. But this diagnosis was incorrect: There are infinite series of sentences (Yablo series) that are not self-referential (each talks about other sentences in the series) and yet collectively yield paradoxes. A better diagnosis is that sentences that fail to be grounded in facts about the world can yield paradoxes.

We discovered two further facts in our discussions. First, some ungrounded sentences are not paradoxical and yet display a very odd behavior. This is the case of Truth-tellers (e.g., *This very sentence is true*). Their problem isn't that they can't be treated as *true* or *false* (or for that matter *indeterminate*), but rather that the choice is arbitrary and impossible to justify on the basis of empirical facts. We also discovered that whether a sentence is ungrounded or not might itself depend on some empirical facts. Some sentences that seem rather innocuous might turn out to be paradoxical under some empirical conditions. This means that excising paradoxical sentences (and nothing else) from the rest of the language is no easy task—and thus fully extending the semantic approach to them is a real challenge, which we address in chapter 17.

# 17 THE LIMITS OF TRUTH II: SOLVING THE RIDDLE OF PARADOXES

## 17.1 THE CHALLENGE

Knowledge of meaning is knowledge of truth conditions—this has been our motto throughout this book. But what *is* truth? We thought we had an answer: The truth conditions of individual words are given by our mental dictionary, and semantic rules extend them to the entire language (this was the topic of chapter 9). For instance, once you know the truth conditions of *p*, and of *q*, the meaning of *and* ensures that *p and q* is true just in case *p* is true and *q* is true. Other cases were less simple, but the core idea was the same, and it yielded a definition of truth for an entire language.

Alas, this was before we investigated paradoxes. These challenge our approach to truth, for two reasons. First, we now know that there are more truth values than we initially thought: Besides *true* and *false*, sentences may be *indeterminate*—that is, neither true nor false. Since the Liar's paradox (*This very sentence is false*) cannot coherently be treated as true, nor as false, it must be indeterminate. But there is a second and deeper problem. Earlier, we could take empirical facts to determine the semantic status of elementary expressions. So, if we wanted to compute the truth value of this statement, *It's raining and it's cold*, we could turn to the external world to give us the truth value of *it's raining* and of *it's cold* (treating these as elementary expressions), and then we could turn to our semantic rule for *and* to compute the truth value of the entire sentence. But when you replace *it's cold* with *this very sentence is true*, this procedure won't do. To know whether the latter clause is true, we must first know the truth value of the entire sentence. But to compute it, we need to first know the truth value of its component parts!

We will now find a way out of this quandary. The solution will be to *construct* the meaning of the word *true* in such a way that it reflects facts about the world and is consistent with the semantic rules we have outlined to evaluate the truth conditions of sentences. We will then turn to a surprising application of this theory of truth: It will yield a possible analysis of one of the most puzzling arguments in philosophy and theology, Anselm's proof of the existence of God (we'll see that it contains a hidden self-reference that might make it indeterminate). But, by the end of the chapter, we will have to remain very modest: despite our best efforts, there will remain paradoxes, called Revenge Liars, which are not easily dealt with by the present approach (or any approach, for that matter).

### 17.2  WHAT IS THE MEANING OF 'TRUE'?

Paradoxes (e.g., *This very sentence is false*) demonstrate that we need more truth values than we thought: not just *true* and *false*, but also *indeterminate*. Truth-tellers (e.g., *This very sentence is true*) show that sometimes the truth value of a sentence is arbitrary and doesn't depend on facts about the world. So we will need to *construct* some aspects of truth. This has nothing to do with the claim, in some circles, that 'truth is a social construct,' or related ideas, which pertain to statements about the world. The problem we are faced with is that some sentences are ungrounded, and their truth value is not determined by facts about the world. But, as was foreshadowed above, this also means that our usual way of handling the meaning of sentences will have to be refined. Take a very simple conjunction like this one:

It's raining and it's cold.

When we know the meaning of *and*, and we know the truth value of the two component parts (*it's raining, it's cold*), it's easy to determine whether the entire sentence is true or not. But now take a self-referential sentence such as the Empirical Truth-teller (ET):

(ET) It is raining and this entire sentence is true.

If it's not raining, you can stop there and determine without further ado that the conjunction is false. That's easy. But if it *is* raining, everything hinges on the second conjunct. Obviously, you can't just look outside to see whether that conjunct is true. The problem is that the truth value of the entire sentence hinges on the second conjunct . . . but the latter makes reference to the truth value of the entire sentence!

Now you might think that we should solve this chicken-and-egg problem by just taking the second conjunct to have a value determined by extrinsic considerations. After all, that's what we do for this other sentence, which is also self-referential:

It is raining and this entire sentence contains 10 words.

Suppose it's raining, so that the value of the entire sentence hinges on the second conjunct. Now count how many words the sentence contains—it's 10, so *voilà*—what the sentence says is true, end of the story.

But things are different with *true*, because it makes reference to the very result of our semantic procedure. So the chicken-and-egg problem is real: to evaluate clauses that contain the word *true*, we need to know which sentences are *true*, which is determined by our evaluation procedure itself.

We must thus find a way to *construct* the meaning of *true*. But this construction should obey some constraints: For the meaning of *true* to be as intended, *true* should hold true of the sentences that are evaluated as true by our semantic rules. In chapter 7, to distinguish words from their denotations, we used boldfacing, thus writing **Nixon** as standing for the person Nixon and **resigned** as standing for the set of people who resigned. The value of **resigned** was determined by facts about the world. In the case of **true**, we want our semantic procedure to be coherent, and thus we want **true** to denote the set of sentences that are in fact evaluated as true by our rules. So we can state the following conditions (how it will be satisfied is the topic of the rest of this chapter):

**true** = the set of true sentences (as evaluated by our semantic rules)

This condition seems obvious enough, but it need not be easy to satisfy. As we saw in chapter 16, when we have just two truth values, the Liar sentence just cannot satisfy the condition: We need a third truth value, which we wrote as #. And we sketched a systematic way of extending to the three-valued case the earlier rules we used when we had just two truth values: We took #, 'neither true nor false,' to mean 'indeterminate'—that is, 'it cannot be determined whether the sentence is true or false.' We extended our earlier rules in a cautious way so that any value *true* or *false* assigned to a sentence never has to be overturned in case we learn that a component that was initially indeterminate turns out to be true or turns out to be false.

But can we be certain that, with three truth values, we can find a coherent interpretation for English? Things are now more complicated than before. *True* will be true of certain sentences (we continue to write this set of things as **true**), false of others (we can write this set of things as **false**), and neither true nor false of still other sentences (those that are neither in **true** nor in **false**).

With this setup, for *true* to have the desired meaning, it should be true of all sentences that are in fact evaluated as true by our semantic rules, and it should be false of all sentences that are evaluated as false by our rules. In other words, when we have three truth values, the following two requirements should be satisfied:

**true** = the set of true sentences
**false** = the set of false sentences

If and when these two requirements are satisfied, we'll know by elimination that the word *true* is neither true nor false (i.e., it is indeterminate) of the sentences that are neither true nor false, which means that we will have found the right meaning for the word *true*. To put it differently, for *true* to have the right meaning, it should be true of all the sentences that are in fact evaluated as true, it should be false of all the sentences that are in fact evaluated as false, and it should be indeterminate of all the others. But the last requirement follows by elimination from the first two, which is why we just have two cases to check.

## 17.3  CONSTRUCTING THE MEANING OF 'TRUE'

So now we know what requirements must be met by the meaning of the word *true*. But can we be sure that such a meaning can be constructed? Given the headaches caused by paradoxes, some caution is called for. Fortunately, a positive answer can be given, as was shown by the philosopher Saul Kripke in 1975.[1]

The main idea is this: We will initially take all clauses that contain the word *true* to be potentially ungrounded and thus 'risky,' as they might not be based on facts about the world (for instance, in case they talk about their own truth). We will thus treat them as being indeterminate, with the value #. All other sentences that don't contain the word *true* just talk about the world and are thus safe (either definitely true or definitely false, as in the procedure described in chapter 7 and chapter 9). But we will devise a procedure to gradually mark as 'safe' many of the clauses that contain the word *true*. First, we mark as 'safe' (definitely true or definitely false) those sentences that talk about sentences about the world (since these are safe, by definition). Then we'll mark as 'safe' sentences that talk about sentences that were marked as safe in the previous step. And we'll iterate the procedure until we know we've marked as 'safe' everything that could be.

An analogy might help. Suppose there has been a big earthquake and the Eiffel Tower has been affected. Any part of the structure (which is made of iron pieces) could be loose—except those that directly rest on the ground. If I need to climb on the tower, it would be prudent to initially take all pieces except those that are on the ground to be potentially unstable. But then I can mark some pieces as 'safe' using the following method: First, pieces that are on the ground are safe. Second, pieces that firmly rest on pieces that were marked as 'safe' in the first step are themselves safe. Third, pieces that rest on pieces that were marked as 'safe' in the second step are themselves safe. And so on and so forth, until no new pieces are marked as safe by the procedure. Chances are that not all parts of the tower will be marked as safe—there has been an earthquake, after all. But those pieces that are marked as safe won't run the risk of being loose.

Kripke's procedure works in a similar way, taking a clause to be safe if its truth value firmly rests on facts about the world, while it is risky if it could generate a paradox. At stage 0, our starting point, only clauses that just talk about the world rather than about other sentences have a normal value—they correspond to the pieces of the Eiffel Tower that are directly on the ground. All clauses that talk about the truth of other sentences are initially deemed risky and get the value #. But then we mark some of them as safe by stages: At stage 1, we mark as safe those clauses that talk about sentences deemed safe at stage 0; at stage 2, we do the same for clauses that talk about sentences that were marked as safe at stage 1, and we continue until the procedure doesn't change the status of any new sentence.

Let me illustrate with a couple of examples. At stage 0, the sentence $N_0$ that claims that *NYC is in the United States* gets the value *true*, while the sentence $P_0$ that claims that *Paris is in Germany* gets the value *false*. At this point, we take each sentence containing the words *true* or *false* to have the third truth value # and thus to be indeterminate. So at stage 0, the sentence $N_1$ which says that $N_0$ *is true* is deemed indeterminate, as is the sentence $P_1$ which says that $P_0$ *is true*. Likewise, the sentence $N_2$ which says that $N_1$ *is true* is indeterminate, since it too contains the word *true*, and the same applies to the sentence $P_2$ claiming that $P_1$ *is true*. The same treatment applies to the Liar L and to the Truth-teller T.

The analogy with the Eiffel Tower will be clearer if we arrange the sentences graphically so that those that are grounded in the world appear toward the bottom: They are the stable parts of the construction (as they rest on facts about the world), and we will gradually deem as stable those that rest on them. The Liar L and the Truth-teller T don't rest on anything firm, so they will remain forever indeterminate.

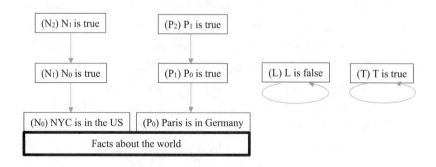

Kripke's trick is to suggest that we revise our cautious assignment of values to clauses containing *true* in the same way as we did for the potentially loose parts of the Eiffel Tower. How so? We start flipping # to *true* when this is warranted by the results of the previous step (= stage 0). The sentence $N_0$ that claims that *NYC is in the United States* got the value *true*, so now $N_1$, which claims that $N_0$ *is true*, is indirectly grounded on a fact about the world. Thus, at stage 1, it can be marked as safe: Its value can be flipped from # to true. Similarly, since $P_0$ ('Paris is in Germany') is false, $P_1$, which claims that $P_0$ *is true*, can also be marked as safe at stage 1, this time by flipping its value from # to false. Since at the previous step $N_1$ and $P_1$ had the value #, the sentences $N_2$ and $P_2$ that talk about them remain indeterminate. And since the Liar L and the Truth-teller T only talk about themselves, their truth values don't get affected and remain indeterminate.

Just as we did with the Eiffel Tower, we then repeat the procedure, now at stage 2. Importantly, our cautious semantic rules ensure that when we flip some values from # to true or false, we never have to revise the standard values we had assigned: All that can happen is that some sentences that were indeterminate become true or false. This is what now happens to $N_2$, which says that $N_1$ *is true*. At the previous step $N_1$ was evaluated as true, so now $N_2$ can be deemed true. Similarly, at the previous step $P_1$ was evaluated as false, so now $P_2$ can be deemed false. And as before, the Liar L and the Truth-teller T remain unaffected.

We can summarize these three steps with a diagram, still preserving the Eiffel Tower metaphor on which the sentences that rest on empirical facts are lower down. At stage 0, only $N_0$ and $P_0$ had a normal value, while all other clauses were indeterminate because they contained the word *true*. But $N_1$ and $P_1$ talk about the truth of $N_0$ and $P_0$ (I've represented this with an arrow in the next figure), so at stage 1 they received a normal value (underlined). And since $N_2$ and $P_2$ talk about the truth of $N_1$ and $P_1$, at the next stage, it is their turn to receive a normal value. On the other hand, since L and T are ungrounded and talk only about themselves, they remain indeterminate throughout.

Stage 0

| $N_2$ | $P_2$ | | |
|---|---|---|---|
| # | # | | |
| ↓ | ↓ | | |
| $N_1$ | $P_1$ | | |
| # | # | | |
| ↓ | ↓ | | |
| $N_0$ | $P_0$ | L | T |
| true | false | # | # |

Stage 1

| $N_2$ | $P_2$ | | |
|---|---|---|---|
| # | # | | |
| ↓ | ↓ | | |
| $N_1$ | $P_1$ | | |
| true | false | | |
| ↓ | ↓ | | |
| $N_0$ | $P_0$ | L | T |
| true | false | # | # |

Stage 2

| $N_2$ | $P_2$ | | |
|---|---|---|---|
| true | false | | |
| ↓ | ↓ | | |
| $N_1$ | $P_1$ | | |
| true | false | | |
| ↓ | ↓ | | |
| $N_0$ | $P_0$ | L | T |
| true | false | # | # |

Just considering these sentences, if we revised truth values a third time, nothing would change: The values *true* and *false* are never revised (because our procedure was designed to be maximally cautious), and since the Liar L and the Truth-teller T don't talk about other sentences, their value remains indeterminate. This is a momentous result: While after stages 0 and 1 the meaning of *true* needed to be corrected, this is not the case anymore after stage 2. Taking **true** to include the sentences $N_0$, $N_1$, $N_2$, and **false** to include the sentences $P_0$, $P_1$, $P_2$, our semantic rules derive exactly the result that $N_0$, $N_1$, and $N_2$ are true, while $P_0$, $P_1$, and $P_2$ are false, and the rest (namely, L and T) are indeterminate. Since no corrections are needed, the challenge has been met: By way of successive corrections, we have constructed an appropriate meaning for *true*. In the end, then, *true* as constructed is true of precisely the true sentences, false of precisely the false sentences, and neither true nor false of all other sentences—precisely the requirements we defined in section 17.2.

As Kripke proved, this is a very general fact: Through successive corrections of this type, we can be assured that we will always be able to find an appropriate meaning for *true*. Furthermore, this doesn't just hold for the simple sentences we considered in this example, but also for empirical Liars and Empirical Truth-tellers. The proof contains more details than you might care to see, but a more articulated example can be found in appendix I.

## 17.4  UNGROUNDED STATEMENTS: LIARS VERSUS TRUTH-TELLERS

The outcome of the procedure I just outlined is that the Liar L and the Truth-teller T both end up with the value #. That's not a bad thing, since both are logically odd, in a way. Still, there is a difference between them: The Liar can *only* have the third value #, whereas the Truth-teller could have any value whatsoever (remember that its value can be set in an arbitrary fashion). Is there a way to capture this distinction?

Yes. We can get an equally coherent interpretation if we add the Truth-teller T to **true**, which gives this result:

**true** = the sentences $N_0$, $N_1$, $N_2$, T
**false** = the sentences $P_0$, $P_1$, $P_2$

Nothing changes, except that T, which asserts its own truth, gets the value *true* (underlined in the graphic); this is alternative A to stage 2.

|  | Alternative A |  |  |
|---|---|---|---|
| $N_2$ | $P_2$ |  |  |
| true | false |  |  |
| ↓ | ↓ |  |  |
| $N_1$ | $P_1$ |  |  |
| true | false |  |  |
| ↓ | ↓ |  |  |
| $N_0$ | $P_0$ | L | T |
| true | false | # | <u>true</u> |

An equally coherent interpretation would be obtained if we decided instead that the Truth-teller T belongs in **false**:

**true** = the sentences $N_0$, $N_1$, $N_2$
**false** = the sentences $P_0$, $P_1$, $P_2$, T

As before, the Truth-teller asserts its own truth, but since we've just decided that T is in **false**, this assertion is false, and we get a second alternative to stage 2, now with T evaluated as false (underlined again).

|  | Alternative B |  |  |
|---|---|---|---|
| $N_2$ | $P_2$ |  |  |
| true | false |  |  |
| ↓ | ↓ |  |  |
| $N_1$ | $P_1$ |  |  |
| true | false |  |  |
| ↓ | ↓ |  |  |
| $N_0$ | $P_0$ | L | T |
| true | false | # | <u>false</u> |

So this is the difference between Liars and Truth-tellers: In every conceivable interpretation in which *true* has the intended meaning, Liars have the third truth value #, whereas for Truth-tellers, things are more flexible. In some coherent interpretations, they have the value #; in others, they have the value *true*; and in still others, they have the value *false*.

One remarkable consequence is that even when we know everything there is to know about the world, we have not yet determined the truth value of all the sentences of English. Some—namely, the Truth-tellers—remain indeterminate, and we need to make an arbitrary decision about their value: true, false, or #. You might think that this only applies to one sentence type, but that's not so: Just like there are empirical Liars, there are Empirical Truth-tellers (as we saw in chapter 16 with the sentence *It's raining and this very sentence is true*), and so there are lots of sentences whose truth value has to be determined in an arbitrary fashion.

Stepping back, our original goal has been met, at least in a simplified case: We have constructed by stages an interpretation for *true* that is adequate—true of the true sentence, false of the false sentences, and neither true nor false of the sentences that are indeterminate. And in the process, we have gained a precise understanding of the difference between Liars and Truth-tellers.

## 17.5 DOES THE THIRD TRUTH VALUE REALLY MATTER?

With all the efforts we just invested, you might wonder whether we really need to worry about paradoxes. Not *really*, and contemporary semantics has happily left them to philosophical logicians, with little damage done in the process (other than missing out on the beauty of ungrounded sentences, be they Liars or Truth-tellers). Still, there are cases in which we might be seriously led astray if we forget about the existence of the third truth value.

A case in point is a purported proof of the existence of Santa Claus (I do realize that only the very youngest readers might fully appreciate its significance). Let's call this sentence SCP (for the Santa Claus proof):

(SCP) Either this entire sentence is false, or Santa Claus exists.

If SCP is true, then the first disjunct is false (since it wrongly claims that SCP is false), so for the sentence as a whole to be true, the second disjunct must be true—*voilà*, Santa Claus exists. Alright, but what if SCP is false? Well, that couldn't be, because that would make the first disjunct of SCP true, and as a result SCP would be true, not false. Conclusion: SCP can only be true. This implies that the first disjunct is false, and therefore that the second disjunct is true: Santa Clause must exist! But wait—while it's nice to 'prove' that Santa Claus exists, you can replace *Santa Claus exists* with any proposition you wish, such as *God exists*, or *2 + 2 = 5*, or anything really. Something has gone wrong.

The source of the error is that we reasoned as if there are only two truth values, but we now know that there are three. And here the third value really helps: On the assumption that Santa Claus doesn't exist, we can without incoherence treat the sentence as being indeterminate. Since the second disjunct is false, everything hinges on the first: SCP is true just in case its first disjunct is true (i.e., just in case SCP itself is false), and so SCP ends up being a variant of the Liar, and it too should be assigned the indeterminate value #.[2]

While only the youngest readers might be interested in a proof of Santa Claus's existence, different cases are occasionally of interest to more mature audiences. One of nerdiest pickup lines ever goes like this (the original is racier):

> If I ask you on a date, will you give me the same answer as the answer to this question?

(We'll assume that the addressee, who is probably intended to be logician-friendly, can only answer with 'yes' or 'no.')

The addressee who answers *yes* is thereby committed to a further *yes* should the speaker then ask: 'Will you go on a date with me?' But the addressee who answers *no* is in an equally precarious situation because if the speaker asks, 'Will you go on a date with me?', the second answer must be different from the first one, so it has to be a *yes* again! How did we get ourselves in this quagmire?

The logical trick is somewhat different from that involved in the proof of Santa Claus's existence, but here too the mistake is to reason as if there were just two truth values rather than three. Things will get a bit clearer if we take it as given that the next question is indeed about the date (that's a fair simplification because there's little doubt about the speaker's intentions). So now the addressee is asked to answer the following two questions:

> If I ask you on a date, will your answer be the same as your answer to the present question?
> Will you go on a date with me?

Since we know that the next question is indeed about the date, there's no need for the *if* qualification, so we can simplify this further to the following pair of questions:

> Will your answer to the next question be the same as your answer to this question?
> Will you go on a date with me?

To simplify things even further, we can restate the question *Will you go on a date with me?* as a demand to assign a truth value to the proposition: *You will go on a date with me.* (Think of the question as *You will go on a date with me—true or false?*) When we transform the first question in a similar way, the speaker in effect asks the addressee to assign values to the propositions (1) and (2) below:

> (1) (2) has the same truth value as (1).
> (2) You will go on a date with me.

Now the unfortunate addressee is caught in a predicament. If (1) is true, then (2) must have the same value as (1), so it must be true as well—and the addressee must grant the date. But if (1) is false, (2) shouldn't have the same value as (1), so (2) must be true—and there's no way to avoid the date either. (Alright, you might just as well replace *Will you go on a date with me?* with *Does Santa Claus exist?* This would yield a rather different 'proof' that Santa Claus exists. But you won't find the Santa Claus version on social media, just the racier version of what I cited.)

The reasoning is, of course, spurious. But what is the source of the error? We have again reasoned as if sentences could only be true or false. Here, the third value saves (from an unwanted date) because when (1) is indeterminate, no inference can be drawn about (2), and no contradiction arises either: whatever the actual value (true or false) of (2), if (1) is indeterminate, it is indeed indeterminate whether it has the same value as (1). Problem solved.

To the layperson, there is a more direct way of remaining noncommittal: Just answer 'maybe' to the first question, and you can answer *yes* or *no* with equal ease when the actual invitation comes. But this more expeditious solution doesn't come with the important lesson we learned in our more pedestrian way. Even in sentences that are not directly paradoxical, forgetting about the existence of the third truth value can lead to reasoning errors, such as the 'proof' that a false sentence is true.

## 17.6 HIDDEN SELF-REFERENCE: BERRY'S PARADOX

Sometimes one encounters ungrounded sentences without realizing it, and they too may lead us astray. By forgetting that they may be *indeterminate* besides *true* and *false*, we can be led to incorrect conclusions.

To convince you of this fact, I'll discuss a particularly devious case of self-reference. It starts from an unexceptionable observation: With sentences of at most 280 characters (the length of a tweet), you can produce unambiguous descriptions of only a finite number of things (I'll assume for simplicity that the characters are letters and spaces, not digits). The reason is that there are just 26 letters in English, so although you can form many sentences with sequences of 280 letters, there is only a finite number of them. As you'll soon see, the details don't matter much. You may, for instance, include or exclude spaces, digits, and punctuation marks in the count, and this won't affect the reasoning, nor does the fact that there is a *very* large number of possible tweets.

Since there are only finitely many things you can describe with a sequence of at most 280 letters, there are only finitely many integers you can describe in words in this way. So one of them is the largest. If we were restricted to sequences of at most three letters, we could define *one*, *two*, *six*, and *ten* (three characters each) but not *nine* or *eleven* (four and six characters, respectively). Other integers have longer names, so the largest integer that can be defined with at most three characters is *ten*. The largest integer that can be defined with 280 characters rather than three will of course be far, far larger, but there will still be such a thing as *the largest integer that can be described in at most two hundred eighty characters.*

But here something odd happens: What about the description *the integer that follows the largest integer that can be described in at most two hundred eighty characters?* If you replace *at most two hundred eighty characters* with *at most three characters*, the description singles out *eleven* (since *ten* is the largest integer that can be defined with at most three characters, the integer that follows it is *eleven*). Similarly, there should be an integer denoted by the description: *the integer that follows the largest integer that can be described in at most two hundred eighty characters.* Of course, this integer shouldn't be describable in at most two hundred eighty characters. But here comes the problem: I've just done so, because the italicized description itself contains fewer than 280 characters (it's about 100, so it would fit comfortably in a tweet, for instance). And now we just don't know what to do.

It turns out that there is a hidden self-reference in this reasoning: The expression *the greatest integer that can be described in at most two hundred eighty characters* makes reference to many descriptions, including itself. Of course, this case of self-reference is far harder to spot than in our earlier example, such as the Liar and the Truth-teller, which involved explicit names of individual sentences. The issue is more subtle here: Through the expression 'described,' the italicized expression 'talks about' multiple descriptions of integers, and among all these descriptions is the italicized expression itself.

Pretty devious—and the reasoning gives rise to a genuine paradox. It is called 'Berry's paradox,' and it was discussed in the early twentieth century by the British philosopher and logician Bertrand Russell, who attributed it to an Oxford librarian by the name of Berry. The conclusion is that there is one component of the reasoning that's indeterminate—neither true nor false. The details might be more than what you bargained for when you bought this book, and they are sketched out in appendix II. To tell you the gist of it, the idea is that Berry's paradox can be expressed by the following reasoning, and that step B is indeterminate because it involves a subtle case of self-reference.

A. Only a finite number of things can be described in at most two hundred eighty characters.

B. So there is something that is *the greatest integer describable in at most two hundred eighty characters*.

C. But then I can also describe *the integer that follows the greatest integer describable in at most two hundred eighty characters*.

D. And I have just done so in fewer than 280 characters!

The basic idea is that the italicized description in B makes reference to all sorts of descriptions of integers (in order to assess what is the greatest integer appropriately describable). But among all these descriptions is the italicized expression itself, hence an instance of (devious!) self-reference.

## 17.7 ANSELM'S ARGUMENT

In the case of Berry's paradox, you have every reason to conclude that paradoxes can be hard to spot and are really confusing, but that otherwise they are of little general interest. However, here is an argument that's considerably more momentous but arguably involves some hidden self-reference as well. It purports to prove from first principles the existence of God. It is a beautiful piece of reasoning, which has left many enthralled and many more unconvinced.

Anselm of Canterbury was an Italian monk and the archbishop of Canterbury from 1093 to 1109. He was understandably interested in proving that God exists, and invented the following ingenious argument. It goes like this: I have the concept of *the greatest thing I can imagine* (call this thing *God*). Of course, having the concept of something doesn't mean that this thing exists. I can easily imagine a unicorn, but unicorns don't exist. However, there is something special about the concept of *the greatest thing I can imagine*: If this thing didn't exist, I could imagine something even greater—namely, that thing *with existence added*. But then *the greatest thing I can imagine* wouldn't be the greatest thing I can imagine (since by adding existence to it I can imagine something greater). This is a contradiction, which shows that our assumption (*if this thing didn't exist*) is false. In other words, the greatest thing I can imagine (also known as God) exists.

Here it's really hard to suggest that the reasoning doesn't matter. For some people, this might be the most important argument they'll ever come across! And on initial inspection, it has nothing whatsoever to do with the Liar or the Truth-teller. But on closer inspection, it can be brought closer to Berry's paradox, especially if you state it like this:

A. There is only a finite number of things I can describe in my imagination.

B. So there is something that is *the greatest thing I can describe in my imagination*.

> Now, to obtain a contradiction, suppose that this thing doesn't exist.

C. Then I can imagine something greater—namely, *the greatest thing I can describe in my imagination with existence*.

D. And I have just described it, so we have a contradiction.

> This shows that the greatest thing I can imagine does exist (since we have obtained a contradiction from the assumption that *this thing doesn't exist*).

As it turns out, on one interpretation at least,[3] this reasoning is incorrect for the very reason that blocked the contradiction in Berry's paradox. (I write 'on one interpretation' because there have been centuries of discussion of Anselm's argument and multiple reconstructions of it; the one I am discussing is interesting in the present context, but it doesn't purport to be the final word on Anselm's argument.[4]) The key is that in step B, the italicized expression *the greatest thing I can describe in my imagination* makes reference to all sorts of descriptions of things (in order to assess what is the greatest appropriately describable). But here, too, among all these descriptions is the italicized description itself. This is the same kind of subtle self-reference involved in Berry's paradox, and in this case too this step ends up being neither true nor false but rather indeterminate (further details are sketched out in appendix II).

If this reconstruction of the argument is right (a highly controversial point!), Anselm made a mistake, but an extraordinarily subtle one: He reasoned as if language (in his case, Latin rather than English) contained just two truth values, whereas we now know that it contains three. What he understandably failed to imagine, in other words, was that a crucial step of his argument could turn out to be indeterminate because of a subtle form of self-reference. This is the same kind of mistake we originally made in our purported 'proof' of the existence of Santa Claus, except that in the case of Anselm's argument, the self-reference is *far* harder to spot. In the end, then, theologians might have to be semanticists (whether semanticists have something momentous to contribute to theology remains to be seen).

## 17.8 THE LIAR'S REVENGE

The construction I sketched in section 17.3 was intended to avoid further headaches with paradoxes. In Kripke's version, it guaranteed that we can find an interpretation for the word 'true' that is as intended, and hence true of the sentences that are in fact evaluated as true by our semantic rules, and false of those that are in fact evaluated as false (and neither true nor false of those that are indeterminate). But this isn't quite the end of our troubles: There are so-called revenge paradoxes that arise in English—paradoxes that we cannot handle in our analysis, and which suggest that it isn't entirely correct.

The simplest example can be stated as follows:

(RL) This sentence is something other than true.

RL, the Revenge Liar (also called the Strengthened Liar), differs from the standard Liar in an inconspicuous way: Instead of saying of itself that it is false, it says of itself that it is something other than true. This subtle difference really matters. According to the treatment we have developed so far, it makes much sense to treat the claim that *sentence S is false* as being indeterminate in case S is indeterminate. The reason is that 'indeterminate' really means 'possibly true and possibly false.' If S is indeterminate, the claim that *S is false* is itself indeterminate (true if S is false, false if S is true). But with the Revenge Liar, things are different because the following reasoning applies:

If RL is true, the claim it makes (namely, that it's something other than true) is false, so RL should be false;

if RL is false, the claim it makes is true, so RL should be true;

**and if RL is indeterminate, it is something other than true, so the claim it makes is true, and thus RL should once again be true.**

The key is the third line (boldfaced). Because of how RL is stated, when it has the third truth value #, the claim it makes ('I am something other than true!') should be true, not indeterminate. As a result, now we cannot assign *any* value to this sentence: our theory is stumped.

Our original analysis was designed to avoid such cases, and it was intended to ensure that whenever we learn that an indeterminate sentence in fact has a standard value (true or false), we might have to revise indeterminate values we assigned but never standard ones, because these were assigned in a maximally cautious fashion. Alas, the expression *is something other than true* makes it impossible to stick to this policy. Take a sentence S, which is initially indeterminate. We can say truly about it that *S is something other than true* (since if S is indeterminate, it is in fact something other than true). But now suppose that S turns out to be true (which is a possibility since it is initially indeterminate). In that case, the sentence *S is something other than true* becomes false. So it just isn't the case any longer that standard truth values (*true* and *false*) don't have to be revised once they have been assigned.[5]

Now you might be tempted to think that what the Revenge Liar shows is that we need more than three truth values, and indeed this solution has been tried. So you could think that RL really means something like:

This sentence is something other than true *among the values true, false, #.*

And we could get out of our predicament by assigning to RL a fourth value, call it $\#^2$ (with the superscript $^2$ to distinguish $\#^2$ from our first indeterminate truth value #). But then nothing will prevent you from defining a Super Revenge Liar (SRL), stated as:

(SRL) This sentence is something other than true *among the values true, false, #, and $\#^2$.*

It is clear that you'll have to continue ad infinitum, positing a new truth value each time. This might be cause for wonder or horror, depending on whether you like or hate the proliferation of truth values. But in any event, at the end of the long day (or sleepless night), you will still have the ability to state a Super Duper Revenge Liar (SDRL), one that talks about *all* the truth values there are:

(SDRL) This sentence is something other than true *among all the values there are.*

If SDRL is true, what it says is false, so it should be false. But if it has any value whatsoever other than true, what it says is true, so it ought to be true. There is just no way to assign a value to *that* sentence.

We might have reached one of the current limits of semantic knowledge. While there are many theories of Revenge Liars, none is entirely satisfactory. But we might also have reached the limits of the standard methodology of semantics (which might explain why linguists are not too keen on discussing such problems). Throughout this book, we took for granted some relatively clear intuitions about the truth conditions of various sentences, but when it comes to paradoxes, particularly in complicated cases, these intuitions become rather shaky. Our primary 'data' might really be a mix of naive and theory-laden intuitions, and our beliefs about how many truth values there 'ought' to be might play a role in what we take the data to be.

There might be a silver lining, however. Just as there is a Strengthened Liar (the Revenge Liar), there is a strengthened 'proof' of the existence of Santa Claus, which goes like this:

Either this entire sentence is something other than true, or Santa Claus exists.

The entire sentence couldn't be false, for if so, its first disjunct would be true, making the entire sentence true as well. But, by the same reasoning, the entire sentence couldn't have an indeterminate truth value, for if so, it would be 'something other than true,' making the first disjunct and hence the entire sentence true again. The only possibility is thus that the entire sentence is true; and since this makes the first disjunct false, the second disjunct must be true: Santa Claus exists.

Of course, this might be . . . too good to be true (you can replace *Santa Claus* with *2 + 2 = 5* and you'll get an equally valid, or rather invalid, reasoning).

## 17.9 CONCLUSION

*To know the meaning of a sentence is to know under what conditions it is true.* This has been the motto of contemporary semantics, and of this book.

Paradoxes raise a huge challenge for it, since they are sentences that cannot coherently be assigned the value *true* or the value *false*. But semantics has an elegant way of meeting the challenge: Posit that there are three truth values, not two. On this view, paradoxes have the third truth value, #, and in simple cases no incoherence arises. The Liar is indeterminate, and it claims of itself that it is not true. On the assumption that the negation of an indeterminate statement is itself indeterminate, we can assign the Liar the value # without risk of incoherence. The Truth-teller can be assigned the same value, again without risk of incoherence. But there is nonetheless an important difference between the Truth-teller and the Liar: unlike the Liar, the Truth-teller could just as well be assigned the value *true* or the value *false*.

Since the word 'true' (unlike the words 'long' or 'resigned') talks about the very properties that our semantic rules define, the meaning of 'true' must satisfy a nontrivial condition: It should be true of the sentences that are in fact evaluated as true by our semantic rules. With just two truth values, this condition cannot be satisfied, as the Liar's paradox demonstrates. But Kripke's procedure shows that we can construct a meaning for 'true' that's appropriate when there are three truth values. It's not the only possible meaning, however: The fact that Truth-tellers can be assigned arbitrary values also shows that there are some arbitrary choices to be made in the construction. Nonetheless, the riddle of paradoxes can be solved in a semantics with three truth values.

Still, this success is not complete, as the Liar eventually comes back with revenge: *This sentence is something other than true* can't be coherently assigned the values *true* or *false*, just like the standard Liar. But in addition, it can't be assigned the value #, because if so, what it asserts would be true. While multiple solutions have been proposed, none is entirely satisfactory: the Liar will continue to haunt semantics.

## APPENDIX I: ILLUSTRATING KRIPKE'S CONSTRUCTION

As promised in the text, I'll now illustrate in greater detail Kripke's construction. To keep things simple, we'll take all the normal predicates (i.e., those verbs or adjectives that are different from the word *true*) to behave as before. *Short* is true of some things and false of all other things (you may think that there are unclear cases in which one doesn't know whether someone does or doesn't count as 'short,' and that is indeed something that semanticists worry about, but we'll disregard this fact here—with paradoxes to deal with, we already have a full plate). By contrast, *true* may be true of certain things (for instance, *2 + 2 = 4*), false of others (for instance, *2 + 2 = 5*), and neither true nor false of still others, such as the Liar sentence (and here too, we disregard the status of things that are not sentences and couldn't have a truth value to begin with). To simplify matters, we evaluate all sentences relative to a certain world so that each sentence can be given a truth value (e.g., *Robin is short* will be true).

We'll start by taking **true** (i.e., the sentences that the word *true* is true of) and **false** (i.e., the sentences that *true* is false of) to be empty, which means that every clause that contains the word *true* (for instance, $S_1$ *is true*) will start out as having the indeterminate value # (neither true nor false). In this way, we'll start maximally cautiously, which is a reasonable attitude since paradoxes are neither true nor false. But we'll revise the procedure in stages, and with enough patience, we'll come to a correct interpretation.

So, let us suppose that **Robin** (the denotation of the word *Robin*) is in **short**, the set of short entities. The sentence (S1) below will of course be evaluated as true, since our semantic rules ask us to check whether **Robin** is in **short**, and this is indeed the case.

(S1) Robin is short.     true

But what about the other sentences below? Each of them starts out with the value #, because at this stage **true** and **false** are both empty: we are being extremely cautious by treating every elementary clause that includes the word *true* as being indeterminate.

(S2) S1 is true.          #
(S3) S2 is not true.      #
(S4) S4 is not true.      #
(S5) S5 is true.          #

There is one final case to discuss: In S6 below, the first conjunct is true and the second has the value # (since it contains *true*, and all clauses of the form *x is true* are initially treated as indeterminate).

(S6) Robin is short and S6 is not true.      #

Remember that # means 'indeterminate' (we just can't tell whether the sentence is true or false), and because the first conjunct of S6 is true, everything hinges on the second. Since it contains the word *true*, the second conjunct is indeterminate, and this infects the entire conjunction. (If Robin were tall, not short, the first conjunct would be false and we wouldn't need to worry about the second, as a conjunction is false as soon as one of its conjuncts is: in that case, S6 would be false rather than indeterminate.)

At the next stage, we correct our overly cautious initial choices for **true** and **false** (both empty!) by adding to **true** the sentences that were evaluated as true at the previous step, and by adding to **false** the sentences that were evaluated as false at the previous step. Since we proceeded very cautiously, sentences we put in **true** or **false** are certain to remain there forever, and hence the only potential corrections are of two sorts: A sentence that was previously treated as indeterminate (neither in **true** nor in **false**) turns out to be true, so we need to add it to **true**, or it turns out to be false, and we need to add it to **false**. If none of these two cases arise, there are no errors to correct and we have reached our goal!

S1 got evaluated as true in the first step, so we add it to **true**, while no sentence is added to **false**. So now we reevaluate all sentences with this new value:

**true** = the sentence S1
**false** = empty

The sentence S1 doesn't need to be reevaluated because it doesn't contain the word *true*. The value of the sentence $S_2$ needs to be revised, however:

since our new meaning for *true* guarantees that S1 is in **true**, the sentence *S1 is true* (i.e., S2 itself) is now evaluated as true. The other sentences don't change values because they don't talk about S1. So, after this initial revision, we get the following result, with the change underlined:

| | |
|---|---|
| (S1) Robin is short. | true |
| (S2) S1 is true. | <u>true</u> |
| (S3) S2 is not true. | # |
| (S4) S4 is not true. | # |
| (S5) S5 is true. | # |
| (S6) Robin is not short and S6 is not true. | # |

That's not quite the end of the process, because this new distribution of values means we must now add S2 to **true**:

**true** = the sentences S1, S2
**false** = empty

Since we are very patient, we again evaluate all our sentences. No need to worry about S1, which doesn't contain the word *true*. No need to worry about S2 either, because once a sentence is in **true** it remains there forever (remember that our semantic rules were designed cautiously in order to enforce precisely this result). But we need to revise S3, which talks about S2. Given our new value for **true**, S3 should be evaluated as false, as it is the negation of *S2 is true*, which is evaluated as true. The other sentences don't mention S2, so nothing changes for them; they keep the value they had at the previous stage (the change of value for S3 is underlined).

| | |
|---|---|
| (S1) Robin is short. | true |
| (S2) S1 is true. | true |
| (S3) S2 is not true. | <u>false</u> |
| (S4) S4 is not true. | # |
| (S5) S5 is true. | # |
| (S6) Robin is not short and S6 is not true. | # |

Being really *very* patient, we evaluate once again our sentences with the corrected values below.

**true** = the sentences S1, S2
**false** = the sentence S3

We already know that changes to the evaluation of sentences could only arise if we found out that a sentence with the initial value # was now true, or false. But this doesn't happen because the only candidates are S4, S5, and S6, and they only talk about themselves, not about S1, S2, or S3. So this can count as our final try. With respect to the sentences we have considered, there is nothing more to correct, because **true** is the set of true sentences and **false** is the set of false sentences, which is exactly the condition that must be satisfied for the word *true* to have the intended meaning. We are done, at least with respect to these sentences.

But can we be sure that when a full language is considered (rather than just six sample sentences), the same result will be obtained? Yes, and the reason is this: At any step in the procedure, one of two things happens: (i) some sentences change their value from # to a standard value (true or false) and keep it forever, or (ii) nothing changes. There are no further possibilities because we only put in the set **true** sentences that we knew were certain to be true and in the set **false** sentences that were certain to be false. So the only possible revision is that some sentences flip from # to *true* or from # to *false*. If nothing changes—case (ii)—**true** is already the set of true sentences and **false** is already the set of false sentences, so we have the result we wanted. If there is a change—case (i)—at least one sentence moves from the 'neither true nor false' basket to one of the other two baskets and stays there forever. How many times can this change happen? At most as many times as there are sentences in the language, since for some change to happen, at least one sentence must move to the **true** or **false** basket (and stay there forever). So, with enough patience, we can be certain that our procedure will come to an end and that we will find an appropriate interpretation for *true*.

You may rightfully object that English (or for that matter Predicate Logic) has infinitely many sentences (for instance, for any English sentence *S*, you can obtain a longer one by saying *It's raining and S*; we considered many more interesting cases in chapter 8). How can we apply a procedure more than an infinite number of times? Here mathematics comes to the rescue: One of the discoveries of the nineteenth century (by the mathematician Georg Cantor) was that there are different sizes of infinity; in particular, there is such a thing as applying a procedure more times than there are sentences in English. This is the sense in which the procedure we outlined requires *a lot* of patience, but from God's perspective, so to speak, or at least from that of a logician, this can be done.

### APPENDIX II: BERRY'S PARADOX AND ANSELM'S ARGUMENT

Let me now provide further details about the relation between Berry's paradox and Anselm's argument. To reiterate, Berry's paradox can be stated in four steps:

A.  There is only a finite number of things that can be described in at most two hundred eighty characters.
B.  So there is something which is *the greatest integer describable in at most two hundred eighty characters.*
C.  But then I can also describe *the integer that follows the greatest integer describable in at most two hundred eighty characters.*
D.  . . . and I have just done so in fewer than 280 characters!

Once we have experience with paradoxes, we know that expressions that directly or indirectly refer to themselves may not just yield truth and falsity but also indeterminacy (i.e., they may yield the value #). The description *greatest integer describable in at most two hundred eighty characters* makes reference to all sorts of descriptions, including that very description itself, so it might well be indeterminate of some objects. And, in fact, B cannot be true (or else we get the contradiction in D), and it also cannot be false, for if so, there would be infinitely many integers describable in at most 280 characters, which cannot be. So B must be indeterminate, and once this is seen, this will block the rest of the reasoning.

If we didn't know that there are infinitely many integers, step C might fail. In fact, the reasoning above could be interpreted (wrongly!) to prove that there is such a thing as *the greatest integer.* The argument would go like this: Suppose (with the goal of obtaining a contradiction) that every integer is followed by a greater one. Then the reasoning in steps A to D would go through. It leads to a contradiction, so the assumption that every integer is followed by a greater one is wrong: There is a greatest integer. This conclusion is rubbish, of course. The problem with the argument is not the assumption that every integer is followed by a larger one (clearly true!); rather, the problem is that the argument involves a subtle kind of paradoxical self-reference, which makes step B indeterminate (neither true nor false). This blocks the rest of the reasoning, and our initial hypothesis (every integer is followed by a greater one) isn't refuted in the end.

One way to look at Anselm's argument is that it makes the same kind of mistake. (This is only one interpretation among many; as I mentioned in the text, there have been countless studies of this extraordinary argument, and I make no claim that this interpretation is the 'right' one, although I think it makes an interesting point.) Instead of talking about integers, the reasoning talks about things I can describe in my imagination. To highlight the similarity, we'll need to fill in some blanks. Anselm assumes that if something I can imagine (say, a unicorn) doesn't exist, I can imagine something greater (namely, that unicorn with existence). Of course, if the unicorn exists, then the unicorn with existence shouldn't count as greater. But if the unicorn doesn't exist, I have one concept of a unicorn and another concept of a unicorn with existence, which counts as greater . . . but why stop here? The concept of a unicorn with existence could itself be endowed with existence, in which case it should count as greater, and so on ad infinitum:

$$🦄 < (🦄 + \text{existence}) < ((🦄 + \text{existence}) + \text{existence}) < \ldots$$

The details don't matter much as long as we can guarantee that when the greatest thing I can imagine doesn't exist, there is an infinite series of greater things. In effect, Anselm's argument purports to show that there is a maximum in a certain series of concepts (of things I can imagine), and this maximum will have to come with the property of existence, otherwise one could always go higher in the series.

With this in mind, we can reproduce the four steps we defined in our flawed proof that there are only finitely many integers. The connection will be easier to see if you keep in mind that we are replacing *the greatest integer describable in at most two hundred eighty characters* with *the greatest thing I can describe in my imagination.*

Suppose that the greatest thing I can imagine doesn't exist (and thus that there is an infinite series of concepts as above, with the unicorn replaced with the greatest thing I can imagine).

A. There is only a finite number of things I can describe in my imagination.

B. So there is something which is *the greatest thing I can describe in my imagination.*

C. But then I can imagine something greater, namely *the greatest thing I can describe in my imagination with existence.*

D. . . . and I have just described it, so we have a contradiction.

This shows that the greatest thing I can imagine exists: God exists!

The reasoning is just as mistaken as the one that led to the incorrect conclusion that there is a finite number of integers. And the error lies again in step B, which is in fact indeterminate (as was the case with step B in Berry's paradox). So, at the end of the day, it is because we wrongly thought that there are just two truth values that (this version of) Anselm's argument could seem to be convincing.

# Conclusion

*To know the meaning of a representation is to know under what conditions it is true.* Repeatedly, this key idea of contemporary semantics has been our guiding principle in a journey that started with primate alarm calls and ended with logical paradoxes. Originally, the dictum applied to sentences alone, but we've seen how fruitful it was to extend it to further types of representations. The connection between meaning and truth made it possible to harness the clarity and precision of logic to understand extraordinarily diverse phenomena in nature, from animal communication to human speech, signs and gestures, and even to music. It is time to reflect on what we discovered.

## THE DIVERSITY OF MEANING OPERATIONS IN NATURE

We started our journey with an investigation of the meaning of primate alarm calls and gestures. An intriguing enterprise—but how much more expressive is human language in comparison! The alarm calls we studied were drawn from a very small inventory, and with one limited exception (the suffix *-oo* in Campbell's monkeys), there was no nontrivial way to combine them: Each call functioned as a separate utterance, although some additional complexity was afforded by competition among calls ('Be as informative as possible!'—also known as the Informativity Principle). For ape gestures, we found a rich vocabulary of innate 'words' and the tantalizing possibility that they might be related to gestures used by human infants, but there was no evidence that these gestures can be combined to create complex meanings.

At the other extreme, human language, in its signed and spoken varieties, has rich means to refer to objects and to situations, and to categorize them as close or far, as singular, plural, or mass. Its syntax makes it possible to combine words in countless ways, and it provides sentences with a Logical Form reminiscent of formal logic. As we process language, we are in effect logic machines. Along several dimensions, however, human language is more expressive than standard logical languages such as Predicate Logic, both in terms of the logical tools it employs and the way it divides information among a rich inferential typology that includes entailments, implicatures, presuppositions, supplements, and expressives, each with characteristic linguistic properties and interpersonal consequences.

Analyzing meaning in terms of truth conditions came with a challenge: Can semantics deal with paradoxes, which are usually thought to be resistant to any truth value? Yes, but to do so we must recognize that there are more truth values than we thought: not just *true* and *false* but also *indeterminate*. The resulting theory of truth is exciting in its own right (for instance, with the discovery of Truth-tellers, whose value does not depend on facts about the world), but it is also faced with challenges that remain open (the Revenge Liar).

### THE IMPORTANCE OF SIGN LANGUAGES

In most of our journey, sign languages played a key role. They are vitally important for Deaf people, and access to sign language is thus essential for Deaf children and their families. Sign languages are also a cultural treasure, both for Deaf communities and for humanity at large. But in addition, they have a unique scientific role to play. Besides deepening our understanding of what human language is, and enriching the typology of human languages, they make two essential contributions to the investigation of meaning. First, in some cases, sign languages reveal in a particularly perspicuous way the Logical Form of sentences in general (logical variables realized as loci were a case in point). Second, they often include far richer means of iconic enrichment than spoken languages. Sign languages are thus a particularly important window into human meaning in general: without them, we would partly miss out on some key components of meaning.

## VARIETIES OF ICONIC ENRICHMENTS

Spoken languages are not fully devoid of iconic enrichments, however. There are occasional cases in which conventional words can be modulated in iconic ways (as in *loooong* being used to mean 'very long,' just like a broadened sign for *GROW* can mean 'grow a lot' in American Sign Language). And there are many more cases in which iconic gestures can be added to speech.

Should we conclude that sign with iconicity is, from a semantic perspective, the same thing as speech with gestures? Not quite—but to see why not, we had to investigate in some detail the typology of iconic enrichments in spoken and in signed languages. While this is a topic of lively debate, two exciting results arguably stand out. First, the typology of gestural meanings falls neatly within the typology of inferences that we found with conventional words. In particular, the meaning of new pro-speech (that is, speech-replacing) gestures is divided on the fly among slots of this typology, which suggests that it is not just an arbitrary property of words: we have sophisticated mental rules that allow us to perform this division in a productive fashion.

Second, co-speech gestures don't always have the same status as iconic modulations. The latter are often at issue (i.e., presented as the main point), whereas the former rarely are. If this conclusion is correct, there are, in the end, systematic differences between sign with iconicity and speech with gestures, which only makes it more important to take into account sign languages in our investigation of linguistic meaning.

## BEYOND LANGUAGE

Our journey also took us beyond language proper, for a simple reason: The motto of contemporary semantics can be applied to any representation that conveys information about the world. Our explorations into Super

Semantics (the extension of semantic methods beyond traditional linguistic objects) were in a way necessitated by the strong interconnection between speech and gestures, and also between signs and iconicity: It just seemed impossible to have a good understanding of linguistic meaning without including in our investigations some instances of pictorial meaning. This point only became more striking when we noticed that several properties of gestures (notably the division of their content among slots of the inferential typology) could be replicated with visual animations embedded in sentences.

How far can and should we go in extending semantic investigations beyond language as standardly conceived? Possibly quite far, as was suggested by the case of music. While the meaning of music is often thought to lie solely in the emotions it evokes in the listener, we saw that this view is overly restrictive: Music can genuinely convey information about the extra-musical world, although this information is very abstract. And there seem to be systematic means by which music does it, some lifted from normal auditory cognition and some more specifically musical. These means are admittedly completely different from the logical tools of language, and if anything, they are reminiscent of the semantics of abstract visual animations. With the proviso that these investigations are in their infancy, there seem to be genuine prospects for a music semantics.

Our explorations were by no means exhaustive. Pictures and comics are now investigated with sophisticated methods partly inspired by linguistics—a thrilling line of research.[1] This is also the case of dance, both in the abstract form it takes in ballet and in more narrative forms that it can find across cultures.[2] There are more frontiers for Super Semantics to conquer than are discussed in this book.

### THE SCIENTIFIC HUMANITIES

This enterprise has broader ramifications as well. There was a time, in the 1960s, when 'semiotics' (defined as the general theory of signs) was seen as the queen of the human and social sciences, and it was applied to everything from anthropology to psychoanalysis to fashion.[3] But few if any scientific fields currently appeal to its results, which have not given rise to well-formalized theories tested with experimental means. At the time, formal semantics, the study of meaning with logical tools, just didn't exist. It arose later, after Noam Chomsky's revolution in syntax made it plausible that one could treat human language as a formal system, and after Richard Montague added that it could be analyzed as an *interpreted* formal system. While syntax and semantics were initially developed in rather different circles, they became more unified in the 1980s, and they now share a key idea: human language is simultaneously a formal and a cognitive system, and its properties are best studied by combining tools from formal language theory and from psycholinguistics.

This research program, which has proven extraordinarily successful, is based on a three-pronged methodology. First, it starts with sophisticated introspective data about the form and meaning of various sentences: good linguistics always starts with good grammatical analysis. Second, one constructs very explicit formal models, which seek to derive and explain the generalizations obtained in the first stage. Third, the predictions of these models are further tested with experimental methods within cognitive psychology. Because the field is so interested in what is and what isn't universal about language, this approach has had a strong comparative and typological component, and thus it offers a theory of language variation: contemporary linguistics is intrinsically comparative in nature (we followed this very program when we compared spoken to signed languages, for instance).

Semantics plays a special role in this program, both because of its topic and of its methods. As was already the case for semiotics, a theory of meaning ought to be of general interest to diverse fields. And the methods of semantics borrow from grammar and philosophy, but also from mathematical logic and cognitive science: semantics thus combines insights from the humanities and from the sciences.

If it has been such a scientific success, why is semantics relatively unknown among the sciences, and why doesn't it have the appeal that semiotics once had? One reason might be that semantics is . . . well, hard (the field is called 'formal' for a reason). But another reason is that semantics might have remained a bit too modest, studying objects that have the same general properties as those the founders (philosophers and logicians) had in mind. Not just English, of course—semantics is comparative—but primarily spoken languages. Since no serious linguist doubts that sign languages are full-fledged languages and present great scientific interest, they too became a natural object of study. But they led to new questions, and new objects, thus playing a role in motivating the development of Super Semantics: it fulfills some of the goals of a general theory of (human and nonhuman) signs, but from the perspective of a well-established scientific field (formal semantics).

In this way, semantics can do its part to bridge part of the gap between the 'two cultures,'[4] science and the humanities. While its methods are squarely scientific, it does not achieve its goals by sidestepping the contributions of humanistic studies or by simplifying them beyond recognition (there is a reason semantics is rooted in grammar and in philosophy). Rather, it starts from exquisitely detailed case studies and, in successful cases, integrates them into ambitious scientific theories, stated with great formal rigor and tested with experimental means. It thus offers a model of how knowledge from the humanities and methods from the sciences can, and should, be fruitfully integrated.

# Appendix: Phonology, Morphology, and Syntax in Speech and in Sign

This book is devoted to meaning, but its twin objects of study, semantics and pragmatics, are only part of language. Any meaning is the meaning of a form. The investigation of linguistic form is divided into three parts: phonology, morphology, and syntax. Phonology studies the nature and combination of the elementary perceptual units of language: audible ones in spoken language, visible ones in sign language. Morphology studies the nature and combination of the elementary meaningful units from which words are made (such as roots, prefixes, suffixes). And syntax studies the ways in which words can be combined to form sentences.

In this appendix, I'll try to give you a bird-eye's view of these other modules of language, with an emphasis on the similarities between spoken language and sign language; as we'll see, they are two sides of the same coin, with interesting differences. (This discussion is based on existing surveys that are referenced in the Going Further section.)

**Phonology:** The articulation of language is the realm of phonology. *Phono* comes from the word φωνή (= phōnḗ) in Ancient Greek, which means *sound*, but the term *phonology* is equally applied to visible articulators in sign language, for good reason: as we will now see, there are striking similarities between phonological rules found in spoken language and in sign language.

Starting with speech, one might initially think that the elementary components of words are the sounds encoded by letters in orthography. But this is not a promising idea: English spelling is notoriously capricious, as was illustrated in a humorous poem (by T. S. Watt), which included the following lines:[1]

> Beware of heard, a dreadful word
> That looks like beard and sounds like bird . . .

The point was that each underlined *ea* sequence has its own pronunciation; and to top it off, that of *heard* is shared with that of *bird*! Dictionaries helpfully use phonetic transcriptions to encode the pronunciation of these words, with different *conventions*, depending on the dictionary. Merriam-Webster uses the following: ə for the vowel of *heard*, e for the first vowel of *dreadful*, and i for that of *beard*, with stress encoded by Merriam-Webster with an apostrophe (') before the stressed syllable.

| | |
|---|---|
| heard: | 'hərd |
| dreadful: | 'dred-fəl |
| beard: | 'bird |
| bird: | 'bərd |

A more promising view is that it is these elementary sounds (those encoded in phonetic transcriptions, not letters in orthography) that are the elementary components of pronunciation—the atoms of phonology, so to speak. But an important discovery of the twentieth century was that the real atoms of sound are even smaller. They are what are called 'features.' As a first approximation, features are articulatory instructions that encode how sounds are made; several such instructions are necessary for each sound, which is why features are in a sense 'smaller' than elementary sounds. For instance, the vowel transcribed as *e* for *dreadful* and *bet* is articulated with the front of the tongue (so it's a front vowel), and the tongue is toward the middle of the mouth (it's a mid vowel). The *i* of *bit* is also a front vowel, but the tongue is higher: It is a high vowel. The *a* of *bat* is also a front vowel, but the tongue is lower than for *bet*, so it's a low vowel. It is a series of articulatory instructions of this type (e.g., front, mid for *e*; front, high for *i*) that define the mental representation of linguistic sounds.

This kind of decomposition into articulatory instructions can be applied to all vowels, but also to consonants. For instance, *b* (as in *lab*) is almost produced in the same way as *p* (as in *lap*): Both are produced with the lips. But there is an important difference—*b* has the vocal folds vibrating, while *p* doesn't. For this reason, *b* is called 'voiced' while *p* is called 'voiceless.' The same difference is found between *d* (as in *kid*) and *t* (as in *kit*): They are almost the same consonant, produced with the tip of the tongue, but the vocal folds vibrate in *d* but not in *t*; thus *d* is voiced and *t* is voiceless. Similarly, *g* (as in *rig*) and *k* (as in *Rick*) are both produced with the body of the tongue, but only in *g* do the vocal folds vibrate: *g* is voiced, *k* is voiceless. Many consonants similarly come in pairs, with a voiced and an unvoiced member. Thus *z* as in *buzz* is almost the same consonant as *s* as in *bus*, with the important difference of voicing. If you produce a very long *zzzzz* with your hand on your throat, you'll feel the vocal folds vibrating (*z* is voiced); if you produce a very long *sssss* instead, there will be no similar vibration (*s* is voiceless). And you can perform the same experiment with *v* as in *save* (voiced) and its voiceless counterpart, *f* as in *safe*. You can feel your vocal folds vibrating in a long *vvvv* but not in a long *ffff*. (Unlike *s*, *z*, *f*, *v*, the consonants *p*, *b*, *t*, *d*, *k*, *g* can't be held continuously, which makes the same experiment with your hand on your throat a bit less striking.)

An important claim of phonology is that the laws that govern linguistic sounds make reference to these articulatory instructions (i.e., to features) rather than to unanalyzed units such as *p*, *b*, *t*, *d*, *k*, *g*. (I am simplifying a bit. Further features pertain to the perception rather than to the articulation of sounds, but we can leave this aside.) To give you a feel for the argument that sounds are represented as sets of features, consider the pronunciation of the English past tense suffix -*ed*, restricting attention to the two cases below (I'll continue to use Merriam-Webster's conventions to encode pronunciation):

1. After the sounds *b* (scru<u>b</u>), *g* (pe<u>g</u>), *z* (bu<u>zz</u>), *v* (sa<u>ve</u>), *zh* (camoufla<u>ge</u>), <u>*th*</u> (bathe), the suffix is pronounced *d*: scrubbed, pegged, buzzed, saved, camouflaged, bathed.

2. After the sounds *p* (ma<u>p</u>), *k* (li<u>ck</u>), *s* (ki<u>ss</u>), *f* (lau<u>gh</u>), *sh* (squi<u>sh</u>), *th* (fro<u>th</u>), the suffix is pronounced *t*: mapped, licked, kissed, laughed, squished, frothed.

One could state the rule by just listing the sounds after which the suffix is pronounced as *d* and those after which it is pronounced *t*, as I just did. But there is a much simpler and more elegant statement of the rule, which makes crucial use of the fact that *d* and *t* are almost the same consonant but differ by one articulatory instruction (i.e., by one feature): the vocal folds vibrate for *d* but not for *t*; in other words, *d* is voiced, *t* is voiceless.

> **Voicing assimilation:** The past tense suffix *-ed* is pronounced *d*, unless the preceding sound is a voiceless consonant; if so, *d* is changed into its voiceless counterpart, *t*.

You can check by putting your hand on your throat that the consonants listed in rule 1 above are indeed produced with vibrating vocal folds. The rule states, in essence, that the past tense suffix *d* (written as *-ed*) may get turned into *t* in order to agree with the voiceless feature of the preceding consonant. This is called an assimilation rule: a certain feature of a consonant, such as the voiceless feature of *k* in *lick*, gets extended to a neighboring consonant, here the *d* of the past tense suffix, yielding the sound *t*.

The upshot is that a rule stated in terms of features (here, assimilation to a preceding voiceless sound) is simpler and more elegant than one stated in terms of sounds. But there is more: The rule based on features makes predictions for sounds that are not usually found in the English language. Linguists like to cite a beautiful example of precisely this. The name of the composer Johan Sebastian Bach is often uttered with a borrowing of the German consonant *x* for *ch* (this sound is also used in *loch*, for instance, to refer to a lake in Scotland). Now the sound *x* is not part of the consonants I listed above, but you can check that it is produced without vibrating vocal folds: It is voiceless. Now when you say that a certain composer *outBached Bach himself*, you have no choice but to pronounce the past tense suffix after the sound *x* of *outBach*. And lo and behold, the past tense suffix gets pronounced exactly as is predicted by the assimilation rule discussed here: since *x* is voiceless, *d* is changed to its voiceless counterpart *t*. This is exactly what we find.[2]

Strikingly, linguists have concluded that in essential respects, sign language has the same kind of phonological organization as spoken language.

Of course, *phonology* doesn't pertain to sounds in this case, but rather to the visible articulators of sign language. If you think about it, this needn't be so surprising in view of our earlier discussion: If sound is linguistically encoded as features, construed as articulatory instructions (as in the case of the vowels and consonants discussed above), features could work just as well to encode manual or facial articulations. This is precisely what is found in sign language. In fact, we'll see in a minute that rules of assimilation (illustrated above with the pronunciation of the past tense suffix) have counterparts is sign language.

But first, what do features look like in sign language? Just like spoken language features are instructions to vocal articulators (shown on the left in the figure below), sign language features are instructions to the hands and other visible articulators (shown on the right below).

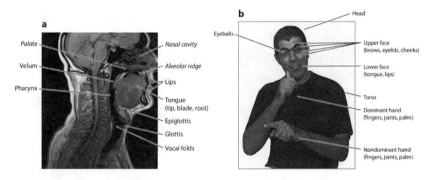

**Figure 17.11.1**
*Articulatory system in spoken language (left) and sign language (right)*

Focusing for simplicity on the hands, these features are of three main types, pertaining to (i) hand configuration, (ii) location, and (iii) movement. And just like *kit* and *kid* differ by just one feature—namely, the fact that the vocal folds vibrate in the final consonant of *kid* but not of *kit*—so similarly one can find sign language words that differ just by hand configuration, or just by location, or just by movement, as in the examples below from Israeli Sign Language (for present purposes, we can think of the differences as involving just one instruction, although this is a simplification).

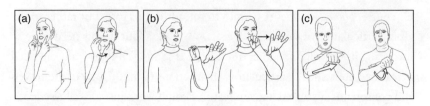

**Figure 17.11.2**

*Signs of Israeli Sign Language that differ with respect to (a) hand configuration, (b) location, and (c) movement*

(a) MOTHER, NOON are distinguished by hand configuration features. (b) SEND, TATTLE are distinguished by location (place of articulation) features, (c) ESCAPE/FLEE, INSULT are distinguished by movement features.

The analogy between sign language and spoken language features runs deeper. We saw previously that spoken language phonology involves rules of feature assimilation—for instance, with respect to voicing (the voiced consonant $d$ gets turned into its voiceless counterpart $t$ when it follows a voiceless consonant, as in *licked*). To see an assimilation rule in sign language, let's look at the first-person pronoun in ASL. For a right-handed person, it is realized by pointing the right index toward oneself. But when saying *I cook*, the next ASL word, *COOK*, involves a flat right hand flipping over the left hand, realized like this (think of flipping a patty):

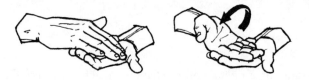

**Figure 17.11.3**

*The sign COOK in ASL*

Assimilation of *I* to *COOK* happens by optionally replacing the index pointing for *I* with a full hand pointing, as in the rightmost realization below (so the pointing index is replaced with a pointing hand):

| No assimilation | | Assimilation of the handshape of the sign for *I* | |
| --- | --- | --- | --- |
| I (normal handshape) | COOK | I (assimilated handshape) | COOK |

**Figure 17.11.4**
*Optional assimilation in I COOK (ASL)*

A similar case arises with the ASL compound that means *believe* and is literally made of *THINK* followed by *MARRY* (maybe a belief is a thought you are married with . . .). *THINK* involves an index pointing toward and touching one's forehead. *MARRY* is realized with a full open hand. Here, too, an optional rule of assimilation turns the index of the first part into a full open hand, as shown on the right below:

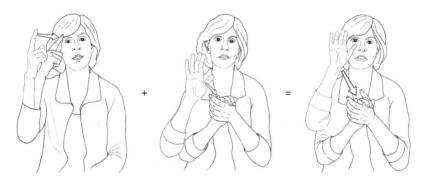

**Figure 17.11.5**
*Optional assimilation in BELIEVE (ASL)*

The upshot is that sign language has a phonology just like spoken language does, and furthermore that phonological organization is in some respects similar in the two modalities. This might initially have been a bit unexpected. But since even spoken language sounds are linguistically encoded as articulatory instructions or features, it is in the end unsurprising that features lie at the core of sign language as well. They are just instructions for a different set of articulators—primarily the hands and face, rather than the vocal apparatus.

**Morphology:** Words often have meaningful parts. The simplest case in English is that of compounding. In some cases, you can merge two words and obtain a new one that has its own characteristic semantic and phonological properties. *Blackboard* is thus formed from *black* + *board*, but a *blackboard* isn't just a *black board*: It should be used for writing with chalk (no such requirement for a *black board*) . . . and it needn't even be black (some blackboards are green, for instance). The compound *blackboard* also has its own stress pattern: The stress is on the initial syllable (*blackboard*), whereas if one is talking of *a black board*, it is often more natural to stress the final syllable. You'll find the same contrast between *a dark room* (a room that's dark) and *a darkroom* (a room for developing photographs, from which normal light is excluded).

A second way to create new words is by adding suffixes or prefixes to existing words to modify their meaning and often their syntactic category; this is called 'derivational morphology.' For instance, *unhappiness* is made of three components. From the adjective *happy* you can form *unhappy*, which is its opposite; the prefix *un-* occurs in numerous other words—for instance, in *unwise*, which is the opposite of *wise*. And to the adjectives *happy* or *unhappy* you can add *-ness* to obtain nouns: *happiness, unhappiness*. Here, too, the suffix *-ness* occurs in numerous further words. Just like *happiness* and *unhappiness* refer to the state of being happy and unhappy, respectively, *strangeness* refers to the state of being strange. The derivation can change the grammatical category of the modified noun. *Happy* is an adjective, but *happiness* is a noun. Similarly, *learn* and *teach* are verbs, but *learner* and *teacher* are nouns. The suffix *-er* turns a verb into a noun. Sometimes the derivation primarily involves a change of stress from the final to the initial syllable. Manufacturers may *discount* prices (verb, stress on the final syllable), and one then obtains a *discount* (noun, stress on the initial syllable). Similarly, students may learn to *construct* a theory (verb, stress on the final syllable), and if they succeed they'll have produced a *theoretical construct* (noun, stress on the initial syllable).

Finally, some morphological processes just modify the grammatical properties of a word; this is called 'inflectional morphology.' From *dog* you can form *dogs* to obtain a plural, and from *lick* you can form the third-person present tense *licks* and the past tense *licked* (to pronounce the result, you still need to apply phonological rules: the assimilation rule we saw above guarantees that *licked* gets pronounced with a final *t*).

Strikingly, all three types of morphology exist in sign language. We already saw an example of compounding. ASL for *believe* is formed from *THINK + MARRY*—and an assimilation rule may be applied in the phonology. An example of derivational morphology is reminiscent of the *learn-learner, teach-teacher* pattern in English. To form the word for *student*, you start from the verb for *learn* and immediately add to it a suffix meaning *person* (two flat hands going down):

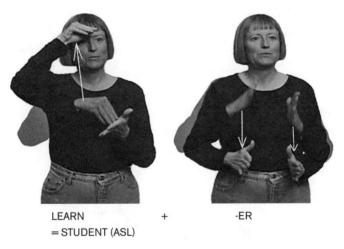

LEARN          +          -ER
= STUDENT (ASL)

**Figure 17.11.6**
*STUDENT in ASL*

And to form *teacher* . . . well, you start from the verb *teach*, and you add the same *person* suffix:

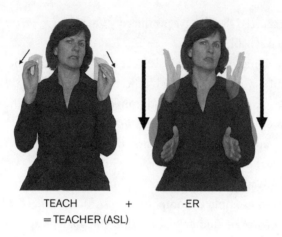

TEACH       +       -ER
= TEACHER (ASL)

**Figure 17.11.7**
*TEACHER in ASL*

A further example of derivational morphology is a bit reminiscent of
the stress rule in English verb-noun pairs in that it turns a verb into a noun
without adding a separate prefix or suffix. The derivation doesn't involve a
stress change but a repetition. One such pair is *SIT* versus *CHAIR*: The verb
for *sit* involves a large single movement ([**AVApp.1**]); the noun for *chair*
involves a short double movement ([**AVApp.2**]). Similarly, for the verb/
noun pair *FLY* versus *AIRPLANE*, the verb *fly* (in an airplane) is realized with
the 🤙 handshape, representing an airplane, moving through signing space
([**AVApp.3**]). The noun *airplane* is realized by a very short double movement
involving the same hand configuration ([**AVApp.4**]).

Finally, there are interesting cases of inflectional morphology in ASL.
Some verbs, called agreement verbs, involve a movement to and/or from a
locus (i.e., a position used to denote an entity in signing space). As discussed
in chapter 2, these loci play an important role in the realization of pronouns:
*I* is realized by pointing toward oneself, *you* by pointing toward the addressee,
and *he, she, it* by pointing toward various positions that correspond to various entities (using their real location if they are present in the context).
Agreement verbs make use of these loci in their very shape. For instance,
ASL for *I give you* resembles a giving gesture that starts from the signer and
goes toward the addressee:

**Figure 17.11.8**
*I-GIVE-YOU in ASL*

If a third-person locus has been established on the signer's right (say, to refer to Sam) and another third-person locus has been established on the signer's left (for instance, to refer to Robin), then *s/he gives him/her* resembles a giving gesture going from right to left:

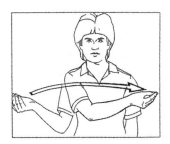

**Figure 17.11.9**
*S/HE-GIVE-HIM/HER in ASL*

(As discussed in chapter 2, in French Sign Language, LSF, something similar happens with the verb *TELL*. If a locus for Sarkozy was established on the left and a locus for Obama on the right, one can sign that Sarkozy told Obama something by having *TELL* start from the Sarkozy locus on the left and move toward the Obama locus on the right.)

Similarly, if a third-person locus was established on the signer's right, *you give him/her* resembles a giving gesture that starts from the addressee position and moves toward the right—so this is a movement from the center to the right rather than from the right to the left, as was the case for *s/he gives him/ her* in the preceding example.

**Figure 17.11.10**
*YOU-GIVE-HIM/HER in ASL*

**Syntax:** Different languages have different word orders. In English, the verb comes before its complement (hence one *eats apples*). In Japanese, the complement comes before the verb (hence, literally, one *apples eats*). The rules by which words are put together to form sentences is the realm of syntax.

Just as different spoken languages have different basic word orders, different sign languages use different word orders as well. ASL primarily has the order SVO (subject–verb–object), like English. By contrast, LIS (Italian Sign Language) primarily has the order SOV (subject–object–verb), so literally, *GIANNI COFFEE ORDER* would mean that Gianni orders a coffee.[3] You might think that the difference between the ASL word order and the LIS word order arises because English and Italian have different word orders, but this is entirely incorrect. Just like English, Italian has a basic order of SVO, so this can't explain the SOV order found in LIS. While sign languages may be influenced by the surrounding spoken languages, they have entirely autonomous histories and structures, just like Quebec French does in Canada, despite being surrounded by English speakers.

In chapter 9, we saw that the specification of basic word orders isn't enough. Sometimes words get moved around to achieve certain effects, as in the case of the following sentence, which makes clear that John is the topic of the conversation:

John, I like ___ .

When it comes to questions, languages differ. As we also saw in chapter 9, English usually moves interrogative expressions to the beginning of the sentence:

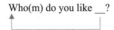

Who(m) do you like ___?

Mandarin Chinese doesn't move interrogative words:

Mandarin Chinese:

| Nǐ | xǐhuān | sheí? |
|-----|--------|-------|
| you | like | who |

And French can, in some cases at least, use either option:

French:

| Tu | aimes | qui? |
|-----|-------|------|
| you | like | who |

| Qui | tu | aimes? |
|-----|-----|--------|
| who | you | like |

Movement rules exist in sign language as well, but often with a twist. One such twist is that facial expressions can have a grammatical function that interacts with these rules. The ASL counterpart of the English sentence above also involves movement of *JOHN* to the beginning of the sentence, but in addition, *JOHN* appears with raised eyebrows to indicate that this word is the topic of the conversation (raised eyebrows have rather diverse functions in sign language; as briefly noted in section 10.3, they can also serve to mark focus, sometimes in conjunction with word movement).

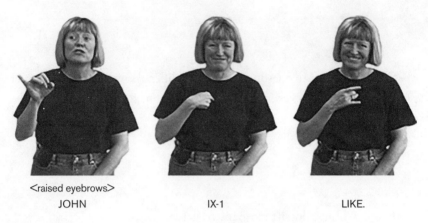

<raised eyebrows>
JOHN                    IX-1                    LIKE.

**Figure 17.11.11**

JOHN, signed with raised eyebrows.

**Figure 17.11.12**

Raised eyebrows are also used for yes/no questions. But for wh-questions, such as *What did John buy?*, ASL uses lowered eyebrows instead. As in Mandarin Chinese, the interrogative word can be left after the verb, just as a normal object (e.g., *CAR*):

&lt;lowered _____ eyebrows&gt;

JOHN                 BUY               WHAT?

**Figure 17.11.13**

But in some situations (and for some signers), you can also find the interrogative word at the beginning of the sentence, as in English:

&lt;lowered   eyebrows&gt;
WHAT JOHN BUY?

And you can also find the interrogative word moved to the end of the sentence, even when this is not its normal position, as when the *WHO* is used as the subject of *BUY*:

&lt;lowered eyebrows&gt;
BUY CAR WHO?

On top of this, the interrogative word may occur twice, at the beginning of the sentence *and* at the end of the sentence:

&lt;lowered_____eyebrows&gt;
WHAT NANCY BUY YESTERDAY WHAT

And these are just some of the possibilities! You'll understand why the formation of questions in sign language is a topic of active research. But two things are rather clear: ASL can leave interrogative words in their original position (as is the case in Mandarin) or move them (as is the case in English); and facial expressions (lowered eyebrows in ASL) play an important role as well.

This is part of a larger pattern. The syntax of sign languages has numerous properties in common with that of spoken languages, and there are interesting properties that are characteristic of sign languages as well—for instance, those that pertain to facial expressions.

# Glossary

While technical terminology is kept at a minimum in the book, the following definitions might be helpful at various junctures (they are all introduced in the main text, however).

**Agreement:** Modification of a word that indicates that it stands in a particular grammatical relation to another (for instance, the appearance of a plural on the verb in *My friends are meeting nearby*).

**ASL:** American Sign Language.

**Assertive, assertion:** The assertive component of a clause is its main point, which gets negated by *not* and interrogated by questions. 'Assertive component' is used in this book as a synonym for 'at issue component.'

**Assimilation rule:** A rule by which a feature of a phonological unit gets extended to a neighboring one. For instance, in English, the voiceless feature of the sound *k* in *lick* gets extended to the past tense suffix *d*, which is thus pronounced as *t* (voiceless) in *licked*. There are also assimilation rules in sign language phonology; they pertain to features as well, but in the visual rather than vocal modality.

**Atelic:** A verb (and more generally a verb phrase) such as *run* is atelic because it describes events without reference to an intrinsic endpoint. For this reason, atelic verbs satisfy the Divisibility test. Atelic verbs are more natural with *in* than *for*, hence *Ann ran for one hour*, not *Ann ran in an hour*.

**At issue:** The at issue component of a clause is its main point, which gets negated by *not* and interrogated by questions. 'At issue component' is used in this book as a synonym for 'assertive component.'

**Co-speech gesture:** A gesture that co-occurs with the word or words it specifies (and thus a co-speech gesture does not have its own time slot).

**Count nouns:** Nouns, such as *coin*, which refer to things that have clearly identifiable minimal parts that satisfy the expression—in this case, individual coins. Unlike mass nouns, count nouns fail the Divisibility test: A part of a coin isn't a coin anymore. In English, count nouns can appear after the determiners *a*, *every*, and *many*, but not after *much*.

**Counterfactual:** Something that runs counter to established facts. A counterfactual situation is one that is known not to be the actual one. A counterfactual conditional (e.g., *if earth were the size of a nickel, the moon would be about as big as a coffee bean*) is one whose *if*-clause is known to be false. In English, it can involve the subjunctive (in this case, *were*).

**CSL:** Chinese Sign Language.

**Definite descriptions:** Descriptions preceded by the definite determiner *the* (e.g., *the winner, the winners)* or by a possessive (e.g., *your mother, my parents*). A definite description *the blah* presupposes that there exists a unique maximal group that satisfies *blah* (in the context), and if so, it denotes that group. *The winner* thus presupposes that there exists a unique singular winner and denotes that person. *The winners* presupposes that there exists a maximal group of winners and denotes that group. Similarly, *the beer* presupposes that there exists a maximal group of beer portions and denotes that group—hence all the beer there is.

**Denotation:** Whatever a linguistic expression refers to.

**Determiner:** An expression such as *the, some, a, every, many, much, most* that precedes a noun phrase and determines the quantity of the objects it makes reference to.

**Divisibility test:** A test that can be applied to nouns (and noun phrases) as well as to verbs (and verb phrases) and goes like this: For any thing that qualifies as *blah* (where *blah* is nominal or verbal), any part of it also qualifies as *blah*. Mass nouns such as *water* satisfy the Divisibility test: Any part of water still qualifies as water. Count nouns such as *coin* fail the test because a proper part of a coin isn't a coin. Atelic verbs such as *run* satisfy the Divisibility test: Any part of an event of running still qualifies as an event of running. Telic verb such as *arrive* fail the test because a part of an arrival that just precedes the 'finish line' doesn't qualify as an arrival.

**Dynamic logic:** A variety of logic developed in the 1980s. It was inspired in part by the observation that in natural language, a pronoun/variable can depend on an existential quantifier that appears in an earlier sentence or conjunct, as in: *[Some senator]$_x$ x came and he$_x$ gave a speech*. In standard Predicate Logic, this dependency fails in analogous formulas (such as *[∃x x came] and x gave-a-speech)*. By contrast, dynamic logic allows for this very dependency.

**Economy Principle:** A principle of communication that prohibits expressions from being verbose, in the sense that they could be eliminated without changing the overall meaning; in particular, one should not state the obvious. An example of a violation: *Ann is in Southern Italy. She is in Italy.* The second sentence is trivial (obvious) after the first sentence has been uttered and thus could be eliminated without changing the overall meaning.

**Entailment:** A sentence *S* entails a sentence *S'* if every conceivable situation that makes *S* true also makes *S'* true. An example: *Robin will go to Paris* entails *Robin will go to France*. Similarly, *Ann is in Southern Italy* entails *Ann is in Italy*. When *S* entails *S'*, one can infer *S'* from *S* on the basis of the literal meaning of the words alone. In case *S* entails *S'* but not conversely, the entailment is asymmetric.

**Expressive:** A meaning component that is not at issue and provides information about the speaker's attitude toward certain things or individuals (slurs are a prime example of words with an expressive component). *Frog* refers to French people but carries the expressive component that the speaker dislikes the French. Like presuppositions, expressives trigger inferences that are preserved in a variety of environments from which entailments disappear—for instance, questions (e.g., *Do any Frogs oppose Brexit?* still suggests that the speaker dislikes the French). But they are also preserved in some environments from which even presuppositions seem to disappear (e.g., *If I really hated the French, I wouldn't hire a Frog* suggests that the speaker dislikes the French, whereas this is not the case with the presupposition trigger *know*, as in, *If I really hated the French, Robin would know that I do*).

**Grounded, ungrounded:** In the theory of paradoxes, a sentence is said to be grounded if it can be assigned the value *true* or the value *false* on the basis of facts about the world. Sentences that are not grounded are ungrounded and come in many varieties, including the Liar's paradox, Yablo's paradox, and (different versions of) the Truth-teller.

**Iconicity:** A property of a representation that refers to things by virtue of resembling them. The sound of the word *cat* does not in any way resemble cats (the animals), and so the word isn't iconic. The sound of the word *meow* somewhat resembles the crying sound of a cat, so *meow* is somewhat iconic.

**Implicature:** An inference that does not follow from the meaning of the words alone but rather from a reasoning on the speaker's intentions. A scalar implicature arises when one compares the sentence uttered to a more informative alternative that wasn't uttered. One may assume that this is because the more informative alternative was false. For instance, *Most of my friends are honest* evokes the more informative alternative, *All of my friends are honest*, and thus implicates that the latter is false.

**Informativity Principle:** A principle of communication by which one assumes that the speaker uttered the most informative sentence possible among a set of alternatives. It is used to derive scalar implicatures: *Most of my friends are honest* evokes the more informative alternative, *All of my friends are honest*, and thus uttering the former suggests (by the Informativity Principle) that the latter is false.

**Introspection principle:** A principle by which if I believe something, I believe that I believe it.

**Islands:** A syntactic island is an expression out of which words cannot be moved. Conjunctions and disjunctions are examples of syntactic islands. One can say, *Sam, I will invite __*, thus moving *Sam* from the object position to the beginning of the sentence; however, one cannot say, *Sam, I will invite **Robin and** __*, as movement out of the boldfaced conjunction is blocked. Nor can one say, *Sam, I will invite **Robin or** __*, as movement out of the boldfaced disjunction is blocked as well.

**Liar's paradox:** A sentence such as *This very sentence is not true*. Like other paradoxes, it cannot coherently be assigned the value *true*, nor the value *false*. Under some assumptions, it may coherently be assigned a third truth value, # (sometimes called *hash*), 'neither true nor false.' The Revenge Liar (also called Strengthened Liar) is stated a bit differently—for instance, *This very sentence is something other than true*. It is hard to deal with because it cannot be coherently assigned the value *true*, nor the value *false*, nor the value # (if it is 'neither true nor false,' it is something other than true, which should make its content true!).

**LIS:** Italian Sign Language (for: *Lingua Italiana dei Segni*, now called *Lingua dei Segni Italiana*).

**Locus (plural: loci):** In sign language, a locus is a position in signing space used to refer to an object or individual. A pronoun may then be realized by pointing toward that position. In some cases, loci can be used to refer to situations as well. Some theories take loci to be a visible instantiation of logical variables.

**Logical Form:** A level of syntactic representation in which quantifiers appear in the positions in which they are interpreted. According to some theories, the Logical Form of a sentence may be mentally derived by moving words to different positions from their apparent ones. For instance, the sentence *Some voter called every senator* can give rise to different Logical Forms that correspond to different meanings: *[some voter]$_x$ [every senator]$_y$ x called y; [every senator]$_y$ [some voter]$_x$ x called y*.

**LSF:** French Sign Language (for *Langue des Signes Française*).

**Mass nouns:** Nouns, such as *water*, which refer to things that do not have clearly identifiable minimal parts that satisfy the expression. Unlike count nouns, mass nouns satisfy the Divisibility test: Any perceptible part of water still qualifies as water. In English, mass nouns can appear after the determiner *much* but not after *a*, *every*, and *many*.

**Modal statement, modal auxiliary:** Modality pertains to situations that are possible (conceivable) rather than just to those that are real. A modal statement such as *It might be raining* makes reference to possible situations, and it may involve a modal auxiliary (here, *might*).

**Mood:** A modification of a verb that specifies how similar the situations it refers to are to the actual one (or rather to what is known of the latter). For instance, the subjunctive *were* marks the situations described by the *if*-clause as incompatible with what is known of the actual situation, as in: *If earth were the size of a nickel, the moon would be about as big as a coffee bean.*

**Moore's "paradox":** A type of puzzling statement (discussed by the philosopher G. E. Moore) that cannot be coherently uttered even though it is not logically contradictory. An example is: *It's already past midnight but I don't believe that it is.* Third-person counterparts of the statement are coherent; for example: *It's already past midnight but Moore doesn't believe that it is.* The first-person version is odd because one cannot coherently hold both beliefs (*'It's already past midnight,' 'I don't believe that it's already past midnight'*) at once. This is not a paradox in the technical sense (pertaining to sentences that cannot coherently be assigned the value *true* nor the value *false*).

**Morphology:** The study of the nature and combination of elementary meaningful units from which words are made.

**Movement (syntactic):** An operation by which some words are displaced from their base position, as in *Sam, I will invite __* (*Sam* originates from the object position of *invite*, represented as __) or in *Who(m) do you like __?* (*who(m)* originates from the object position of *like*).

**Negative polarity item:** An expression such as *ever* and *at all*, which is acceptable in negative but not in positive environments (for instance, one can say *Robin won't ever go to France*, but not *\*Robin will ever go to France*). A commonly accepted generalization is that negative polarity items are acceptable in environments that are negative-like in logical terms; they are environments that reverse informativity relations (i.e., entailment relations).

**Paradox:** In the logical sense, a paradox is a sentence that cannot coherently be assigned the value *true* nor the value *false*.

**Phonology:** The study of the nature and combination of the elementary perceptual units of language: audible ones in spoken language, visible ones in sign language.

**Pluractional:** A marker that indicates that a verb makes reference to a plurality of events. Sometimes pluractionality is marked by repetition, both in spoken and in sign languages. In sign language, the repetition may have an iconic component—for example, in LSF, if the iterations of the verb *GIVE* are signed at an accelerating pace, one understands that the giving events took place more and more quickly as well.

**Post-speech gesture:** A gesture that follows the word or words it further specifies (and has its own time slot).

**Pragmatics:** The study of inferences (beyond the literal meaning of words) that can be derived by reasoning on the speaker's motives for uttering one sentence rather than another.

**Predicate Logic:** A logic made of the connectives *and, or, not,* and the quantifiers $\forall$ (universal quantifier, read as 'for all') and $\exists$ (existential quantifier, read as 'there exists' or 'for some').

**Presupposition:** A meaning component that is presented as being redundant (i.e., uninformative) in view of the beliefs of the speaker and addressee and of the linguistic environment. For example, *John knows that he is incompetent* presupposes and thus presents as established that John is in fact incompetent. Presuppositions are preserved in many linguistic environments from which entailments disappear—for instance, in the presence of a negation (*John doesn't know that he is incompetent*) or a question (*Does John know that he is incompetent?*).

**Pro-speech gesture:** A gesture that fully replaces a word or some words (and thus has its own time slot).

**Proximate, obviative:** In some Algonquian languages, if two third-person noun phrases are used, one is typically marked as 'proximate,' which means that it refers to an object that is close to the center of attention and is thus most salient, while the other is marked as 'obviative,' which means that it refers to a less salient object.

**Quantifier:** In Predicate Logic, quantifiers are expressions such as $\forall$ (universal quantifier, read as 'for all') and $\exists$ (existential quantifier, read as 'there exists' or 'for some'). $\forall x\, Px$ can be read as *for all things x, P holds of x*; $\exists x\, Px$ can be read as *there exists a thing x such that P holds of x* (or *for some thing x, P holds of x*). In natural language, quantifiers are expressions such as *some student, every professor, most politicians,* and by extension *some, every, most* (which are also called 'determiners').

**Recursion:** Cases in which a category $S$ is found under another $S$ in a syntactic tree. Whenever this happens, if you have built a structure with an S under another S (i.e., $S \ldots S$), you can copy the $S \ldots S$ part once again to obtain a larger sentence (i.e., $S \ldots S \ldots S$).

**Scale:** In pragmatics, a set of words that evoke each other and are ordered by informativity. For instance, <or, and> is a scale: Each of these two words evokes the other, and in an unembedded sentence, *p and q* entails *p or q* but not conversely. Scales play a role in the derivation of scalar implicatures.

**Semantics:** In a broad sense, the study of meaning. In a strict sense, the study of meaning as it is encoded in words. Semantics in a broad sense includes semantics in the strict sense, together with pragmatics.

**Sincerity:** The assumption that the speaker believes what she says (this assumption plays a role in the analysis of Moore's "paradox").

**Supplement:** A meaning component which is not at issue, but which is presented as informative (unlike presuppositions). A prime example of supplements are non-restrictive relative clauses, as in: *Does this guy, who is incompetent, have an awareness of it?* Unlike presuppositions, supplements are deviant in some negative environments. But like presuppositions, supplements are preserved in a variety of environments from which entailments disappear.

**Syntax:** The study of the ways in which words can be combined to form sentences.

**Telic:** A verb (and more generally a verbal construction) such as *arrive* is telic because it describes events with reference to an intrinsic endpoint—in this case, the arrival. For this reason, telic verbs do not satisfy the Divisibility test. Telic verbs are more natural with *in* that *for*, hence: *Ann arrived at the finish line <u>in</u> five minutes*, not *Ann arrived at the finish line <u>for</u> five minutes*.

**Tense:** A modification of a verb that specifies how the situations it refers to are temporally ordered relative to the time of utterance (or sometimes other moments mentioned in a sentence). In English, the modification can be effected by a suffix (*Robin smokes*, *Robin smoked*) or by an auxiliary (*Robin will smoke*).

**Truth-teller:** A sentence such as *This very sentence is true*, which can coherently be assigned the value *true* or the value *false* (or the value *neither true nor false*) irrespective of the facts about the world.

**Variable:** In logic, a variable is a logical expression such as $x$ in $\exists x\; x > 1$ ('for some x, x is greater than 1'), which serves to connect a quantifier to the formulas it specifies. By extension, variables are overt or covert elements of natural language that encode referential dependencies. Pronouns are often thought to be a primary exponent of variables, although in spoken language the variables themselves are not expressed, hence the ambiguity of the statement *Sarkozy told Obama that he would win the election*. Depending on whether *he* refers to Sarkozy or to Obama, the sentence is thought to be mentally represented as *Sarkozy$_x$ told Obama$_y$ that **he**$_x$ would win the election*, or as *Sarkozy$_x$ told Obama$_y$ that **he**$_y$ would win the election*. In sign language, variables have been argued to be (sometimes) realized by loci.

**Yablo's paradox:** A paradox that does not involve self-reference but is based on an infinite series of sentences that each talk about other sentences in the series.

# Going Further

What follows are suggestions for further reading; some of these works are introductory, but several are technical in nature, in which case this is highlighted. Bibliographies of the works cited should be consulted for more extensive references, which are not included here.

## ON LANGUAGE IN GENERAL

There have been multiple books on language in general, often with special attention to sound (phonology), word formation (morphology), syntax, and language acquisition. The following are excellent and highly readable introductions:

Jackendoff, Ray. 1994. *Patterns in the Mind: Language and Human Nature*. New York: Basic Books.

Pinker, Steven. 1994. *The Language Instinct*. New York: Harper Perennial Modern Classics.

For more recent introductions, see:

Adger, David. 2019. *Language Unlimited: The Science Behind Our Most Creative Power*. Oxford: Oxford University Press.

Roberts, Ian. 2017, *The Wonders of Language: Or How to Make Noises and Influence People*. Cambridge: Cambridge University Press.

For introductions to semantics and pragmatics from the perspective of the philosophy of language, see, for instance:

Gendler Szabó, Zoltán, and Richard Thomason. 2018. *Philosophy of Language*. Cambridge Textbooks in Linguistics. Cambridge: Cambridge University Press.

Taylor, Kenneth. 1991. *Truth and Meaning: An Introduction to the Philosophy of Language*. Oxford: Wiley-Blackwell.

For a meditation on linguistics and the notion of possible versus impossible languages, see:

Moro, Andrea. 2016. *Impossible Languages*. Cambridge, MA: MIT Press.

There are numerous linguistically informed discussions of language use at this website curated by linguists:

Language Log. https://languagelog.ldc.upenn.edu/nll/.

For a list of online resources, see for instance:

https://allthingslinguistic.com/post/164874346205/how-to-teach-yourself-linguistics-online-for-free.

### INTRODUCTION

On the history of semantics as a field, the following offers a somewhat specialized introduction:

Partee, Barbara H. 2011. "Formal Semantics: Origins, Issues, Early Impact." In *Formal Semantics and Pragmatics: Discourse, Context, and Models*. Vol. 6 of *The Baltic Yearbook of Cognition, Logic, and Communication*, edited by B. H. Partee, M. Glanzberg, and J. Skilters, 1–52. Manhattan, KS: New Prairie Press.

Detailed textbook introductions to semantics include:

Altshuler, Daniel, Terence Parsons, and Roger Schwarzschild. 2019. *A Course in Semantics*. Cambridge, MA: MIT Press. (recent technical introduction)

Chierchia, Gennaro, and Sally McConnell-Ginet. 2000. *Meaning and Grammar: An Introduction to Semantics*. Cambridge, MA: MIT Press. (technical introduction)

Coppock, Elizabeth, and Lucas Champollion. 2020. *Invitation to formal Semantics*. Unpublished draft manuscript, August 21, 2021. http://eecoppock.info/bootcamp/semantics-boot-camp .pdf. (recent technical introduction)

Heim, Irene, and Angelika Kratzer. 1998. *Semantics in Generative Grammar*. Malden, MA: Blackwell. (standard technical introduction)

Larson, Richard K. 2022. *Semantics as Science*. Cambridge, MA: MIT Press. (recent step-by-step undergraduate introduction)

Larson, Richard K., and Gabriel Segal. 1995. *Knowledge of Meaning: An Introduction to Semantic Theory*. Cambridge, MA: MIT Press. (technical and philosophical introduction)

An older reference is:

Bach, Emmon. 1989. *Informal Lectures on Formal Semantics*. SUNY Series in Linguistics. NY: State University of New York Press. (informal introduction)

For a more logic-oriented introduction to semantics, see:

Gamut, L.T.F. 1991. *Logic, Language, and Meaning*. Chicago: University of Chicago Press. (volume 1, An Introduction to Logic; volume 2, An Introduction to Semantics)

Shorter and less technical introductions to semantics include:

De Swart, Henriëtte. 1998. *Introduction to Natural Language Semantics*. CSLI Lecture Notes. Stanford, CA: CSLI Publications.

Elbourne, Paul. 2011. *Meaning: A Slim Guide to Semantics*. Oxford Linguistics. Oxford: Oxford University Pres. (brief introduction)

Portner, Paul H. 2008, *What Is Meaning? Fundamentals of Formal Semantics*. Malden, MA: Wiley-Blackwell.

A survey of some topics in Super Semantics can be found in:

Schlenker, Philippe. 2019. "What is Super Semantics?" *Philosophical Perspectives* 32, 1: 365–453.

## CHAPTER 1

For an introduction to animal signals, one may consult:

Zuberbühler, Klaus. 2009. "Survivor Signals: The Biology and Psychology of Animal Alarm Calling." *Advances in the Study of Behavior* 40: 277–322.

For an excellent textbook introduction to the theory of animal signals from the perspective of behavioral ecology, see:

Searcy, William A., and Stephen Nowicki. 2005. *The Evolution of Animal Communication: Reliability and Deception in Signaling Systems*. Princeton, NJ: Princeton University Press.

On monkey calls, a more detailed presentation of the main ideas of this chapter can be found in the following encyclopedia article:

Schlenker, Philippe, Emmanuel Chemla, and Klaus Zuberbühler. 2017. "Semantics and Pragmatics of Monkey Communication." In *Oxford Research Encyclopedia of Linguistics (Online, paywalled)*. http://linguistics.oxfordre.com/view/10.1093/acrefore/9780199384655.001.0001/acrefore-9780199384655-e-220.

On ape and human infant gestures, the following research articles are highly relevant:

Hobaiter, Catherine, and Richard W. Byrne. 2017. "What Is a Gesture? A Meaning-Based Approach to Defining Gestural Repertoires." *Neuroscience & Biobehavioral Reviews* 82:3–12.

Kersken, Verena, Juan-Carlos Gómez, Ulf Liszkowski, Adrian Soldati, and Catherine Hobaiter. 2018. "A Gestural Repertoire of 1- to 2-Year-Old Human Children: In Search of the Ape Gestures." *Animal Cognition* 22: 577–595. https://doi.org/10.1007/s10071-018-1213-z.


## CHAPTER 2

On sign languages, the following is a recent introductory textbook:

Hill, Joseph C., Diane C. Lillo-Martin, and Sandra K. Wood. 2018. *Sign Languages: Structures and Contexts*. London: Routledge.

The following is an advanced textbook on sign language linguistics:

Sandler, Wendy, and Diane Lillo-Martin. 2006. *Sign Language and Linguistic Universals*. Cambridge: Cambridge University Press.

For a discussion of the history of American Sign Language, see:

Supalla, Ted, and Patricia Clark. 2015. *Sign Language Archaeology: Understanding the Historical Roots of American Sign Language*. Washington, DC: Gallaudet University Press.

On the importance of giving deaf children access to sign language, see:

Napoli, Donna Jo, Nancy K. Mellon, John K. Niparko, Christian Rathmann, Gaurav Mathur, Tom Humphries, Theresa Handley, Sasha Scambler, and John D. Lantos. 2015. "Should All Deaf Children Learn Sign Language?" *Pediatrics* 136 (1): 170–176.

A recent survey of sign language semantics can be found in the following research article:

Schlenker, Philippe: 2018. "Visible Meaning: Sign Language and the Foundations of Semantics." *Theoretical Linguistics* 44 (3–4): 123–208.

A shorter piece summarizes the main results pertaining to sign language pronouns:

Schlenker, Philippe. 2017. "Sign Language and the Foundations of Anaphora." *Annual Review of Linguistics* 3:149–177.

The data discussed from Nicaraguan Sign Language originally appeared in:

Senghas, Ann, Sotaro Kita, and Asli Özyürek. 2004. "Children Creating Core Properties of Language: Evidence from an Emerging Sign Language in Nicaragua." *Science* 305 (5691): 1779–1782.

On the neuroscience of spoken and sign language, see:

MacSweeney, Mairéad, Cheryl M. Capek, Ruth Campbell, and Bencie Woll. 2008. "The Signing Brain: the Neurobiology of Sign Language." *Trends in the Cognitive Sciences* 12 (11): 432–440.

On the idea of a 'Universal Grammar' in syntax, the following is an excellent general audience introduction, focusing both on language universals and language variation:

Baker, Mark C. 2002. *The Atoms of Language*. Oxford: Oxford University Press.

## CHAPTER 3

A clear but specialized (and pioneering) philosophical discussion of perspectives can be found in:

Lewis, David. 1983. "Attitudes De Dicto and De Se." In *Philosophical Papers*, vol. 1., edited by D. Lewis, 133–159. Oxford: Oxford University Press.

An advanced presentation of the contents of this chapter can be found in the following (technical) survey article:

Schlenker, Philippe. 2011. "Indexicality and De Se Reports." In *Semantics: An International Handbook of Natural Language Meaning*, vol. 2, edited by C. Maienborn, K. von Heusinger, and P. Portner, 1561–1604. Berlin: De Gruyter Mouton.

## CHAPTER 4

The analogy between the nominal and the verbal domain is discussed at an introductory level in chapter 9 of:

Fromkin, Victoria A., ed. 2001. *Linguistics: An Introduction to Linguistic Theory*. Malden, MA: Wiley-Blackwell.

For an excellent general audience (but high level) introduction to the count/mass distinction, see:

Chierchia, Gennaro. 2010. "Language, Thought, and Reality after Chomsky." In *Chomsky Notebook*, edited by J. Bricmont and L. Franck, 142–169. New York: Columbia University Press.

A detailed but specialized study of event semantics in English can be found in the following book:

Parsons, Terence. 1990. *Events in the Semantics of English*. Cambridge, MA: MIT Press.

A nontechnical discussion of non-signers' ability to guess the telicity of sign language verbs can be found in the following article:

Strickland, Brent, Carlo Geraci, Emmanuel Chemla, Philippe Schlenker, Meltem Kelepir, and Roland Pfau. 2015. "Event Representations Constrain the Structure of Language: Sign Language as a Window into Universally Accessible Linguistic Biases." *Proceedings of the National Academy of Sciences* 112 (19): 5968–73.

## CHAPTER 5

The seminal (and highly readable) article on the tense/pronoun analogy is the following piece by one of the pioneers of the field:

Partee, Barbara H. 1973. "Some Structural Analogies between Tenses and Pronouns in English." *Journal of Philosophy* 70 (18): 601–609.

An advanced textbook in progress on temporal and modal dependency (in the spirit of Heim and Kratzer's 1998 book cited above, under 'Introduction') can be found online:

Heim, Irene, and Kai von Fintel. 2020. *Intensional Semantics* (Spring Edition). Lecture notes, MIT. https://github.com/fintelkai/fintel-heim-intensional-notes.

The role of situations in semantics is discussed in the following online survey article:

Kratzer, Angelika. 2019. "Situations in Natural Language Semantics." In *The Stanford Encyclopedia of Philosophy* (Summer Edition), edited by Edward N. Zalta. https://plato.stanford.edu/archives/sum2019/entries/situations-semantics/.

Temporal and modal pronouns in ASL are discussed in the following research article:

Schlenker, Philippe. 2013. "Temporal and Modal Anaphora in Sign Language (ASL)." *Natural Language & Linguistic Theory* 31 (1): 207–234.

## CHAPTER 6

The following advanced survey article on time and modality is congenial to the perspective of this chapter, with an emphasis on similarities between nominal, temporal, and modal reference. In several cases, it adopts standard views from the literature, but within a framework that makes comparison across domains particularly easy:

Schlenker, Philippe. 2006. "Ontological Symmetry in Language: A Brief Manifesto." *Mind & Language* 21 (4): 504–539.

The idea that *if*, *when*, and *the* can be given a unified semantics goes back to the following book:

Lewis, David K. 1973. *Counterfactuals*. Cambridge, MA: Harvard University Press.

## CHAPTER 7

For a textbook introduction to Predicate Logic, see volume 1 of:

Gamut, L.T.F. 1991. *Logic, Language and Meaning*. Chicago: University of Chicago Press.

For a brief history of the idea that human language can be treated as a formal language (especially with respect to its semantics), see:

Partee, Barbara H. 2013. "On the History of the Question of Whether Natural Language Is 'Illogical.'" In *History and Philosophy of the Language Sciences* (Blog), edited by James McElvenny. https://hiphilangsci.net/2013/05/01/on-the-history-of-the-question-of-whether-natural-language-is-illogical/.

## CHAPTER 8

The origin of Richard Montague's interest in semantics is discussed in the following article:

Partee, Barbara H. 2011. "Formal Semantics: Origins, Issues, Early Impact." In *Formal Semantics and Pragmatics: Discourse, Context, and Models*. Vol. 6 of *The Baltic Yearbook of Cognition, Logic, and Communication*, edited by B. H. Partee, M. Glanzberg and J. Skilters, 1–52. Manhattan, KS: New Prairie Press.

The following website, created by Ivano Caponigro, reports interesting facts about Richard Montague's life:

"The Simplicity of Language, the Complexity of Life: Richard Montague 1930–1971." https://www.richardmontague.com/.

For a detailed presentation of the syntax/semantics interaction in the spirit of this chapter, one may consult the following textbook introduction:

Heim, Irene, and Angelika Kratzer. 1998. *Semantics in Generative Grammar*. Malden, MA: Blackwell.

## CHAPTER 9

For a brief introduction to Logical Form (with examples from Hungarian that are close to the ones we discuss in the text), the reader may consult chapter 8 of:

Fromkin, Victoria A., ed. 2001. *Linguistics: An Introduction to Linguistic Theory*. Malden, MA: Wiley-Blackwell.

There has been a vibrant debate on the need (or lack thereof) to posit an abstract syntax (one with quantifier movement) for purposes of semantic interpretation. An alternative to the view presented in this chapter is called 'direct interpretation,' without any invisible movement of quantifiers; a technical discussion can be found in sections 1.1–1.3 of the introductory chapter of:

Barker, Chris, and Pauline I. Jacobson. 2007. *Direct Compositionality*. Oxford: Oxford University Press.

On negative polarity items and entailments (and more generally on semantics), this introductory article is useful:

Larson, Richard K. 1990. "Semantics." In *Invitation to Cognitive Science*, vol. 1. *Language*, edited by D. Osherson. Cambridge, MA: MIT Press.

On the connection between negative polarity items and reasoning, experimental data are discussed in:

Chemla, Emmanuel, Vincent Homer, and Daniel Rothschild. 2011. "Modularity and Intuitions in Formal Semantics: The Case of Polarity Items." *Linguistics & Philosophy* 34:537–570.

## CHAPTER 10

A technical survey of the topics of this chapter (and chapter 11) can be found in:

Schlenker, Philippe. 2016. "The Semantics/Pragmatics Interface." In *The Cambridge Handbook of Formal Semantics*, edited by Maria Aloni and Paul Dekker, 664–727. Cambridge: Cambridge University Press.

A seminal article on the acquisition of scalar implicatures is:

Noveck, Ira. 2001. "When Children Are More Logical than Adults: Experimental Investigations of Scalar Implicature." *Cognition* 78 (2):165–188.

For a detailed presentation of pragmatics from an experimental perspective, see:

Noveck, Ira. 2018. *Experimental Pragmatics: The Making of a Cognitive Science*. Cambridge University Press.


## CHAPTER 11

A technical survey of the topics in this chapter (and chapter 10) can be found in:

Schlenker, Philippe. 2016. "The Semantics/Pragmatics Interface." In *The Cambridge Handbook of Formal Semantics*, edited by Maria Aloni and Paul Dekker, 664–727. Cambridge: Cambridge University Press.

A technical survey of presupposition theory can be found online:

Beaver, David I., Bart Geurts, and Kristie Denlinger. 2014. "Presupposition." *The Stanford Encyclopedia of Philosophy* (Winter Edition), edited by Edward N. Zalta. https://plato.stanford.edu /archives/win2014/entries/presupposition/.


## CHAPTER 12

For an introduction to gestures in linguistics, see:

Abner N., K. Cooperrider, and S. Goldin-Meadow. 2015. "Gesture for Linguists: A Handy Primer." *Language and Linguistics Compass* 9 (11): 437–449.

For a comparison between speech with gestures and sign with iconicity, see:

Goldin-Meadow, Susan, and Diane Brentari. 2017. "Gesture, Sign, and Language: The Coming of Age of Sign Language and Gesture Studies." *Behavioral and Brain Sciences* 40. https:// doi.org/10.1017/S0140525X15001247.

A technical presentation of ideas directly related to those of this chapter can be found in:

Schlenker, Philippe. 2018. "Iconic Pragmatics." *Natural Language & Linguistic Theory* 36 (3): 877–936.

For a dissertation on related topics, see:

Esipova, Maria. 2019. *Composition and Projection in Speech and Gesture*. PhD diss., New York University. https://ling.auf.net/lingbuzz/004676.

Relevant experimental data on co-speech gestures can be found online:

Tieu, Lyn, Robert Pasternak, Philippe Schlenker, and Emmanuel Chemla. 2018. "Co-speech Gesture Projection: Evidence from Inferential Judgments." *Glossa* 3 (1): 109. 1–21. https://doi.org /10.5334/gjgl.580.

On emojis and their relation to gestures, see, for instance, chapter 5 of the following book (much recent research is still in progress and will likely appear in the near future):

McCulloch, Gretchen. 2019. *Because Internet: Understanding the New Rules of Language.* New York: Riverhead Books.

For some emojis that trigger presuppositions similar to those of co-speech gestures, see:

Pasternak, Robert, and Lyn Tieu. 2020. "Co-linguistic Content Projection: From Gestures to Sound Effects and Emoji." *Quarterly Journal of Experimental Psychology* (2022): https://journals .sagepub.com/doi/full/10.1177/17470218221080645.

Pierini, Franceso. 2021. "Emojis and Gestures: A New Typology." *Proceedings of Sinn und Bedeutung* 25. https://doi.org/10.18148/sub/2021.v25i0.963.

## CHAPTER 13

For a technical presentation of ideas that are similar to those of this chapter, see:

Schlenker, Philippe. 2020. "Gestural Grammar." *Natural Language & Linguistic Theory* 38:887–936.

An experimental study of plurals in homesigners appears in:

Coppola, M., E. Spaepen, and S. Goldin-Meadow. 2013. "Communicating about Quantity without a Language Model: Number Devices in Homesign Grammar." *Cognitive Psychology* 67:1–25.

## CHAPTER 14

An experimental study of several key points discussed in this chapter can be found in:

Tieu, Lyn, Philippe Schlenker, and Emmanuel Chemla. 2019. "Linguistic Inferences without Words." *Proceedings of the National Academy of Sciences* 116 (20): 9796–9801.

For a theoretical (and technical) presentation of the same topics, see:

Schlenker, Philippe. 2019. "Gestural Semantics: Replicating the Typology of Linguistic Inferences with Pro- and Post-speech Gestures." *Natural Language & Linguistic Theory* 37 (2): 735–784.


## CHAPTER 15

For a highly readable introduction to music cognition (in its experimental and formal aspects), see:

Patel, Aniruddh. 2008. *Music, Language, and the Brain*. Oxford: Oxford University Press.

For an introduction to music cognition from a formal perspective, see:

Jackendoff, Ray, and Fred Lerdahl. 2006. "The Capacity for Music: What Is It, and What's Special about It?" *Cognition* 100 (1): 33–72.

The following book was a seminal contribution to formal music cognition:

Lerdahl, Fred, and Ray Jackendoff. 1983. *A Generative Theory of Tonal Music*. Cambridge, MA: MIT Press.

Leonard Bernstein's early views on musical meaning can be found in the following book (first and foremost, this material was a TV series, which may be found online):

Bernstein, Leonard. 2005. *Young People's Concerts*. Foreword by Michael Tilson Thomas. Pompton Plains, NJ: Amadeus Press, ch. 1, "What Does Music Mean?" (Concert No. 1, CBS Television Network, original broadcast date January 18, 1958).

The ideas of this chapter are presented in condensed form in:

Schlenker, Philippe. 2017. "Outline of Music Semantics." *Music Perception: An Interdisciplinary Journal* 35 (1): 3–37. https://doi.org/10.1525/mp.2017.35.1.3.

For a longer presentation, see:

Schlenker, Philippe. 2019. "Prolegomena to Music Semantics." *Review of Philosophy & Psychology* 10 (1): 35–111. https://doi.org/10.1007/s13164-018-0384-5.

For a technical introduction to Western tonal harmony for musicians, see:

Payne, Dorothy, Stefan M. Kostka, and Byron Almén. 2018. *Tonal Harmony* (8th Edition). New York: McGraw-Hill.

A logical and philosophical introduction to the Liar's paradox can be found in chapter 1 of:

Simmons, Keith. 1993. *Universality and the Liar: An Essay on Truth and the Diagonal Argument.* Cambridge: Cambridge University Press.

One of the preeminent specialists of paradoxes, Roy T. Cook, has a blog about paradoxes:

Paradoxes and Puzzles with Roy T. Cook. https://blog.oup.com/category/series-columns /paradoxes-puzzles-roy-cook/.

## CHAPTER 17

The seminal paper on theories of truth for paradoxes is:

Kripke, Saul. 1975. "Outline of a Theory of Truth." *Journal of Philosophy* 72:690–716.

A technical but pedagogical presentation is included in chapter 3 of:

Simmons, Keith. 1993. *Universality and the Liar: An Essay on Truth and the Diagonal Argument.* Cambridge: Cambridge University Press.

The connection between Berry's paradox and Anselm's proof is made in the following technical paper:

Schlenker, Philippe. 2009. "Anselm's Argument and Berry's Paradox." *Noûs* 43 (2): 214–223.

## CONCLUSION

The connection between semantics and Super Semantics is discussed in:

Schlenker, Philippe. 2019. "What Is Super Semantics?" *Philosophical Perspectives* 32 (1): 365–453.

There are numerous further investigations of the linguistics/semantics of nonstandard objects.

Very interesting analyses of comics can be found in:

Cohn, Neil. 2013. *The Visual Language of Comics: Introduction to the Structure and Cognition of Sequential Images.* London: Bloomsbury.

McCloud, Scott. 1993. *Understanding Comics: The Invisible Art.* New York: Harper Collins.

A framework for picture semantics is developed in:

Greenberg, Gabriel. 2013. "Beyond Resemblance." *Philosophical Review* 122 (2): 215–287.

Pioneering work on the formal semantics of visual narratives is surveyed in:

Dorit Abusch, "Possible World Semantics for Pictures," in *The Wiley Blackwell Companion to Semantics*, ed. L. Matthewson, C. Meier, H. Rullmann, and T. E. Zimmermann (Oxford: Wiley, 2020), https://doi.org/10.1002/9781118788516.sem003.

The semantics and pragmatics of film is discussed in:

Cumming, Samuel, Gabriel Greenberg, and Rory Kelly. 2017. "Conventions of Viewpoint Coherence in Film." *Philosophers' Imprint* 17 (1): 1–29.

The syntax of a variety of dance (ballet) is discussed in:

Charnavel, Isabelle. 2019, "Steps toward a Universal Grammar of Dance: Local Grouping Structure in Basic Human Movement Perception." *Frontiers in Psychology* 10:1364.

The semantics of a different variety of dance (a narrative Indian dance) is discussed in:

Patel-Grosz, Pritty, Patrick Georg Grosz, Tejaswinee Kelkar, and Alexander Refsum Jensenius. 2018. "Coreference and Disjoint Reference in the Semantics of Narrative Dance." In *Proceedings of Sinn und Bedeutung* 22 (2): 199–216.

## APPENDIX

The presentation given in the appendix is particularly indebted to the works of Halle, Pinker, Sandler, and Lillo-Martin and Sandler.

On spoken language phonology, the following general audience introduction was written by one of pioneers of contemporary linguistics, Morris Halle:

Morris, Halle. 1978. "Knowledge Unlearned and Untaught: What Speakers Know about the Sounds of Their Language." Reprinted in: Halle, Morris: 2013, *From Memory to Speech and Back: Papers on Phonetics and Phonology 1954—2002*, Berlin: De Gruyter Mouton.

On sign language phonology, one may consult the following introduction:

Sandler, Wendy. 2012. "The Phonological Organization of Sign Languages." *Language and Linguistics Compass* 6 (3): 162–182.

The following book offers an excellent introduction to linguistics as practiced in the 1990s (see also the other works listed at the beginning of this section):

Pinker, Steven. 1994. *The Language Instinct*. New York: Harper Perennial Modern Classics.

On morphology (and further aspects of linguistics), the following is a highly readable general audience introduction:

Pinker, Steven. 1999. *Words and Rules: The Ingredients of Language*. New York: Basic Books.

On sign languages, the following are, respectively, a recent introductory textbook and an advanced textbook:

Hill, Joseph C., Diane C. Lillo-Martin, and Sandra K. Wood. 2018. *Sign Languages: Structures and Contexts*. London: Routledge.

Sandler, Wendy, and Diane Lillo-Martin. 2006. *Sign Language and Linguistic Universals*. Cambridge: Cambridge University Press.

# Notes

## INTRODUCTION

1. I adopt the common convention of using the capitalized word *Deaf* to refer to deaf people who identify as members of a community of deaf people (in particular through sign language). Without a capital, *deaf* refers to a person's audiological status.

2. Taylor Lorenz, Erin Griffith, and Mike Isaac, "We Live in Zoom Now," *New York Times*, March 17, 2020, https://www.nytimes.com/2020/03/17/style/zoom-parties-coronavirus-memes.html; Shira Springer, "For Some, Zoom Bar and Bat Mitzvahs Highlight 'Most Meaningful and Memorable Moments,'" *NPR*, May 16, 2000, https://www.npr.org/2020/05/16/856819558/for-some-zoom-bar-and-bat-mitzvahs-highlight-most-meaningful-and-memorable-momen.

3. Steven Pinker, *The Language Instinct* (New York: Harper Perennial Modern Classics, 1994).

## CHAPTER 1: MEANING IN THE WILD

1. I am indebted to Guillaume Dezecache for this anecdote.

2. This comparison is used in Luigi Luca Cavalli-Sforza and Francesco Cavalli-Sforza, *The Great Human Diasporas: The History of Diversity and Evolution* (New York: Addison-Wesley, 1995).

3. R. M. Seyfarth, D. L. Cheney, and P. Marler, "Monkey Responses to Three Different Alarm Calls: Evidence of Predator Classification and Semantic Communication," *Science* 210 (1980): 801–803.

4. K. Zuberbühler, Cheney, and R.M. Seyfarth, "Conceptual Semantics in a Nonhuman Primate," *Journal of Comparative Psychology* 113, no. 1 (1999): 33–42.

5. A. Lemasson, K. Ouattara, E. J. Petit, and K. Zuberbühler, "Social Learning of Vocal Structure in a Nonhuman Primate?" *BMC Evolutionary Biology* 11, no. 362 (December 2011), https://doi.org/10.1186/1471-2148-11-362.

6. See page 16 of H. Bouchet, M. Laporte, A. Candiotti, and A. Lemasson, "Flexibilité vocale sous influences sociales chez les primates non-humains," *Revue de Primatologie* 5 (2013),

document 53, http://journals.openedition.org/primatologie/1794, https://doi.org/10.4000/primatologie.1794.

7. W. D. Hopkins, J. Taglialatela, and D. A. Leavens, "Chimpanzees Differentially Produce Novel Vocalizations to Capture the Attention of a Human," *Animal Behaviour* 73 (2007): 281–286.

8. C. Cäsar, K. Zuberbühler, R. J. Young, and R. W. Byrne, "Titi Monkey Call Sequences Vary with Predator Location and Type," *Biology Letters* 9 (2013): 20130535.

9. Here my discussion mirrors the following article: P. Schlenker, E. Chemla, C. Cäsar, R. Ryder, and K. Zuberbühler, "Titi Semantics: Context and Meaning in Titi Monkey Call Sequence," *Natural Language & Linguistic Theory* 35, no. 1 (2016): 271–298, https://doi.org/10.1007/s11049-016-9337-9.

10. A word of caution is in order: this specific pattern—a single A call followed by a series of B-calls—was not replicated in later research, so this is currently a point of debate.

11. Here my discussion mirrors the following article, which in turn builds (among others) on Ouattara's dissertation and on Kate Arnold's and Sumir Keenan's work: P. Schlenker, E. Chemla, K. Arnold, A. Lemasson, K. Ouattara, S. Keenan, C. Stephan, R. Ryder, and K. Zuberbühler, "Monkey Semantics: Two 'Dialects' of Campbell's Monkey Alarm Calls," *Linguistics & Philosophy* 37, no. 6 (2014): 439–501, https://doi.org/10.1007/s10988-014-9155-7.

12. One might initially think that *hok-oo* ('weak non-ground alert') is more informative than *krak-oo* ('weak alert'). But on closer inspection this is not so: If non-ground alerts tend to be rather serious (e.g., because they involve raptors), something may count as 'weak' for a non-ground alert while still counting as 'serious' relative to alerts in general. (By the same logic in a very different domain, something may be a 'cheap diamond' without counting as a 'cheap object.')

13. K. Zuberbühler, "A Syntactic Rule in Forest Monkey Communication," *Animal Behaviour* 63 (2002), 10.1016/anbe.2001.1914.

14. H. Rainey, K. Zuberbühler and P. Slater, "Hornbills Can Distinguish between Primate Alarm Calls," *Folia Primatologica*, 74 (2003): 214.

15. See section 7.3 of P. Schlenker, E. Chemla, A. Schel, J. Fuller, J.-.P Gautier, J. Kuhn, D. Veselinovic, K. Arnold, C. Cäsar, S. Keenan, A. Lemasson, K. Ouattara, R. Ryder, and K. Zuberbühler, "Formal Monkey Linguistics," *Theoretical Linguistics* 42, no. 1–2 (2016): 1–90, https://doi.org/10.1515/tl-2016-0001.

16. See, for instance: Jean-Pierre Gautier, "Interspecific Affinities among Guenons as Deduced from Vocalizations," in *A Primate Radiation—Evolutionary Radiation of the African Guenons*, ed. A. Gautier-Hion, F. Bourlière, J. P. Gautier, and J. Kingdon (Cambridge: Cambridge University Press, 1988), 194–226.

17. C. Crockford, R. M. Wittig, R. Mundry, and K. Zuberbühler, "Wild Chimpanzees Inform Ignorant Group Members of Danger," *Current Biology* 22, no. 2 (2012): 142–146.

18. R. W. Byrne, E. Cartmill, E. Genty, K. E. Graham, C. Hobaiter, and J. Tanner, "Great Ape Gestures: Intentional Communication with a Rich Set of Innate Signals," *Animal Cognition* 20, no. 4 (2017): 755–769.

19. See p. 756 of R. W. Byrne, E. Cartmill, E. Genty, K. E. Graham, C. Hobaiter, and J. Tanner, "Great Ape Gestures: Intentional Communication with a Rich Set of Innate Signals," *Animal Cognition* 20, no. 4 (2017): 755–769.

20. K. C. Kirchhofer, F. Zimmermann, J. Kaminski, and M. Tomasello, "Dogs (*Canis* familiaris), But Not Chimpanzees (Pan troglodytes), Understand Imperative Pointing," *PLoS ONE* 7, no. 2 (2012): e30913, https://doi.org/10.1371/journal.pone.0030913.

21. M. Bohn, J. Call, and M. Tomasello, "Comprehension of Iconic Gestures by Chimpanzees and Human Children," *Journal of Experimental Child Psychology* 142 (2016): 1–17, https://doi.org/10.1016/j.jecp.2015.09.001.

22. R. M. Yerkes, *Chimpanzees: A Laboratory Colony* (New Haven: Yale University Press, 1943), 192.

23. Emily Genty and Klaus Zuberbühler, "Spatial Reference in a Bonobo Gesture," *Current Biology* 24, no. 14 (2014): 1601–1605.

24. See p. 16 of D. Leavens and K. Bard, "Environmental Influences on Joint Attention in Great Apes: Implications for Human Cognition," *Journal of Cognitive Education and Psychology* 10, no. 1 (2011): 9–31, https://doi.org/10.1891/1945-8959.10.1.9.

25. P. Douglas and L. Moscovice, "Pointing and Pantomime in Wild Apes? Female Bonobos Use Referential and Iconic Gestures to Request Genito-Gential Rubbing," *Scientific Reports* 5 (2015): 13999, https://doi.org/10.1038/srep13999.

26. K. E. Graham, C. Hobaiter, J. Ounsley, T. Furuichi, and R. W. Byrne, "Bonobo and chimpanzee gestures overlap extensively in meaning," *PLoS Biology* 16, no. 2 (2018): e2004825, https://doi.org/10.1371/journal.pbio.2004825.

27. R. W. Byrne, E. Cartmill, E. Genty, K. E. Graham, C. Hobaiter, and J. Tanner, "Great Ape Gestures: Intentional Communication with a Rich Set of Innate Signals," *Animal Cognition* 20, no. 4 (2017): 755–769.

28. Verena Kersken, Juan-Carlos Gómez, Ulf Liszkowski, Adrian Soldati, and Catherine Hobaiter, "A Gestural Repertoire of 1- to 2-Year-Old Human Children: In Search of the Ape Gestures," *Animal Cognition* 22 (2018): 577–595.

## CHAPTER 2: VISIBLE LOGIC: SIGN LANGUAGE AND PRONOUNS

1. Wayne H. Smith, "Taiwan Sign Language Research: An Historical Overview," *Language and Linguistics* 6, no. 2 (2005): 187–215; Wikipedia, "Taiwan Sign Language," last modified November 7, 2021, 07:05 UTC, https://en.wikipedia.org/wiki/Taiwan_Sign_Language.

2. Emily Shaw and Yves Delaporte, *A Historical and Etymological Dictionary of American Sign Language* (Washington, DC: Gallaudet University Press, 2015), x.

3. Pierre Desloges, *Observations d'un sourd et muèt sur un cours élémentaire d'éducation des sourds et muèts publié en 1779 par M. l'Abbé Deshamps, Chapelain de l'Église d'Orléans* (1779).

4. Shaw and Delaporte, *A Historical and Etymological Dictionary of American Sign Language*.

5. Yves Delaporte, *Dictionnaire étymologique et historique de la langue des signes française. Origine et évolution de 1200 signes* (Paris: Editions du Fox, 2007), 17.

6. Margret A. Winzer, *The History of Special Education: From Isolation to Integration* (Washington, DC: Gallaudet University Press, 1993).

7. Nora Ellen Groce, *Everyone Here Spoke Sign Language: Hereditary Deafness on Martha's Vineyard* (Cambridge, MA: Harvard University Press, 1985).

8. Shaw and Delaporte, *A Historical and Etymological Dictionary of American Sign Language*, xi.

9. Harlan Lane, *When the Mind Hears: A History of the Deaf* (New York: Vintage, 1989).

10. Donna Jo Napoli, Nancy K. Mellon, John K. Niparko, Christian Rathmann, Gaurav Mathur, Tom Humphries, Theresa Handley, Sasha Scambler, and John D. Lantos, "Should All Deaf Children Learn Sign Language?" *Pediatrics* 136, no. 1 (2015): 170–176; Iva Hrastinski and Ronnie B. Wilbur, "Academic Achievement of Deaf and Hard-of-Hearing Students in an ASL/English Bilingual Program," *Journal of Deaf Studies and Deaf Education* 21 (2016): 156–170.

11. Shaw and Delaporte, *A Historical and Etymological Dictionary of American Sign Language*, xiii.

12. Carlo Cecchetto, Carlo Geraci, and Sandro Zucchi, "Strategies of Relativization in Italian Sign Language," *Natural Language & Linguistic Theory* 24, no. 4 (2006): 945.

13. Ann Senghas, Sotaro Kita, and Asli Özyürek, "Children Creating Core Properties of Language: Evidence from an Emerging Sign Language in Nicaragua," *Science* 305, no. 5691 (2004): 1779–1782.

14. Mairéad MacSweeney, Cheryl M. Capek, Ruth Campbell, and Bencie Woll, "The Signing Brain: The Neurobiology of Sign Language," *Trends in the Cognitive Sciences* 12, no. 11 (2008): 432.

15. Mark C. Baker, *Lexical Categories: Verbs, Nouns and Adjectives* (Cambridge: Cambridge University Press, 2003).

16. Pointing toward people to refer to them doesn't quite work in virtual meetings on Zoom, for instance. One and the same person may appear in different parts of the screen for different participants, so pointing could be very misleading. Under such circumstances, signers may make greater use of proper names to avoid ambiguities.

17. For example, see C.-T. James Huang, "Remarks on the Status of the Null Object," in *Principles and Parameters in Comparative Grammar*, ed. R. Freidin (Cambridge, MA: MIT Press, 1991), 56–76.

18. See, for instance, Diane Lillo-Martin, *Universal Grammar and American Sign Language: Setting the Null Argument Parameters* (Dordrecht: Kluwer, 1991), 63; Jeremy Kuhn, "Discourse Anaphora—Theoretical Perspectives," in *The Routledge Handbook of Theoretical and Experimental Sign Language Research*, ed. Josep Quer, Roland Pfau, and Annika Herrmann (London: Routledge, 2021), 458–479, example (2).

19. See, for instance, Elena Koulidobrova, "SELF: Intensifier and 'Long Distance' Effects in American Sign Language (ASL)" (unpublished manuscript, University of Connecticut, 2011). An earlier reference is Ronnie Wilbur, "Focus and Specificity in ASL Structures Containing *SELF*" (presentation, Linguistic Society of America Annual Meeting, San Diego, CA, January 1996).

20. Susanne Fuchs, Egor Savin, Stephanie Solt, Cornelia Ebert, and Manfred Krifka, "Antonym Adjective Pairs and Prosodic Iconicity: Evidence from Letter Replications in an English Blogger Corpus," *Linguistics Vanguard* 5, no. 1 (2019).

21. Philippe Schlenker, "Visible Meaning: Sign Language and the Foundations of Semantics," *Theoretical Linguistics* 44, no. 3–4 (2018): 123–208.

22. *Detective L*, episode 11, starring Bai Yu, You Jing Ru, Ji Chen, He Yong Sheng, premiered May 5, 2019, video, 15:26, https://www.youtube.com/watch?v=VvfcRVtC_jY&t=15m26s.

23. Philippe Schlenker, "Sign Language and the Foundations of Anaphora," *Annual Review of Linguistics* 3 (2017): 149–177.

24. Philippe Schlenker, Jonathan Lamberton, and Mirko Santoro, "Iconic Variables," *Linguistics & Philosophy* 36, no. 2 (2013): 91–149.

## CHAPTER 3: ME, ME, ME! PERSPECTIVES IN LANGUAGE

1. For a brief synthesis on Oedipus in myth and literature, see Wikipedia, "Oedipus," last modified November 10, 2021, 09:18 UTC, https://en.wikipedia.org/wiki/Oedipus.

2. One notable source (which contains further references) is David K. Lewis, "Attitudes De Dicto and De Se," *Philosophical Review* 88, no. 4 (1979): 513–543.

3. One can sometimes disambiguate by using two pronouns *(he himself)* rather than one *(he)*. Thus *Rudolf Lingens thinks that he himself is locked in the Harvard library* typically attributes to Lingens a first-person thought. But *he himself* does not invariably carry this function, as noted by Hazel Pearson ("He Himself and I," *Snippets*, 31 (2017): 20–21). She considers a story in which John, unaware that he is looking in a mirror, thinks 'that guy is an idiot.' Bill says: *I don't understand the story. Who does John think is an idiot?* Ann replies: *John thinks that he himself is an idiot.* Here Ann's use of *he himself* just serves to answer the question, without attributing to John a first-person thought.

4. Héctor-Neri Castañeda, "'He': A Study in the Logic of Self-Consciousness," *Ratio* 8 (1966): 130–157.

5. George N. Clements, "The Logophoric Pronoun in Ewe: Its Role in Discourse," *Journal of West African Languages* 10 (1975): 141–177; Hazel Pearson, "The Interpretation of the Logophoric Pronoun in Ewe," *Natural Language Semantics* 23, no. 2 (2015): 77–118; Abigail Anne Bimpeh, "Default De Se: The Interpretation of the Ewe Logophor," in *Proceedings of TripleA 5: Fieldwork Perspectives on the Semantics of African, Asian and Austronesian Languages,* ed. M. Ryan Bochnak, Miriam Butt, Erlinde Meertens, Mark-Matthias Zymla (Universitätsbibliothek Tübingen, 2019). Here I follow the description of the data by Bimpeh rather than by Pearson. (The French version of the term 'logophoric pronoun' was coined by Claude Hagège, "Les Pronoms logophoriques," *Bulletin de la Société de Linguistique de Paris,* 69 [1974]: 287–310.)

6. Larry M. Hyman and Bernard Comrie, "Logophoric Reference in Gokana," *Journal of African Languages and Linguistics* 3, no. 1 (1981): 19–37.

7. Clements, "The Logophoric Pronoun in Ewe."

8. While there is a large literature on this topic, two particularly important sources for semantics are Lewis, "Attitudes De Dicto and De Se," and Gennaro Chierchia, "Anaphora and Attitudes 'De Se,'" in *Semantics and Contextual Expressions,* ed. R. Bartsch, J. van Benthem, and P. van Emde Boas (Amsterdam: Kluwer/Reidel, 1989), 1–31.

9. "Trump's 'I Love WikiLeaks' Praise Fades as U.S. Charges Julian Assange," *Japan Times,* April 12, 2019, https://www.japantimes.co.jp/news/2019/04/12/world/crime-legal-world/u-s-charges-u-k-arrested-wikileaks-founder-julian-assange-hacking-conspiracy-chelsea-manning/#.XL23L5MzaRs; Mark Hosenball, "Update 5: U.S. Charges WikiLeaks' Assange with Hacking Conspiracy with Manning," Reuters, April 11, 2019, https://www.reuters.com/article/ecuador-assange-usa/update-1-u-s-charges-wikileaks-founder-assange-with-conspiracy-idUSL1N21T0IL.

10. Cleve R. Wootson Jr., "Trump Tweets 'Covfefe,' Inspiring a Semi-Comedic Act of Congress," *Washington Post,* May 31, 2017, https://www.washingtonpost.com/news/the-fix/wp/2017/05/31/trump-tweets-covfefe-inspiring-a-semi-comedic-act-of-congress/.

11. Pranav Anand and Andrews Nevins, "Shifty Operators in Changing Contexts," in *Proceedings of Semantics and Linguistic Theory* (= SALT) XIV, ed. K. Watanabe and R. B. Young (Ithaca, NY: CLC Publications, 2004), 20–37.

12. Pranav Anand, "De De Se" (PhD diss., MIT, Cambridge, MA, 2006).

13. Anand and Nevins, "Shifty Operators in Changing Contexts."

14. Anand, "De Se Se."

15. Diane Lillo-Martin, "Utterance Reports and Constructed Action," in *Sign Language—An International Handbook,* ed. R. Pfau, M. Steinbach, and B. Woll (Berlin: De Gruyter Mouton, 2012), 365–387.

16. Philippe Schlenker, "Super Monsters I: Attitude and Action Role Shift in Sign Language," *Semantics & Pragmatics* 10 (2017); Philippe Schlenker, "Super Monsters II: Role Shift,

Iconicity and Quotation in Sign Language," *Semantics & Pragmatics* 10 (2017); Kathryn Davidson, "Quotation, Demonstration, and Iconicity," *Linguistics & Philosophy* 38, no. 6 (2015): 477–520, https://doi.org/10.1007/s10988-015-9180-1.

## CHAPTER 4: NOUNS AND VERBS: OBJECTS AND EVENTS

1. Here and throughout, I restrict attention for simplicity to cases in which nominal constructions refer to objects and verbal constructions refer to events/situations. But there are cases in which the distinction is blurred, as in *Ann's arrival*, which might be taken to refer to whatever *Ann arrived* refers to: this might be a case in which a nominal expression refers to events. My main point—namely, that the nominal domain and the verbal domain display far-reaching grammatical and semantic analogies—is not directly affected by this complication.

2. For a summary, see Mark Joseph Stern, "Neil Gorsuch's Persnickety Libertarianism Gave Immigrants a Win at the Supreme Court," *Slate*, April 29, 2021, https://slate.com /news-and-politics/2021/04/gorsuch-libertarian-textualist-immigrant-rights.html. The majority opinion, delivered by Justice Neil Gorsuch, can be found in "Niz-Chavez v. Garland, Attorney General, Certiorari to the United States Court of Appeals for the Sixth Circuit," No. 19–863, argued November 9, 2020, decided April 29, 2021, https://www.supremecourt .gov/opinions/20pdf/19-863_6jgm.pdf. Justice Brett Kavanaugh filed a minority opinion, arguing in particular that some count nouns, such as *a manuscript* or *a job application*, can refer to things that come in parts. Both sides agreed that context matters. (I am indebted to Benjamin Spector for a reference to the Niz-Chavez case.)

3. David G. Nash, *Topics in Warlpiri Grammar* (New York: Garland, 1986), cited in R. Pfau and M. Steinbach, "Pluralization in Sign and in Speech: A Cross-Modal Typological Study," *Linguistic Typology* 10 (2006): 135–182.

4. On American Sign Language plurals, see Philippe Schlenker and Jonathan Lamberton, "Iconic Plurality," *Linguistics & Philosophy* 42, no. 1 (2019): 45–108, https://doi.org/10.1007 /s10988-018-9236-0.

5. Suzi Lima, "All Notional Mass Nouns Are Count Nouns in Yudja," *Proceedings of Semantics and Linguistic Theory* (= SALT) XXIV (2014): 534–554.

6. Jeremy Kuhn and Valentina Aristodemo, "Pluractionality, Iconicity, and Scope in French Sign Language," *Semantics & Pragmatics* 10, no. 6 (2017), http://dx.doi.org/10.3765 /sp.10.6, citing Paul Newman, "Pluractional Verbs: An Overview," in *Verbal Plurality and Distributivity*, ed. Patricia Cabredo Hofherr and Brenda Laca (Berlin: De Gruyter Mouton, 2012), 185, 209, http://dx.doi.org/10.1515/9783110293500.185.

7. Kuhn and Aristodemo, "Pluractionality, Iconicity, and Scope in French Sign Language."

8. Susan Rothstein, *Structuring Events: A Study in the Semantics of Lexical Aspect* (Malden, MA: Blackwell, 2004).

9. Ronnie B. Wilbur, "Representations of Telicity in ASL," *Chicago Linguistic Society* 39 (2003): 354–368.

10. Philippe Schlenker, "Visible Meaning: Sign Language and the Foundations of Semantics," *Theoretical Linguistics* 44, no. 3–4 (2018): 123–208.

11. Brent Strickland, Carlo Geraci, Emmanuel Chemla, Philippe Schlenker, Meltem Kelepir, and Roland Pfau, "Event Representations Constrain the Structure of Language: Sign Language as a Window into Universally Accessible Linguistic Biases," *Proceedings of the National Academy of Sciences* 112, no. 19 (2015): 5968–5973.

12. Inspired by the connection between count/mass and telic/atelic, a team of linguists and psychologists did something even more devious. They showed (non-signing) subjects the same type of verbal signs—for instance, *RUN* (atelic, no sharp boundaries) and *DECIDE* (telic, sharp boundaries). But instead of giving them a choice between two verbal meanings, as in the text, they offered two nominal meanings, a count one and a mass one. For instance: Does this mean *coin* (count) or *rain* (mass)? From the perspective of sign language, either answer was wrong! But for telic verbs, which came with a boundary in their realization, subjects preferred the count meaning, while for atelic verbs, they preferred the mass meaning. In other words, the intuitive mapping rules that non-signers used drew a connection between count and telic and between mass and atelic. See Jeremy Kuhn, Carlo Geraci, Philippe Schlenker, and Brent Strickland, "Boundaries in Space and Time: Iconic Biases across Modalities," *Cognition* 210 (2021): 104596.

13. Donald Davidson, "The Logical Form of Action Sentences," in *The Logic of Decision and Action*, ed. Nicholas Rescher (Pittsburgh: University of Pittsburgh Press, 1967); Terence Parsons, *Events in the Semantics of English: A Study in Subatomic Semantics* (Cambridge, MA: MIT Press, 1990).

## CHAPTER 5: BEYOND THE HERE AND NOW I: FROM OBJECTS TO SITUATIONS

1. In chapter 3 (section 3.2), I wrote that "a possible world, a way things are, is entirely specific: It determines the truth value of every imaginable sentence." Situations can be thought of as parts of possible worlds; conversely, a possible world may be defined as a maximally large situation. Since situations are more discriminating than possible worlds (because they are smaller), nothing will be lost by talking about situations rather than possible worlds (on the other hand, a situation may not be entirely specific, as it is does not provide information about other situations in the same possible world).

2. We discussed a similar example to the same effect in chapter 1 (section 1.5): *It is possible, and in fact even certain, that Russia influenced the 2016 election.*

3. Barbara H. Partee, "Some Structural Analogies between Tenses and Pronouns in English," *Journal of Philosophy* 70, no. 18 (1973): 601–609.

4. Matthew Stone, "The Anaphoric Parallel between Modality and Tense" (University of Pennsylvania Department of Computer and Information Science Technical Report No. MS-CIS-97-09, 1997).

5. Here I follow the version of the site allmusical.com (retrieved on January 11, 2022), https://www.allmusicals.com/lyrics/fiddierontheroof/ifiwerearichman.htm.

6. Philippe Schlenker, "Temporal and Modal Anaphora in Sign Language (ASL)," *Natural Language & Linguistic Theory* 31, no. 1 (2013): 207–234.

7. For a discussion of timelines in Chinese Sign Language, see Hao Lin, Jeremy Kuhn, Huan Sheng, and Philippe Schlenker, "Timelines and Temporal Pointing in Chinese Sign Language," *Glossa: A Journal of General Linguistics* 6, no. 1 (2021), https://doi.org/10.16995/glossa .5836. See also https://www.youtube.com/playlist?list=PLs9JnJPtVhZOpd73x_do8nt6 UELdLeXz8. (Thanks are extended to Hao Lin for this discussion.)

## CHAPTER 6: BEYOND THE HERE AND NOW II: DESCRIBING AND CLASSIFYING OBJECTS AND SITUATIONS

1. Conditionals analyzed in this way are called *strict conditionals*. On this view, *if p, q* (sometimes written as $p \rightarrow q$) is true in a situation s just in case for every situation s′ accessible from s, whenever p is true in s′, q is also true in s′ (the notion of 'accessibility' corresponds to the 'salient domain' discussed in the text). An older and less plausible view was that natural language conditionals are *material conditionals*. On this view, *if p, q* (sometimes written as $p \Rightarrow q$) is true in a situation s just in case p is false in s or q is true in s (or both). This analysis was later taken to be implausible because it makes all conditionals true as soon as the *if*-clause is false—which predicts, absurdly, that *if there had been a nuclear war in 1962, nobody would have died* has to be true (because there was in fact no nuclear war in 1962). We won't discuss the material conditional analysis in this book.

2. Robert Stalnaker, "A Theory of Conditionals," in *Studies in Logical Theory: American Philosophical Quarterly Monograph 2*, ed. Nicholas Rescher (Oxford: Blackwell, 1968), 98–112.

3. Philippe Schlenker, "Conditionals as Definite Descriptions (A Referential Analysis)," *Research on Language and Computation* 2 (2004): 417–462.

4. Wikipedia, "Bo (Dog)," last modified November 18, 2021, 01:24 UTC, https://en.wikipedia .org/wiki/Bo_(dog).

5. This version is from Paul Waldman, "The True Grit of Hillary Clinton," *The Week*, June 9, 2016, https://theweek.com/articles/628601/true-grit-hillary-clinton. For a version in which Hillary and Bill Clinton are replaced with Michelle and Barack Obama, respectively, see "Funny Story: The Obamas Go to Dinner," *HuffPost*, last updated December 6, 2017, https://www.huffpost.com/entry/funny-story-the-obamas-go_n_884146.

6. Rajesh Bhatt and Roumyana Pancheva, "Conditionals," in *The Blackwell Companion to Syntax*, vol. I, ed. Martin Everaert and Henk van Riemsdijk (Oxford: Blackwell, 2006), 638–687.

7. I am simplifying a bit. *The man* is really *which man*, but the latter construction behaves like a definite description.

8.    Philippe Schlenker, "Ontological Symmetry in Language: A Brief Manifesto," *Mind & Language* 21, no. 4 (2006): 504–539.

9.    Charles F. Hockett, "What Algonquian Is Really Like," *International Journal of American Linguistics* 32 (1966): 59–73.

10.   Some researchers treat *had* in Yiddish *I have had said* (= *ix hob gehat gezogt*) as an adverb rather than as a past participle. See, for instance, Elaine Gold, "Aspect, Tense and the Lexicon: Expression of Time in Yiddish" (PhD diss., University of Toronto, 1999), 133.

11.   Johann Wolfgang von Goethe, *Wilhelm Meister's Apprenticeship*, 5th book, ch. 12.

12.   Philippe Schlenker, "Conditionals as Definite Descriptions (A Referential Analysis)," *Research on Language and Computation* 2 (2004): 417–462.

13.   See, for instance, Toshiyuki Ogihara and Yael Sharvit, "Embedded Tenses," in *Handbook of Tense and Aspect*, ed. R. Binnick (Oxford: Oxford University Press, 2012), 638–668; and (for a Russian example) Philippe Schlenker, "A Plea for Monsters," *Linguistics & Philosophy* 26 (2003): 29–120.

14.   For the similarity between the Konjunktiv I and the Ewe logophoric pronoun (discussed in chapter 3, section 3.3), see Schlenker, "A Plea for Monsters," section 6.2.

## CHAPTER 7: LOGIC MACHINE I: PREDICATE LOGIC

1.    Margaret A. Boden, *Mind as Machine: A History of Cognitive Science*, 2 vols. (Oxford: Oxford University Press, 2006), 781.

2.    Barbara H. Partee, "Formal Semantics: Origins, Issues, Early Impact," *Baltic International Yearbook of Cognition, Logic and Communication* 6 (2011): 13, 23. On Richard Montague, see also Ivano Caponigro's website and ongoing work toward a biography: https://www.richardmontague.com/.

3.    Partee, "Formal Semantics," 25.

4.    The joke appears in the 1930 Marx Brothers film *Animal Crackers*. See Wikipedia, "Animal Crackers," https://en.wikipedia.org/wiki/Animal_Crackers_(1930_film); 1linequotes, November 23, 2012, YouTube, 0:07, https://www.youtube.com/watch?v=GC73XxZDtpg.

5.    Here and elsewhere, I often use the term *logic* to refer to a system with sophisticated inferential rules. There is a more narrow notion on which logical expressions are ones whose semantic effect does not depend on empirical facts. See, for instance, Alfred Tarski, "What Are Logical Notions?" *History and Philosophy of Logic* 7 (1986): 143–154.

6.    Here I am cutting some corners in the interest of simplicity. A key innovation of semantics (originating with the Polish logician Alfred Tarski in the 1930s) was a procedure that made precise the underlined part in *for every object, if we call it x, the statement x ≥ 0 is true*. The procedure involved assignment functions, which were so-called because they assigned objects to variables and in effect treated them as temporary names of these objects. If $x$ is a temporary name of 0 (written as x → 0), then $x > 0$ is false. On the other hand, if $x$ is a

temporary name of 1 (written as x → 1), then *x > 0* is true. An assignment function assigned a value to every variable (e.g., x → 1, y → 0, z → 2, etc.). The first lines of the definition (pertaining to to *not A*, *(A and B)*, *(A or B)*) should thus be understood as specifying the truth values of formulas *relative to an assignment function*, as in (i), where I have added the boldfaced parts:

(i)  If *x* is any variable, if *A* and *B* are formulas, and **if f is an assignment function**, *not A* is true **relative to f** just in case *A* is false **relative to f**.
    *(A and B)* is true **relative to f** just in case *A* is true **relative to f** and *B* is true **relative to f**.
    *(A or B)* is true **relative to f** just in case *A* is true **relative to f** or *B* is true **relative to f** or both.

The rules for quantifiers consider various possible denotations for the variable *x* (that's why I called it a *temporary* name). So, starting from an assignment function f (e.g., x → 1, y → 0, z → 2, . . . as above), we must make reference to other assignment functions that are identical to f except that they assign other values to x (thus keeping constant the parts y → 0, z → 2, . . .). For instance, we can write as f[x → 0] the function that is just like f except that it treats *x* as a temporary name of 0 rather than of 1 (so this function is **x → 0**, y → 0, z → 2, . . .), and we can write as f[x → 2] the function that is just like f except that it treats *x* as a temporary name of 2 rather than of 1 (this is now the function **x → 2**, y → 0, z → 2, . . .). The last lines of the definition (pertaining to ∀*x A*, ∃*x A*) should be understood as in (ii):

(ii)  ∀*x A* is true **relative to f** just in case for every object d, *A* is true **relative to f[x → d]**.
    ∃*x A* is true **relative to f** just in case for at least one object d, *A* is true **relative to f[x → d]**.

for every object d, *if we modify f so that x names d* (i.e., 'if we call the object d *x*'), *A* is true relative to this modified assignment function.

## CHAPTER 8: LOGIC MACHINE II: ENGLISH AS A FORMAL LANGUAGE

1.  This has become a folklore example—usually unsourced, alas. This version is cited by Richard Lederer in *Anguished English* (Charleston: Wyrick, 1987), 65. A related case is cited by Steven Pinker in *The Language Instinct* (New York, NY: Harper Perennial Modern Classics, 1994), 210: "The judge sentenced the killer to die in the electric chair for the second time."

2.  See Marrey Bikes, Facebook, January 17, 2020, https://www.facebook.com/marreybikes/photos/a.236118565766/10157622412135767/?type=3&theater.

## CHAPTER 9: LOGIC MACHINE III: THE EXPRESSIVE POWER OF HUMAN LANGUAGE

1.  Nicholas Kristof and Stuart A. Thompson, "How Much Worse the Coronavirus Could Get," *New York Times*, March 13, 2020, https://www.nytimes.com/interactive/2020/03/13/opinion/coronavirus-trump-response.html.

2. Multiple references exist for this joke, especially in syntax and semantics homework. This particular version was cited by Suzana Fong in MIT slides, December 7, 2018.

3. See for instance Øystein Linnebo, "Plural Quantification," *The Stanford Encyclopedia of Philosophy* (Summer 2017 Edition), Edward N. Zalta (ed.), https://plato.stanford.edu/archives/sum2017/entries/plural-quant/, footnote 2.

4. For references on the logical properties of natural language quantifiers, see for instance: Westerståhl, Dag, "Generalized Quantifiers," *The Stanford Encyclopedia of Philosophy* (Winter 2019 Edition), Edward N. Zalta (ed.), https://plato.stanford.edu/archives/win2019/entries/generalized-quantifiers/.

5. For related Hungarian examples, see chapter 8 in Victoria A. Fromkin, ed., *Linguistics: An Introduction to Linguistic Theory* (Malden, MA: Wiley-Blackwell, 2001). I am indebted to Anna Szabolcsi and Zoltán Gendler Szabó for this discussion.

6. For a right-handed signer, loci are alphabetized from right to left (conventions would be reversed for a left-handed signer). So, the *a* on *Obama$_a$* indicates that it is signed on the (right-handed) signer's right, while the *b* on *Sarkozy$_b$* indicates that it is signed on the signer's left.

7. The ASL example is, for instance, cited in Philippe Schlenker, "Visible Meaning: Sign Language and the Foundations of Semantics," *Theoretical Linguistics* 44, no. 3–4 (2018): 123–208.

8. The expression *logic in grammar* is used by Gennaro Chierchia, one of the leading specialists of the semantics/grammar interaction; see Gennaro Chierchia, *Logic in Grammar: Polarity, Free Choice, and Intervention* (Cambridge, MA: MIT Press, 2013).

9. To be a bit more precise, *has been to Paris* is more informative than *has been to France* in the following sense (which involves what is called 'generalized entailment'): *For every x, if x has been to Paris, then x has been to France* (but not conversely). So, starting from *every [student who ___] speaks good French*, replacing ___ with a more informative expression (e.g., replacing *has been to France* with *has been to Paris*) yields a less informative result: the environment in which ___ appears reverses informativity (i.e., entailment) relations.

10. See, in particular, Emmanuel Chemla, Vincent Homer, and Daniel Rothschild, "Modularity and Intuitions in Formal Semantics: The Case of Polarity Items," *Linguistics & Philosophy* 34 (2011): 537–570; and also Milica Denić, Vincent Homer, Daniel Rothschild, and Emmanuel Chemla, "The Influence of Polarity Items on Inferential Judgments," *Cognition* 215 (2021): 104791.

**CHAPTER 10: NOT QUITE SAYING IT: FOCUS AND IMPLICATURES**

1. George Edward Moore, "A Reply to My Critics," in *The Philosophy of G. E. Moore*, ed. P. A. Schilpp (Evanston, IL: Northwestern University Press, 1942), 535–677.

2. For a logical discussion, see, for instance, Adam Rieger, "Moore's Paradox, Introspection and Doxastic Logic," *Thought: A Journal of Philosophy* 4, no. 4 (2015): 215–227.

3. This example has been discussed with minor variations for dozens of years. One source is Andrew Matthews, *Making Friends* (New York: Being Happy/PSS: Price Stern Sloan, 1991).

4. B. K. Dichter, J. D. Breshears, M. K. Leonard, and E. F. Chang, "The Control of Vocal Pitch in Human Laryngeal Motor Cortex," *Cell* 174, no. 1 (2018): 21–31.e9.

5. For additional ways of marking focus in ASL, see, for instance, Philippe Schlenker, Valentina Aristodemo, Ludovic Ducasse, Jonathan Lamberton, and Mirko Santoro, "The Unity of Focus: Evidence from Sign Language," *Linguistic Inquiry* 47, no. 2 (2016): 363–381. On the broader category of stress (not discussed here) in ASL, see, for instance, Ronnie Wilbur, "Stress in ASL: Empirical Evidence and Linguistic Issues," *Language and Speech* 42 (1999): 229–250.

6. Ricardo Miguel Godinho, Penny Spikins, and Paul O'Higgins, "Supraorbital Morphology and Social Dynamics in Human Evolution," *Nature Ecology and Evolution* 2 (2018): 956–961, https://doi.org/10.1038/s41559-018-0528-0.

7. For a linguistic discussion, see Judith Degen, Daisy Leigh, Brandon Waldon, and Zion Mengesha, "A Linguistic Perspective: The Harmful Effects of Responding 'All Lives Matter' to 'Black Lives Matter,'" *ALPS Lab* (blog), Stanford University, June 23, 2020, http://alpslab.stanford.edu/posts/blm/2020-06-23.html.

8. Rasmussen Reports, "Black Lives Matter or All Lives Matter?" August 20, 2015, https://www.rasmussenreports.com/public_content/politics/general_politics/august_2015/black_lives_matter_or_all_lives_matter.

9. Why should strong focus matter? In a nutshell, linguists believe that it helps one insert an unpronounced version of *only*, with the effect that *I doubt that I'll invite Robin OR Sam* could mean something like *I doubt that I'll invite <only> Robin OR Sam*. The theory of unpronounced *only* has given rise to very important research in semantics and psycholinguistics, but it lies outside the scope of this book. See, for instance, Emmanuel Chemla and Benjamin Spector, "Experimental Evidence for Embedded Scalar Implicatures," *Journal of Semantics* 28, no. 3 (2011): 359–400.

10. You may be surprised that I included the rider "as soon as there are people in the first place," but the reason is this: On the assumption that no people exist (!), *everyone sings* is predicted by the semantic rules in section 9.2, partly copied below, to be vacuously true: If there are no $N$'s (here, no people), it is true that every object x which is an $N$ (here, a person) sings. But in this very special case, it doesn't follow that at least one person sings (since there are no people!). So it is only when there are $N$'s in the first place (here, people) that the entailment from *every N VP* to *some N VP* holds.

    *[Every N]$_x$ VP* is true just in case for every object x which is an $N$, *VP* is true.
    *[Some N]$_x$ VP* is true just in case for at least one object x which is an $N$, *VP* is true.

11. The French version of this story is cited in Julien Colliat, *Anthologie de la répartie* (Paris: Cherche-Midi, 2019), 155.

12. Ira A. Noveck, "When Children Are More Logical than Adults: Experimental Investigations of Scalar Implicature," *Cognition* 78, no. 2 (2001):165–188. (The title of this section is borrowed from Noveck's article.)

13. See, for example, Gennaro Chierchia, Stephen Crain, Maria Teresa Guasti, Andrea Gualmini, and Luisa Meroni, "The Acquisition of Disjunction: Evidence for a Grammatical View of Scalar Implicatures," in *Proceedings of the 25th Annual Boston University Conference on Language Development* (Somerville, MA: Cascadilla Press, 2001), 157–168.

14. Chierchia et al., "The Acquisition of Disjunction."

15. Lewis Bott and Ira. A. Noveck, "Some Utterances Are Underinformative: The Onset and Time Course of Scalar Inferences," *Journal of Memory and Language* 51, no. 3 (2004): 437–457.

16. James M. Markham, "For Spain, 'Guernica' Stirs Memory and Awe," *New York Times*, November 2, 1981, https://www.nytimes.com/1981/11/02/arts/for-spain-guernica-stirs-memory-and-awe.html; Laurence R. Horn, "Telling It Slant: Toward a Taxonomy of Deception," in *The Pragmatic Turn in Law: Inference and Interpretation in Legal Discourse*, ed. D. Stein and J. Giltrow (Berlin: De Gruyter Mouton, 2017), 23–55.

17. Peter Tiersma and Lawrence Solan, *Speaking of Crime: The Language of Criminal Justice* (Chicago: University of Chicago Press, 2010), 213.

## CHAPTER 11: NOT AT ISSUE: PRESUPPOSITIONS, SUPPLEMENTS, AND EXPRESSIVES

1. In the case of *know*, there are additional complexities because *x knows that p* doesn't just mean: *p and x believes that p*. The reason is that knowledge isn't just true belief: there are usually further requirements as well—for instance, the belief should be justified in addition to being true. I disregard this point here.

2. From *New York Magazine*, December 2, 1985, 33.

3. Victor Raskin, *Semantic Mechanisms of Humor* (Dordrecht: D. Reidel Publishing, 1985), 217.

4. Raskin, *Semantic Mechanisms of Humor*, 217.

5. In chapter 10 (section 10.3), we discussed constructions in which focus helps determine which alternatives are false—for instance, *I only drink RED wine* suggests that I do not drink white wine.

6. Abby Ohlheiser, "The Woman behind 'Me Too' Knew the Power of the Phrase when She Created It—10 Years Ago," *Washington Post*, October 19, 2017, https://www.washingtonpost.com/news/the-intersect/wp/2017/10/19/the-woman-behind-me-too-knew-the-power-of-the-phrase-when-she-created-it-10-years-ago/.

7. Barry Dougherty and H. Aaron Cohl, *The Friars Club Encyclopedia of Jokes: Revised and Updated* (New York: Black Dog & Leventhal Publishers, 2009), 416.

8. Wikipedia, "List of U.S. Presidential Campaign Slogans," last modified November 20, 2021, 12:08 UTC, https://en.wikipedia.org/wiki/List_of_U.S._presidential_campaign_slogans.

9. Justin Davidson, "The Leader of the Free World Gives a Speech, and She Nails It," *New York Magazine*, March 18, 2020, https://nymag.com/intelligencer/2020/03/angela-merkel-nails -coronavirus-speech-unlike-trump.html.

10. This "More from the Campaign trail" headline appeared on the *USA Today* website at https://www.usatoday.com/story/news/politics/onpolitics/2016/05/13/record -trump-and-paul-ryan-now-seeing-each-other/84308106/.

11. Cited in Raskin, *Semantic Mechanisms of Humor*, 254. Raskin cites Harvey Mindess, *Laughter and Liberation* (Los Angeles: Nash, 1971), 45.

12. "Homophobia in Football: 'One Plays it by Ear and just Says That the Supporters Are Homophobic,' Laments One of Their Lawyers," *Radio France*, August 29, 2019, https:// www.francetvinfo.fr/societe/lgbt/homophobie-dans-le-football-on-navigue-a-vue-et-on-se -borne-a-dire-que-les-supporters-sont-homophobes-deplore-un-de-leurs-avocats_3594993 .html.

13. Camille Caldini, "We Explain to You Why 'Enculé' Is a Homophobic Insult," *FranceInfo Sport*, September 22, 2019, https://www.francetvinfo.fr/sports/foot/ligue-1/on-vous- explique-pourquoi-encule-est-une-insulte-homophobe_3620089.html; "Five Questions on Homophobic Insults in the Stands, Which Have Become a Headache for French Football Authorities," *Radio France*, August 29, 2019, https://www.francetvinfo.fr/societe/lgbt/cinq -questions-sur-les-injures-homophobes-en-tribunes-devenues-un-casse-tete-pour-les -instances-du-foot-francais_3595205.html.

## CHAPTER 12: ICONICITY REVISITED: SIGN WITH ICONICITY VERSUS SPEECH WITH GESTURES

1. "I Want There to be an Italian Hand Emoji. #justiceformarzia #justiceforitaly #world- peace," *Change.org*, petition started by Seiko Miyamoto, n.d., accessed November 19, 2021, https://www.change.org/p/apple-i-want-there-to-be-an-italian-hand-emoji-justiceformarzia -justiceforitaly-worldpeace; "Make the Italian Hand Gesture an Emoji," *Change.org*, petition started by John Appleseed, n.d., accessed November 19, 2021, https://www.change.org/p /reddit-make-the-italian-hand-gesture-an-emoji.

2. "The Best Partner," episode 24, January 3, 2020, YouTube, 42:27, https://www.youtube.com /watch?v=pgY3rrXXv40&feature=youtu.be&t=31m50s.

3. The examples, pictures, and theories discussed in this section appear in Philippe Schlenker, "Gesture Projection and Cosuppositions," *Linguistics & Philosophy* 41, no. 3 (2018): 295– 365; Philippe Schlenker, "Iconic Pragmatics," *Natural Language & Linguistic Theory* 36, no. 3 (2018): 877–936.

4. This discussion is from Robert Pasternak and Lyn Tieu, "Co-linguistic Content Projection: From Gestures to Sound Effects and Emoji," *Quarterly Journal of Experimental Psychology*

(2022): https://journals.sagepub.com/doi/full/10.1177/17470218221080645. Pasternak's sounds effects can be found on SoundCloud ("Examples, 'The Projection of Co-speech Sound Effects,'" n.d., SoundCloud, audio, https://bit.ly/2Je6Sto.)

5. On the emoji-gesture connection, see L. Gawne and G. McCulloch, "Emoji as Digital Gestures," *Language@Internet* 17 (2019). For a recent work that is close in spirit to the present discussion, see Francesco Pierini, "Emojis and Gestures: A New Typology," *Proceedings of Sinn und Bedeutung* 25 (September 2021), https://doi.org/10.18148/sub/2021.v25i0.963. On face-related versus non-face-related emojis, see Patrick G. Grosz, Elsi Kaiser, and Francesco Pierini, "Discourse Anaphoricity and First-Person Indexicality in Emoji Resolution," *Proceedings of Sinn und Bedeutung* 25 (September 2021), https://doi.org/10.18148/sub /2021.v25i0.941.

6. One might ask about emojis that follow a sentence, as in *I didn't train* 🏊. Here the swimmer emoji suggests that the training under discussion pertained to swimming. Pierini argues that such emojis are ambiguous between the role of co-speech and of post-speech gestures. The reason is that unlike gestures, emojis cannot co-occur with text, and as a result the post-posed position can do double duty, encoding co-speech or post-speech behavior. The discussion appears in Pierini, "Emojis and Gestures: A New Typology."

## CHAPTER 13: GRAMMAR IN GESTURES

1. Unless otherwise noted, this entire discussion is from Philippe Schlenker, "Gestural Grammar," *Natural Language & Linguistic Theory* 38 (2020): 887–936.

2. M. Coppola, E. Spaepen, and S. Goldin-Meadow, "Communicating about Quantity without a Language Model: Number Devices in Homesign Grammar," *Cognitive Psychology* 67 (2013): 1–25.

3. M. Coppola and W. C. So, "The Seeds of Spatial Grammar: Spatial Modulation and Coreference in Homesigning and Hearing Adults," in *Proceedings of the 30th Boston University Conference on Language Development*, ed. D. Bamman, T. Magnitskaia, and C. Zaller (Boston: Cascadilla Press, 2006), 119–130.

4. Bill Vicars, "TELL: The American Sign Language (ASL) Sign for 'Tell,'" ASL University, n.d., accessed November 20, 2021, https://www.lifeprint.com/asl101/pages-signs/t/tell.htm.

5. This discussion of gestural loci is from Philippe Schlenker and Emmanuel Chemla, "Gestural Agreement," *Natural Language & Linguistic Theory* 36, no. 2 (2018): 587–625, https:// doi.org/10.1007/s11049-017-9378-8.

## CHAPTER 14: MEANING IN GESTURES

1. If you take into account the more informative alternative that *not many of my friends are dishonest*, you will also derive the inference that *many/most of my friends are dishonest* (by negating that alternative). The reasoning is similar to one discussed in chapter 10 (section

10.6) in connection with the statement, *Quite a few Congressmen are dumb as rocks. Not all of them GOP.*

2. Related but slightly more complicated examples were tested experimentally in Lyn Tieu, Philippe Schlenker, and Emmanuel Chemla, "Linguistic Inferences without Words," *Proceedings of the National Academy of Sciences* 116, no. 20 (2019): 9796–9801. The experimental examples were longer than those I discuss in the text because they sought to establish clear contrasts among the alternative gestures, which is important to trigger implicatures. Writing *TURN-WHEEL* for the partial wheel-turning gesture and *TURN-WHEEL-COMPLETELY* for the complete wheel-turning gesture, some of the crucial examples were the following (they appeared in videos rather than in writing):

(i) John is training to be a stunt driver. Yesterday, at the first mile marker, he was taught to TURN-WHEEL-COMPLETELY. Today, at the next mile marker, he will **TURN-WHEEL.**
(inference due to the boldfaced gesture: he will turn the wheel but not completely)

(ii) John is training to be a stunt boat driver. Out by the first buoy, he decided to TURN-WHEEL-COMPLETELY, but at the second one he did not TURN-WHEEL. At the next buoy, he will not **TURN-WHEEL.**
(inference due to the boldfaced gesture: he will not turn the wheel at all)

(iii) John is training to be a stunt boat driver. Out by the first buoy, he decided to TURN-WHEEL-COMPLETELY, but at the second one he did not TURN-WHEEL. At the next buoy, he will not **TURN-WHEEL-COMPLETELY.**
(inference due to the boldfaced gesture: he will turn the wheel but not completely)

3. Tieu, Schlenker, and Chemla, "Linguistic Inferences without Words."

4. Judith Tonhauser, "How to Cut the Projective Content Pie" (slide presentation, University of California, San Diego, December 4, 2017).

### CHAPTER 15: MEANING IN MUSIC

1. Alex Ross, "Monument Man," *New Yorker*, July 24, 2014, https://www.newyorker.com /culture/cultural-comment/richard-strauss-and-the-american-army.

2. Alfred Maskeroni, "You've Never Seen a Food Commercial Quite as Otherworldly as This One," *Adweek*, April 4, 2014, https://www.adweek.com/creativity/youve-never -seen-food-commercial-quite-otherworldly-one-156806/.

3. "Tropicana Essentials Probiotics TV Commercial, 'Start Your Day with a Billion Active Cultures' Song by Richard Strauss," *iSpot.tv*, n.d., accessed November 20, 2021, https:// www.ispot.tv/ad/IfNc/tropicana-essentials-probiotics-feel-like-a-billion.

4. "Carlsberg-Lite (Reklame)," April 12, 2008, YouTube, 00:35, https://www.youtube.com /watch?v=0W7QN-oYrtg.

5. "Pampers Pooface," c. 2015, Vimeo, 01:15, https://vimeo.com/131077537.

6. Unless otherwise stated, this chapter follows three articles: Philippe Schlenker, "Outline of Music Semantics," *Music Perception: An Interdisciplinary Journal* 35, no. 1 (2017): 3–37, https://doi.org/10.1525/mp.2017.35.1.3; Philippe Schlenker, "Prolegomena to Music Semantics," *Review of Philosophy & Psychology* 10, no. 1 (2019): 35–111; Philippe Schlenker, "Musical Meaning within Super Semantics," *Linguistics & Philosophy* (forthcoming).

7. For some recent experimental work on universals of music, see, for instance, S. A. Mehr, Manvir Singh, Dean Knox, Daniel M. Ketter, Daniel Pickens-Jones, S. Atwood, Christopher Lucas, Nori Jacoby, Alena A. Egner et al., "Universality and Diversity in Human Song," *Science* 366, no. 6468 (2019): 1–17.

8. F. Heider and M. Simmel, "An Experimental Study of Apparent Behavior," *American Journal of Psychology* 57 (1944): 243–259.

9. For the comparison of meaning effects in music to Heider and Simmel's animations, see Fred Lerdahl, *Composition and Cognition: Reflections on Contemporary Music and the Musical Mind* (Oakland: University of California Press, 2019), ch. 3.

10. For a written version, see Leonard Bernstein, *Young People's Concerts*, foreword by Michael Tilson Thomas (Pompton Plains, NJ: Amadeus Press, 2005).

11. Bernstein, *Young People's Concerts*, 8.

12. Bernstein, *Young People's Concerts*, 27.

13. Bernstein, *Young People's Concerts*, 14.

14. For a somewhat related but distinct discussion of real versus virtual sources in music, see Albert S. Bregman, *Auditory Scene Analysis* (Cambridge, MA: MIT Press, 1994).

15. Peter Desain and Henkjan Honing, "Physical Motion as a Metaphor for Timing in Music: The Final Ritard," in *Proceedings of the International Computer Music Conference* (San Francisco: International Computer Music Association, 1996), 458–460.

16. Henkjan Honing, "The Final Ritard: On Music, Motion, and Kinematic Models," *Computer Music Journal* 27, no. 3 (2003): 66–72.

17. For a cross-cultural discussion, see Mehr et al., "Universality and Diversity in Human Song." This article cautiously argues that the notion of a 'tonic center' might be applicable across musical styles and cultures.

18. There are still ongoing debates about the acoustic and cognitive sources of consonance and dissonance. Explanations are usually rooted in the overtone series. Every note is made of a fundamental frequency and a series of overtones, which are multiples of the fundamental frequency. For instance, a C whose fundamental frequency is f = 65 Hz has overtones at frequencies 2f (= 130 Hz), 3f (= 195 Hz), and so on. As a result, C contains other notes as overtones: 2f yields a C one octave higher; 3f yields a G; 4f yields a higher C; 5f yields an E. For this reason, G and E are contained as overtones in C. One possible theory is that a chord such as C E G (= the C major chord) is particularly consonant because it resembles a simple note in the following sense: It is made of a C and of further notes, E and G, which are among

the first overtones of C. The C minor chord CE♭G is arguably a bit less consonant because, unlike E, E♭ is not one of the first overtones of C.

For a particularly pedagogical presentation of the overtone series, see, for instance, Leonard Bernstein, *The Unanswered Question: Six Talks at Harvard (The Charles Eliot Norton Lectures)* (Cambridge, MA: Harvard University Press, 1976); see also "Harmonic Series—Explained," December 10, 2016, YouTube, 08:48, https://www.youtube.com/watch?v=3TlQryUBz3E.

For a scientific study of the cognitive roots of consonance and the role played by musical experience, see Josh McDermott and Andrew Oxenham, "Individual Differences Reveal the Basis of Consonance," *Journal of the Acoustical Society of America* 127, no. 1949 (2010), https://doi.org/10.1121/1.3384926.

19.  *WALL-E*, directed by Andrew Stanton (2008; Walt Disney Pictures), 1:38:00; "WALL-e," *Internet Movie Database (IMDb)*, accessed November 20, 2021, https://www.imdb.com/title /tt0910970/?ref_=tttr_tr_tt.

20.  See the references in endnote 18.

21.  See Schlenker, "Musical Meaning within Super Semantics," for a discussion of the specific musical means that trigger inferences in the Strauss's Variation II; some salient excerpts are rewritten (by Arthur Bonetto) to show that when the musical form changes, so do the inferences.

### CHAPTER 16: THE LIMITS OF TRUTH I: THE RIDDLE OF PARADOXES

1.  For a biography containing much information about Tarski's life but also about his scientific contributions, see Anita Burdman Feferman and Solomon Feferman, *Alfred Tarski: Life and Logic* (Cambridge: Cambridge University Press, 2014).

### CHAPTER 17: THE LIMITS OF TRUTH II: SOLVING THE RIDDLE OF PARADOXES

1.  Saul Kripke, "Outline of a Theory of Truth," *Journal of Philosophy* 72 (1975): 690–716.

2.  This paradox is called Curry's paradox, and it is usually presented in a different form: *If this very sentence is true, Santa Claus exists.* (It is equivalent to the disjunctive version on the assumption, often made in logic but not in this book, that *if p, q* is equivalent to *not p or q*. This is the material conditional discussed in endnote 1 of chapter 6.)

3.  Here we follow Philippe Schlenker, "Anselm's Argument and Berry's Paradox," *Noûs* 43, no. 2 (2009): 214–223.

4.  A different objection to the argument is that imagining a thing x with existence is no 'greater' than just imagining x. But even if one grants Anselm's assumptions in this respect, the problem mentioned in the text arises.

5.  To make things concrete, let's see how our revision procedure would treat the Revenge Liar RL. At stage 0, it gets the indeterminate truth value (because it contains the word *true*). At

stage 1, we evaluate RL (which says that *RL is something other than true*) on the basis of the truth values obtained at stage 0—so now RL is evaluated as true, since # is something other than true. But doing the same revision at stage 2 leads to the result that . . . RL is false (since true isn't something other than true!). And if we continued at stage 3, RL would be evaluated as true, and then the value of RL would oscillate forever between *true* and *false*. This is the problem when *is something other than true* is part of the language: the standard values *true* and *false* may need to be revised—in this case, forever.

| Stage 0 | Stage 1 | Stage 2 | Stage 3 | Stage 4 |
|---------|---------|---------|---------|---------|
| RL | RL | RL | RL | RL |
| # | true | false | true | false |

## CONCLUSION

1. For pioneering work on the semantics of pictures, see Gabriel Greenberg, "Beyond Resemblance," *Philosophical Review* 122, no. 2 (2013). For very exciting work on the semantics of visual narratives, see Dorit Abusch, "Possible World Semantics for Pictures," in *The Wiley Blackwell Companion to Semantics*, ed. L. Matthewson, C. Meier, H. Rullmann, and T. E. Zimmermann (Oxford: Wiley, 2020), https://doi.org/10.1002/9781118788516.sem003. Groundbreaking work on formal and experimental analysis of comics has been conducted by Neil Cohn, *The Visual Language of Comics: Introduction to the Structure and Cognition of Sequential Images* (London: Bloomsbury, 2013).

2. For pioneering approaches to the study of dance syntax and semantics, see the following references: Isabelle Charnavel, "Steps toward a Universal Grammar of Dance: Local Grouping Structure in Basic Human Movement Perception," *Frontiers in Psychology* 10 (2019): 1364; Pritty Patel-Grosz, Patrick Grosz, Tejaswinee Kelkar, and Alexander Refsum Jensenius, "Coreference and Disjoint Reference in the Semantics of Narrative Dance," *Proceedings of Sinn und Bedeutung* 22, no. 2 (2018): 199–216.

3. The term has been used by different authors and invoked by multiple fields of the humanities; for a list, see, for instance, Wikipedia, "Semiotics," last modified November 20, 2021, 07:37 UTC, https://en.wikipedia.org/wiki/Semiotics#:~:text=Semiotics%20(also%20called%20semiotic%20studies,itself%20to%20the%20sign's%20interpreter.

4. The expression is used by Charles Percy Snow and his eponymous book; see Charles Percy Snow, *The Two Cultures* (Cambridge: Cambridge University Press, 2001).

## APPENDIX: PHONOLOGY, MORPHOLOGY, AND SYNTAX IN SPEECH AND IN SIGN

1. The poem can be found in the following discussion at the Linguist List; see Steve Moran, ed., "Summary: Pronunciation Poem," *Linguist List* 13.3353 (December 18, 2002), https://linguistlist.org/issues/13/13-3353/.

2. Our discussion disregards one important case: After *t* and *d*, the past tense suffix is pronounced *əd*, as in coat → coated, code → coded. The reason is that the vowel *ə* is inserted to avoid a sequence of consonants (*td, dd*) that are identical except possibly for voicing (i.e., for the vibration of the vocal folds). A more extensive analysis, presented for a general audience in Steven Pinker's *Words and Rules* (1999, 34)—see the Going Further section—would go as follows; remember that it applies to the pronunciation, not to the spelling:

Step 1: Insert *d* for the past tense of regular verbs.

Step 2: If this gives rise to a sequence *td* or *dd* (= a sequence of two consonants that are identical except possibly for the vibration of the vocal folds), insert *ə*—hence *əd* (as in *coded*).

Step 3: If Step 1+Step 2 give rise to a sequence of consonants that differ in voicing (e.g., *k*, voiceless, followed by *d*, voiced), apply a rule of assimilation: extend the voiceless feature of the first consonant to the second, thus turning *d* into *t* (as in *licked*).

3. On Italian Sign Language, see, for instance, Carlo Geraci, "Italian Sign Language," in *Sign Languages of the World: A Comparative Handbook*, ed. Julie Bakken Jepsen, Goedele De Clerck, Sam Lutalo-Kiingi, and William B. McGregor (Berlin: De Gruyter Mouton, 2015), 473–510.

# Illustration Sources

**Page 3, Figure 1.2.1**

Human Origins Program, Natural Museum of Natural History (NMNH), Smithsonian Institution, https://humanorigins.si.edu/evidence/genetics.

**Page 10, Figure 1.4.1**

Original figure (redrawn and modified here) from Cristiane Cäsar, "Anti-Predator Behaviour of Black-Fronted Titi Monkeys (*Callicebus nigrifrons*)" (PhD diss., University of St Andrews, 2012). A correction to one call transcription is due to Mélissa Berthet.

**Page 19, Figure 1.6.1**

Author's figure using Campbell's monkey: © UR1/Dircom/JLB, with permission; Amur leopard: Art G. from Willow Grove, PA, USA, https://commons.wikimedia.org/wiki/File:Amur_Leopard _(1970226951).jpg.

**Page 24, Figure 1.8.1**

Figure redrawn from P. Schlenker, E. Chemla, A. Schel, J. Fuller, J.-P. Gautier, J. Kuhn, D. Veselinovic, K. Arnold, C. Cäsar, S. Keenan, A. Lemasson, K. Ouattara, R. Ryder, and K. Zuberbühler, "Formal Monkey Linguistics," *Theoretical Linguistics* 42, no. 1–2 (2016): 1–90, https:// doi.org/10.1515/tl-2016-0001. The original figure is from Katerina Guschanski, Johannes Krause, Susanna Sawyer, Luis M. Valente, Sebastian Bailey, Knut Finstermeier, Richard Sabin, Emmanuel Gilissen, Gontran Sonet, Zoltán T. Nagy, Georges Lenglet, Frieder Mayer, and Vincent Savolainen, "Next-Generation Museomics Disentangles One of the Largest Primate Radiations," *Systematic Biology* 62, no. 4 (2013): 539–554.

**Page 31, Figure 1.10.1**

Catherine Hobaiter, Richard Byrne, and colleagues, *The Great Ape Dictionary*, University of St Andrews, accessed October 28, 2021, http://greatapedictionary.ac.uk/. Figures drawn by Kirsty E. Graham.

**Page 45, Figure 2.1.1**

Ann Senghas, Sotaro Kita, and Asli Özyürek, "Children Creating Core Properties of Language: Evidence from an Emerging Sign Language in Nicaragua," *Science* 305, no. 5691 (2004): 1780.

**Page 47, Figure 2.2.1**

Mairéad MacSweeney, Cheryl M. Capek, Ruth Campbell, and Bencie Woll, "The Signing Brain: The Neurobiology of Sign Language," *Trends in the Cognitive Sciences* 12, no. 11 (2008): 433.

**Pages 55, 61, and 62, Figures 2.4.1, 2.6.1, and 2.6.2**

Illustrations by Marion Bonnet reprinted under Creative Commons CC BY 4.0, redrawn from Philippe Schlenker, "Iconic Features," *Natural Language Semantics* 22, no. 4 (2014): 330.

**Page 63, Figure 2.6.3**

Emily Shaw and Yves Delaporte, *A Historical and Etymological Dictionary of American Sign Language* (Washington, DC: Gallaudet University Press, 2015), 117.

**Page 64, Figure 2.7.1**

Jeremy Kuhn, with permission.

**Pages 66, 98, 249, 250, 252, 264, 277, 323–324, and 331, Figures 2.7.2, 4.2.2, 4.2.3, 12.1.1–12.1.3, 12.2.1, 12.6.1, 13.3.1, 15.8.2, 15.8.3, 15.8.4, and 15.10.2–15.10.4; Pages 253–256, 258–260, 262, 268, 271–272, 274, 275, 277–278, 280–281, 283, 290–292, and 294–295, unnumbered figures**

Illustrations by Marion Bonnet reprinted under Creative Commons CC BY 4.0.

**Page 87, Figure 3.7.1**

Diane Lillo-Martin, "Utterance Reports and Constructed Action," in *Sign Language—An International Handbook*, ed. R. Pfau, M. Steinbach, and B. Woll (Storrs, CT: Sign Linguistics & Language Acquisition Lab, University of Connecticut, 2012), 365–387.

**Page 97, Figure 4.2.1**

Signing Savvy, https://www.signingsavvy.com/sign/TROPHY/7122/1.

**Page 105, Figure 4.5.1**

Clayton Valli, *The Gallaudet Dictionary of American Sign Language* (Washington, DC: Gallaudet University Press, 2005).

**Page 105, Figure 4.5.2**

Clayton Valli, *The Gallaudet Dictionary of American Sign Language* (Washington, DC: Gallaudet University Press, 2005).

**Page 106, Figure 4.5.3**

*La langue des signes—dictionnaire bilingue LSF-français* (Paris: IVT—International Visual Theater, 1986).

**Page 206, Figure 10.4.1**

(a) Lord Kitchener Wants You, published in *London Opinion*, 1914, public domain, https://en.wikipedia.org/wiki/Lord_Kitchener_Wants_You; (b) Uncle Sam, poster by J. M. Flagg, 1917, public domain, https://en.wikipedia.org/wiki/Uncle_Sam.

**Page 271, Figure 13.2.2**

Bill Vicars, "TELL: The American Sign Language (ASL) Sign for 'Tell,'" ASL University, n.d., accessed November 20, 2021, https://www.lifeprint.com/asl101/pages-signs/t/tell.htm.

**Page 273, Figure 13.2.6**

Philippe Schlenker and Emmanuel Chemla, "Gestural Agreement," *Natural Language & Linguistic Theory* 36, no. 2 (2018): 587–625.

**Pages 298 and 300, unnumbered figures**

Lyn Tieu, Philippe Schlenker, and Emmanuel Chemla, "Linguistic Inferences without Words," *Proceedings of the National Academy of Sciences* 116, no. 20 (2019): 9796–9801.

**Page 311, Figure 15.4.1**

Henkjan Honing. Video of the final ritard machine. Discussed in Henkjan Honing, "The Final Ritard: On Music, Motion, and Kinematic Models," *Computer Music Journal* 27, no. 3 (2003): 66–72.

**Page 313, Figure 15.5.1**

Philippe Schlenker, "Prolegomena to Music Semantics," *Review of Philosophy & Psychology* 10, no. 1 (2019): 35–111, on the opening sequence of Stanley Kubrick's *2001: A Space Odyssey*.

**Page 393, Figure 17.11.1**

Wendy Sandler, "The Challenge of Sign Language Phonology," *Annual Review of Linguistics* 3 (2017): 46; Sign Language Research Lab, University of Haifa. Leftmost picture cited by Sandler from John Kingston.

**Pages 394 and 395, Figures 17.11.2 and 17.11.5**

Wendy Sandler, "The Challenge of Sign Language Phonology," *Annual Review of Linguistics* (2017): 47; Sign Language Research Lab, University of Haifa.

**Page 394, Figure 17.11.3**

Bill Vicars, "COOK: The American Sign Language (ASL) sign for 'cook,'" ASL University, n.d., accessed November 24, 2021, https://www.lifeprint.com/asl101/pages-signs/c/cook.htm#:~:text =The%20sign%20for%20%22cook%22%20uses,then%20turn%20the%20food%20over.

**Page 395, Figure 17.11.4**

Diane Brentari, *Sign Language Phonology* (Cambridge: Cambridge University Press, 2019), 247, fig. 8.2.

**Pages 397, 402, 403, Figures 17.11.6, 17.11.11–13**

Wendy Sandler and Diane Lillo-Martin, *Sign Language and Linguistic Universals* (Cambridge: Cambridge University Press, 2006), 66, fig. 4.9; 291, fig. 18.1; 442, fig. 23.6; 436, fig. 23.1; Sign Linguistics and Language Acquisition Lab, University of Connecticut.

**Page 398, Figure 17.11.7**

Mark Aronoff, Irit Meir, and Wendy Sandler, "The Paradox of Sign Language Morphology," *Language* 81, no. 2 (2005): 301–344; Sign Language Research Lab, University of Haifa.

**Pages 399 and 400, Figures 17.11.8–17.11.10**

Carol A. Padden, *Interaction of Morphology and Syntax in American Sign Language* (London: Routledge, 2017), 61, viewed in Google Play Books. First published 1988 by Garland. Also cited in Wendy Sandler, "The Phonological Organization of Sign Languages," *Language and Linguistics Compass* 6, no. 3 (2012): 162–182.

# Index

Abbé de l'Épée, 41–43
Adjective, 91–92, 107–112, 213, 396
Adverb, 91–92, 107–110, 112, 161,
  166–168, 213
Agreement, 57–58, 191, 268–275, 398, 405
  verb, 50, 270, 273, 398
Algonquian (language), 136, 142
Alternative, 197–222, 231–232. *See also*
  Implicature
Ambiguity, 49, 51, 64, 83, 86, 122, 124,
  148–152, 155–156, 169–175
  lexical, 149
  of loudness interpretation, 318–320, 328
  structural, 165–170
American Sign Language (ASL), 39–67,
  203–204, 234, 271–282, 394–404,
  405
  context shift in, 86–88
  facial expression in, 256, 261–263
  modal pronoun in, 123–125
  plural locus in, 64–67, 409
  pointing sign in, 122–123, 186–189
  quantifier in, 186–190
  repetition in, 95–100
  telicity in, 104–106 (*see also* Telic/atelic)
  temporal pronouns in, 121–123
Amharic (language), 82, 85, 88, 136,
  141–142
Anand, Pranav, 84

Anselm of Canterbury, xix, 356, 369
Anselm's argument, 369–371, 379–381
Antecedent, 57–58, 116–124, 268–269,
  273–274
Ape, xiii, xvii, xix, 1–4, 14, 25–34
  African, 32–33
  call, 25–27, 34
  family tree, 2–3, 23–24, 32
  gesture, 2, 27–30, 33–34
Arnold, Kate, 17
Articulation, 389–394, 396. *See also* Feature
Assertion, xvi, 119, 202, 215, 227–234, 298,
  405. *See also* At issue
Assimilation rule, 392–397, 405
Atelic. *See* Telic/atelic
At issue, xiii, xvi, xviii, 7, 225–234, 251–254,
  261–264, 288–290, 298–300, 385,
  405
  entailments, 228, 288, 300, 407
Auxiliary, 113, 118, 122, 138, 168

Bernstein, Leonard, 307–309, 334–337
Berry's paradox, 367–370, 379. *See also*
  Paradox
Bilingualism, 21–22
Bonobo, 2, 26–34, 204, 297. *See also* Ape
Boundary (gestural), 104–107, 110,
  280–281. *See also* Telic/atelic
Bulgarian (language), 136, 139

Burke, Tarana, 232
Byrne, Richard, 27

Call (animal communication), xiv, xix, 1–28,
    33–37, 48, 54
  alarm, xii, xvii, xxiii, 1, 4–6, 9, 17–19, 26,
    35–37, 297, 383
  sequence, 10–15, 21, 48
  suffix, 34
Campbell's monkey, 7–8, 15–26, 34–35
Carroll, Lewis, 69
Cäsar, Cristiane, 9
Castañeda, Héctor-Neri, 76–77, 79, 82, 84
Causal source, 309
Cheney, Dorothy, 3–5
Chierchia, Gennaro, xv
Chimpanzee, 1–2, 8, 18, 25–35, 204,
    230–231, 297. See also Ape
Chinese Sign Language, 41, 123, 406
Chomsky, Noam, xiv–xviii, 47, 52, 63, 157,
    284, 387
Chopin, Frédéric, 318
Common ancestor, 2–7, 21–25, 30, 33. See
    also Evolution; Family tree
Complementizer phrase, 158–159
Compounding, 396–397
Conditional, 119, 127, 132–134. See also
    If-clause
Conditionalized presupposition. See
    Presupposition
Conjunction ('and'), 108–110, 150–154,
    164–166, 182–185, 200, 214, 228, 290,
    345–348, 376
Consonance/dissonance (music), 314,
    321–322, 325, 329–336, 391–394
Consonants, 390–393
Context, 71–75, 79–90, 116–119, 127–134,
    207, 210, 215, 231–232, 261, 268, 271,
    278, 288
  dependency, 71, 84
  linguistic, 234–237, 242, 296, 299–300
  negative, 239, 259–261, 289

non-linguistic, 235
  shift, 82–90, 281–284
Counterfactual, 38, 118–120, 128, 140–141,
    406. See also Mood; Tense
Count/mass distinction, 92–104, 110, 406,
    409
Crescendo/decrescendo. See Loudness

Deaf Awakening, 42
Deaf people, xi–xvii, 39–46, 266, 384
Definite description, 129–131, 139, 226, 406
Delaporte, Yves, 41–43
Denoted object/event, 96–102, 108–110,
    252, 309–312, 327–334, 406
Desain, Peter, 311
Determiner, 92–93, 178, 406
Diana monkey, 5–7, 21–24
Dickens, Charles, 148
Direct discourse, 76, 80
Disjunction ('or'), 150–153, 177, 182–185,
    207–214, 348–349
  exclusive, 154, 208–213, 222, 297
  inclusive, 154, 208–210, 213–216, 219,
    222, 348
Divisibility test, 93, 103–104, 406. See also
    Telic/atelic
DNA, 3, 23, 25. See also Evolution; Family
    tree
Dynamic logic. See Logic

Economy Principle, 26–27, 35, 230, 407. See
    also Pragmatics
Ellipsis, 273–276
Emoji, 248–249, 256–258
Emoticon, 247–248
Emotion, xix, 175, 248, 305, 309, 321,
    329–334, 337
Entailment, xvi, 145, 192–195, 215, 228,
    287–288, 407
Epimenides paradox, 341. See also Paradox
Evolution, 22–25, 30–33. See also Ape, family
    tree; Common ancestor; Family tree

of ape gestures, 30–32
of monkey calls, 22–25
Ewe (language), 76–79, 84, 136, 141–142
Existence of God, 356, 369. *See also* Anselm's
    argument
Expressive, 240–245, 249, 287–290,
    295–297, 300, 407
Eyebrow raising, 203–204, 401–404. *See also*
    Facial expression

Facial expression, xii, 203–204, 247,
    255–263, 278, 401, 404
    post-sign/post-speech, 260–261
Family tree (phylogeny), 2–3, 23–24, 32
Feature, 389–396
Final ritard. *See* Tempo
First person, 37, 74–84, 118, 140, 142,
    207
    perspective, 69, 73, 76–84, 90 (*see also*
    Perspective)
    pronoun, 37, 71, 75, 82–85, 141, 394
Focus, 197–209, 222, 256
Formal language, xii–xviii, 72, 90, 149, 153,
    156–157, 163–164, 171–172, 175, 179,
    189, 195, 343
Formula (logic), 147, 150–158, 174, 176,
    179–180. *See also* Predicate logic, syntax
    of
French (language), 79, 127–128, 135, 183,
    400–401
French Sign Language (LSF) 40–44, 49–60,
    64–67, 86–88, 102, 105–106, 123, 134,
    234, 262–263, 267, 270–271, 276,
    279–282, 399, 409
Frequency. *See* Pitch

Gallaudet, Thomas Hopkins, 39–43
Gender distinction, 56
German (language), 71, 80, 88, 138,
    141–142, 197–199
Gesture, xii–xxiii, 26–37, 44–46, 204–206,
    245–304, 383–386, 398–399

co-speech, 253–258, 265–268, 287, 293,
    385, 406
expressives in, 295–297
grammar, 265–285
implicatures in, 291–293, 408
post-sign, 261
post-speech, 258–265, 287–290, 411
presuppositions in, 293–295, 411
pro-speech, 261–265, 268–269, 279, 290,
    293, 411
supplements in, 289–290, 412
Gokana (language), 77–79, 84
Gorilla, 2, 25–26, 32–34. *See also* Ape
Grammar
    gestural, xix, 268, 274–281
    logic in, 190–196
    of English, 90, 102, 124, 128, 158, 163,
    275
    Universal, 47–48, 52, 284 (*see also*
    Chomsky, Noam)
Grammatical agreement, 191
Grice, Paul, xvi, 13, 198, 208
Groundedness/ungroundedness, 339,
    343–367, 408
Guaraní (language), 299

Hand configuration, 393–394, 398
Harmony (music), 320–324
    and stability, 312, 315, 321–322, 325–328,
    360
Hebrew (language), 141
Heider, Fritz, 306, 316
Heim, Irene, xv, 188
Herrmann, Bernard, 321, 329
Higginbotham, James, xv
Hitchcock, Alfred, 321–322, 329
Hobaiter, Catherine, 27, 33
Homesigners, 44, 265–268, 285
Honing, Henkjan, 311
Horn, Laurence R., 221
Hungarian (language), 179–181,
    184–185

Iconicity, xvii–xviii, 44, 53–56, 64–68, 97–99, 106–107, 245–247, 255–261, 276–280, 295–299, 325, 384–386, 408
Iconic enrichment, 245, 249–250, 263–264, 385
Iconic gesture, 29–30, 287
Iconic modulation, 54–55, 251–252, 258–264, 289
Iconic variable, 55–68
If-clause, 119–120, 131–139, 235-237, 242, 296. *See also* Conditional
Implicature, xvi–xviii, 13, 145, 197, 208–223, 287–293, 297–300, 408
Indexical, 71–75, 79, 83–85, 88–89
  pronoun, 88
Indicative (mood), 118–121, 139–140
Indirect discourse, 75–90, 141, 282
Infant gesture, 33–34
Inferential typology, xvi–xix, 245, 251, 264, 287–290, 297, 300–301, 384–386
  linguistic, xvi, 251, 287–288, 300
  of iconic enrichments, 264
Infinitive (mood), 78–79, 82, 84, 90
Informational content, 72, 287, 297–300
Informativity Principle, 13–21, 26, 34–35, 208, 408. *See also* Pragmatics
International Sign, 44
Introspection Principle, 201, 408
Island. *See* Syntactic island
Italian (language), 40–43, 47–48, 248
Italian Sign Language (LIS), 40–43, 248, 400, 409
Iteration. *See* Repetition

Japanese (language), 95, 183, 400
Japanese Sign Language, 40–41
Johnson, Gary, 233

Kamp, Hans, 188
Keenan, Sumir, 17
Kerry, John, 233
Kratzer, Angelika, xv

Kripke, Saul, 359–362, 371, 374–375
Kubrick, Stanley, 303–304, 313–314

Laertius, Diogenes, 148
Language family, 44, 48
Lesion studies, 46
Lexicon, 159–163
Liar, Liar's paradox, xii, 339, 341–343, 349–375, 384, 408–409. *See also* Paradox
  empirical, 351–353
  infinite, 350
  strengthened, 371–373, 408–409
Literal meaning, xv–xvi, 13, 35, 148, 198–200, 211, 220–223
Locus (plural: loci), 49–55, 59–67, 86–89, 97–100, 122–124, 186–190, 267–270, 275–276, 282–284, 398–399, 409
Logic, xii–xx, 115, 147–172
  dynamic, 188–190, 407
  Predicate, 147–156 (*see also* Predicate Logic)
Logical Form, 179–186, 409
Logophoric marker, 77–79, 82–84, 89, 136
Loudness (music), 309–310, 313, 318–320, 325–328

MacSweeney, Mairéad, 46
Major/minor mode (music), 312–314, 318–324, 330–334, 341
Mahler, Gustav, 318–320, 332
Mandarin (language), 40, 51–53, 56, 122, 183, 248, 401–404
Marathi (language), 134
Marler, Peter, 4, 7
Minsky, Marvin, 147
Modal statement/auxiliary, 113, 409
Monkey, xii–xvii, xxiii, 2–9, 12–26, 34–35
  call, xvii, 2–8, 22–25
Montague, Richard, xiv–xviii, 147–148, 153, 157, 163, 343, 387
Mood, xiii–xviii, 115, 118–125, 128, 135–145, 409–410

Moore's "paradox", 199–201, 342, 410. *See also* Paradox

Moore, George Edward, 199–202

Morphology, 16, 21, 35, 389, 396–398, 410
derivational, 396–398
inflectional, 397–398

Movement
direction and manner of, 45
island to, 182–183, 408 (*see also* Syntactic island)
melodic (music), 314–315, 336
quantifier, 184–186
syntactic, 169, 182–186, 195–196, 410

Mozart, Wolfgang Amadeus, 317

Music, xii–xix, xxi, 245, 303–339, 386
-external reality, 305–309, 315, 320
inferences from, 316–324
meaning in, 303–337
semantics, 304, 316, 329

Natural language, xii, 79, 147–156, 176–177, 180, 189, 196

Natural unit, 168–171

Negation, xvi, 59, 112, 116–117, 150–154, 165–166, 243–244, 254–262, 347–348, 374–377

Negative environments, negative-like environments, 213–217, 222–223, 240–241, 292–294

Negative polarity item, 190–196, 213–214, 410

Neuroimaging, 46

Nicaraguan Sign Language, 44–45

Non-restrictive relative clause, 238–241, 259–265, 289–290. *See also* Supplements

Nontriviality condition, 230

Normal auditory cognition, 310–324

Noun, xiii, xviii, 91–112, 129–130, 163–164, 276–279, 396–398
count (*see* Count/mass distinction)
phrase, 158–159, 177–178, 189–194

/verb analogy, 101–102

Noveck, Ira, 217

Object classification, 135–143

Object marker, 275

Obviative. *See* Proximate/obviative

Onomatopoeia, 268

Orangutan, 2, 25, 28, 32. *See also* Ape

Ouattara, Karim, 15

Paradox, xix, 339–384, 410
Berry's, 367–370, 379–381
empirical Liar's, 351–353
Epimenides, 341
infinite Liar's, 350
Liar's, xii, 156, 339, 341–343, 349–375, 408–409
Moore's, 199–201, 342, 410
strengthened Liar's, 371–373, 409
Yablo's, 345–346, 353, 413

Partee, Barbara, xv

Pasternak, Robert, 256-257

Perspective, 37, 61–62, 69–90, 93, 136–137, 141–143, 281–284

Phonology, 389–397, 410

Pictorial representation, 251

Pitch (music), 311–320, 326, 332

Pluperfect (tense), 137–142. *See also* Tense
double, 137–138

Pluractional, 101–102, 110, 279–281, 410–411

Plural, 56–58, 64–68, 91–103, 129–131, 175–176, 188–191, 266–267, 276, 279
locus, 64–67, 99, 409
marking, 95–99, 139
pronoun, 56–57, 64–68
repetition-based, 96, 100, 252

Pointing
gesture, 28–30, 71, 206, 267–270
sign, 50–67, 87–88, 122–125, 176, 188–189, 268–282, 394–395

Portuguese (language), 48

Possible world, 72
Post-speech gesture. *See* Gesture
Potawatomi (language), 136
Pragmatic contradiction, 200–201, 342
Pragmatic enrichment, 199–201
Pragmatic reasoning, 13, 199–201, 208, 210
Pragmatic rule/principle, 21, 35. *See also*
    Economy Principle; Informativity
    Principle
Pragmatics, xvi–xxiii, 13–15, 26–27, 34–35,
    199, 411
Predicate Logic, 145–164, 173–181,
    184–186, 189–190, 195–196, 411
    semantics of, 152–155
    syntax of, 149–152
Prefix, 389–396, 398
Presupposition, xvi–xxi, 56–57, 129–130,
    145, 225–244, 251–264, 287–301, 411
    conditionalized, 255–258
    in gestures, 293–296
Primate, xix–xxiii, 1–25, 33–35. *See also* Ape
    call, xix, xxiii, 8–34
    communication, xxiii, 2, 15, 34
    semantics, 4
Pro-speech gesture. *See* Gesture
Pronoun, xiii–xviii, 75–82, 85–89, 91,
    115–125, 176, 187–190, 234, 267–268,
    398–400
    first person, 37, 71, 75, 82–85, 141, 394
    (*see also* First person)
    logophoric, 75–77, 141–142
    modal, 118–121, 123–125
    personal, 135–136
    reflexive, 51–52, 187
    relative, 81
    second person, 85
    sign language, 39–68
    temporal, 121–123
    third person, 76–77, 89 (*see also* Third
    person)
Proof theory, 153
Proper name, 48, 61–63, 74–75, 158

Proximate/obviative, 136, 411
Proximity
    classifying by, 135–141
    modal, 138–142
    object, 135–137
    temporal, 132, 137–139
Psycholinguistics, xx, 217, 266–267
Puccini, Giacomo, 333

Quantifier, 108, 112–118, 151–154, 176–
    178, 180–181, 184–190, 195–196, 411
    movement, 184–186
Quotation, 75–77, 80–84, 88–89

Reagan, Ronald, 229–230, 233
Recursion, 162, 412
Repetition, 95–102, 116–119, 122–124,
    266–267, 276–280, 398
    -based plural, 96, 100, 252
    in music, 319–320
    punctuated/unpunctuated, 96–102,
    266–267, 276–280
    verbal, 279
Role Shift, 86–89, 282–284
Roosevelt, Franklin D., 233
Rossini, Gioachino, 307–309
Russell, Bertrand, 368
Russian (language), 43, 141–142, 204

Sacks, Oliver, 73
Saint-Saëns, Camille, 317–329
Salience, 130–134, 137–138
Scale
    musical, 210–213,
    pragmatic, 312–331, 412
Second person, 272–275
    pronoun, 85
Self-reference, 343–346, 350–353, 356–357,
    367–371, 380
Semantics, xiii–xxiii, 21, 34–35, 101, 147,
    152–157, 171–172, 383–389, 412
    music, 304, 316, 325, 329

of monkey calls, 3–8
of paradoxes, 339, 342–343, 353, 364,
    373–374, 410
of Predicate Logic, 152–155
primate, 5
Semantic rule, xv, 154–155, 166–168,
    347–348, 353–358, 361–362,
    374–377
Semiotics, 386–387
Seyfarth, Robert, 3–5
Shaw, Emily, 43
Shift
    body, 87–89, 282
    context, 84–90, 281–284
    Role, 86–89, 282–284
Sign language, xi–xix, 98–106, 186, 245–252,
    265–270, 384–388, 398–404
    and pronouns, 39–68
    context shift in, 86–89
    facial expression in, 256
    focus in, 203–204 (*see also* Facial expression,
        eyebrow raising)
    history of, 40–45
    modal pronouns in, 123–125
    temporal pronouns in, 121–123
    repetitions in, 95–98
    Role Shift in, 282–285
Signing space, 49, 52–53, 57, 86, 96, 123,
    266–276, 398
Simmel, Marianne, 306, 316
Sincerity, 200–202, 215, 412. *See also* Moore's
    "paradox"
Situation, 111–145, 305–316, 325–327
    -denoting pronouns, 119, 123
    possible, 111–141
    temporal, 137–138
Slur. *See* Expressive
Socrates, 148, 170
Spanish (language), 44–48
Speed
    in music, 310–311, 316–321, 328, 332 (*see
        also* Tempo)

in sign language, 252, 262
Spoken language, xviii–xx, 64–67, 190, 245,
    249–250, 263–264
    context shift in, 82–86 (*see also* Amharic
        (language); Zazaki (language))
    eyebrow raising in, 204
Strauss, Richard, 303–304, 308–309,
    312–316, 326
Stress, 232, 390, 396–398
Subjunctive (mood), 118–120, 141–142
Suffix, xxiii, 59, 77, 140, 391–393, 396–398
    in monkey calls, 16, 21, 34
    logophoric, 77
Super Semantics, xvii, 245, 388
Supplement, 238–244, 258–264, 289–290,
    294, 412
Syntactic category, 396
Syntactic island, 184–186, 195, 408
Syntactic rule, 15, 21, 34, 163–164
Syntax, xv, 8–13, 35, 178, 389, 400–404, 412
    of English, 157–163
    of Predicate Logic, 149–152 (*see also*
        Predicate Logic)
Systems of classification. *See* Object
    classification
Swahili (language), 299

Taiwan Sign Language, 40–41
Tarski, Alfred, xiv–xviii, 153, 342–343
Telic/atelic, 103–110, 280–281, 405, 410,
    412
Tempo (music), 309–311, 318–320
    past, 137–143
    present, 140–142
Temporal expressions, 112
Tense, xv, 109, 112–125, 391–393, 397,
    412
Third person, 56–60, 200–201, 269,
    272–276, 397–400
    locus, 269, 399, 409
    pronoun, 76–77, 89 (*see also* Third person)
Tieu, Lyn, 256–257

Titi monkey, 8–15, 35
Tree
   family, 2–3, 23–24, 32 (*see also* Evolution)
   syntactic, 159–162, 167–169 (*see also*
      Syntax)
Trump, Donald, 233
Truth, xii–xxii
   conditions, xiv, xix, 147, 153, 163, 166,
      175–177, 186
   limits of, 341–374
   musical, 324–329, 353–356
   value, xiv, xix, 72, 153–154, 339,
      344–375
Truth-teller, 349—364, 368–370, 374, 413
   empirical, 353, 356–364
   infinite, 350–351

Ungroundedness. *See* Groundedness
Universal Grammar, 47–48, 52, 284. *See also*
   Grammar; Chomsky, Noam.

Variable, 37–40, 48–53, 116–121, 151–155,
      176–178, 184–190, 267–268, 413
   iconic, 55–68
   logical, 39–40, 55–68, 90, 97, 188–189
Veditz, George, 43
Verb, 38–50, 54–55, 77–82, 91–113,
      273–281, 396–402
   mass/count, 103 (*see also* Mass/count
      distinction)
   phrase, 158–168, 192–194, 273–274
Verdi, Giuseppe, 329–332
Vervet monkey, 3–8, 15, 18
Vidal, Gore, 229–130
Voiced/voiceless (phonology), 391–394
Von Stechow, Arnim, xv
Vowel, xviii, 53–55, 261–263, 390, 393
   lengthening, 53 (*see also* Iconic modulation)

Warlpiri (language), 96
When-clause, 131–132
Word order, 8, 43, 50, 180–181, 195, 400

Yablo, Stephen, 345
Yablo's paradox, 345–346, 353, 413. *See also*
   Paradox
Yerkes, Robert, 29
Yiddish (language), 128, 138
Yudja (language), 101

Zazaki (language), 82–90, 136, 141–142,
   281–282
Zuberbühler, Klaus, 5